Top Dog

Top Dog

THE SCIENCE OF
WINNING AND LOSING

PO BRONSON
&
ASHLEY
MERRYMAN

TWELVE

NEW YORK   BOSTON

The authors previously published a version of their Chapter Two discussion of the "N-Effect," as "New Research: Taking the SAT in a Crowded Room Means Lower Scores," a 2009 essay for their *NurtureShock* blog for *Newsweek*.

The image from the "Reading the Mind in the Eyes" test used in Chapter Nine appears courtesy of Simon Baron-Cohen. The selected questions from the Taiwanese Basic Competency Test included in Chapter Four were provided courtesy of Chun-Yen Chang.

Twelve
Hachette Book Group
237 Park Avenue
New York, NY 10017

www.HachetteBookGroup.com

Printed in the United States of America

RRD-C

First Edition: February 2013
10 9 8 7 6 5 4 3 2 1

Twelve is an imprint of Grand Central Publishing.
The Twelve name and logo are trademarks of Hachette Book Group, Inc.

The Hachette Speakers Bureau provides a wide range of authors for speaking events. To find out more, go to www.hachettespeakersbureau.com or call (866) 376-6591.

The publisher is not responsible for websites (or their content) that are not owned by the publisher.

Library of Congress Cataloging-in-Publication Data
Bronson, Po, 1964–
    Top dog : the science of winning and losing / Po Bronson & Ashley Merryman.—1st ed.
        p. cm.
    Includes bibliographical references and index.
    ISBN 978-1-4555-1515-8 (hbk.)—ISBN 978-1-4555-2955-1 (large print hbk.)—ISBN 978-1-4555-1516-5 (ebook)—ISBN 978-1-61113-012-6 (audiobook)
    1. Competition (Psychology) 2. Success—Psychological aspects. 3. Failure (Psychology) I. Merryman, Ashley. II. Title.
    BF637.C47B76 2013
    302'.14—dc23   2012033767

CONTENTS

"What counts is not necessarily the size of the dog in the fight—it's the size of the fight in the dog."

—President Dwight D. Eisenhower

Top Dog

PART I

Foundations

"A horse never runs so fast as when he has other horses to catch up and outpace."

—Ovid

CHAPTER ONE

Introduction /
Parachutists and
Ballroom Dancers

1

Scholars didn't get away with these kinds of experiments in the United States. Why the University of Trier's Ethics Board approved of her experiment, we still don't completely understand.

What we do know is that, at some point, Renate Deinzer received her university's blessing. And there she stood—in the middle of a tiny airfield in the Mosel wine region of Germany—facing sixteen terrified people she had convinced to go skydiving for the very first time.

In a single day, each was going from "Total novice who had never done anything like this," to "Mastering advanced free fall."

Scaring people to death was exactly the point of Deinzer's experiment. She was trying to discover how the body responds to incredible stressors: she wanted to know if there was a biochemical expression of fear to match the frightened expressions she saw before her.

Before and after their jumps, Deinzer asked each person to chew a small gauzy sponge and then spit the sponge into a test tube. From these saliva samples, Deinzer could discern exactly how the acute stress of skydiving manifested itself, biologically: she could measure the telltale psychoendocrine cocktail of the skydiving rush.

Three to four people went up in the small plane each time— buckled into the floor. Their hearts felt as if they'd pound right out of their chests if not restrained by the straps of their chute packs.

In just five minutes, the plane reached 10,000 feet in altitude over the drop zone. As nervous as they were, for the greater good of science, none chickened out. As the plane slowed to a hundred miles per hour, one by one they climbed onto the rails and dropped off the trailing edge. They tumbled once, then stabilized in the arch position— their bellies and faces to the earth—free-falling at 120 miles per hour.

For a long minute, the newborn parachutists felt the extraordinary sensation of hurtling toward the vineyards below.

In a first free fall, people can get so scared that they forget to breathe—or they hyperventilate. Which is a particular concern because at a 10,000-foot altitude, people already start to feel the effects of the reduced oxygen supply, and the air pressure alters how arteries function. If severe enough, this can trigger hypoxia, a condition that results in temporary blindness and impairment in memory and reasoning. The moment of pulling the ripcord to save oneself is sometimes so intense that, for some, they faint just as their canopy opens and remain unconscious for part of the flight down.

None of Deinzer's subjects experienced complications, though. Hearing instructions via radio sets in their crash helmets, they were guided toward the landing strip, where most were able to glide in standing up.

However, this wasn't a "Do this once and check it off the bucket list" day. Instead, they had to do it *again*. Deinzer had asked each person to make three separate jumps that very day: after they'd landed, they chewed a sponge and waited their turn to go back up. For some, they did all three jumps within the span of a single hour.

Why did they have to jump three times?

Deinzer was also interested in whether people habituate to the rush of skydiving—do you get used to it, such that it doesn't trigger the same degree of blast?

Analyzing the jumpers' saliva samples, Deinzer wasn't surprised to learn that they had a huge rush response to the first jump. But with each subsequent jump, the rush was reduced by about a quarter. By just the third jump, there was still a pronounced rush of stress, but (on average) it was now only half the first jump's intensity. It was more akin to the stress you get from driving in slow traffic that's making you late.

Apparently, hurtling to the earth in a free fall is something you can get acclimated to, rather quickly.

Now, there are many people who go skydiving frequently and love it. But if repeated skydiving doesn't reliably trigger a massive surge in natural hormones—then what's the ongoing appeal? Stephen Lyng is a scholar who studies *edgework*, a term borrowed from Hunter S. Thompson's description of anarchic human experiences. During the 1980s, Lyng was a jump-pilot at a local skydiving center. He contrasted what he learned there from skydivers with what he learned later by studying car racers, downhill skiers, combat soldiers, and business entrepreneurs. Lyng eventually concluded that the true "high" of skydiving, and other edgework, stems from the way skilled performance brings control to a situation most people would regard as uncontrollable. All of the safety rituals used to minimize the danger (in situations of extreme risk) engender this sense of control, but edgeworkers' fundamental skills are the ability to avoid being paralyzed by fear and the capacity to focus their attention on the actions necessary for survival. The feeling of self-determination they get from conquering the risks is the real payoff. It's not pure thrill they seek, but the ability to control the environment within a thrilling context.

Now let's compare parachuting against...ballroom dancing.

2

Hunter S. Thompson would never have described ballroom dancing as edgework. There's nothing anarchic about it. It's not an "uncontrollable" situation. Death is not a potential outcome.

About 280 miles northwest of the previous study, this time near Dortmund, Germany, there was another scholar also interested in the psychoendocrine cocktail induced by vigorous experience. Nicolas Rohleder was himself equipped with sponges to chew. In much the same way as in the skydiving study, he also analyzed results of subjects, comparing practice days and rest days to contest days. But his subjects were ballroom dancers—for the most part, couples who'd been doing this for years. They were competing in the Nordrhein-Westfalen Regional Ballroom Dance Competition.

There was no money at stake whatsoever, just bragging rights. Dancers had flown in from all over Europe for the fun. Held on a Saturday, the contest stretched for hours and ran continuously—with only minor breaks for the winners of each preliminary heat to be announced. In the Modern category, the men wore white tie and tails, with their hair gelled back; the women were attired in silk and sequined ball gowns, with stage makeup. When they heard their number called, each couple joined the others on the dance floor, performed a slow waltz for about 90 seconds, then rushed off for a drink of water and waited to be called again. Next was a tango, then a Viennese waltz, a slow foxtrot, and a quickstep.

During the competition, the couples were referred to only by their number—their names were not used until the final winners were announced at the end of the day. But this anonymity provided little safety; the sense that any mistake in their posture or floorcraft would be seen by the five judges was palpable. Every gesture counted: the smoothness with which they stroked their feet across the floor during the foxtrot; the staccato action of their tango; the extension of their ankles and pointing of their toes to enhance their line; the rise and fall of their waltzes.

During each round, as well as in the hours prior and after, the couples chewed a sponge. By the end of the night, Rohleder's refrigerator was filled with almost 900 saliva samples.

Back at his lab, Rohleder froze and then thawed the saliva samples, to prevent mold growth. He spun the saliva samples in a centrifuge at 3,000 rpm, and then, with a pipette, transferred 25 microliters from each dancer's sample onto an assay plate that had been coated with goat antirabbit antibodies. He added enzymatic peroxide and antiserum to each sample, then rinsed away all the free-floating molecules with a phosphate bath. Transformed by the chemicals, the assay plate now glowed, eerily. Finally, a luminometer measured the glow strength from each sample, which gave Rohleder a precise account of the chemical messengers of stress he was looking for.

Just how much stress had the dancers been under?

The pressure of ballroom dancing induced a stress rush just as strong as someone's second parachute jump. Many of the ballroom dancers' stress response was every bit as high as *a first parachute jump*.

Don't forget—this was not the dancers' first competition, or second. On average, the competitors had been in 131 competitions, and they had been going to dance contests for eight years. Yet even with all that experience competing, plus thousands of hours of practice, ballroom dancing was still enormously stressful.

Rohleder ran the data, specifically looking for experience effects. He broke the dancers into three groups, sorted by their level of experience. The first group were the dancers who'd attended fewer than 80 competitions; most had just a couple years of experience. The second group had competed more than 80 times, and they had been dancing for a number of years.

The third group had been to more than 173 competitions: they were the masters who'd practiced and performed repeatedly for over ten years. One dancer had been in over 400 competitions. In theory, these were the true experts. According to what science tells us, dancing at that point in their lives should have required very little cognitive control. All the muscle memory should have been driven down into the cerebellum region of their brains, where it was automated. There should have been no worry over forgetting to vary the inside and outside of their feet to create style and line.

But that wasn't the case. The intense stress reaction was no different between the three groups. The psychoendocrine cocktail didn't lie. The cutthroat world of the ballroom remained terrifying no matter how long they'd been at it. The contestants did not habituate.

Even ballroom dancers with over ten years of continuous experience might as well have spent that Saturday in northwestern Germany jumping out of an airplane.

Why might that be the case? How is it that someone can immediately get used to skydiving but can never get used to ballroom dancing?

Because the real difference between skydiving and dancing isn't defined by the physical environment of the activities. It's not even about the actual jeopardy to life and limb.

The real difference was the *psychological* environment. The expert dancers were in a competition, and the novice parachutists were not. To be more precise, it wasn't the *dancing* that was stress-inducing. It was being judged. It was winning and losing.

Competition is special. It has a danger and excitement all its own.

Let's think about what that means in the big picture.

The last few years, it has been argued that the secret to success in any activity is accumulating ten years' worth of deliberate, effortful practice. It's practice that makes you an expert. Stick at it, and you'll have a chance to succeed.

As that argument was spread far and wide, we felt that something was missing from the success formula. People aren't judged on how they *practice*.

Practicing is not the same as competing. You can rehearse a speech about how you deserve this job a thousand times—but how do you respond when you see 30 other people in a waiting room all vying for your same spot?

A broker can have a Ph.D. and ten years spent studying stock valuation—will that be enough when a portfolio's lost half its value overnight, and the client wants to know why he shouldn't move his account to the other trader down the street?

You can pitch a million baseballs to your child until he perfects his swing—but wait until he faces a pitcher who wants him to miss. Practicing the piano may develop finger dexterity, but that alone won't remedy the sick twisting feeling in your stomach the first time you are in front of an audience.

To be successful, you have to be able to perform when it counts. You have to be able to handle that pressure. You need to not wilt in the competition.

We wanted to know—what makes someone good at that?

What the ballroom dancing study tells us is that the stress of competition doesn't go away with experience. The inescapable conclusion is that years and years of practice are not, automatically, enough. In addition to the deliberate practice, success also depends on how well people compete. It hangs on how well they handle that psychoendocrine stress response, manage it, and even harness it. What we'll learn later in this book is that everyone has that stress response, but we can interpret it differently, which drastically affects our performance.

Ten years of practice may make you an expert. But even then, it just gets you in the door. You'll still have to dance against other experts—most of whom have put in their ten years, too. The winner is not the person who practiced more. It's who competes better. It's who lives up to the moment when the band is playing, the lights are bright, and judges are watching.

The same fundamental skills that matter in edgework turn out to matter in any competitive situation: the ability to avoid being paralyzed by fear, and the capacity to focus attention.

And the truth is, nobody puts in ten years of experience *before* he starts competing. The world doesn't work that way. We all are thrown into competitive situations, long before we've had enough practice. Our results are still judged; our fate is still determined by how we do. To survive these trials, we need more than practice. We need competitive fire.

This book is an investigation into competitive fire—what it is, and how to get it.

3

Competition makes the world go round. It is the engine of evolution and the foundation of democracy. It prompts innovation, drives global markets, and puts money in the pocket.

Still, there are those who have argued that competition is a source of evil. They see competition in terms of destructiveness: they don't believe it's a constructive activity. They assert that competition inherently kills off more prosocial behaviors, such as cooperation and respect.

First, we think that the assumption that competition is the opposite of cooperation is missing something crucial. To compete, both opponents have to cooperate on the rules: there's a mutual agreement of cooperation that governs the competition. As well, competitions are commonly among teams; each individual needs to cooperate with team members in order to compete effectively. Healthy competition can't happen without cooperation. In fact, the hormones that drive us to compete are the same hormones that drive us to collaborate.

Admittedly, competitions do occasionally bring out the worst in us. But bad behavior is not a long-term strategy for competitive success. Kids don't want to play with the kid who steals all their toys. You don't get repeat customers if you rip people off or make them sick. Bad behavior leads to isolation: no one wants to work with someone he can't trust. Furthermore, competitors who spend their time cheating their way into a victory don't develop the necessary skills to win on their merits. Again, cheating is a short-term strategy. It's not a winner over the long haul.

We also think that some of the anticompetition view can be pinned on a vocabulary problem. We don't hesitate to declare that countries have to remain competitive in business and in academics. A corporation that is not competitive is behind economically, but it is also failing in its duty to shareholders and employees alike. Season ticket holders of sports teams have an unquestioned right to complain when their local team isn't competitive. Their teams don't have to win every time, but they have to at least push their opponents and never fail to give their all.

It's when "competitive" is applied to individuals that the connotation gets murky. "Competitive" is a compliment when describing Magic Johnson on the basketball court and in his real estate empire— but it's probably a warning sign when depicting a girlfriend's behavior during a casual night of board games.

We need to make a distinction between *adaptive competitiveness* and *maladaptive competitiveness*. Adaptive competitiveness is characterized by perseverance and determination to rise to the challenge, but it's bounded by an abiding respect for the rules. It's the ability to feel genuine satisfaction at having put in a worthy effort, even if you lose. People with adaptive competitiveness don't have to be the best at everything—they only strive to be the best in the domain they train for. They might be perfectionists at work, but they don't care if they're the worst at tennis and shuffleboard. They are able to defer gratification, meaning they accept that it can take a long time to improve.

Healthy competitiveness is marked by constant striving for excellence, but not desperate concerns over rank. It's adaptive competitiveness that leads to the great, heroic performances that inspire us all.

The maladaptive variety is what gives competitiveness its bad name. Maladaptive competitiveness is characterized by psychological insecurity and displaced urges. It's the individual who can't accept that losing is part of competing; it's the person who competes when others around him are not competing. He has to be the best at everything, and he can't stop comparing himself to others even when the competition is over. He doesn't stop when the whistle blows. He drags others into competitions they don't want to be in, by provoking them. And he will resort to cheating when he can't win.

It's this maladaptive type of competitiveness that people usually have in mind if they say, "I'm not competitive." They're picturing those who seem desperate to turn even the most innocuous event into blood sport—those who want to compete for no reason other than as an opportunity to humiliate the other guy. But hypercompetitiveness is the maladaptive aberration: adaptive competitiveness is that productive agent of change. When you pick and choose your battles, recognizing which are important and which are just a distraction. The adaptive form is our focus for most of this book.

But that left us tongue-tied.

In the English language, the distinction between the maladaptive and adaptive is ignored by the catch-all "competitiveness." The linguistic workaround is to turn to metaphor—an attempt to capture the valor of being a great competitor without the negative aftertaste. We say someone has "ice in his veins," "killer instinct," "nerves of steel," and the "heart of a champion." They have a "take no prisoners" attitude, or are "going for broke" or "taking the bull by the horns" or "giving 110 percent." They walk the talk, storm the gates, champ at the bit, and gird their loins. Top Dogs come out swinging, will it to happen, put their noses to the grindstone, and show up when it counts.

Our search for the right word eventually led us to the first culture that truly celebrated competition: the Ancient Greeks. The gymnasium, where men trained athletically, was the center of Greek life. Men came together and argued ideas; through contest and challenge, their ideas evolved. Ancient Greeks played dice, marbles, knucklebones, and checkers, all very seriously. The stage tragedies of Aeschylus, Sophocles, and Euripides were entrants in government-created dramatic competitions. They held the Olympic Games, Isthmian Games, and Heraea Games for women.

The virtue of competing all the time was that it honed a person's mind and body. The ultimate goal was to achieve something the Greeks called *aretas*. (Its pronunciation rhymes with *gravitas*.)

Today, you may see English translations of *aretas* as "excellence." However, that is just a fraction of its true significance.

In the Homeric Age, to describe someone as having *aretas* was to say that he had competitive fire. According to historian J. E. Lendon, competition was the outlet for all other virtues—courage, loyalty, trustworthiness. In the heat of battle, someone with *aretas* had proven himself to be a fearless opponent and brilliant strategist. When tested, he was a leader, masterfully skilled, knowledgeable, and persuasive among his peers. He had *metis*—a cunning intelligence. He was physically strong, fast on his feet, and agile with a sword. He was brave and steadfast in character.

Thus *aretas*—attaining excellence through competition—became the supreme Grecian virtue. *Aretas* was something that the gods had and mere mortals sought to achieve.

Originally, the Olympic Games were a religious festival—a way to demonstrate one's *aretas*. Sports were not merely an entertainment, or a distraction, or a mimicry of war: all the events were said to have been contested first by the gods and heroes of Greek myths. The human competitors were hoping to demonstrate traits associated with the gods: through the events, the athletes were following the path of the gods to the divine. Competition brought out the best and taught athletes to be their absolute best. It was a chance to show honor and valor among rivals. It was during these contests that you earned *kudos* for all your glorious deeds.

In many ways, Homer's *The Iliad* and *The Odyssey* are paeans to *aretas*. Both Achilles (in *The Iliad*) and Odysseus (in *The Odyssey*) are heroic figures who hone their *aretas* over the duration of the epic poems. In *The Iliad*, the questions of why we fight, whom we fight for, and how we maintain honor while fighting help define *aretas*. Through the endless trials of Odysseus on his route home, *The Odyssey* portrays sports prowess, endurance, self-control, cunning, and diplomacy as elements of *aretas*.

The Ancient Greeks did not fear that competition bred immoral behavior. They believed that competition *taught* moral behavior. Only by competing could people come to attain the full nobility of the human spirit. In simplest terms, they learned to fight fair, with honor and mutual respect for opponents. *Aretas* meant that competing had shaped you into a better person: competition challenged you to become the best you could be.

4

Some 2,900 years after Homer's time, the modern Olympics were being held in Beijing, China. It was August 11, 2008, at the Water Cube, China's National Aquatics Center. The French team was favored in the 4 × 100 meter men's freestyle finals. Going into the race, Alain Bernard had predicted his French team would "smash" the Americans. The two teams would be racing side by side, in lanes five and four. There was also a long history of rivalry between the Americans and Australians—who had made the finals and would be in lane three.

The Olympics are almost always the highest-profile, highest-pressure meets of an athlete's career—but in this case, the expectations were stratospheric. There would be a dozen world record holders in the pool including the entire American team of Michael Phelps, Cullen Jones, Garrett Weber-Gale, and Jason Lezak, as well as France's Bernard and Frédérick Bousquet. World record holder Eamon Sullivan would lead the Australians, while South Africa had reunited its entire freestyle team from the Athens Games—the team that had set a world-record time to win the 2004 gold. And the entire sports world was following the storyline of whether Phelps would win eight gold medals—breaking Mark Spitz's record haul of seven. For Phelps to get to eight, the Americans would have to win this race.

The Americans knew that every one of their swimmers would need a perfect race to win. By perfect race, that meant each swimmer would have to record a lifetime personal best during his leg.

As expected, the first leg was dominated by Australia's Sullivan, who finished in 47.24. (Two days later, he would establish a new world record in the solo 100-meter freestyle of 47.05 seconds.)

Phelps was 3/10 of a second behind, and the French team just behind Phelps. But over the second and third legs, the French overtook the USA and built a body-length lead.

The American anchorman was 32-year-old Lezak, the oldest male swimmer at the Olympics. On that final leg, he swam near the lane line, drafting on the wave created by Bernard, who was out in front. "For a 100-meter race, most swimmers will pace themselves somewhat," he told us. "They're still breathing. In the 50, they're not. Typically, when I go max for 100, I die in the last ten meters."

In the 2004 Olympic solo event in Athens, Lezak had ever-so-slightly conserved energy in the semifinals and didn't even qualify for the finals. That miscalculation had eaten at him for years. Four years later, trailing Bernard, "I had to go as hard as I could from the get-go."

When he flipped and turned, Lezak was still 3/4 of a body length behind. He peered to his right and saw Bernard ahead of him. Briefly, he abandoned hope. His muscles and lungs hurt intensely. He knew his speed was about to fade. "I told myself there was no way I could do this. He was the world record holder." It seemed the USA would be happy if it could even hold on to the silver medal. "I told myself just to swim my own race." But the fade he expected didn't happen. He felt strong and told himself so. "I got a little confidence back from getting up to his hip, little bit by little bit. And then I thought I actually had a chance." Right at the point where Lezak expected his body to die in the water, the recognition that he had a chance generated a super-charge in his body.

"I'd never felt it before."

Over the last 15 meters, Lezak caught Bernard and took the gold medal by an outstretched arm.

It was one of the most exciting relays in history and one of the closest. Fans around the world were stunned by Lezak's time: 46.06 seconds—a second faster than the world record and almost two seconds faster than he'd ever swum in a solo race. No matter how his race was dissected, it was still considered the swimming equivalent of a mom lifting up a car to save her trapped child.

How did he do it? What caused this phenomenal demonstration of competitive fire?

By the time you are done with this book, you will recognize that dozens of factors came together and contributed to that very special 46 seconds. Yes, dozens of factors, each one taking a few hundredths of a second off his time.

First and foremost, the tightness of the race was inseparable from the result—without Bernard to chase, it never could have happened. You'll learn how important it was that the Americans had a fierce rivalry with the other nations in the pool. You'll learn why it was crucial the Americans were underdogs—that Lezak could swim to win, but wouldn't be faulted if he lost, and how this altered his body's physiology. The roaring crowd contributed. Another element in the win was that the Americans had not won the gold medal in the prior two Olympics; their silver in Sydney was considered not "second best," but an absolute failure. To win, it was essential that Lezak believed he had a chance, both before the race and at that critical moment when he reached Bernard's hip.

There were biological factors in Lezak that made this moment possible—from the gene variation he likely carries that enables him to perform better under intense pressure, to the levels of hormones that were present in him when he was just a gestating fetus in his mother's womb. Other biochemicals kicked in the day before this race, which switched on genes in his cells and altered the production rate of neurotransmitters he'd need on race day. Then there was a surge of hormones the hour before the race, followed by different hormones at the starter's gun, which he would burn up in seconds. You'll learn what happened to his lungs and his blood vessels, to his pain sensitivity and his decision making and his attentional focus.

Then there were team effects. On his own, in the solo final two days later, he'd finish in a comparatively slow 47.67 seconds. Were there two kinds of people: those who perform best solo, and those who perform their best only on a team? Lezak knew how to compete *with* his teammates. He'd taken them all aside to talk about the importance of being a team, not four separate individuals. Subliminal cues they gave one another bolstered their confidence and sense of support, which turned on yet other hormones for the collaborative effort. He was doing this for himself, his teammates, and his country, all at once.

That Lezak was an unranked sprinter during his teens and early college years, yet kept training, wired him to be persistent and made him refuse to quit on that back leg. It's fair to say that even Lezak's childhood contributed to that moment, by forging him into the competitive kid who would one day swim in the Olympics. All his early years playing basketball and water polo with other boys served as a training ground for his competitive psyche.

The factors that came together in that pool are at work during almost any great performance—when a singer belts it out onstage, or a student aces the SAT, or a negotiator secures an incredible deal for her company, or a soldier has to survive an ambush, or a chess master reaches the finals of a tournament. Any time that your commitment and ability are challenged by other human beings who are trying to beat you—these same factors are relevant.

Over the course of this book, all these factors will be discussed and more. These factors make a difference in all types of competitions, from sporting contests to sales contests, from academic pursuit to creative pursuit, from political ambition to entrepreneurial ambition.

5

As a general rule, the research has found that the Greeks had it right: most of us do improve in competition. We do naturally rise to the occasion. (In fact, everyone in that Beijing pool had done just that: five of the eight teams finished ahead of the world-record time.)

Competition spurs motivation, one way or another—whether it's because a competitor wants to win or because a competitor simply doesn't want to come out on the bottom. Even when we are dragged into competitions we'd rather not be in, the fact we are being compared to others triggers our competitive instinct and we try harder.

For decades, social science theory has professed that, in competition against others, our motivation is extrinsic, while when we perform an activity on our own, motivation is *intrinsic*. Thus the concern is that competition skews people to be extrinsically motivated, and they'll lose touch with their natural intrinsic love for an activity. But it's not really that simple: some people *love* to compete. For them, competing makes an activity *more fun*. A study of distance runners, for instance, reveals that those who compete at the national level (for money, medals, and glory) have the greatest intrinsic motivation. It's only the intermediate runners who are externally focused. Similarly, ROTC cadets learning to shoot rifles develop more love of it—*and* more respect for their opponents—when they are part of a team-based competition than when they are taught to master and excel at rifle shooting without competition.

It's even true that competition increases *creative* motivation. While our society upholds an ideal that creative genius is most prolific when it's untainted and uninfluenced by petty outside forces—such as comparison to others, deadlines, or financial rewards—we conclude quite the opposite. Competition doesn't kill creativity: it facilitates creative output by supplying motivational drive. Competition also teaches people to be comfortable with conflict and opposition, which is a necessary building block for developing the creative psyche.

There are a few people who seem comparatively immune to a contest. But they are the exception—not the rule—and for them, there doesn't seem to be a downside to their participation in a competition. It neither hurts nor helps their performance. And there are those whose performances do suffer in competitive environments. They become overwhelmed by the intensity of the event, until they emotionally withdraw.

What's fascinating is how the science can predict which category you will fall into. And the science also shows how people can improve their performance in competition, no matter which of those categories they began in.

Success in competition requires taking risks that are normally held back by fear. The first risk is entering the competition itself—choosing to compete. Everyone has his own personal threshold where the benefits of competing outweigh the fears. Those who focus on what they'll win choose to compete far more. Those who focus on their odds of winning choose to compete far less.

As humans, we all are driven by a desire to experience pleasure and to avoid pain. But people differ in how much of each they need and can bear. This book describes these two biases as "gain-oriented" or "prevention-oriented." And these biases significantly impact whether people compete or not. You'll also learn that women choose to compete less than men do, but it's not because men are bigger risk takers per se—it's that men tend to be overconfident of their abilities and thus are blind to some of the risk. This gets men into more contests, but it doesn't necessarily help them win.

This same decision point—whether to join a contest in the first place—repeats itself in miniature thousands of times *during* a contest. Every competitor is vulnerable to a tendency to conserve energy; going all out with total focus is virtually impossible to do continuously. We all constantly calculate whether to continue investing our energy and our hopes in the competition; we constantly keep track of our odds of winning and the expected value return on digging deeper. Again and again, we choose whether to go for it or not. We decide whether to lie back and protect ourselves, or whether to put our egos on the line.

Religious scholar James Carse makes a distinction between *finite* and *infinite* games. Finite games have a beginning and an ending, with the goal of winning. Between games there is recuperation and restoration. Infinite games never end, and since no winner is ever declared, the goal instead is to get ahead. With infinite games, there is no end to the comparisons, only a waxing and waning of competitive intensity. It turns out that women handle infinite competitions better than men, often because they find ways to recuperate while still competing. Men, unable to shield their egos, do best in shorter competitions of a discrete length.

Competitive fire is a consequence of both nature and nurture coming together. Typically, we tend to think of biological factors as determinative, or permanent, but that, too, isn't so clear-cut. Often biology and psychology are in a war for control. When biology gets the upper hand, your mind can't turn the tide, and you are its victim, whipsawed by the effects of your body's response. But when people say that the difference between an elite competitor and an intermediate competitor is all mental, that's accurate: becoming a better competitor is about controlling your psychological state, which in turn alters your underlying physiology. Most simply put, if you can control your fear, then you can control your biology, too.

Yet it's a myth that remaining calm is the answer for everyone. Only some people need to remain calm; others conquer anxiety by going to the other end of the spectrum—by being highly aroused, animated, and even angry. A recurring note in this book is that there are two kinds of people: those who need to avoid stress to do well, and those who actually need stress to perform their best. Being told to chill out, relax, and think positively is fundamentally counterproductive for some people.

What it takes to compete is not the same as what it takes to maintain well-being and to live a happy, contented life. To wade further into this book, one has to accept that the mental states, behaviors, and intensity of top competitors would be socially taboo if not for the competition. (Notice men don't pat each other on the butt *after* the game.) But the rules of the game give them a pass; in fact, one could argue that it's *only* during competitions that we are socially permitted to try our absolute hardest, uncloak our desire to win, and be at our most intense.

No wonder we like it so much.

CHAPTER TWO

The Competition Machine

1

If you go back to the first published research ever done in the field of social psychology, the year was 1898, and the author was a 37-year-old high school teacher named Norman Triplett, who had returned to Indiana University to pursue his master's degree.

Triplett had an idea that competition somehow galvanizes a person's performance: the mere presence of another person doing the same task makes someone work harder. In the right circumstances, competition teases out people's best.

Competition had always been at the cornerstone of political and economic theory—Sun Tzu, Machiavelli, Hobbes, Adam Smith. Just 40 years earlier, Darwin had suggested that competition was the engine of evolution. But Triplett was the first to measure its effect, rather than just theorize about it.

Triplett's hobby was long-distance bicycling, at a time when cycling had captured the national imagination. Chain-driven bicycles with pneumatic tires had been invented, but Ford's Model-T was still a few years away. There was spectacular press coverage on every lowering of a cycling world record—over distances from 20 miles to 100 miles. Some cyclists attempted to go faster in an individual time trial by employing a series of pacers—usually skilled tandem teams that alternated—putting the trailing solo rider on a record pace. Other cyclists raced against competitors.

Triplett pored over all the 1897 season data from the Racing Board of the League of American Wheelmen, trying to ascertain whether cyclists were faster racing against the clock or against other cyclists. He concluded that competition against other cyclists took off five seconds per mile compared to racing alone against the clock. He posited that the presence of another rider aroused competitive instinct, "releasing or freeing nervous energy for him that he cannot of himself release."

But it was still unclear if this speed increase could really be separated from the role of pacers and air/wind friction.

Triplett designed an experiment to get to the meat of the issue. For his master's thesis, he wanted a unique task, something that no person could have practiced before. He built a metal contraption in his advisor's laboratory that he called "the Competition Machine."

The size of a rowing scull, the machine was an odd combination of two anchored reels at the end of long arms, a pulley, and a spindle loaded with a long reel of silk cord. Triplett recruited 225 subjects of all ages to run multiple trials on his machine; they did it sometimes alone, sometimes in competition with another person. At a signal, the stopwatch began, and each participant turned an arm-size reel as fast as possible, pulling the silk cord through a 16-meter-long path. Bright flags sewn to the cords indicated their progress. They would finish in around 150 turns of the reel; the whole thing would be over in approximately 40 seconds.

While his summaries were recorded, much of Triplett's raw data is lost to history. The exception is the performances of 40 children: each ran six trials over a number of days. He wrote about these kids in his

1898 paper, listing every trial time. Most subjects were between 9 and 13 years old.

Triplett had turned to children to answer several questions that intrigued him. Was competitive fire innate? Was there something special about competition that could help one child succeed, while another crumbled? Did it matter how old the kids were? What about gender? Would there be differences in how girls and boys reacted to the race?

All the children had a little practice with the Competition Machine, then did a time trial, pushing themselves to finish as fast as they possibly could. They were racing against the clock. Then, after a rest, 20 of them were matched up in ten head-to-head competitions, against another child who'd clocked a similar time.

Here were their times.

	First and Second Time Trial	
	Alone	*Head-to-Head*
Albert P	29.0	28.0
Anna P	67.0	57.0
Bessie V	46.2	41.0
Emma P	38.4	42.0
Genevieve M	36.0	36.0
Harry V	32.0	32.0
Harvey L	49.0	42.6
Helen F	44.0	51.0
Howard C	42.0	36.4
Inez K	37.0	35.0
Jack R	44.2	44.0
John T	30.2	30.8
Lois P	53.0	45.6
Lora F	40.4	35.0

Mary M	48.0	44.8
Milfred V	36.4	29.0
Robert H	31.4	31.4
Violet F	54.4	42.6
Warner J	41.6	43.6
Willie H	37.8	38.8

The pattern is not immediately clear, is it? Several kids were considerably faster, and a few slower—and one much slower. Was there a pattern at all?

The second group of 20 kids did two time trials by themselves, without competition. Just with the extra practice, they reduced their times on average by 2.5 seconds. At that point, they went head-to-head, to see if competition further reduced their times.

	Second and Third Time Trial	
	Alone	*Head-to-Head*
Anna F	31.8	32.4
Bertha A	49.0	48.0
Carlisle B	35.4	35.0
Clara L	44.0	46.0
Clyde G	35.0	32.4
Dona R	37.2	36.0
Eddie H	29.2	27.6
George B	36.0	37.6
Gracie W	50.0	42.0
Hazel M	35.8	38.2

(continued)

| | Second and Third Time Trial | |
	Alone	Head-to-Head
Helen M	45.6	35.8
Lela T	37.4	36.8
Lucile W	50.0	43.0
Lura L	39.0	38.0
Mary B	46.0	43.4
Mary W	53.0	45.8
Mollie A	30.0	28.0
Ora R	30.0	29.0
Pearl C	43.0	40.0
Stephen M	50.0	43.0

The pattern's still not evident, but one is emerging. In that second list, it looks like *most* kids put out more effort when competing.

By the end, every child had three solo times against the clock, and three times induced by competition. Looking across all six trials, a general finding did emerge. Triplett concluded that competing head-to-head, on average, took a couple seconds off a child's time. He observed, "The desire to beat, if it did nothing else, brought them to a sense of what was possible."

But that wasn't the case across the board.

For example, in each list above, there was a Helen—one was Helen M., a ten-year-old girl. The other was Helen F., who was nine. Helen M.'s three solo times were all between 45 and 46 seconds. But head-to-head competition brought out significantly harder efforts in her. She was *five to ten seconds faster* in each trial when competing head-to-head.

One way to describe competitive fire is that it's being able to turn up the effort when challenged. Not just turn it up a little bit. Competitive fire is what you see when you dial the effort knob up to 11.

Helen F. had the opposite experience. She wilted in the face of competition and worked far less, losing spirit. Her first head-to-head race was seven seconds slower than her solo time. She didn't do as poorly in later rounds, but competition never lowered her time.

Triplett stood by during all the children's trials, keeping notes on their moods and facial expressions, recording their agony and triumph. Ten of the children he labeled as "stimulated adversely" by competition—they really did not enjoy it, and many crumbled. Their breath was labored, their faces flush with distress. They had so much tension in their arm muscles that they had trouble working rapidly. Their times reflected this struggle. Kids of every age—even a fourteen-year-old—were among those who crumbled. Overall, girls benefitted *more* from having the competition trials—their times got disproportionately faster. But some girls suffered more from it as well.

Triplett broke apart the kids by category, based on his observations of how they seemed to handle his Competition Machine. He found a 50%/25%/25% split—half the kids benefitted *a lot* from being made to compete. Another quarter of the kids were largely unaffected, barely lowering their times over the three competitive trials. The last quarter of the kids did not handle the competition trials well at all.

That turned out to be the pattern.

In just about every study of competition effects on a normal population, the majority improve their effort level in competitive circumstances, while some are immune and some reduce their effort.

The real benefit of competition is not winning—it is improved performance. Competition liberates, or generates, hidden reserves of additional effort. Competitors discover an extra gear. And in the right circumstances, this happens *even if you ultimately don't win the contest.* Competition facilitates improvement.

But the tradeoff is that competition doesn't benefit everyone.

There are many reasons that some people wilt under competitive pressure. Later in the book, the biological and psychological factors will be dissected. But it'd be a mistake to jump ahead, since sometimes the result has nothing to do with an individual's failings at all.

This section of the book is about how the will to compete is affected by structural factors. As you'll see, the number and strength of competitors can alter who crumbles and who excels.

Triplett had his children race head-to-head against a single, relatively equal competitor, but it's a different story when there's a whole field of competitors, of varying ability. A few basic lessons will be deduced here, from a variety of competitive settings: the U.S. Air Force Academy, corporate sales contests, SAT test-takers, and the global market for industrial packaging machines. Together, they prove a singular point: to keep the competitive fire lit bright, nothing is more important than that the contest be *close*.

2

Like every class to come before, the 2011 graduating cadets of the U.S. Air Force Academy threw their hats into the air at the precise moment the Air Force Thunderbirds flew over Falcon Stadium.

But in one pivotal way, the 2011 graduates were different. Though they were never told, they were lab rats in a large-scale experiment in social engineering designed by a few economists.

The Academy's military mission means cadets must be willing to go to war. Cadets' ability to compete is—very literally—a matter of life and death. So everything at the Academy is a competition, meant to instill competitive fire into the future officers.

The freshmen are called "fourth-class" and go by the nickname "doolies," from the Greek word for "slave." They have little freedom: if not in a required activity, they are restricted to their dorms, the library, and athletic fields. Privileges are earned only through performance. Your status is worn on your breast, with pins earned by succeeding at everything from grades to being a crack shot. At graduation, the faculty ranks every cadet. High rankings turn into plum assignments; low grades get Minot, North Dakota.

The students—and the school—are largely top rung. In 2011, *Forbes* magazine rated it the tenth-best university in the country. Aerospace engineering is one of the most popular majors. SAT scores are high, and only 14% of applicants are admitted. Just to apply, students need to be nominated by a member of the U.S. Congress.

Despite all this screening of applicants, every year there are freshman cadets who don't handle the competitive environment very well. Like Triplett's "adversely stimulated" kids, some crumble. This manifests most significantly in cadets' falling behind academically. Cadets with a 2.0 grade point average (GPA) go on academic probation, and many drop out.

In the mid-2000s, the Academy commandant became concerned that the number of students in trouble was steadily on the rise. He was looking for solutions.

As it happened, economist Scott Carrell was already working in partnership with the Academy on several studies. Carrell was a major in the Air Force Reserves and a graduate of the Academy. His close friend, economist James West, had long been on the Academy faculty. They'd done one study on the connection between sleep duration and academic performance at the Academy; another study had helped the Academy combat cheating—which had been rampant a couple years earlier.

Carrell and West's newest study was on a particular peer effect. They'd noticed a pattern: cadets with lower grades improved academically if they socialized with, and spent more time around, cadet friends with high GPAs. The high-performers rubbed off on the low-performers, dragging them upward. Having friends whose SAT scores were 100 points higher than yours led to a half-grade improvement in GPA.

Carrell proposed that leveraging this known peer effect could prevent the lowest-performing cadets from going on academic probation and dropping out of school. It wouldn't cost a dime. All the Academy had to do was intelligently seed the next incoming class.

Mimicking the military, all cadets are assigned to squadrons. Each squadron is made up of roughly 110 cadets—35 freshmen, 30 sophomores, 25 juniors, and 20 seniors. The freshmen in each squadron eat together, sleep together, train together, and study together. By changing who would be in each squadron, the peer effect would kick in.

Carrell and West started by identifying which of the 1,314 incoming cadets had lower SAT scores and GPAs. These were the students most at risk of dropping out. They were assigned to special squadrons with a makeup of extra numbers of high-achievers. Compared with normal squadrons, these socially engineered squadrons had a few more low-performers, many more high-performers, and—to make room—fewer middle-performers.

Many of these middle-performers were assigned to their own, fairly homogenous squadrons.

Based on his calculations, Carrell predicted that the number of students on academic probation would be sizably reduced. The new groupings just had to lift cadets' GPAs above that 2.0 cutoff.

After the first semester, when Carrell eagerly ran the numbers, his first impulse was denial. *This can't be happening*, he thought to himself.

More of the at-risk cadets were crumbling, not fewer.

For the spring semester, freshman cadets get to pick their own roommates. So Carrell inquired after those choices. He saw a trend that low-performers were rooming up with other low-performers. The more he asked around, the more he realized what was going on. Within a test squadron, the low-performers were self-segregating into cliques, to insulate themselves from the endless ranking and comparison. Even though each squadron ate every meal at the same table in Mitchell Hall, the low-performers would sit together in clumps. They would study at McDermott Library in different carrel areas. Competition works when it pushes everyone to new heights. But in this case, the very subjects meant to be helped by competition were retreating from it.

Still, Carrell hoped this was temporary, and the team-building forces of squadron life would eventually win out. But after the spring academic data came in, Carrell grieved. The experiment was backfiring.

Squadrons are reassigned after the freshman year and then become permanent. Thus when the experimental groupings of the 2011 class were unwound, this change wasn't considered unusual. None of the students ever detected that they'd been part of some master plan.

Meanwhile, the incoming 2012 class had already been seeded and sorted into the new test squadrons. That class, too, went through an experimental year. Once that data came in, Carrell was in a state of acceptance. The results replicated themselves. The at-risk cadets were actually more at risk of dropping out if they'd been placed in the test squadrons.

Even though he got the opposite result he wanted, Carrell still published his study, for two reasons. First, he thought it was a useful cautionary tale that would warn off others from making the same mistake. Second, there was a saving grace.

Remember those squadrons comprised of leftover middle-performers? It turned out that their academic performance dramatically *surpassed* expectations. Subjected to the daily competitive grind, these middle-rankers all responded well. They turned it up a notch, across the board. Both in the class of 2011 and 2012.

Originally just an afterthought—barely on the economists' radar—the middle-performers became a new point of interest.

Why did they do so well?

Perhaps part of the answer lies in the pattern seen elsewhere: in sales competitions.

Now, salespeople and Air Force Cadets might not seem like they have anything in common, but in one particular way, they do.

All over the world, economists and business professors have studied corporations' sales contests. In some cases, the professors have even been allowed to design the contests. Ordinarily, salespeople are already compensated with some commission structure—the contests are above and beyond that, attempting to induce additional effort out of employees.

When done right, the effort materializes. Studies generally confirm this—in everything from lending officers at French bank branches to immigrant strawberry pickers in England to retail clerks in a Dutch clothing chain. The sales contests boosted productivity from 10% to 50%.

But those gains aren't always seen. The rule of thumb in sales research is that contests only work when it's an even matchup, or a close race, such that the extra effort becomes the decider between winning and losing. People need at least a fighting chance.

When leaders are not challenged, they coast a little. Those too far behind stop trying as hard, lacking any sense that winning is feasible.

Sales contests should almost always be designed with contestants stratified into groups with a similar historical track record. They may also be tweaked so that more contestants have the sense that winning is still possible.

For instance, the French bank branches were given daily feedback during a two-month contest. Each day, the banks learned which locations around the country had made the most personal loans the day prior. (Personal loans contributed 90% of the bank's pretax profit.) Because the loan volume fluctuated a great deal, at one point or another, many of the branches were proclaimed a "Daily Leader," even if they were still far from winning cumulatively. Nevertheless, getting recognized as the Daily Leader reset those branches' reference point. Those banks worked harder from then on. For the rest of the contest, their sales volume was up 28%.

If you think again about the Air Force Cadets, the middle-performers were surrounded by competitors similar in academic ability. They never felt far behind, and many on one test or another no doubt felt like a "daily leader." The competition brought out their best, and they never fell so far behind that they felt like quitting.

The low-performing cadets were surrounded by top students who made them feel inadequate day in and day out. Rather than cajoling them to work harder, the endless comparison to an impossible benchmark was defeating. These low-performers therefore created a clique—finding refuge in their identity as low-performers—but this safety inadvertently gave them permission to not excel.

3

For most of us, competitive fire is hugely impacted by what we feel our odds of success are. It's a big difference if you're competing against ten people or competing against 100. When the field is too large, and the chance to be near the top is slim, people don't try as hard.

Here's a remarkable example: when taking the SAT, the number of other students taking the test at the same location has a significant impact on the average score. Professors Stephen Garcia and Avishalom Tor analyzed every single SAT score for 2005. They discovered that teens who take the SAT in big venues with lots of other test-takers score worse. Conversely, teens in smaller venues with fewer test-takers score better. (For stats aficionados out there, the correlation between the number of test-takers at a venue and SAT scores is a whopping $r = -.68$.)

These kids know darn well that the entire country is taking the test that day; however, having so many at the same place, often in the same room, is intimidating. It's a stark reminder of just how many other students are competing with you for college spots. And that, in turn, affects concentration and effort.

Take a look at this chart of several states' mean SAT scores.

2011 SAT Scores by State

If we asked you to guess which state has the highest average SAT scores in the country, you probably wouldn't guess Arkansas, Alabama, or Montana. In the rural, less populated states, test-takers have to drive farther to get to a test-taking venue, but there are still fewer students at any given venue. In the graph, the states on the left have the lowest *test-taker density*. The states on the right have the highest test-taker density.

It's also true that, in rural states, more students take the ACT. It could be that only the best and the brightest take the SAT in those states. But Garcia and Tor included ACT/SAT prevalence (and ACT scores) in their analysis. Even controlling for the ACT, the kids in the low-density states still had higher scores. Garcia and Tor also addressed other between-state differences. They made statistical adjustments for parental education and the percentage of kids who were a minority. They included more systemic controls, including the states' rate of SAT score improvement over the past decade and the amount of state and federal funding going into schools.

With all these things taken into account, the kids who were taking the SAT in smaller, less crowded venues still had higher scores.

Garcia and Tor found the same phenomenon in test scores of Michigan undergrads taking the Cognitive Reflection Test (CRT). They also reproduced it in lab experiments. Subjects finished a test faster when they were told they were competing against nine other people. Telling them they were competing against 99 people reduced their effort.

Garcia and Tor call this phenomenon the "N-Effect." The larger the N—the number of participants involved in a task—the worse the outcome for the individuals who are participating.

According to Garcia, "How we compare ourselves to other individuals is the engine that drives how we compete against others." When there are only a few people in the race, we put our foot on the gas, working harder and harder to outpace our competitors. And the competition becomes very personal, a referendum on our own ability.

"In contrast, when we are against many, many competitors," says Garcia, "we don't care as much about how we stack up against one other competitor." Once the crowd is large enough that we don't feel the element of personal competition, the result doesn't feel like a personal statement of our worth, so we don't try as hard.

In the school reform debate, the buzz about small classroom size is based on an idea that smaller classrooms facilitate more teacher-student interaction. But Garcia wonders if the reason students do better in smaller classes is because of more intense peer relations and more competition between the students; the frame of reference is narrower. It really has nothing to do with the teacher.

In 1898, Norman Triplett found that competition against one person is better than competing against no one at all.

Garcia and Tor have discovered that competing against too many others has the opposite effect—effort suffers.

4

What does one do, then, when facing a large field of competitors? If the N-Effect of a large field dampens competitive fire, how do you compensate, to keep the fire stoked?

In college football, not every team can compete for the national title, or even compete to be in the Top 25, and this might dampen their spirit, since there's no chance. But a lot of teams can be in the running for their conference title. By narrowing their focus, by framing the race to be among fewer competitors, the athletes try harder. The ultimate narrowing of focus is the annual rivalry game, where even if a team has a losing record, and is limping its way to the end of the season, the team's players still manage to summon competitive fire and give their all to spoil their rival's bowl aspirations.

Take the Harvard-Yale football rivalry, which began in 1875 and since 1959 has been known as "The Game." A century ago, these two teams were national powers; today, not so much. But the outcome of the game still feels just as consequential. Yale holds the historic advantage, 65-56, with eight ties, though Harvard has been victorious the last six. Each team is the benchmark the other measures itself against. Nobody doubts that this annual matchup gives rise to more intense competitive spirit than an ordinary game on any other Saturday, but the *proof* of that observation is in how often the lowly underdog manages to spoil the favorite's season. On paper, it shouldn't even be a fair fight in these years: one team has a great winning record, and the other team is mired in mediocrity. Yet upsets are common.

On ten different occasions in the last century, Yale went into The Game with an *undefeated* record. But look at the outcomes:

November 23, 1912: Yale 0, Harvard 20
November 19, 1921: Yale 3, Harvard 10
November 24, 1923: Yale 13, Harvard 0
November 22, 1924: Yale 19, Harvard 6
November 20, 1937: Yale 6, Harvard 13
November 19, 1960: Yale 39, Harvard 6
November 23, 1968: Yale 29, Harvard 29
November 23, 1974: Yale 16, Harvard 21
November 17, 1979: Yale 7, Harvard 22
November 17, 2007: Yale 6, Harvard 37

Yale came away with a victory only three times. There are always Cinderella stories in sports, but they're random; you never know when they're going to happen. Except with rivalries. Rivalries seem to create *reliable* upsets.

Rivalry is like competition squared: it fans the flames of competitive fire.

In industry, too, there is usually a large number of competing firms in any field. Following the basic principles of capitalism, these firms compete in an open market, pushing one another to create value and grow. What's overlooked, though, is that even in business— even in industries with a large *N* of competitors—feelings of rivalry intensify competitive effort. The rivalry effect has been studied in many arenas, including Scottish knitwear companies, Norwegian groceries, video game producers, and banks. But it's in the Emilia-Romagna region of Northern Italy that local rivalries are producing economic value in surprising ways.

Around the historic city of Bologna, a new, modern industry has sprouted up and managed recently to dominate the $28.6 billion world market—for packaging machinery. This region has earned the nickname "Packaging Valley."

That plastic clamshell your phone charger came in, or the foil blister pack your heartburn pill pops out of, or the six-pack box of bouillon-cube dice in your pantry—there's a good chance the machine that pressed it came from Packaging Valley. This little region has become the world's leader in packaging innovation. The rise of Packaging Valley has led people to wonder what its secret is, much like they wonder why Silicon Valley has dominated high technology.

One of the main reasons that so many packaging machines get exported from Italy today is the intense feelings of rivalry between specific companies located right there in Packaging Valley.

There are about 200 companies in the valley that make industrial packaging machines. You might think they all compete against one another, but a local scholar, economist Cristina Boari from the University of Bologna, went around interviewing employees from the firms. Companies didn't see themselves as competing against 200—the average firm viewed itself as pitted against just four or five other firms. But two of them, often located in another country or somewhere else in Italy, were distant both geographically and psychologically. Their real competitor, their rival, was just one—maybe two—other local firms. They measured themselves against the other guys down the road who also built machines to cut and foil-wrap cheese, or cigarettes, or cosmetics.

This concentration of competitive focus has magnified the psychological involvement for employees. The striving to outdo each other has led to one innovation after another. The Italian companies have made it clear that, whatever idea a designer can envision for a package, they can build the machine to execute the dream. Whether it was biodegradable bottles or bottles of unusual shapes to be easy to grip, they wanted the job. They built superfast robots and freeze-dryers to turn liquids into powders and aseptic systems that let no air in. Every single container that rolled off an assembly line became trackable.

Machines to prefill syringes with polio vaccine were shipped to India, while elsewhere around the world, people began making espresso from single-use pods.

We've said that what drives competitive fire is a close race; well, the closeness is psychological, too. The fact that these packaging firms are geographically close has been inextricable from their success: they've been better able to keep tabs on their competitors, imitate their innovations rapidly, and respond in kind. But Boari found that it's more than that. Feelings of pride and the need for respect have come into play. The threat of losing honor, the drive to not be beaten on home turf, has surged. These companies have a shared value: to build high-end, complex machines that are extremely reliable. They've bought parts from similar suppliers, also in the region. The firms are closely tied in other ways—they steal employees from one another, with 10% turnover every year.

It's a work culture where there's no slacking off, where employees genuinely care, all the way down to the machine-shop floor.

As one engineer told Boari, "Some of our rivals sent charming ladies here, trying to steal our best technicians, but they did not succeed. Here we are able to make beautiful machines and to motivate our technicians."

One could argue that the cross-country move of Facebook, from Cambridge to Palo Alto—memorialized in *The Social Network*—was crucial not just for the access to venture capitalists and programmers in Silicon Valley, but also because it stirred up deeper, rivalrous feelings between Facebook employees (then in Palo Alto) and Google employees (next door in Mountain View). When Top Dog is at stake—not just in some abstract way, but every time you make a reservation for dinner, every time you open the newspaper, every time you tell someone at a party where you work—and they nod, knowingly—employees take the competition more seriously. They try harder.

This same factor of *closeness* is at the core of college rivalries. Harvard and Yale haven't just competed at football all these years. What makes this an enduring rivalry is the way they are so closely tied together in all dimensions—competing over top applicants, Nobel Prizes, alumni who become American presidents, endowments, and the pride of New England. They share very similar values and have similar aspirations, such as offering financial aid to make their schools affordable to any student, no matter how poor. With all that at stake, their rivalry is sure to perpetuate and, no matter how awful a team is on the gridiron in any given year, when it comes to late November, the mostly unnoticed lineman in the trenches is still going to give his all.

The term *Matthew Effect* was coined by sociologist Robert Merton in 1968; it refers to the dynamic that the early leaders in a competition tend to get showered with resources that make them even better, increasing the gap on weaker competitors over time. For instance, the best students get sent to the best schools, where they have the best teachers; in the same way, the best players get sent to the best teams, where they get trained by the best coaches. The term was inspired by a quote from the Gospel According to Matthew: "For to everyone who has, more will be given and he will grow rich; but from the one who has not, even what he has will be taken away."

Whenever we try to counteract this—whenever we try to redistribute resources to prop up the weaker competitors—we're applying the *Mark Effect*. This term was coined in 2009 by the University of Chicago's Matthew Bothner, drawing from the Gospel According to Mark: "But the first will be last, and last will be first." In our society, there's an almost unlimited number of ways we try to assist, or intervene, when competitors are unequal. We take it as a given that competition is predicated on a level playing field—that the rules apply to all, and if some redistribution isn't done now and then, the rich will just get richer, to the point there's no competition left.

What's easy to overlook is that sometimes, all any competitor needs is an equal match and a fighting chance. That, alone, can do wonders to revive his spirit.

The next chapter will look at a few common structural factors that can alter performance. Crowds, prizes, and home field advantage can all increase competitive fire. It might seem obvious that they all do, yet *why* they work, and why they commonly backfire, is not as obvious.

CHAPTER THREE

What Goes Down When the Stakes Go Up

1

The home advantage operates in almost any form of negotiation, whether formal or informal, and at every level of the corporate and political world.

In the fall of 1998, our friend Kirk Hanlin was on Air Force One, as it was making its final approach into Tokyo.

Hanlin was President Bill Clinton's Trip Director—responsible for literally guiding Clinton through every meeting and event of the president's day. And as the mammoth plane neared its destination, Hanlin became increasingly concerned about what might happen during the first few minutes of the president's arrival. The president was to proceed immediately to Emperor Akihito's personal residence. Clinton was the first American president ever invited to meet the emperor at his private home, and Hanlin knew that even the slightest delay could cause an international incident.

The location of a diplomatic event is often seen as a reflection of the entire negotiation process. Ideally, it all happens in a neutral territory, where no one can claim any sort of home field advantage. Napoleon I of France and Tsar Alexander I of Russia met on a raft in the middle of a river when they signed the Treaty of Tilsit. President George Bush and Russian leader Mikhail Gorbachev ended the Cold War with a summit held on two ships.

Clinton's meeting with the emperor was coming at an incredibly sensitive time. The United States was in the midst of an ongoing conflict with Japan over a number of trade issues, and, to make matters worse, many Japanese were still furious over a U.S. military-involved rape that had occurred two years earlier in Okinawa. There were around 50,000 U.S. military personnel in Japan, and 40% of the Japanese public wanted all of them to leave.

On all levels, the Japanese seemed to be saying that Americans were little more than unwelcome intruders. By going to Japan, the president's entire trip was thus an effort to, in word and deed, change that view.

As the jet began its descent, Hanlin recalled an earlier trip to Japan, when he had been responsible for many of the logistical arrangements for the presidential visit.

At the time, the Japanese tried to use their home field advantage by always holding the meetings in small, airless rooms. Knowing that many Americans were avid nonsmokers, the Japanese smoked throughout the sessions. They'd hoped that the Americans would be so eager to get out of the smoke-filled rooms that they'd quickly agree to their requests. (It didn't work. Instead, Hanlin was just amused by the attempt.) The biggest bone of contention Hanlin had to overcome had been that the Japanese didn't want the American press corps included in the president's motorcades. It just wasn't done that way in Japan, for security concerns. It would have been easy for Hanlin to concede, just so as not to offend his hosts. But Hanlin persisted, because members of the press corps are always included in American presidential motorcades.

There's a dark, unspoken reason for this. The assassination of President John F. Kennedy was one of the biggest events in American history, and not a single news camera was there. Soon after, the White House press corps instituted what's quietly known as "the body watch." The president can barely step one foot outside the White House without at least a couple reporters there to document it.

Now, two years later, Hanlin had heard that the Japanese were once again refusing to let the press into the presidential motorcade. Hanlin knew that if he failed to ensure the American press corps a ride to the imperial residence, *that* would have become the news back home. Hanlin would be responsible for headlines probably something to the effect of "American Press Shut Out of Meeting with Clinton and Emperor." (Add conspiratorial overtones as needed.)

Hanlin decided there was only one thing to do: tell President Clinton about the situation. In the Air Force One version of the Oval Office, Hanlin quickly brought the president up to date on the motorcade issue.

Once the plane had landed, however, Hanlin breathed a sigh of relief. Among the line of cars was a van marked "Press," and Hanlin watched as the White House traveling press climbed in.

On Hanlin's cue, the motorcade departed, at a pell-mell rate. But the cars hadn't made it out of the airport grounds when Hanlin received a frantic call. The Japanese had pulled a double-cross. Yes, the press were in a van—but the Japanese security wouldn't let the van go anywhere. The furious reporters were still parked next to the plane.

Hanlin sighed. At this point, the motorcade was nearly off the airport grounds. It would be easy enough to just let the Japanese win this one, but Hanlin decided to take a stand. On the spot, he concocted a ploy. Hanlin called Clinton's driver, telling him to pull over and stop the car.

Secret Service agents parked the presidential limousine. Hanlin ran from his car to Clinton's. Hanlin opened the limo door, and he leaned in.

"Mr. President, I just need them to see you talking to me." He quickly relayed his plan to the president.

"Here's the thing: I can't be late for the emperor," Clinton responded. Both knew that while Clinton was famously late for events, Emperor Akihito was equally famous for being exactingly punctual.

Hanlin insisted that he had the drive timed to the minute. There were about two or three minutes to spare in the schedule.

"It's a deal, but I can't be late."

"You won't be, Sir. I promise."

As he ran back toward the staff cars, Hanlin knew he was minutes away from having not one, but two heads of state furious with him.

"I just spoke to President Clinton," Hanlin announced to the Japanese staff. "And he wants to know who on your staff stopped the press from getting in the motorcade. The president gave me this piece of paper, and he wants you to write on it that person's name in Japanese. And he's going to give that paper to the emperor, so that the emperor knows exactly who on his staff was responsible for President Clinton being late to meet him."

He handed them the scrap of paper and waited for their response. Seconds Hanlin did not have ticked by.

Hanlin wasn't given a name. Instead, he received a call that the American reporters were suddenly joining the motorcade.

With seconds to spare, Clinton made it to the imperial residence on time.

Later that day, Clinton began a series of bilateral talks with the Japanese prime minister, Keizo Obuchi. At the talks' conclusion, the two nations affirmed the importance of a continued U.S. military presence in Japan.

At a dinner gathering of Japanese and American dignitaries, Clinton said: "At the center of all our efforts is the strong bond between the people of the United States and the people of Japan. Our security alliance is the cornerstone of Asia's stability. Our friendship demonstrates to Asia and to the world that very different societies can work together in a harmony that benefits everyone."

Reminded of the fact that there were bigger, more imminent threats to Japanese sovereignty than a few U.S. troops (e.g., China, North Korea), the Japanese and the Americans toasted their renewed commitment.

Ah, location, location, location.

It may seem obvious that the home field advantage is so strong in high-level diplomacy that it takes exceptional stubbornness, and ingenuity, to still accomplish what you came for. What's not as obvious is how this same dynamic is operating every time two companies, or two people, sit down to negotiate.

University of British Columbia professor Graham Brown once asked pairs of college students to take part in a mock contract negotiation. But he staggered the arrival of the students, taking early-arriving students to an unused office. There, Brown handed the early bird a key to the office, told her she was free to use the computer, even encouraged her to hang up a poster or two as decoration. Then he gave the early bird 20 minutes to get comfortable in the space. Once the other student arrived, they proceeded with the negotiation. It wasn't even close. The students who made themselves at home in the office got everything they wanted, and more.

Brown concluded that those who are on their home turf receive a huge windfall. Their takeaway may be worth up to *160% more* than what the away-team opponents will bring home.

Someone asking his boss for a raise is more likely to be successful if he's in own office than in his boss's, according to Brown. When two teams at a firm work together on a project, the team hosting the coffee and bagels in their conference room is more likely to take charge of the entire endeavor.

Researchers have been studying the home field advantage in sports since the 1970s. Around the world, from American baseball to Chinese curling, competitors are more likely to win at home. It isn't a slam dunk, but the home team in a NBA game wins about 63% of the time. Similar advantages have been found in ice hockey, rugby, Australian football, and speed skating. The downside from an away game isn't just the loss. In Iran, soccer players are significantly more likely to become injured during an away game than if they were home.

Being at home changes the style of play. In studies of collegiate and professional basketball teams, the home teams are led by centers and forwards. The home teams are better at blocks, steals, turnovers, and have more successful field-goal attempts. The away team is led by guards' defensive tactics: they are better at assists, three-point shots, rebounds, and intentional fouls. The differences in team play are so striking that scholars have concluded that coaches should be taking location into account when preparing for games.

The home advantage is stronger when the result seems uncertain. It's stronger at the beginning of a season, at the start of a game, or if the home team's behind at the halfway mark.

While everyone agrees that the home advantage is real, what has remained a mystery is why this is so.

Theories abound. There is some support for referee bias. (The yells of the home team crowd apparently sway referees' calls.) But that doesn't explain why the players themselves would be changing their strategies.

Another popular explanation is that away teams may be worn out from airplanes, time changes, and sleeping in weird hotel rooms. That, too, could explain some of it—but it can't be the entire explanation because home field advantage can be lost by the home team, without any difference in the away team's practices. Statistician Richard Pollard looked at the win-loss records of 37 professional teams that moved to shiny new stadiums across town. You'd think that the new and improved facilities help the teams, but Pollard's results show that, at least at first, teams are actually less likely to win in the new stadium than they were at the old park.

If you ask the fans, they say that the home advantage comes from the excitement of the crowd. But that doesn't seem to be the answer, either. A few years ago, violence in the stands of Italian soccer games became so pronounced that some teams chose to play in empty stadiums: not a single fan was allowed in to watch the game.

But the home teams still kept winning.

Perhaps the most interesting take is that the crowd acts much like a boss or supervisor, monitoring the players, seeing every move. Players can't shirk off, or the crowd will call them on it. This might explain why the home advantage has been shrinking over time. In decades past, a team could conserve its energy during an away game, and few fans would know. But the rise in televised games means that the home crowd is always watching, demanding that its team perform at its best at all times.

Still, the flaw in all these arguments is that these explanations mostly just apply to sports. They don't help explain why the advantage has been found in all those other competitive contexts—where there's no referee, no travel, and no crowd.

For example, preschoolers playing a game are more likely to win if they're playing in their own classroom: a kid from down the hall is on defense and more willing to give away his chocolate chip cookies.

People are more likely to vote for a school bond initiative if their polling place is an actual school building: they just can't say no to schools when they're in one. College students are more likely to win arguments with their peers if the argument takes place in their own dorm rooms.

Given findings such as these, researchers have increasingly come to the conclusion that the home advantage is an evolutionary one, rooted in territorialism—a deeply rooted, innate need to control one's own space. And once this sense of territorialism is activated, you become more competitive; you're more willing to challenge potential intruders. You're more confident, more motivated, and more aggressive when you perceive a potential threat. You have a higher sense of self-efficacy, controlling the environment in a way that best suits your needs. Researchers are still working out the neuroscience of the home advantage—but so far the data suggest that home victories light up the brain's reward center in a different, more pronounced way. Thus winning at home is more thrilling to pursue and more fulfilling once achieved.

As Professor Brown has explained, territorialism is inherently a social process, born out of excluding others. In other words, it isn't enough to claim something is "Mine!" Instead, territorialism is saying, "Mine! Not yours!" And this claim—whether it's of an airport tarmac or office cubicle—brings security, a statement of identity, and a sense of belonging.

Even the smallest sense of ownership can trigger a profound sense of territorialism. And it doesn't take years for it to occur. It's instantaneous. In video game experiments, if a player arrived at the game's target destination *just ten seconds* before his opponent, he was more likely to win the game.

People accept others' sense of ownership just as quickly: late arrivals accept that they are the visitors and usually defer to this prior residency. Latecomers are the ones more likely to flee than stand their ground. Territorialism explains why pedestrians naturally say, "Excuse me," when walking past a perfect stranger. On a subconscious level, it feels as if the other person already "owns" the sidewalk in front of him, and someone needs permission to take the sidewalk away.

And once held, the desire to hold onto that space is powerful. In an Atlanta shopping mall, researchers timed how long it took for cars to exit parking spots. If another car was waiting for the space, people took twice as long to exit. Even though their goal was to get out of the parking lot, they still took longer to leave, if leaving meant they had to surrender their turf to someone else.

2

About a decade ago, researchers at the University of Trier made twenty-somethings get up in front of a very stern panel and give a speech about why they were the best candidate for a job opening. They had to stand at a microphone, while a video camera was pointed right at their faces, recording every nervous gesture and glance.

Some of the job applicants were allowed to bring a boyfriend, girlfriend, or spouse for support.

After the job interview, each participant had to chew a piece of gauze, so the scholars could determine from saliva samples just how stressful the job interview had been.

The scholars had entirely expected that having a supportive partner there would diminish the stress of giving a speech. And that did happen for the men; having their girlfriend or wife there calmed them considerably.

But to the researchers' surprise, it was the exact opposite for the women. Having their boyfriend or husband there aggravated their stress levels. It made them self-conscious, rather than comfortable. They felt *more* judged, not less.

This finding isn't meant as a comment on the state of marital relations. Instead, it neatly frames a conundrum: sometimes when you're performing or competing, it really helps to have a loved one there to support you. And sometimes it doesn't.

This will stir memories in anyone who grew up playing a sport, performing in dance recitals, or participating on a debate team. Some really wanted their parents in the stands. Some hated it. It only increased the pressure to look good. It made them more afraid to disappoint.

While it's confidence-building to have someone believe in you, when those beliefs also come with high expectations, it can increase the sense of difficulty. Those high expectations are harder to fulfill. This forces a competitor to think too much, rather than rely on automatic processes.

The riddle is: why is this sometimes the case while sometimes the opposite is true? Why does being watched—really, by anyone—sometimes help performance, and sometimes hurt it? Previously, we mentioned that crowds are like the effort police, ensuring you don't slack off. But in this case, we aren't talking about the amount of effort you put in. We're talking about the psychological effect—why sometimes an audience emboldens you, and other times it just makes you anxious.

The consensus among the "Ice Moms" of youth figure skating is that you need to watch enough of your daughter's practices that she gets used to your presence and you don't become a mental distraction on competition day. Showing up only for the big events may hurt more than help. Of course, the benefit in having Mom at practice isn't just for the daughter. It's also that, by watching practice, Mom sees the falls and slipups, and she stops having unrealistic expectations for the competition.

The workplace has its version of this same conundrum: sometimes, employees' effort level goes up if a boss frequently monitors them. But it's also true that being monitored can stress out employees and become a distraction, causing them to lose concentration and be *less* productive.

Back in 1925, University of Iowa's Lee Travis reported that freshmen undergrads performed much better on a manual labor task if they were being watched by a small group of upperclassmen. Even though this audience wasn't judging the performance—they were just watching intently—an environment of evaluation was inherent to the situation, because the undergrads didn't want to look bad in front of upperclassmen. The subjects focused more and worked harder.

Travis was, briefly, put on a par with Norman Triplett. Competition improved performance, but so did an audience. The excitement over Travis's work spurred a slew of other experiments, with a variety of tasks and audiences. The tasks researchers came up with were always novel—nothing as ornate as Triplett's "Competition Machine," but the main idea was the scholars didn't want a task that a subject had prior experience with. Researchers had factory workers learning mazes, National Guard troops signaling light failures, students memorizing nonsense syllables—always with and without an audience, boss, or teacher. Many of these studies replicated Travis's finding. But the problem was, quite a few studies showed negative effects from an audience. Eventually, with so many conflicting findings, the entire line of inquiry fell out of favor.

In 1965, Robert Zajonc, then at the University of Michigan, resuscitated the question. He noticed a dividing line in all the research, a consistency that explained when being watched helped or hurt performance. He theorized that the key variable was whether people were in a learning phase or had already mastered the skill. If they were learning the skill, the presence of spectators hampered performance. If they had mastered it, the presence of spectators improved performance. "To put the statement in conventional psychological language," Zajonc wrote, "performance is facilitated and learning is impaired by the presence of spectators."

Learning is already stressful enough as it is. But once you've mastered something, you may benefit from additional pressure to perform at your best.

At the time, Zajonc called his idea a "tentative generalization." He looked at early physiological studies of rats and monkeys to speculate that the presence of an audience raised the arousal level, increasing motivational drive and dominance.

Since then, Zajonc's parse has become the rule. Study after study has found that even a supportive audience can be a distraction when someone is trying to learn a new skill, even something like a new video game. It doesn't matter if the audience is quiet and doesn't disturb—the mere presence of others creates an environment of evaluation. The idea that novices and experts respond to an audience divergently is consistent with other work that shows that novices get the most out of positive feedback, but experts benefit from criticism—they need that discerning scrutiny in order to improve.

Pushing this line of research even further, Jack Aiello of Rutgers University has shown that simple tasks improve under supervision. But the more complicated the job, the worse people perform when being monitored. Data entry productivity goes up when a boss is watching, but people can't solve as many difficult anagrams if a spectator is looking over their shoulder. Aiello did a study of IBM telecommuters—they actually worked an hour more per day, when at home and unsupervised.

Think about this for a moment. If some IBM computer scientists didn't need any supervision at all, and their productivity rose when they were left alone to work, this raises a provocative question. For the sophisticated kinds of work our economy increasingly relies on—complex and creative work that takes more brainpower than muscle power—do employees need to be monitored at all? Sure, they need to be managed, in the sense that members of a team need to coordinate their work, but does anyone truly need to be checked up on, just to make sure she's working? Can you just hire people who are driven and motivated, and turn them free?

Well, there's a short answer and a long answer. The short answer is that Aiello and his team have found that intermittent supervision works even better than continuous supervision. Checking in on employees randomly creates a residual presence that motivates, without creating a mental distraction. It's also true that introverts work most productively without supervision; they find any level of monitoring to be distracting.

But extroverts crave the extra stimulation and interaction; without it, they get bored and lose focus on their work.

The long answer begins by first recognizing that this question (whether employees must be interrogated with the adult equivalent of "Have you done your homework yet?") is inextricably tied up with another question: how should employees be compensated and incentivized?

We can't consider one issue without the other because, in many ways, they're two sides of the same coin. Monitoring and supervising are more punitive, compensation inherently more rewarding—but the goal of both is to promote better performance. The age-old wisdom has been that, when employees' pay is strongly tied to their performance, that's usually enough to get them to work hard. High compensation should bring higher productivity: if low-productivity is felt in the wallet, then employees won't slack off.

However, there's recently been an idea in the zeitgeist challenging the connection between productivity and compensation. According to this argument, people want to do things that matter—that are intrinsically motivating. When people work on things they believe are significant, that importance can have a value more meaningful than the zeros on their paychecks. Thus, at least for a certain intrinsically driven cohort, you don't even need incentive pay. Because incentive pay, much like monitoring, is seen as just another insult—another cattle prod when none is needed. Ironically, if you trust professionals to do their job, they reward you with even greater productivity.

If that's all true, then we probably don't need to closely supervise people, either. But *is* it true? Can we take it as the new given that, when high-caliber people are competing, you don't even need prizes and financial bonuses? Are people naturally driven to excel, whether there's money on the line or not?

Do you have to pay people more to induce great performances?

That's the next topic we must tackle.

3

In the movie version of *Glengarry Glen Ross*, Alec Baldwin plays Blake, a sales strategist brought in to light a fire under the office's real estate agents. "We're adding a little something to this month's sales contest," he announces. "As you all know, first prize is a Cadillac Eldorado. Anybody want to see second prize? Second prize is a set of steak knives. Third prize is you're fired."

How the economists describe this is the *prize spread*. The question they're interested in is how wide a spread is needed to intensify competitive fire and improve performance, versus at what point does the spread just cause people to crumble, or even break the rules to get ahead?

Sunday, February 18, 1979, was one of the coldest days ever recorded in New York State: it hit minus 52 degrees in Old Forge. The storm swept up from Georgia, leaving the Peach State covered in four inches of ice. Washington, D.C., was under two feet of snow. Just about everyone in the east would spend the day watching television.

As it happened, the Daytona 500 was being held that day, the first NASCAR race ever televised live from start to finish. It was 75 degrees in Daytona, but overnight rain had made the track slippery. On lap 32, Donnie Allison lost control of his car and forced his brother Bobby, as well as Cale Yarborough, into a spin into the backstretch infield. Yarborough was forced to repair his car, and he fell two laps behind the leader. He made up both laps through a series of caution periods.

Donnie Allison led for 93 of the ultimate 200 laps. But on the final lap, Yarborough was right behind him.

What happened next is NASCAR legend. With such a large television audience, it was considered the moment stock racing was born as a national sport.

The winner of the Daytona 500 that year would get $73,900.

Finishing a second later, after more than three hours on the track, would cost the next driver almost $15,000. The third driver, right behind, would be out 35 grand. (By comparison, a month later, in a Richmond race, the winner took home only $16,275, and the spread at the top was about $5,000 per place.) Certainly, drivers are naturally competitive. It's also true that they'll fight their hardest in the most prestigious events. But to what extent does the money push them to risk their lives for a win?

Since the 1990s, economists have looked at historical race data and have concluded that when payoffs are high, as at Daytona, wider spreads indeed lead to riskier, faster driving and more crashes. The economists have concluded that prize spreads were so wide back then that they were past the point of diminishing returns. They'd juiced the drivers all they could, and then some.

At Daytona, as the two cars whipped onto the 3,000-foot back-stretch for the final time, Yarborough tried to slingshot under Allison's Oldsmobile. Allison skipped down two lanes and blocked the move, forcing Yarborough off the track and down onto the dirt. Without lifting the throttle, Yarborough came back on the track and collided with Allison. Both cars fused together and plowed into the third turn wall.

The national television cameras shifted to Richard Petty, who took the checkered flag over Darrell Waltrip by a car length. A moment later, the cameras cut back to Yarborough and the Allison brothers, out of their cars and in a brawl, smashing each other with their helmets, tempers overflowing. The visible competitiveness of the drivers—in both the wreck and the brawl—turned the country on to the sport.

To be clear, it wasn't just the $15,000 spread at work. The bragging rights value of the Great American Race, the glory of winning before a live television audience, and the innate competitiveness of NASCAR drivers all added to the equation. To top it off, the Allison brothers—nicknamed the "Alabama Gang"—had an acrimonious rivalry with Yarborough going back to 1973, when Donnie Allison challenged the legality of Yarborough's engine after the National 500 in Charlotte. But what the economists were looking for was a pattern of risk taking for the field of drivers over several years. And they found it. Drivers went *faster* when the spreads were wider; they continuously took more chances flying around the track.

To flip that around, the drivers didn't take the same chances when the prize wasn't sweetened with the extra cash reward. The races weren't nearly as thrilling to watch. The performances weren't quite as great, in the particular way we want NASCAR races to be great.

Philosophers and social observers have long theorized about whether you need to reward competitors with bonuses and prizes. But it's not a theoretical question—it's an empirical one. One has to look at the data and look at the performances of the contestants. If competitors are truly maximizing their effort, and truly giving it their all, then prize spreads aren't necessary. If they are going so far as to cheat, then the prizes and spreads are probably too big. If competitors are being conservative and not trying quite hard enough, then prizes and spreads might need tweaking.

On the PGA Tour, the data shows that in the tournaments with bigger purses and the widest prize spreads, the men respond—they pull out their drivers on a narrow hole despite the risk, and, on par 5s they shoot for the green rather than lay up, and so on. The greater the purse and spreads, the more the men take chances to win, and winning scores are lower as a result. But the opposite is the case on the women's tour, the LPGA. The LPGA data shows that their golfers are actually more cautious in the biggest tournaments. The women try to win not by taking risks, but by avoiding them.

The LPGA's purses are comparatively meager—about $1.75 million per event for the women versus $6 million for the men—and the spreads between finishers work out to a lot less cash. It's not surprising, then, that women golfers don't take as much risk to win. Whether this makes the women's game more or less desirable to follow is a matter of personal taste, but the spreads need to widen if more risk taking is desired. To test this, the LPGA is doing an experiment of its own. Typically, the winner of LPGA events receives 15% of the total purse. However, starting in November of 2011, there was a significant change to the event that crowns the season, the LPGA Titleholders Championship. For that tournament, the winner now gets *one-third* of the total purse. Nothing like that is seen on the men's tour. The year before the change, the winner finished five strokes below par. In 2011, on the same course—with the larger purse at stake—the winner finished nine strokes below par.

Immediately, one thinks of the Olympic Games—a situation where heroically great performances are induced for medals instead of cash prizes. But that's a contest staged once every four years, and most who make it to the Olympics go once in a lifetime. The glory of it is enhanced by its rarity. It would be a very different story if the Olympics were held 40 weekends of the year, like NASCAR. The more frequently people have to compete, often against the same field, the lower the psychological value of the bragging rights and other intangibles. When people have to compete continuously, such as in the workplace, incentive pay becomes a bigger factor in how hard they compete.

People may say they don't compete for the money, and that the job is its own reward. However, motivation rarely operates on a single level. There's a motivational hierarchy, with intrinsic motivation at the core—doing something just for the love of it. Once you're with others, participating in a common activity, being better than the others can motivate you. Once there's a structured competition, then winning is a reward. Trophies and titles act as symbolic rewards, which can, in many cases, be just as powerful as any financial reward. Prizes and financial bonuses are merely the last layer.

The reason people can't be trusted to know what truly motivates them is that awareness of rewards is as much an unconscious recognition as a conscious one. In numerous studies done by Dr. Henk Aarts's team in the Netherlands, subjects are given tasks to do on a computer. On the screen, an image may appear to tell participants if they'll get a cash reward for doing this particular task; if there's no image shown, there will be no cash. If the participants know they'll be rewarded, they work harder—and even harder for bigger rewards. That's not surprising. What's amazing about Aarts's work is that, some of the time, the image of the reward is displayed for only 17 milliseconds—that's 1.7 *hundredths of a second*. It's so brief that it never enters consciousness; the subjects "think" they are not being rewarded for this task, but their resulting behavior shows otherwise. They focus more, work harder, and try to win, just as much when they've been shown the reward overtly. It's important to understand that the reward center of the brain is an *extremely* sensitive instrument; 1.7 hundredths of a second of exposure to the possibility of a reward is all it takes to get recorded, even when the rest of the conscious brain doesn't process it. This makes people extremely unreliable self-reporters as to what drives their motivation.

As well, the reward center of the brain readjusts constantly, continuously, every second—in response to every layer of reward. One second, the joy can be intrinsic, and a second later the drive could be fueled by the need for status, and then back again.

The downfall of financial rewards is well known—they sometimes displace or destroy intrinsic motivation. The sense of unfairness that stems from unequal pay can often be detrimental among coworkers. And financial rewards become a treadmill you can't escape—if you stop paying people, they stop trying as hard.

Hundreds of social science studies make these points, but there's a fundamental omission in them that too often goes unrecognized.

In the real world, people are not captive subjects. They are free agents who choose what kind of workplace they want to work in, or choose what kind of school to attend. They self-select; they sign up for the competition or they don't. The point is that highly talented, ambitious people have a strong attraction to incentive-laden, financially rewarding workplaces, schools, and teams.

While there are sometimes detrimental effects from making people compete, and rewarding some more than others—these concerns are more than offset by the fact that you attract higher performers over time. A workplace can be egalitarian and noncompetitive, but it will repel the stars, who fear they won't get the recognition and compensation for their superior value.

The question posed earlier was if can you just hire driven, motivated people, and turn them loose, without supervision or bonus pay to prod them. Sure, if you can find those people and hold on to them. If you can't, usually you have to sweeten the pot. Again, in all these cases, it's not a theoretical question: it's an empirical one.

From here onward, this book leaves behind the foundational factors that impact all competitors and picks up the formational factors— biological and psychological—that define how competitors perform. This includes gender differences as well as family dynamics in childhood that lead to competitiveness as adults. Even conditions in the womb during fetal gestation have a lasting impact. But let's start with the source code: our DNA. This next chapter is about the gene that determines how people respond to the stress and pressure of performing.

PART II

Formation

"I have been up against tough competition all my life. I wouldn't know how to get along without it."

—Walt Disney

CHAPTER FOUR

How the Worriers Can Beat the Warriors

1

For half a century, after the discovery of the genome, it was commonly assumed that there was a gene for this and a gene for that. Just as a chromosome determined if you were male or female, genes controlled everything else. If you were tall, there was a gene for it; if you were violent, there was a gene for it; if you didn't like spicy food, there was a gene for it. With 3 billion base pairs, the genome controlled the nearly infinite variation between humans.

This notion of a one-to-one relationship between traits and their underlying genes was central to the lore and mythology around genetic determinism.

But it's important to recognize just how misguided that notion is. It is extremely rare that a single gene, all by itself, controls *anything*. Most traits are *polygenic*—controlled by many genes.

Dr. Ross Tucker, a lecturer at the University of Cape Town, explains that something as basic as height is in fact extraordinarily complex. We know that height is 20% a function of your environment (such as your diet) and 80% a function of your genes. Nevertheless, there is no one gene for height. Nor are there ten genes for height, or fifty.

In a study that identified the genomes of around 4,000 people, then cross-referenced these by the people's height, it was found that 294,831 different genes contributed to how tall they were. While genes, in concert, did "control" how tall someone was, no single gene had any control at all. You could not, with the flip of a single genetic switch, change someone's height.

294,831 different genes!

Just as Dorothy believed the Wizard of Oz controlled everything, we've given singular genes way too much credit.

Some human traits are controlled by much smaller constellations of genes. Dr. Claude Bouchard was studying how people's aerobic capacity responds to physical training. He put 473 volunteers through five months of vigorous training, to see how much their aerobic capacity improved.

For instance, the top 24 volunteers had improved their aerobic capacity by an average of 40%. These were the ones who could, presumably, become elite athletes, because exercise changes them drastically. But the 24 at the bottom of the volunteers, they had only improved by 4%. Exercise did nothing for them. It wasn't that they cheated and didn't exercise—it was that their bodies didn't learn and adapt.

Bouchard also had the volunteers' genetic codes sequenced. Then he fed the codes into a computer, hunting for the genes that determined the training response. The computer kicked out 21 genes, or, more specifically, 21 genetic variations.

People with 19 or more of these advantageous variations were high responders; their aerobic capacity improved 26%. People with nine or fewer of those advantageous variations were low responders; their aerobic capacity only improved 9% on average.

Not everybody gets more fit, no matter how much exercise they are forced to do.

To be extra clear, how the genes do their magic is still unknown. Right now, we just know they do *something*. The same goes for height—what each of those 294,831 genes does is not known to science. Yet.

All this helps put this section into perspective. Its main character—the star of this chapter—is a single gene: the COMT gene.

In this case, what this COMT gene does is known, as is how it works. This single gene significantly affects whether people perform well under pressure and stress.

But even as its power will be revealed, do not assume that it works all by itself, like Superman with no sidekicks. Its impact is very important, but don't make the mistake of believing that competitive fire is entirely determined by a single gene.

2

When Dr. Julius Axelrod was awarded the Nobel Prize in Physiology or Medicine, it was 1970. Axelrod was at the National Institutes of Health in Bethesda, Maryland—surrounded by counterculture peace protests against the Vietnam War. The chant "Make Love, Not War" echoed across the country. Because scientific research was being used to engineer bombs and create chemical agents of destruction, there was a shadow cast over all scientific endeavor. Many people felt that technology and science were making the world a worse place, not better. This greatly bothered Axelrod.

At his banquet speech in Stockholm, Axelrod addressed the royalty of Sweden and the Nobel Committee. From the podium, he observed, "This award comes at a time when our young and many of our most influential people believe that basic research is irrelevant or is put to evil uses." He thanked the Committee for making his work highly visible to the general public, "which gives us an opportunity to show how misinformed and mistaken they are." Axelrod promised that his work, and the work of those with whom he shared the Nobel, would one day explain such illnesses as depression, Parkinson's disease, and drug abuse, "and lead the way to the treatment of these terrible afflictions."

The brain is both electrical (along nerve fibers) and chemical (between the nerves). Nerves push neurotransmitters into synapses, then retract and recycle the chemicals: this ebb and flow regulates the level of neural activity.

One of those neurotransmitters is dopamine. In the past few years, dopamine has become famous for its role as the chemical jolt of victory that lights up the brain's reward center.

You want some neurotransmitters in the brain's synapses, but you don't want too many: clearing away dopamine is crucial, or else the brain will overload. It's like flooding the combustion chamber of a car's engine with too much gas. In other areas of the brain, after dopamine floods the synapses, most of it is ushered away by what are called dopamine transporter proteins. But that's not what happens in the prefrontal cortex.

The prefrontal cortex is where we plan, make decisions, anticipate future consequences, resolve conflicts, and orchestrate our thoughts. The massive growth of the prefrontal cortex is what separated us from the Neanderthals. But we evolved in such a way that there aren't many dopamine transporter proteins in the prefrontal cortex. In this preeminent region of the brain, how do we get rid of the excess dopamine?

Back in 1957, this was the question that Julius Axelrod solved.

He discovered the role of a secondary dopamine clearer—an enzyme called *catechol-O-methyltransferase*, or COMT. COMT is only a fraction as effective at clearing dopamine as the transporter proteins; nevertheless, it's responsible for the bulk of the job in the prefrontal cortex. This is a precarious and vulnerable link in the system that maintains mental balance.

It was for discovering the COMT enzyme and how it worked that Julius Axelrod was bestowed the Nobel Prize.

Imagine the brain as a big elementary school, and the kids as the dopamine molecules. Every recess, classes empty and kids are released onto the playground. They go wild, and the energy level on the playground reaches peak intensity very rapidly. When recess is over, the bell rings, and teachers must corral the children back into the classrooms. Around most of the school, the regular teachers are up to the job: they get it done. But in the new wing of the school, where kids have their own playground, substitute teachers are responsible for the task. It's not an easy job for a regular teacher, let alone a substitute. That playground of screaming kids is very susceptible to overload and meltdown.

In the very region of our brain where we do our planning and decision making, and orchestrate complex thought, we are reliant on this inefficient COMT enzyme to keep the brain humming without overloading—to strike the right balance between being alert and melting down under pressure.

There's only one twist: in the late 1990s, it was discovered that there are *two* kinds of COMT enzymes. Some of us have busy, hard-working ones. Some of us have lazy, slow-working ones.

3

Let's zoom in, with the mind's eye. Inside our cells, inside the nucleus, along chromosome 22...to band q11.21, position 19.93...there's a particular codon in a long string of codons, snippets of genetic code. Codon 158. If you looked right there in an electron microscope, you would see...

Well, you wouldn't see anything, because you can't "see" genetic code, visibly. It has to be decoded, or transcribed, to know what it means.

In the lab, scientists transcribe the code as consisting of three letters—the cell's instruction to make a single amino acid. For some of us, the code reads GTG. For others, it reads ATG. This changes the molecule that gets built. In the body, GTG is translated to mean "build a valine amino acid." ATG is translated as "build a methionine amino acid."

When the body builds the COMT enzyme protein, it machines along the genetic code, building hundreds of amino acids chained together. When it gets to codon 158, it builds whichever amino acid the code tells it to. Some of us have COMT enzymes where, in that string of hundreds of amino acids, the 158th one is a valine. For others, it's a methionine.

That, right there—that single-letter code, that single amino acid difference—determines whether your COMT enzyme is hardworking or lazy. The hardworking ones are precisely *four times faster* than the lazy ones. The hardworking enzymes are built with valine, the lazy enzymes with methionine.

We inherit this code from our parents, getting one chromosome from each. In people of European descent, 50% have a combination of both slow and fast enzymes; 25% have only fast enzymes; and 25% have only slow enzymes.

Tying this all together, we can get back to what this has to do with performance under pressure and stress.

In the neocortex of the adult human brain, there are 20 to 25 billion neurons and 164 *trillion* synapses.

Stress floods the synapses of the prefrontal cortex with dopamine. In general, you need dopamine: it's a neural enhancer and a turbo charger, but if there's too much, you overload.

For people whose enzymes work fast, their brains can handle the stress, because the enzymes can get rid of the extra dopamine.

People whose enzymes work slowly can't handle the stress, because their enzymes can't clear the dopamine. Their brains become overexcited, and they become overwhelmed.

Everything we've written thus far makes it sound like fast enzymes are good and slow enzymes are bad. That's not the case. It all depends on whether you are under stress or not.

The fast enzymes work so rapidly that when someone is *not* being stressed—when conditions are normal, and there's just a normal dopamine turnover—the enzymes *clear out too much dopamine*. For people with these fast enzymes, their normal dopamine levels are chronically lowered. There's not enough gas in the combustion chamber. Their prefrontal cortex works, but suboptimally. They actually *need the stress* (and the dopamine) to get up to the optimal level of mental functioning. They need stress to function best. Deadlines, competitions, high-stakes tests, et cetera.

The slow enzymes work poorly, but that's to people's *advantage*—as long as they're not under stress. Dopamine levels remain high, and their prefrontal cortexes are topped off—plenty of gas—performing optimally. On most days, having slow COMT enzymes is actually a good thing. But under stress and pressure, with that extra flood of dopamine, they crack.

So it's a tradeoff. Some people's brains work best in the absence of stress. While others cannot reach peak performance without stress.

According to evolutionary theory, the two COMT genotypes would not both have survived through history unless each variant served some evolutionary advantage under certain conditions. The COMT gene for the fast-acting enzymes is one we share with chimps and apes—it's been in human DNA forever. But the COMT gene for the slow-acting enzymes is ours alone; it's a more recent entrant in the survival-of-the-fittest contest.

What might its purpose be?

Some scholars have suggested that we are all Warriors or Worriers. Those with fast-acting dopamine clearers are the Warriors, ready for threatening environments where maximum performance is required despite threat and pain. Those with slow-acting dopamine clearers are the Worriers, capable of more complex planning and thinking ahead about likelihoods and consequences. Both Warriors and Worriers were necessary for human tribes to survive.

While you might think the Warriors are the aggressive ones, that's not accurate. With higher levels of dopamine, the Worriers are always near the threshold for an aggressive response. It's easy to set them off; they're very temperamental. They get angry more easily and act out. But their aggression isn't necessarily *successful*. The meaning of "successful aggression" is correctly reading and interpreting other people's aggressive intentions, and matching them. Worriers tend to see aggression when it's not there, and they miss it when it is. The Warriors are ready for the real thing.

It doesn't get any more real than the 1994 Rwandan Civil War. In 2006 and 2007, a team of scholars repeatedly visited the Nakivale Refugee Camp in southwestern Uganda, where survivors of the Rwandan genocide had been living for nearly thirteen years. The scholars tested for the COMT gene in 424 survivors from different families, to get as broad a genetic sample as possible. As you might imagine, posttraumatic stress disorder (PTSD) had been pervasive in this community. But PTSD was significantly moderated by the COMT genotype. For those with the "Warrior" gene, a majority had recovered from their PTSD. And after the researchers had reconstructed their history of trauma, the scholars learned that the Warriors had only developed PTSD after experiencing a number of traumatic incidents. For those with the "Worrier" gene, it was a different story. It had taken only a single traumatic event to cause severe PTSD symptoms. And the majority of the Worriers still had PTSD related to the trauma of the genocide. More than a decade later, they had not yet recovered.

Fifty years after his discovery of the COMT enzyme, Julius Axelrod's prediction that it would one day explain important mental disorders finally paid off.

Let's review a quick list of how people differ based on their genotype:

Warriors	*Worriers*
valine in COMT enzyme	methionine in COMT enzyme
dopamine reabsorption works super fast	dopamine reabsorption 4 times as slow
sub-optimal dopamine levels under normal conditions	optimal dopamine levels under normal conditions
stress raises dopamine to optimal levels	stress overloads dopamine levels
successfully aggressive	unsuccessfully aggressive
handles stress well, even when inexperienced	handles specific stressors very well when experienced with it
better task switching	better working memory
more attuned to novelty	less attuned to newness
malfunction leads to schizophrenia	malfunction leads to anxiety
PTSD after multiple traumas	PTSD after a single trauma

4

A brand-new study out of Taiwan shows just how powerfully this genetic factor can affect academic performance. In the ninth grade, all Taiwanese children take the Basic Competency Test (BCT), which determines if they'll get to attend senior high school. The questions are much harder than American SAT questions, perhaps more equivalent to what Americans might see during a college final exam. And the testing takes *two days*. Only 39% of all Taiwanese ninth-graders manage to pass. It's enormously competitive and stressful.

Just to stress *you* out, let's look at the kinds of questions Taiwanese kids are expected to know the answers to. Here's one from the science section:

John takes 1.4 g of metal (M) to react with sulfuric acid. After the reaction, 3.4 g of MSO_4 was produced. Table 7 is the element table; please use this to identify the metal. (A) Mg (B) Ca (C) Fe (D) Cu

Element	H	O	S	Mg	Ca	Fe	Cu
Atomic weight	1	16	32	24	40	56	64

Yikes! That's a pretty sophisticated, difficult problem. But they're all like that.

As is this riddle from the math section:

In Fig. 12, ABCD is a rectangle and the length of line BC = 18, line AB = $8\sqrt{3}$. Also, point E is on line BC and the length of BE = 6. If we set point E to be the center and draw an arc with radius = 12, there is an intersection point F on line AB. Please determine the area of the shadow in this rectangle
(A) $48\pi + 18\sqrt{3}$ (B) $72\pi - 18\sqrt{3}$ (C)$120\pi + 9\sqrt{3}$ (D) 36π

Man, are we in trouble. That's the kind of stuff a Taiwanese teen must answer—not to get into college or grad school—just to get into tenth grade!

In the first-ever study of its kind, researchers from a major national Taiwanese university took genetic samples from 800 junior high students in four regions of Taiwan. By transcribing the kids' genetic code, they were able to discern which version of the COMT gene each had.

The scholars knew which kids had slow-acting enzymes, which had fast-acting, and which had a mix.

In regular classroom work, on a daily basis, the Worriers have the advantage. Thanks to high dopamine levels, they have better memories and attention and a higher verbal IQ. They're superior planners and can better orchestrate complex thought. But as the BCT nears, the pressure intensifies, and the hours spent studying grow. "Many students go to cram school almost every night to study all the subjects on the test," explained one of the scholars, Chun-Yen Chang.

The very process of learning is changed by this ever-increasing pressure. The Worriers become distressed and frustrated: they become unable to switch strategies or see something in a new way. They have trouble integrating new information. They are prone to panic when given new directions, preferring to stick to familiar ways of solving problems.

They arrive for test day feeling like they have not been their usual selves of late—that their brains haven't been as sharp the last few weeks. But they still think of themselves as top students, because during most of the school year, they're in the top group. The burden of high expectations weighs them down further. They're hoping they just don't mess up.

How do they do on the test?

The Worriers score about 8% lower than the Warriors. The Worriers struggle the most on the academic subjects that tax working memory the hardest: science, social science, and math.

It's as if some of the A students and B students trade places when it's test time.

"Just one or two percentage [points'] difference will drag you from the number one high school down to number three or four," explained Chang.

All these very smart kids don't get into the school they expect, merely because they're being tested in such a high-stakes environment. They probably know the material; if the test wasn't so competitive, they'd probably be able to give the correct answers. Their only fault is they're not good test-takers, on account of being born with a different genotype. "I am not against pressure. Actually, pressure is good to someone," Chang stated. "But the pressure of high-stakes tests in Taiwan is way too high."

Shouldn't society find some other way to evaluate kids' cognitive ability, without so much pressure?

Here's an example of how the stress of an academic test was toned down, with dramatic results.

Drs. Adam Alter and Joshua Aronson gave 124 Princeton University underclassmen a test that drew its questions from the GRE, the graduate school admissions test, so the questions would be somewhat stressful for freshmen and sophomores. As if that wasn't taxing enough, for half of the students, the researchers added to their pressure in two ways. First, the students began by answering some demographic questions: they had to report what high school they'd attended and how many of their high school classmates were also at Princeton. This was intended to make most test-takers feel as if they were alone at Princeton, that they were lucky to be at Princeton, and that they had barely met the bar for admittance. The second way the research team added to students' stress was they labeled the test, "Intellectual Ability Questionnaire." They wanted the test's title to be threatening to the students, to make the students fear that, if they did poorly, the test would reveal they lacked the true ability to be at Princeton.

The students who took the test under all this stress got 72% of the answers correct.

The other students weren't threatened in this way. Their test was labeled "Intellectual Challenge Questionnaire," as if it was brainteasers to wrestle with. Also, they weren't asked about what high school they'd attended until *after* they'd taken the test, when it could no longer affect their performance.

Those students got 90% correct.

By moderating the amount of stress the students were under, Alter and Aronson were able to engineer an 18% difference in their test scores.

Some might argue that real life is full of stress, and if high-stakes tests weed out children who can't handle the stress of performance, maybe the tests are just accurately predicting who will do well in real life.

The problem with this argument is that it fails to recognize that the amount of pressure we put ourselves under is partially within our control. As the Princeton students showed, we can ratchet up or down the stress level of many circumstances. We can also self-sort into fields that fit our stress capacity. To be a trial attorney, you need to be up for a fight; to be a research attorney, you don't. Maybe one type of computer programmer needs to excel under deadline, but another type maintains ongoing systems beautifully. One type of doctor might be better in the emergency room, while another would function well in family practice. But you can still be a lawyer, a programmer, or a doctor.

To put a finer point on it, the research does not say that those with the Worrier gene are doomed when thrown into a stressful situation.

At Stanford, Dr. Quinn Kennedy has led an ongoing study that puts airplane pilots under stress in a series of six flight simulator tests. Recently, her team checked the COMT gene of 172 pilots before they climbed in the simulator.

The pilots were kept constantly busy, flying to new altitudes and new headings, dialing to new frequencies, and punching in new transponder codes—all the while repeating the instructions aloud for confirmation. Severe turbulence rattled the simulator the entire flight. Then the carburetor would ice up, or the engine's oil pressure would drop, just as they hit air traffic and had to veer away from incoming planes. Coming in to land, they were hit by a 15-knot crosswind.

From what we know so far, we would predict that the pilots with the Warrior gene would handle this chaos well. And they did. Even the recreational pilots, pure hobbyists with only a few hundred hours of flight experience and not yet rated for instrument flying at night or in fog, handled the simulator plane as well as professional pilots. As long as they had the Warrior gene.

We'd also predict that the pilots with the Worrier gene couldn't handle the turmoil. (We might predict they don't even become pilots in the first place.)

But that's not what the scholars at Stanford found.

The recreational pilots with the Worrier gene did melt down under the pressure, as predicted. The havoc of the simulator overwhelmed them—but the more flight experience they had, the better they handled it. The Worrier-gene pilots who were professionals did best of all. The increased pressure did not diminish their performance; instead, their genetically blessed working memory and attention advantage kicked in, until they surpassed the performance of all the Warrior pilots.

What this suggests is that Worriers *can* handle stress, and even outperform the Warriors, if they train themselves to handle the specific stress of certain recurring situations. By acclimating to their stressful environment over a long period of time, they learn to perform.

The crucial difference between the pilots and the Taiwanese ninth-graders is the amount of experience they have. The pilots spend years in the cockpit, getting hundreds—even thousands—of repetitions in the stresses of flying a plane. The Taiwanese children get a single shot—one attempt at the Basic Competency Test. Practice tests might cover the same material, but they can't simulate the stress of the actual test day, when a child's future hangs in the balance.

5

In her book *The Female Brain*, Dr. Louann Brizendine calls estrogen the queen of all hormones: "powerful, in control, all-consuming; sometimes all business, sometimes an aggressive seductress." Estrogen is the primary female sex hormone. It increases drive and the ambitious spirit.

Estrogen works by passively entering cells and altering the transcription of a myriad of genes.

One of these is the COMT gene.

Estrogen's effect on the COMT process is quite dramatic. It slows down dopamine reabsorption by 30%, regardless of which genotype a woman is.

In other words, women have higher baseline levels of dopamine than men, especially during the two peaks in estrogen each month, once right before ovulation and also before menstruation. When you add stress to the equation, women are far more likely to overload. Some of the commonly cited differences between men and women are more noticeable under stress, and it's likely the result of these differing levels of dopamine.

At the University of Southern California, Drs. Nichole Lighthall and Mara Mather have done a series of experiments to determine how gender differences become more prominent under stress.

To stress people, Lighthall and Mather do it very differently than the team did at Princeton. They make subjects hold their hand submerged in ice water for as long as they can, or up to three minutes. It's very painful, and it does trigger a very strong psychoendocrine stress response. Physical stress is different from psychological stress, in that it's processed in the brainstem, while psychological stress is processed in the limbic regions— but once the stress reaction has kicked in, the result is the same.

In one early experiment, Lighthall and Mather had people play a risk-taking game where they earned money. The details of the game aren't important, except to understand that the longer you played a round, you ran the risk of suddenly losing all the money you had earned that round. To avoid this, you could play it safe by cashing out and starting a new round. Lighthall and Mather found that the differences between men and women were very small when they just came into the lab and played the game. But if they first had to submerge a hand in ice water, then play, the differences were dramatic. Women took less risk after being stressed; they made decisions more slowly and earned less money for themselves. Meanwhile, for men, the stress actually improved their performance. They took more risk, and it was *smart* risk—the stressed men earned more money overall. They also made faster decisions.

The researchers' work showed exactly the pattern that would be expected from dopamine/COMT research. Stress helped the men and hurt the women.

Lighthall and Mather repeated the study—this time scanning the subjects' brains while they played the game. They concluded that "stress leads to opposite effects in males and females." For women, the emotional regions of the brain increased activity after stress; their decision making became entangled with their emotions. But for men, there was no increase in emotionality—stress made them more calculated.

In further research, the scholars found that, in the back of our brains, in the optical cortex, there's a region where we process the visual look on faces, to read the subtle cues of mood. When women have been stressed, this region markedly increases its activity, but in men, the activity in that region is suppressed.

Under stress, men's brains tune out emotional cues. Women under stress seek out the emotional cues. The lesson from Lighthall and Mather's work is that to manage stress, women and men might go about it differently. Certain things might help calm a woman down; those same things might not even be noticed by men. And risk taking, which is a requisite part of competitiveness, might be maximized under different conditions for women than they are for men.

How might this science translate to a real-life application?

Anson Dorrance has been the coach of the women's soccer team at the University of North Carolina for over thirty years. In that time, he has led the team to twenty-one national championships. He is arguably the single most successful coach in college history, in any sport.

Dorrance's program is a perfect example of both kinds of stress management we've been discussing. He rigorously trains his players to acclimate to the specific stresses of high-stakes, high-speed, high-risk soccer. By making practices even harder and more punishing than games, the

North Carolina women become like the professional pilots in the turbulent flight simulator—so used to the stress that it no longer overwhelms them. But during the Tar Heels' matches, when the stress of competing is not simulated and all-too-real, Dorrance very consciously avoids adding to the women's stress. In those moments, he's like the researchers at Princeton, maximizing performance by taking the stress away.

In practice, he dials the stress way up. In games, he dials the stress down.

Dorrance sits on the U.S. Soccer Federation's player development committee, which makes recommendations and sets priorities for the more than 3 million American children playing in youth leagues. On this committee, there is a debate over whether winning matters. Lately, those who say winning isn't important have been in the rule. This isn't a revival of the self-esteem movement, and they're not sheltering kids. Rather, in youth play, it's easier to win by booting the ball downfield rather than connecting lots of passes. The emphasis on winning is preventing kids from learning how to pass, which is the skill they ultimately need at the highest levels. The proposed solution is for top youth players to *play fewer games.* Fewer games means less booting the ball downfield.

Because Dorrance has won so much, he has automatically been lumped in with those on the committee who say winning is important. However, he doesn't feel he belongs on that side of the argument. Instead, what he's trying to explain is that *competing is important.* Players must learn to compete. They won't succeed if they are just taught technical skill. He has succeeded by teaching girls to compete and to handle the stress of a tight game.

In his book about Dorrance titled *The Man Watching,* journalist Tim Crothers dissects the early years of the UNC Women's Soccer program. In the beginning, Dorrance coached both the men's and women's teams at North Carolina. He was adamant that girls didn't need to be coached any differently than guys: he was equally critical of all his players. Dorrance believed that almost all female players—even the very top recruits who came to UNC—had come from cultures where women were not allowed to put winning over relationships. "Especially in practice, they were afraid to compete against teammates, for fear of jeopardizing their relationships with teammates." Dorrance was inspired by the style of one player, April Heinrichs, who became the first true superstar out of the UNC program, and he decided that the success of his program depended on making the other players more like Heinrichs.

Away from the field, Heinrichs cared deeply about team dynamics and interpersonal relationships. She desperately wanted to be liked. But as Dorrance told Crothers, from her very first preseason practice in 1983, she "was an absolute shark." Whenever she stepped on the field, her sole purpose was to put the ball in the back of the net. As a player, she never sacrificed winning in order to be liked. When Heinrichs's teammates complained to Dorrance about her attitude, he not only defended Heinrichs but told them, "I want you guys to play just like her." He wanted a program where being popular didn't matter. Being respected did.

Inspired by Tar Heel basketball legend Dean Smith, Dorrance decided that the primary way to teach competitiveness was to always keep score, in as many ways as possible. Every game and scrimmage in practice had a score, and that score was written down for season-long rankings. He made his players relentlessly play against each other, in one-on-one, head-to-head competitions, so that they learned the psychological dimension needed to compete. These scores were tallied and posted publicly. He invented a 23-factor matrix that continuously graded the players on every measurable aspect of the game. Saying that he was creating "Natural Born Killers," Dorrance ran practices where the women repeatedly crashed headlong into each other—until they were unafraid of brutal contact. He made players participate even when hurt—with torn knees and broken noses. The players dreaded every week's "Terrible Tuesday," when they'd run fitness drills to the point of collapse. The team's mantra was "No Fucking Babies." Vomiting in the bushes at practice was common.

To this day, Dorrance has never backed away from any of those techniques to teach competitiveness. His teams have been known for a kind of aggressive, physical play never before seen in women's sports. Tactically, he never put four women back on defense or conceded an inch of the field. Knowing that college women players were not strong enough on the ball to handle pressure, he trained his team to close the gaps and smother opponents like a full-court press.

Dorrance concedes there is a limit on how much he has been able to make players more competitive. "They are all on a continuum, and you can move them along that continuum a bit, but most of them you can't totally transform."

One player who transformed him just as much as he transformed her was Carla Werden Overbeck. Dorrance first got to know her when, in the 1984 off-season, he was coaching a regional Olympic Development Team of fifteen- and sixteen-year-olds. A high school sophomore, Overbeck was one of his players.

"We were up in Ypsilanti, Michigan, playing some games," he told us. "I got a call that night from my wife, saying my father had died. I told my team of teens that it was okay that I was there with them, and not with him when he died. My father had wanted me to become his corporate attorney; he'd disapproved when I became a soccer coach instead. But when he saw how much I loved it, and how much richer my life was for it, he changed his perception of me and embraced my choice. I told those teens that my father wanted me to be with them. Then I went to pack, and on the way out to the car, there was a pay phone on the side of the building. Carla Overbeck was on the phone, and tears were streaming down her cheeks. She was calling her family to tell them my father had died. In that moment, I felt incredibly connected to her. Her compassion for me was amazing. She seared herself into the middle of my heart."

In that moment, he finally realized how real—and how important—these connections are for women.

While coaching the men's team, Dorrance had always felt that if he were too nice, the boys would exploit it. "They would sense weakness and take advantage if I let up on my domination of them. But with women, niceness is a sign that you really care about them." It was after seeing Overbeck's reaction that he decided to go in a different direction with the women's team.

Dorrance realized he didn't need to yell at the women, because the matrix numbers on the locker room wall were stress enough. He started calling the women by their first names, when the men were addressed only by their last names. He would put the women through an extremely hard practice, but then he'd invite the team over to his house for pizza or banana splits.

"They didn't need the force of my personality," he said. "They needed my humanity. Above all, they wanted me to care about them as people."

He was still stressing them, but his *de-stressing* toolbox was new. He presented long-stem roses to seniors before their final game, and, every season, he wrote players long, heartfelt letters about their virtues. Often, he read these letters aloud in the locker room, bringing the entire team to tears. On the field, crying was taboo. But off the field, a cry-fest was sometimes just what they all needed.

The single-best example of how Dorrance coaches women is in his halftime speech. When he coached men, Dorrance's best-ever halftime speech was when he got so mad that he kicked a trash can through a window. "I drove that sucker through a window and I stormed out," he recounted in *The Man Watching*. "Let me tell you something about human evolution. That spoke volumes to the men in the room. In the second half everything changed. All of a sudden, we had great energy, tactics, shape, and the game totally turned around."

Some men, he feels, *need* shock to wake them up. Top male athletes are so used to competition that even being on the losing end at half-time is not shock enough.

But he would never treat women that way.

As Dorrance told Crothers, "If they've played poorly, you still come storming in like a caged tiger, but because these are women they can sense immediately that you're upset. The critical thing is tone. You turn to face them and you calmly say, 'Well, what do you think?' Now you can hear a chorus of self-flagellation as every woman in the room is taking full responsibility for the disaster that is taking place. I haven't criticized anybody, and I don't need to because they're their own worst critics. . . . [A]nd now when the halftime talk ends they are willing to die for you because all you've done is support them."

That's all he does. *Well, what do you think?* This winningest coach in history, this rabid collector of inspirational quotations, emotional writer of letters . . . and his halftime speech is . . . "Well, what do you think?"

The stress of the game is already as much as they can handle. By picking his moments to *not* yell at his players, he's won twenty-one championships.

Three years after that training camp in Michigan, Carla Werden Overbeck arrived at North Carolina as a freshman. That first year, she wanted to be everyone's friend, and her play suffered for it. But after a while, she was complaining to reporters that she was "sick and tired" of seeing her name on the bottom of the matrix list on the locker room wall. "Some players only put their toe in it the freshman year. They jump in later," Dorrance remarked. "Carla made a transformation to becoming one of the most competitive players I ever coached."

The Tar Heels won every national college championship from 1986 to 1994. Carla Overbeck became the team captain, then the U.S. team captain, and in the 1999 World Cup—where Brandi Chastain became famous for pulling off her jersey in victory—it was Overbeck who took the first penalty kick. Her journey to being World Champion had begun in compassionate tears as a teen.

CHAPTER FIVE

Even Odds: Why Women Need Them and Men Don't

1

To explore the question of how competitive someone is, or to ask a categorical question such as whether men or women are more competitive, a distinction has to be made between how *hard* someone competes, and how *eagerly* someone chooses to compete in the first place. There's scant evidence that women don't compete as hard as men; however, there is sizable evidence that women, on average, don't jump into competitions as easily as men do, and they don't turn situations into explicit competitions as quickly as men do.

As you'll see in this chapter, that's not necessarily a bad thing.

This chapter will look at female-male differences in several contexts: in political elections, in laboratory experiments, in elite schools, and on Wall Street.

It's a curious quirk of American history. The first woman ever to serve in the U.S. Congress, Jeannette Rankin, was elected to that office in 1916—four years before the constitutional amendment gave women the right to vote. (The suffragist Rankin could vote in her home state of Montana, but women were still barred from full voting rights in more than 30 other states.)

A hundred years later, we still have to cheer as "special" every time a woman wins a seat in Congress. During the 112th Congress, for every five male representatives, there was just one female representative. While women make up half the U.S. population, 44 of the 50 states have male governors, and men are mayors in 92 of the 100 largest cities in the nation.

Why aren't more women in elected office? According to the Pew Research Center, most Americans believe that gender discrimination is to blame. They themselves would vote for a female, but, as a society, they believe that Americans just aren't ready to elect a woman to higher office.

It is undeniably true that sexism persists. For example, talk show host Glenn Beck referred to Senator Mary Landrieu (D-La.) as a prostitute because of a vote she'd made, while Michael Savage maligned then-Senator Olympia Snowe (R-Maine) as a "Jezebel." When Secretary of State Hillary Rodham Clinton held a 2011 press event with Peruvian prime minister Salomon Lerner, the *Huffington Post*'s sole coverage of the event was a poll to see if readers approved of Clinton's hairstyle.

But surprisingly, study after study has shown that when women are on the ballot today, they win just as often as men do. They also raise just as much money in campaign donations. Generally speaking, Democrats vote for their party's nominee, regardless of the nominee's gender. The same goes for Republicans.

If women can win just as often as men, then what's the holdup?

There's an even more fundamental problem: women don't get elected because they refuse to put their names on the ballot in the first place.

They just aren't competing in the political arena in the same numbers as men. This is true despite decades of determined effort encouraging women to become candidates. A number of organizations—such as Yale University's nonpartisan "Women's Campaign School"—train women on everything from giving a persuasive stump speech to hiring campaign staff. There are Democratic and Republican organizations whose sole mission is to help female candidates get elected. Such efforts are treasured by candidates they've supported: Senator Kirsten Gillibrand (D-N.Y.) credits such programs as being a factor in her election.

Nevertheless, according to Rutgers University's Center for American Women and Politics, just four women filled out the forms for a gubernatorial run in 2012. In 1994, that number was 34.

In fact, even when you go down the food chain to survey the kinds of people who might one day run for office—lawyers, businesspeople, community activists, educators—and you ask them if they've ever even contemplated running, men are 35% more likely to say that they've considered it.

The question is, why? Elections are intense, grueling competitions, held in public. Is there something about competing that scares away talented women? Are women just less ambitious than men?

Paul Begala, one of the nation's leading political strategists, knows that women candidates can be just as tough as the men. Begala developed a profound admiration for Senator Dianne Feinstein (D-Calif.) when he worked on Feinstein's brutal reelection campaign in 1994. As grueling as it was, Begala says of Feinstein, "She never flinched. She never panicked." Instead, the senator stated, "I have been through tougher times." Begala had known this was true: it was Feinstein who found the body of murdered San Francisco supervisor Harvey Milk.

Begala was also at the side of Feinstein's Senate colleague, Barbara Boxer (D-Calif.) during Boxer's reelection. Begala was impressed by Boxer's spirit of determination: she was never afraid to fight for her office.

That's what you need, Begala says, to be elected.

In 2006, then-chairman of the Democratic Congressional Campaign Committee Rahm Emanuel had asked Begala for help with recruiting some congressional candidates. Begala traveled around the country meeting with a dozen or so state representatives, party officials, and others who had caught Emanuel's eye. In those meetings, Begala was looking for people ready to do the political equivalent of climbing Mount Everest. You don't want someone showing up with just a windbreaker and a backpack: "You want them to know that it's freezing and a lot of people die on the way up." If Begala sensed any ambivalence in someone about running, he reported back to Emanuel that they should find someone else to run.

"You want someone burning burning burning. If it's against your better judgment, you can't do it. You want someone who wakes up in the morning and says, 'This is a great day to run head first into a brick wall,' and they'll say it again tomorrow." Within the bounds of the law, they have to be willing to do whatever it takes. The one who does whatever it takes is the one who wins.

If we stopped here, we could just leave with the idea that women are just innately less ambitious or less competitive, or both. But Sarah Fulton's research flipped that idea upside down. And in the process, she created a completely new approach to considering gender and competitiveness.

Fulton, a professor of political science at Texas A&M, was doing a sort of scholarly version of Begala's recruiting process. She'd surveyed 835 men and women currently serving in their state legislatures, trying to see how many of them were considering a move up to the U.S. Congress.

Statehouses are considered an "If you can make it there, you'll make it anywhere" scenario. State legislators learn very quickly how noble ideas and campaign promises are ground into the sausage of legislation. Serving in a statehouse requires a punishing schedule: there's little glamour in spending all night in a committee meeting arguing over the wording of a single line in a proposed bill. Some state representatives are in session most of the year, and they have full-time offices handling constituents' personal issues as well as conducting legislative work. Other state legislatures are "part-time," but that just means their representatives usually have full-time regular jobs on top of their duties at the capitol. Then add to all that the constant concern of a reelection campaign.

Survive a term or two as a state legislator, and it can be a stepping stone to national office. According to one analysis, half of those in the U.S. Congress previously served in state legislatures.

Knowing this, Fulton had two main questions for the state representatives. First, how likely is it that you'll run for the U.S. Congress in the next election? And second, if you do run, what are the chances you would win?

State legislators know, on a daily basis, the answers to these questions. They know how in sync their political views are with those of their constituents. They know if their ideas have broad-based support, or if they're on their own with a vote. They know who the likely opponents in a congressional race will be. They know the size of their campaign war chest. They know where they stand in the state's political hierarchy, and if they can expect the support of their political party. In some states, this alone can tip the odds in their favor.

Analyzing the state representatives' responses, Fulton concluded that ambitious male state legislators will run for Congress if they have *any* chance to win. Ambitious female legislators will run for Congress if they have a *good* chance to win.

The tipping point seems to be around 20% odds. When the odds of winning are below that, almost all the candidates will be men. When the odds of winning are better than that, women jump in the race. In fact, when the odds are decent, women will compete in the election even more than men will.

The ambition gap goes away, and even reverses itself, if the odds of success are plausible. Men will gamble on long odds—even stupid odds. Women won't.

Begala was once meeting with a friend of his, Tommy Sowers—at the time a professor at West Point. Sowers was a decorated war hero, armed with two Bronze Stars and a Ph.D. in government from the London School of Economics. He had been an Army Ranger and a Green Beret. Having served two tours in Iraq, he was involved in the first Iraqi elections, in intelligence, and in coordinating efforts with Iraqi civilians.

After eleven years of service, Sowers told Begala that he wanted to retire from the military and become a Democratic candidate for Congress. The question was: from where? Between going to college at Duke and his various military posts, Sowers had a number of places he could legitimately call home. And both he and Begala knew that the district he chose could decide his election.

Eventually, Sowers decided on moving to his childhood home of Rolla, Missouri: he'd run as a candidate for the state's Eighth Congressional District. But the Eighth was likely the most conservative congressional district in the nation. The (literal) birthplace of Rush Limbaugh, no Democrat had won that seat in 30 years. The current Republican incumbent had been in office for seven terms, and it was a foregone conclusion that there'd be an eighth for the Eighth.

Facing a tough midterm election, 2010 wasn't a year Democrats were likely to gain a historically Republican seat. Begala tried to get Sowers to reconsider a Missouri race; he encouraged Sowers to move some place where Sowers had at least a chance of winning. "But there was just no talking him out of it," Begala recalled.

Sowers ran. Some argued that he was the first serious challenger the incumbent had ever faced, but he was still 40 points behind in the polls. Begala and others helped him as much as they could; by November, Sowers had over a million dollars to spend on the campaign. However, Begala knew that no matter what they did, it wouldn't make a bit of difference on Election Day.

And it didn't.

"He got trounced," said Begala.

Sowers received only 29% of the vote.

The war hero had always known it was a losing battle. The odds were against him, but it was his hometown. His family was there. His heart was there. He'd rather have lost there than won somewhere else.

"I'm not saying that men are not strategic, but women are more responsive to the costs and benefits. You could vary the chance of winning, but it isn't going to alter the men's running all that much," explained Fulton. "But for women, it's a really strong, steep slope. They're extremely responsive to the chance of winning."

Fulton's findings changed the paradigm across all the social sciences. It was no longer sufficient to claim that women were inherently less competitive just because they competed in fewer contests. Instead, it was necessary to evaluate the more strategic aspects of tournament entry—how the potential costs and benefits compare to the likelihood of success.

Women do seem to compete less—because they only compete when they know they have a decent chance to win.

"Women are thinking very strategically and proceeding very carefully," Fulton said.

A study of elected Texas judges confirmed Fulton's core finding. As did a study of New York state trial court judges. When the odds are actually good, women will compete (by entering the race) more than men.

As noted earlier, on the whole, the odds of winning are the same for women as for men. So how do we reconcile this and explain why women so rarely run for the U.S. Congress?

The decisive factor is incumbency. Incumbents win about 92–95% of the time, depending on the year. That figure doesn't change much. Even 2010, considered a horrendous year for congressional incumbents, saw 100% of Republicans retain their seats and 82% of Democrats retain theirs. All told, a "terrible" year for incumbents meant that they won 87% of the time, instead of the usual 95%.

"It's pretty risky—and kind of stupid—to challenge an entrenched incumbent," commented Fulton.

Facing those impossible odds, men like Tommy Sowers will run, but women won't. Instead, women will wait until something weakens the incumbent (a change in the economy, a personal scandal). Or they'll wait until the congressional seat is vacant and their odds are a 50-50 toss-up. In the meantime, they will work on building the skills needed to make them even stronger candidates.

When you look at other elected positions, where women have better odds, you see a different story. There are approximately 550,000 elected positions in the United States. (To put that number in perspective—there are 363,000 computer programmers.) The majority of those are for local government positions, perhaps a part-time city council or school board. The odds of winning in those races are much better. And so women hold a much higher percentage of posts—44% of school board posts are held by women. Not quite parity, but much closer.

Once again—the new paradigm becomes apparent. When women are confident they have a chance, they will compete. As much or more than men. They just refuse to waste time with losing.

"I was surprised that women were thinking so much more about the probability of success as opposed to men," said Fulton.

2

For the first time in human history, women and men commonly compete side by side. Most of the aggressive, ambitious, daring things we attempt to accomplish are done together.

But—as Fulton's research dramatically shows—men and women don't compete the same.

From champion tennis players to MBA students to army recruits to *Jeopardy!* contestants—even children just racing across the playground—women and men compete differently. They choose competitors differently. They don't have the same timing in their attacks and withdrawals. They differ in whether they play to win, versus play not to lose. They judge risk differently, even more so when under stress. They attach different meanings to successes and failures—which, in turn, alters whether they choose to compete again. They differ in how they buffer the anxiety of endlessly being ranked against others. Whether they're competing alongside the other sex can really affect how intensely they compete. While men will turn a mundane activity like washing dishes into a race, women have their own social-reputation domains where they compete, and men don't—from who has the best shoes to who is the better mother. Because of this, women feel their lives are every bit as competitive—if not more—than men's lives are.

Working with this science can feel like working with flammable compounds or radioactive materials. But it's paramount to understand these nuances of how men and women compete, and recognize what maximizes their performance.

The first thing we need to appreciate is that to compete means to risk losing: the more you have to invest in the competition (time, money, emotion), the more you can lose. And women—as in the case of the female politicians—judge this risk differently from men.

Take chess, for example. A chess rating of 2200 or higher designates a player as a National Master. Theoretically, there shouldn't be a difference between male and female players at such an elite level, but there is. A Stockholm University study of 1.4 million games over 11 years showed that elite women are less likely to use an aggressive opening move than elite male players. The women devote more deliberative thought to their first 25 moves: they are looking for the best possible move every time, instead of a good move. (That means they often run short on time in tournaments and have to rush at the end.) Women are less likely to arrange a draw when the outcome is predictable—women want to play the game out. If it's a sure win for women, they want to get that win. (Men seem to get bored or decide that the time spent finishing the game is more trouble than it's worth.)

A study of *Jeopardy!* contestants revealed that, on average, women who hit the "Daily Double" square will bet 40% of their pot; men will bet 60%. How much they bet doesn't have anything to do with how well they have played up to this point, or what they'll do after. In a study of 20,000 people's retirement accounts, women were more conservative in pension fund allocations. A gender difference in risk taking is apparent even among gamblers at the horse track: gambling women make smaller bets, so when they lose, they lose less.

But is it wrong to be conservative with pension funds? Is it right to bet lots of money at the horse track?

Stanford economics professor Muriel Niederle has been interested in women's underrepresentation in business boardrooms since she was a high schooler. She was in an advanced math track that was equally populated by boys and girls. "But when they went to college, so many of the women studied comparative literature or theater, while all the guys went to engineering or math or physics," she said. "I thought it was odd." Were women avoiding harder subject areas because those areas were more competitive? When Niederle graduated from Harvard with her Ph.D. in economics, she thought it would be an interesting phenomenon to research.

Niederle's body of research is famous for a simple lab challenge. Reflective of her own background, she asked subjects to do some easy, grade-school arithmetic. They were given sets of five two-digit numbers to add. They had five minutes to get as many done as possible. To make sure they worked hard at it, she paid the subjects by the set: 50 cents for each set completed. Men and women did equally well, averaging about 10 sets completed and earning $5. (Each set took about 30 seconds.)

Go ahead and try a set:

$$
\begin{array}{r}
45 \\
93 \\
26 \\
81 \\
+\,69 \\
\hline
\end{array}
$$

Then two men and two women sat in a room, and they did the task again. This time, the only change was that it was now winner-take-all. Whoever solved the most sets won $2 per set. Under these conditions, much like Norman Triplett's kids on the Competition Machine, Niederle's subjects worked a little harder and on average completed about 12 sets. Again, men and women did equally well. But they didn't know this: they weren't yet told who'd won, and the winner hadn't yet been paid the $25–$30. They had to go into the third round without knowing.

For the third and final round of the math challenge, they had a choice. Did they want to be paid by the set, as in the first round? Or did they want to enter another winner-take-all tournament?

Despite the fact men and women had performed equally well in the previous round, a staggering gap emerged. Seventy-three percent of men entered the tournament, but only 35% of women wanted to play winner-take-all.

Niederle has replicated this time and again, and now many other scholars use her paradigm as well. "The data is so clear, the gap is so big," Niederle said.

At first glance, it looks as if women are afraid of competing in a win-lose situation. And in the thirty or so news articles reporting Niederle's work, that's often been the headline. But think of it rationally for a moment. The odds of winning the tournament round are 1 in 4. For any one player, it's very likely he or she will lose and get nothing. For those average at math, the rational choice is to not enter the tournament.

Those who are brilliant at math and confident of their ability should enter the tournament and go after the quadruple prize. Otherwise, the expected return is higher being paid by the set.

For those 73% of men who want to enter the tournament, one of two things is going on in their heads:

1) They know they'll very likely lose, but they don't mind because they want someone else to get the $25 pot.
2) They are under the illusion that they have a good chance to win.

This is not Lake Wobegon. Seventy-three percent of men are not above average—which means there are a lot of men who falsely believe they're going to win.

By contrast, the women are better judges of their own ability. Most don't enter the tournament because they recognize it's a losing proposition. It's not that women are naturally risk-averse. They perceive risk quite accurately. It's not that women are afraid of the competition itself, or don't enjoy the competition—it's that they're better at recognizing when they will probably lose.

It's men who don't really recognize the odds and are overconfident. They mostly think about what they'll win. Challenged to compete, they can't resist.

Niederle is clear that even among women who ace the math sets, and for whom the likely odds of winning another tournament are high, there's still a reluctance to enter. They play it safe a little more than they should.

However, it doesn't take much to get women to compete more. In a recent study, the classic Niederle experiment was replicated with MBA students. The only change in the protocol was that right before doing the experiment, the MBAs were given one of two short surveys. One survey asked about their gender and family, and how many kids they had. The other survey quizzed them about their professional plans—what was their expected salary after graduation, et cetera. Women MBAs who took the family survey were reluctant to compete in the third round. Women MBAs who took the professional survey had no such reluctance. Even more of them wanted to compete than male MBAs.

To get women to compete, they need to be in a social context where competing is relevant to their success.

When they choose to be overtly competitive, women, it seems, are more attuned to the context than men are. As you'll see in the next section, the ability to turn competitiveness off is just as important as the ability to turn it on.

3

When parents send their children to elite schools, they're often aware of the potential downside: elite schools are competitive cauldrons. What if my child isn't quite up to it? Will the hothouse environment be too much, with my child surrounded by so many high achievers? Parents often wonder if their kids would do just as well going to a good school that drew a wider range of students.

Northwestern University professor C. Kirabo Jackson has discovered that girls handle the hothouse environment differently from boys. Girls tend to thrive in these environments, across the board, and the more elite the school, the better they do.

Not necessarily so for boys.

The first piece of evidence came from his study in the small Caribbean nation of Trinidad and Tobago. Jackson got the data on every fifth-grader in the country in 2000. Virtually all the children there attend a form of public school, modeled on the British system: either a government school or a "government-assisted" school such as a religious school. Every one of these schools is ranked, from the most elite college preparatory boarding schools down to vocational schools, and these rankings are widely published.

Jackson compared students' fifth-grade national test scores against their scores in tenth grade. He noted the ranking of the middle school they attended those intervening five years. Did going to a higher-ranked school mean you improved the most?

After he set up his models and ran all the numbers, "I thought I must have made a mistake," Jackson said. He started over from scratch and ran the numbers again. Same thing. What he found was that boys and girls have different outcomes from attending elite middle schools. "Boys seem to be more discouraged," Jackson said.

Pointedly, Jackson noted that, for boys who went to the most elite schools, their math scores suffered. They would have *learned more math* if they had gone to a slightly easier school. When Jackson looked at single-sex schools, the trend was even stronger.

Could it really be true, Jackson wondered, that boys don't handle the elite competitive cauldrons as well as girls? Aren't boys supposed to be more competitive than girls?

Jackson started asking friends and other researchers if they were seeing a similar pattern in their ongoing studies—was anyone else finding that boys were hurt by being in a more competitive environment?

Papers started coming in from around the world.

One study tracked 2,134 students attending an elite Chinese university. Chinese colleges assign students to dorms: the same three or four people will share one very small room for the entire four years of school. Researchers tracked these quartets over time, and they found that the best-achieving woman served as a "shining light" for her roommates. Over time, she pulled up the grades of her fellow roommates. But the strongest male roommate had the opposite effect; his presence seemed to drive down his roommates' grades year to year. Rather than being inspired by their high-achieving dormmate, "Men seem to be depressed by their strongest peer."

British researchers reached a similar conclusion, after looking at test scores of 1,300,000 children in the British public schools. The very strongest boys, the "Top Five Percenters," tended to have a negative effect on the boys who ranked just below them. When going to an elite school filled with the very best students, boys who scored in the 80th to 94th percentile on national tests didn't continue learning as much as those who went to a slightly easier school. There was no such effect for equivalent girls, who only got benefits from attending a very top school with top students.

A fourth study had researchers from Harvard, Yale, and Dartmouth come together to follow kids who entered public school lotteries for charter school spots. If you've seen movies like *Waiting for Superman*, you know these charter schools are supposed to be saviors, the road to college. On the whole, their data was on impoverished children in the American South. Just as you'd expect, girls who won the lottery and attended their first-choice charter school increased their odds of going to a four-year college. But boys who *lost* the lottery (and didn't go to the charter school of their dreams) had better odds of attending a four-year college than boys who *won* the lottery.

That's astounding. Something was going wrong during high school for many boys who attended these charter schools.

All these researchers were perplexed by their findings at first—they even doubted the accuracy of their data. But looking at the papers together, Jackson saw that each confirmed the other. Around the world, a pattern was becoming clear.

Jackson went back to his data and dug in. He realized that when a child goes to an elite school, there are two major factors on performance. First is the "resource effect." Elite schools have great teachers, an organized curriculum, and administrators who help fine-tune the school each year. Second is the "competitive effect": the presence of other top students, who push one another to excel.

For girls, both factors add to their learning and performance. However, for boys, the two factors conflict and often cancel each other out.

The resource effect drives performance up. But the competitive effect causes boys on the losing end to fall behind. "Being a small fish in a big pond is particularly bad for boys," Jackson added.

"The bottom line is, if you have a girl, I would put her in the best school as possible and have her around the smartest peers possible," Jackson summarized. "If you have a son, you should put them in the school with the brightest teachers, but you should be wary of putting him in a hypercompetitive environment."

Think once more to that study of the Air Force Academy cadets—which backfired when low-performing boys were put in squadrons with high-achievers.

The Air Force Academy was *82% male.*

The irony of the Air Force experiment is that the all-boys environment hid the all-boys result. Suddenly, the experiment's backfiring seems almost inevitable: *Well, of course, it didn't work—weaker boys don't do very well in schools when confronted with higher-achieving peers.*

What's going on?

This is not, as it first seems, a failure to compete on the part of boys. It's an example of how the psyche gets worn down when you *overcompete*—when people compete too much, always interpreting their world through the lens of winners and losers.

When enrolling in these schools, girls tend to be highly aware of the probability that they'll no longer be one of the best. Boys rarely even think about this risk; full of confidence on Day One, most don't truly realize what they're in for, and they're caught off guard by what happens. Then, Jackson suspects, boys who fall behind find it difficult to ask for help, not wanting to admit their troubles. Girls ask for help and get it, bringing them back into the fold.

Most competitions are held over a defined period of time—the 60 minutes of football. When the contest is over, competitors can relax, leave it behind, and separate themselves from how well they did in the game. In elite schools, this isn't the case. The competition for good grades is endless; the comparisons never cease. It's not just a game—it's their life, with real outcomes. Competition is not just about winning; sometimes it's about surviving. To lose in a game is something men can rebound from. But to be losing in life, day in and day out, gets to them. They can't escape it.

As religious scholar James Carse explained, *finite* games have a beginning, an end, and the goal of winning. Between games, there is recuperation and restoration. *Infinite* games, by definition, can never end, and, since no winner is ever declared, the goal instead is to just stay ahead. With infinite games, there's no rest—only a waxing and waning of competitive intensity.

It's in these infinite games, the evidence suggests, that women survive better than men. By *not* always caring about winning and losing, they thrive. Their competitive style is more successful.

All these examples have been in academic settings. But the pattern is still present far away from the hothouse environment of elite schools, somewhere entirely different—such as an office furniture dealership.

A large national office furniture chain decided to test if letting employees know their national sales ranking would motivate them. It didn't work at all—those who learned their rank sold 26% less furniture over the next two years. But there was a gender difference in the decline: almost all that reduction in sales was from bummed-out sales*men*. The men couldn't handle it. They liked the old way, thinking they were the third- or fourth-best salesperson in the local office. It destroyed them to learn they were ranked 239th nationally. Saleswomen just weren't bothered by it. They knew their rank, but were less heedful of it. It didn't get to them.

4

Let's go back to this finding that men tend to be overconfident and think their odds of winning are better than they actually are. It's the lab version of the decision being made by the state legislators whether to run for Congress. Women are savvy about the odds, men are good at ignoring the odds.

Do these optimistic biases show up elsewhere in the real world? What about in an industry such as Wall Street, where judging risk accurately is the name of the game? Do the female financial analysts perform any differently from the men?

The knee-jerk reaction is that of course women don't perform worse than men, and any such thought to the contrary would be sexist. Women broke into Wall Street in large numbers in the 1980s, when investment banks began recruiting talent from the top colleges and business schools. These were high-prestige, high-salaried jobs that the women were trying to nab. (In 2006 the average stock analyst on Wall Street made $590,000 a year.)

During the 1980s, of all the financial analysts covering stocks, 8% were women. This figure rose through the 1990s, and in 2001 it peaked at 20%. Since then, the percentage of female analysts has fallen, to 16%. Were women underperforming?

What if we told you the opposite was the case—that female financial analysts have statistically outperformed men, by a meaningful margin? And that Wall Street, which prides itself on being the greatest financial market, is actually an inefficient *labor* market, because it's going in the wrong direction?

Dr. Alok Kumar, from the University of Texas's McCombs School of Business, became interested in gender and financial projections when he read studies on whether women CFOs were better than male CFOs at maximizing shareholder value. They were, but the dataset was not large enough to be truly conclusive. In search of a larger dataset, he went to the Thomson Reuters' Institutional Brokers Estimate System (I/B/E/S). This had every financial earnings projection made by every Wall Street stock analyst from May of 1983 to June of 2006—a total of 2,856,198 forecasts issued by 18,292 analysts who covered 21,107 stocks. These were not "Buy/Sell" ratings; they were projections of the earnings-per-share each company would gain in future quarterly financial performance. Women made 16% of these projections.

The first thing Kumar found was that women analysts outperform men: their projections are 7.3% *more accurate.* Women also do less "herding," clustering near the industry average to avoid being controversial and sticking out. They also don't revise their estimates just because everyone else on the Street revised the numbers. All-in-all, women are actually bolder in their predictions than men. And to top it off, they do all this despite having fewer years of experience on the job.

Prior to 2000, many Wall Street financial analysts were privy to earnings guidance from CFOs. Cozy analysts had the inside scoop. This ended when the Securities and Exchange Commission instituted Regulation Fair Disclosure. As well, in 2003, a global settlement prevented stock analysts from even talking with the investment bankers in their firms without a compliance officer in the room. It's important to note that Kumar's dataset includes hundreds of thousands of financial estimates made after these rules were in place. His findings held equally true before and after the regulatory changes.

Kumar checked to make sure that women weren't outperforming only in the industry sectors where they made up a larger proportion of the analysts, such as the apparel/clothing sector, where 40% of the financial estimates were made by women. Stocks are normally categorized into 48 different industries. Of those, male analysts outperformed women in only 15 industries. Women analysts beat the men in 33 industries.

The question Kumar was interested in started to change. If women were better at financial estimates, did the market realize this?

In the 1970s, *Institutional Investor* magazine began naming the All-America Research Team, declaring certain stock analysts as "All-Stars." The magazine's All-Stars team has grown, to the point that it now anoints over 300 analysts each year. In 2006, "All-Star" analysts were paid, on average, $1.4 million a year. Kumar found that *Institutional Investor* was recognizing females' ability. Female analysts make up a higher percentage of All-Stars than they do market-wide, and they were the best performers of all.

However, that recognition of the women's superior performance went only so far. The industry applauded the female rock stars, but failed to acknowledge that even the *average* female analyst was equivalent to a male All-Star.

Then, in a far more complicated analysis, Kumar investigated how the market moves after a stock analyst revises his or her earnings projection. Stock prices show more movement after a revision from a woman—suggesting that the Street trusts female analysts more than men.

So if women do better, and the financial markets secretly know this, why do women make up only 16% of the analysts on the Street? Why is the percentage going down, not up? Because Wall Street is indeed an inefficient labor market. Women are underhired; only the very best are getting in. Meanwhile, plenty of inaccurate men are being hired, and they are paid hundreds of thousands of dollars for jobs they aren't good at.

Since Kumar's research was published in 2010, variations on it have been reproduced in Europe, looking at Buy/Sell recommendations. (The lesson: when a woman tells you to sell a stock, listen to her.) Studies have also looked at when women are on the audit committee, and when women are on a company's board of directors. The general pattern is that men drive a company to take more risk, but women are more accurate in projections and are better at keeping companies out of trouble.

It's sometimes hard to say whether these tendencies are a good thing or a bad thing. It's good to stay out of trouble—especially for large companies—but being an entrepreneur is all about taking risk.

The open question remains—is all that risk calculation ultimately to women's benefit? Of course, both men and women do some sort of risk-reward calculation when deciding to enter a competition. But it's women who tend to focus on odds, and it's men who focus on what they'll win.

Researchers have found that the more people focus on their odds of winning, the less likely they'll go for it. But the more they focus on what they'll win if they succeed, the more likely they'll go for it. People standing in line for Powerball don't think that their odds of winning are one in 195 million; instead, they're thinking about the $195 million they would take home. People who write screenplays don't think about the terrible odds (only 1 out of every 363 registered scripts is purchased every year), they think about seeing their story on the silver screen.

The Egyptian men and women who took to Tahrir Square did not decide to act because they believed in the likelihood of success: what pushed them forward was the prize of freedom.

Maybe we need more Tommy Sowerses in the world. Yes, Sowers's race didn't work out. But the odds didn't really look any better for Steve Jobs, and he did just fine. The world needs underdogs who will take a fighting chance. If they dwelled on the odds, they'd never do it.

One of Paul Begala's favorite movie scenes is from *Dumb and Dumber.* Jim Carrey's character asks Lauren Holly's what are the chances of them having a relationship. "Not good," answers Holly's character.

"Not good like . . . one in a hundred?" asks Carrey.

"More like—" Holly replies, "one in a million."

Carrey takes this in for a moment.

Then he responds: "So you're telling me there's a chance." And he screams with delight.

"That's who I want," Begala explained. "I'm drawn to the people who want the million-to-one shot."

If we, too, want more of the men and women willing to go for it, the question we're left with at this point is, what makes people more competitive in the first place—what forces at work in their early lives make them comfortable with winning and losing, make them get up for daring challenges, and what keeps them from quitting when they're behind? In our next chapter, we'll look at just that—some of the underlying mechanisms that light (or extinguish) competitive fire.

CHAPTER SIX

The Utter Importance of Pillow Fights

1

Lord of the Flies was first published in September 1954. While the novel is chilling, at a certain point, readers can find solace in knowing it's a work of fiction, and there was no actual kid named "Piggy" tortured in a forest.

But just three months before its publication, a real-life version of Golding's drama played out in Robbers Cave State Park. Three hours outside of Oklahoma City, there was a real boy called "Fatty" fighting to protect his little corner of the forest.

Fatty's summer didn't start out as dramatically as the plane crash of Golding's telling. Instead, a bus just dropped off twelve boys at the park campground. The eleven-year-old boys were complete strangers, but they began to form fast friendships as they were given free rein of the campground.

A couple of kids left camp from homesickness, and the remaining boys shed a few tears for their missing families. But, by and large, the boys—"the Eagles"—were having a wonderful time. The camp was well worth the $25 each family had paid: the Eagles spent their days hiking, playing baseball, barbecuing, canoeing, exploring caves—even the one Jesse James once used as a hideout. But what the boys didn't know was that they were unwitting guinea pigs in one of the most elaborate psychology experiments ever conducted.

Everything in the camp, from the cabin decoration to the food served, had been artfully arranged to test how strangers become groups and how groups become enemies. The camp counselors were, in truth, psychology grad students and professors. The lead researcher, University of Oklahoma professor Muzafer Sherif, had disguised himself as a janitor to watch events unfold.

After the boys had spent some time bonding, they learned they were not alone: there was another cabin of boys, "the Rattlers." The next day, they overheard the Rattlers playing a game. Instantly, one of the Eagles, Wilson, began hurling racial insults at the unseen Rattlers.

Even after the boys met face-to-face, they continued to taunt each other with racial slurs, despite the fact all the campers were nearly identical towheaded kids with the same backgrounds and abilities. Wilson became "Fatty" as far as the Rattlers were concerned, but Wilson's quick hatred and suspicion of the Rattlers improved his status within the Eagles. He became one of the most powerful kids in the cabin.

To catalyze hatred between the groups, Sherif had organized a tournament between the cabins—with events such as tug-of-war, tent pitching, sports contests, and a treasure hunt. But the staged events weren't needed: skirmishes broke out all on their own.

Within just a couple of days, things were already getting out of hand. The Eagles had stolen and burned the Rattlers' flag. In the common mess hall, every meal turned into a food fight, and the kids weren't laughing. They intended to hurt their foes: they collected rocks to throw next. Fatty and the others plotted their next moves. Within days, kids from each group began breaking into the other group's cabins, stealing and destroying the others' prized possessions. Yelling matches escalated into fistfights, until the researchers concluded that the Eagles and Rattlers had to be physically separated for their safety.

Yet, by the time Fatty was climbing aboard the bus for home, all the Eagles and Rattlers had set aside their differences. They were sitting with one another, joking, and laughing. Fatty had become so attached to all the boys that he didn't want to go home. He wanted everyone to remain with him at camp.

What happened between things spiraling out of control, and all the camaraderie on the bus?

Throughout the camp tournament, part of the reason the kids had become so involved in the competition was that there had been no clear winner: each cabin had a real chance at overtaking the other. What the boys hadn't known was that Sherif's researchers had been rigging events so that each would be a close race. They'd planned for the kids to become frustrated and upset, so the boys would fight harder and harder to win.

However, just as the tournament ended, the camp's water tank broke, and all the kids had to help fix it. A couple of days later, one of the camp trucks stalled, and the kids tried to figure out how to get it moving: after some initial head-scratching, they came up with the idea to pull it with their tug-of-war rope. Then the kids agreed to send the broken truck away to be fixed—which meant they'd all have to ride together on one truck for their return. Then the camp couldn't afford the film rental for the Camp Movie Night: the kids figured out what would be a fair contribution from each boy and made up the difference.

Gradually, working for the success of the entire camp became more important than an Eagle or Rattler identity. The boys' competitiveness no longer led to hatred; in its place was a friendlier sort of opposition. The boys even grew to respect the kids from the other group.

Just as the researchers had planned. Because the events that led the kids to cooperate had been just as elaborately staged as those that had led them to fight like cats and dogs.

When Sherif was running his Robbers Cave experiment, memories of World War II were all too fresh, and the ink had barely dried on the Korean War armistice. In the South, they were beginning to draw the battle lines of the civil rights movement. In light of all that, it's unsurprising that everyone focused on the first half of the Sherif experiment: it confirmed everyone's worst fears. Humans—even young children—preternaturally formed tribes. And all it took for tribes to go to war was to know about the other's mere existence.

However, Sherif's point was not the same as Golding's. Sherif believed that the value in his work was more than a frightening cautionary tale.

Yes, Sherif believed that groups are naturally competitive. But Robbers Cave isn't a dark tale set in a competitive state of nature. It's a story about how much a social environment shapes competition and competitiveness. Robbers Cave is a reminder that competitions have rules for a reason: they limit bad behavior and set necessary boundaries for appropriate conduct.

The real importance of Sherif's work was to shine a light on how groups can be brought together. To understand that rivalries can be set aside in pursuit of a common productive goal.

2

While boys don't usually grow up in a Robbers Cave–type environment, it's true that males do spend most of their lives in groups.

Females, on the other hand, spend most of their time in pairs.

And this may explain gender differences in competitiveness. Group membership may be why men—who compete *more*—are *less* concerned about the outcome. And dyads may be behind women's need to be so hyperrational and sure of a win before they compete.

These two social structures may explain why men blithely stick out their necks, while women turtle.

Joyce Benenson, a Harvard evolutionary biologist, theorizes that the gender difference in social structure dates back to at least the hunter-gatherer era. Men hunted and raided in groups, so in order to succeed—in order to survive—they had to bond quickly as a group. Benenson believes that, through natural selection, this must have bred into men some biological factors that facilitated men's group membership, while women are more naturally drawn to pair-based relationships.

Even six-month-old male infants prefer images of groups to images of individuals or pairs; infant girls show no such preference. Observational studies of preschoolers have found that preschool girls are involved in paired activities twice as much as boys; boys are twice as likely to be playing in groups. By around five or six years of age, boys playing in groups of at least three seems to researchers as preordained. In an experimental setting where children were in a playroom and could interact in any way they wished, six-year-old boys spent 74% of their time in a coordinated group activity; girls played in a group only 16% of the time. Girls played more in dyads, and their dyadic interactions lasted twice as long as the boys' pairings.

While in groups, boys roughhouse and fight to be best. Girls play games that require they take turns. And as the kids grow into adulthood, this pattern—where men socialize in groups, women in pairs—persists.

Group-based friendships usually arise out of a common interest or activity, often a game or other competitive activity. Regardless of the specifics, the group takes on a collective identity; it provides everyone with a unified sense of purpose.

Groups are rarely a collection of true equals. It's expected that, within a group, people will have different experiences, abilities, resources. That's often the group's greatest strength. Therefore, as long as everyone has signed on to the group's larger purpose, its members don't need to conform in other ways. Instead, people can adopt roles within the group hierarchy (Tom is the class clown, George is the organizer, and so on.) that actually promote each's sense of individualism. "As long as you feel you have something unique to contribute.... If there is something a boy can feel appreciated for, then he has a place there," says Benenson.

Occasional challenges to group hierarchy can be welcomed, because they force everyone to improve over time. You've always been the weakest player in Wednesday night's poker club, but you've been working on a new betting strategy that could put you on top.

Self-assertiveness is the natural communication style of groups. People need to be loud enough to be heard. A certain amount of braggadocio is necessary just to get the other guys' attention.

The real safety in numbers doesn't come from a chorus of agreement. Instead, groups allow people to argue. In a conversation between two people, even a mild difference of opinion can be perceived as a threat. In a group of people, a number of competing ideas can be expressed, without an accompanying sense of confrontation.

If there is a real argument between group members, someone else can step in as the neutral mediator. ("I know you can't stand Steve right now, but that doesn't change the fact we're all here to play basketball, so shut up and pass the ball.") Those in conflict can also redirect their focus onto other group members, until the tension dies down—because the group reminds its members that there's value in the group as a whole: the group has a purpose that is more important than the competition on any given Sunday.

Ultimately, groups do encourage competition in day-to-day activities, and, within those, there's usually no real cost for losing. Even if you mess up, explains Benenson, the group still sees you as an overall asset. They recognize the contribution you make, and they still want you there. Since you'll still meet up with everyone next week, regardless of the outcome, why not go for it?

At some point, groups teach us how to compete, and then—win or lose—how to move on.

Compare those lessons to the ones learned in pair-based friendships.

There is no larger purpose to a dyadic friendship—other than the value in the friendship itself. While groups embrace individual differences, in pair-based relationships, the emphasis is on finding commonalities and suppressing differences. Friends must be equals.

The success of a dyad depends on a mutual exchange of feelings, a shared sense of history and experience. In lab experiments, dyadic exchanges are less confrontational. Even paired strangers won't express opposing views; instead, they work to find points of agreement.

Dyadic relationships are egalitarian to the point of anti-hierarchical. Both girls are expected to contribute equally to the relationship. To breach that is a huge violation. ("I'm always there for you, and you never are for me. Why are we even friends? I just feel used.") Indeed, women are more likely to turn on a girlfriend they previously judged as trustworthy, after only a single incidence of unreliability.

Because dyads have no larger purpose, or neutral mediator for disputes, dyads are inherently more fragile than group-based relationships; they are much less likely to succeed over the long term.

Aware of that fragility, the dyad must be self-policing: its members must become keenly sensitive of the other's feelings and needs. They don't want to do or say anything that could be perceived as asserting superiority in the relationship. The natural conversational style of a dyad isn't bragging: it's self-deprecation.

The inherent design of dyads discourages competition. To be willing to compete is to be willing to jeopardize a dyad.

If that's your reference point for relationships, it isn't surprising that women need sure things when they compete. Because if competing means risking a relationship with a loved one, you'd better at least know that you'll come back to that empty home with the trophy in hand.

Thus the lesson of the dyad is that competition destroys relationships.

According to Benenson, women aren't merrier in a larger group. They don't see the additional people as assets, but threats to the intimacy of the dyad. A newcomer might even steal away a woman's closest friend. To protect the relationship, therefore, women may use ostracism as a preemptive first strike. Even the potential of an advantage is enough of a threat for women to begin social exclusion.

In experiments, Benenson has found that girls preserve that equal footing with peers, and they're upset when forced to create a hierarchy. Girls are distressed while waiting to learn who won a game; boys relish the anticipation. Girls struggle when tasked with choosing a group leader; boys don't have any problem with picking a boss.

Adolescent girls are perturbed by the idea that a friend of theirs might get better grades, or one would have a boyfriend when she didn't. But—crucially—they are just as troubled by the possibility that they themselves could be the one with the better grades or the boyfriend.

In one experiment, Benenson asked boys and girls to compete in a word puzzle task. Each child had a list of words to complete, but some children were placed in a dyad, and others in a group.

The boys underperformed in the dyads. In videotaped interactions of their play, Benenson saw that the boys immediately perceived a hierarchy within the pair. And when the puzzle was difficult, the lower-achieving boys became embarrassed and frustrated. The boys would interfere with their partner's work, then give up and just pace around the room until the time was up.

But the boys excelled in the group version of the task. Some spontaneously insisted there was a competition between the groups (there wasn't); the boys needed to help each other to make sure their group came out on top.

It was the opposite for the girls. The girls did better in the dyads. They were focused; they helped each other, but only when asked.

In the groups, the girls were less engaged and solved fewer puzzles. Analyzing their play, Benenson discovered that, instead of working on the puzzles, these girls first spent a lot of the time trying to create friendships within their groups. They wouldn't get to work until one girl set the tone for the rest: they'd follow her example of how much work to do, so there was no risk of any girl showing anyone up or being embarrassed.

In other words, even in groups, the girls still played by the rules of the dyad.

3

John Peter Wagner was born near Pittsburgh in 1874, the fourth of five brothers. Growing up, the brothers played neighborhood baseball at night from March through October, often as a family team. John was clumsy and bowlegged, and his German parents gave him the customary nickname for awkward children: Hans. On the sandlots of Chartiers (now the borough of Carnegie), Hans had to play whatever position wasn't taken by somebody older than he. Without power at the plate, he scrapped out singles and learned to steal bases.

At the age of twelve, eligible to work, Hans joined his father and brothers in the coal mines, loading coal for 70 cents a ton. In their free time, the brothers continued to play baseball. In the late 1880s, Hans carried the equipment for his older brother Al's sandlot team, which played in the Allegheny County League. Al was the star of the family and one of the top prospects in the region. Luke Wagner, the middle brother, also excelled.

During the 1890s in Pittsburgh, minor league baseball leagues were constantly forming and going out of business within a year. In the newly formed Inter-State League, Al Wagner became the first player signed for the Steubenville, Ohio, team. The next year, a manager named Ed Barrow heard about the Wagner brothers from a talent spotter. He rated Al the top prospect, but Al had a reputation that he was hard to manage. Barrow went to find the brothers at their local pool hall. He was told they were down at the railroad yards, having a throwing match.

In his autobiography, *My Fifty Years in Baseball*, Barrow recalled:

> I walked down to meet them, and as I got closer I could make out the young [man] in the van, a derby hat on the back of his head with a chicken feather stuck in the band. He was unmistakable, with his bow legs and long arms and ambling, awkward gait.... He didn't know whether he wanted to play ball at all. As we talked he would stoop over every once in a while and pick up a lump of coal or a stone and heave it up the railroad tracks. He threw with a great sweep and almost no effort, and as I watched the rocks sail a couple of hundred feet up the track I knew I had to have this fellow on my ball club.

Al, Luke, and Hans all eventually played minor league baseball, and Al even had one year in the big leagues. But it was his little brother, Hans, pronounced "HAH-nus," who'd grown up doing a man's job by day and struggling every night for a spot on the sandlot field—who went on to become one of baseball's greatest competitors. Before there was Babe Ruth, and before there was Ty Cobb, Honus Wagner was the greatest position player in baseball. A lifetime .327 hitter over 21 seasons, he was considered the greatest shortstop of his era.

But where he really stood out was on the basepaths. In August 1899, in the fourth inning of a game against the New York Giants, Wagner stole second base, third, and home in succession. He repeated the feat in 1902, 1907, and 1909. When he retired in 1917, he had the record for most steals of home: 27. Over his career, the stocky and barrel-chested Wagner stole 722 bases and scored 1,736 runs—both of which ranked him number one in the history of his league. In 1939, he was inducted into the inaugural class of the National Baseball Hall of Fame.

Frank Sulloway, professor at University of California, Berkeley, has studied the baserunning proclivities of brothers in Major League Baseball. More than 350 pairs of brothers have played since baseball's inception, from the DiMaggios to the Alous. Sulloway finds a clear connection between being laterborn and competitive style.

"There's not a lot in baseball you have control over," said Sulloway. "You can't much control whether you hit a home run. The ability to manipulate performance is modest. But one thing players have considerable voluntary control of is base stealing." Base-stealing is both tactically risky and physically risky—it's the largest cause of significant injury in the sport.

Sulloway found that, for every time they got on base, younger brothers would attempt to steal almost twice as often as their older brothers would have. They were risk takers on the basepaths. They didn't dwell on the odds of being tagged out; they focused on the advantage of getting into scoring position.

Also, because they had been forced to find multiple ways to succeed (not just with their bats), younger brothers tended to have careers that lasted longer—over two years longer, on average. "The length of career finding was impressive," Sulloway noted. Baseball careers don't always end pretty; typically, the end comes after several years of grinding it out, with players debating with themselves whether they can still compete, and whether life on the road is worth it. "Youngsters stuck it out longer."

This same dynamic *within* baseball also applies outside baseball—to the sports the kids choose in the first place. Sulloway discovered that laterborns are 1.48 times more likely to participate in dangerous sports than firstborns.

Sulloway's three decades of research on birth order makes it clear that this trend doesn't just arise from the backyards and sandlots where kids hone their skills. It arises also from the home, where younger brothers develop the risk taking and competitive psyche that they then bring to the field.

Anyone who has been around children knows how easily they withdraw from competition when they're behind. For children to compete, they have to learn to not quit. It's no fun to be shown up. The temptation to stop trying—to end the embarrassment by hiding—is incredibly powerful in their early lives. Overcoming that emotional reflex is a necessary part of their development. As parents, we don't just ask them not to quit: we order them. We equate quitting with moral transgression, a taboo. We try to make it clear that the shame of quitting is far worse than the shame of merely losing. We insist they can't quit on a play, can't quit until the final whistle, can't quit on their commitments. They have to learn to give extra effort at the very moment they lack the desire to give it. They need to learn to circumvent the desire to give in.

For older siblings, they are rarely, if ever, second-best at home. It's only outside the home where they have to deal with being shown up. But this is something younger siblings must confront on a daily basis.

Older siblings often identify with the authority of the parents; they become the responsible ones. Laterborns then have to find their own niche; they tend to be more open to experience, nonconforming, exploratory, and tolerant of risk. When the two fight, the elder can easily take what he wants through physical dominance. Laterborns get used to standing up to someone who is bigger, knows more, and wants to crush them. When they get into a real competition, outside the family, they're less intimidated—it's less of a shock. They're psychologically familiar with the circumstance. It's not the first time they've had to work their butt off or endure being the weaker contestant.

4

Regardless of birth order, sibling competition serves as a training ground for competition in life. Feelings of rivalry, envy, and animus propel kids, and even if they don't want to compete, they get provoked by siblings who do. They compete over toys, video games, television channels, grades, honors, and parental approval. From the age of three to the age of seven, siblings clash 3.5 times per hour, on average—it adds up to ten minutes of every hour spent arguing. Competition is never foreign *terroir*.

Austrian neuroscientist Ernst Fehr went looking for whether competition was innate or learned by children. Fehr had young children play games with stickers and toys, where they could share or steal, collaborate or compete. He discovered that competitiveness was clearly at work in children as young as two and three. Basically, as soon as kids were old enough to understand the game, they played it competitively. They wanted theirs—and they didn't want you to have it. Kids did not start out as angels who learned to be selfish and self-serving. Generosity and cooperation came as children got older. Competitiveness seemed innate; it was cooperation that had to be socialized into a child.

Yet it wasn't quite so clear as all that. Because Fehr also noticed a difference between children who'd grown up as siblings and those who were only children. Contrary to the presumption that only children are more selfish than children raised in larger families, Fehr found the onlies to be the more cooperative and selfless. They were completely untroubled by handing over toys to another child, whereas the siblings flatly refused. Fehr came to the conclusion that the onlies didn't know to be competitive because they'd never had to compete. They'd never experienced a scarcity of resources: there was always more cake left if they wanted another piece. They weren't afraid of sharing toys, because they didn't understand if you gave Barbie to another child, she might come back missing her leg or head.

Fehr was unable to prove that either competition or cooperation are innate, but when it came to learning those behaviors, siblings certainly had a leg up on acclimating to competition.

The one important caveat about all this sibling squabbling is that it gets out of hand, constantly. True competitors know how to compete hard, but still play within the rules. Siblings usually don't stay within the rules for long. Dr. Samantha Punch described sibship as "a relationship in which the boundaries of social interaction can be pushed.... Rage and irritation need not be suppressed, whilst politeness and toleration can be neglected." Only about one out of every eight sibling conflicts ends in compromise or reconciliation—the other seven times, the siblings merely withdraw, usually after the older child has bullied or intimidated the younger.

How can kids learn to go hard, yet also respect the boundaries of fair behavior?

An obvious factor is by being forced to compete fairly, such as through sports and board games and playground games, for many years. Over time, kids learn that winning doesn't earn anybody's respect unless you follow the rules.

Then here's a hidden factor: roughhousing—what the scholars call "rough-and-tumble play." Roughhousing with friends and siblings often gets out of hand, but roughhousing with a parent is where the fine line between playing and fighting can be safely explored.

University of Montréal professor Daniel Paquette upset the social psychology apple cart recently when he made the case that parents wrestling, grappling, and play-fighting with their young children was a good thing, not a bad thing, because it teaches kids competitive skills.

Railing against a generation of bubble-wrapped kids, Paquette has argued that the strong ideology of attachment theory has overvalued a parent's role in providing comfort when children feel insecure, and undervalued the parent's role in fostering exploratory behavior. He noted that studies of animals deprived of rough-and-tumble play show they grow up unable to be successfully aggressive: they perceive threats when there are none, and they do not perceive any when they should. Paquette has looked cross-culturally and found that, in the most competitive societies, there is more rough-and-tumble play between parents and kids, suggesting it plays an adaptive role.

Paquette explains that this kind of play, where the parent can escalate or reduce the aggressiveness, teaches children how to express their aggression but in a modulated and controlled way. Doing so within the context of an emotional bond keeps these displays of aggression safe, yet it also destabilizes children, pushing them and expanding their comfort zone. Kids learn to encode and decode signals that regulate aggressive play.

In his definition of roughhousing, Paquette includes activities such as pretending to be a monster and playfully chasing kids around the couch, tickling back and forth, engaging kids in pillow fights, and playing tug-of-war over cushions. In his surveys, roughhousing peaks at around age three to four, but continues through age ten. 86% of dads and 73% of moms report roughhousing with their young kids at least twice a week. Paquette's argument is that this emotional groundwork helps children later in life be brave in unfamiliar situations, stand up for themselves, and learn to take risks. It gives them training time to get comfortable with the emotional intensity of competition.

The imperative thing about roughhousing is that the parent maintains control, animating children but de-escalating when kids are on the brink of anger or frustration. In one of Paquette's longitudinal studies, he videotaped fathers playing with their young children, and then he scored the tapes for the amount and *style* of roughhousing. Five years later, he looked again at the kids. Paquette found that fathers who'd been "weak-dominant"—who let the roughhousing get out of hand, and whose play lost its warmth—had kids who could not emotionally regulate themselves. They were often overly aggressive. Fathers who had been "strong-dominant"—leading the play—had kids who were successfully able to keep their aggressiveness from boiling over on their own.

5

We can build up children's competitive fire through group play, roughhousing within limits, and teaching them never to quit. And it seems that if we push these buttons correctly, those kids will grow up into strong competitors as adults. Especially in the case of young girls, who often don't get as much group play or roughhousing as boys, might we be able to put in motion the psychological forces that lead them, one day, to duke it out with the boys—to run for Congress, or start companies in Silicon Valley?

The most famous early-era female tech entrepreneur was Sandy Lerner, cofounder of Cisco Systems. She earned a master's degree in statistics and computer science from Stanford in 1981, and in 1984 she and her husband, Len Bosack, began selling the first router, which allowed computers of many sorts to join the Internet. In 1988, she was pushed aside by venture capitalist Don Valentine—then, just two years later, Lerner was fired—largely because, as she put it in the documentary film *Something Ventured*, she had stubbornly blocked changes in the company that would have upset Cisco's early customers. She wouldn't compromise. She argued and ranted and screamed. Her combative management style led to turmoil, and actual fistfights erupted in hallways. Eventually, there was a mutiny: the other senior executives went to the CEO and demanded, "It's her or us."

Historically, the number of female entrepreneurs and female venture capitalists in Silicon Valley had been very low. Today, they're not so hard to find—in 2010, Women 2.0's annual list of "Female Founder

Successes" showcased an impressive 131 entrepreneurs. But that's still only a small portion of the huge number of tech start-ups and venture capital firms operating nationally. There's no evidence that women's percentage of the whole has increased.

Among start-up employees, women are still outnumbered by men two-to-one. Farther up the ladder, the numbers are ever thinner. In 2011, only a dozen companies in the Fortune 500 were headed by women. According to journalist E. B. Boyd, 15% of angel investors are women, but less than 7% of venture capital partners are women. And only 4.3% of venture-funded companies are run by women. Women do create Internet firms, but many of them are home-based and on a shoestring, financed with credit cards and personal loans. The evidence contradicts Silicon Valley's image of itself as a pure meritocracy, free of bias.

The usual suspects blamed for the lack of venture-funded female entrepreneurs are that (1) most women are *not like* Sandy Lerner, with an advanced degree in engineering; and (2) Silicon Valley shuts women out of the networking opportunities prerequisite for start-up creation. The boys don't actually like the Sandy Lerner-types, who are just as stubborn and hardheaded as they are.

What if those factors are both to blame, but they are not the whole story, either? Earlier, we showed that women will run for political office (even more than men will) when the odds of winning are decent, but when it's a long shot, very few women will enter political contests. Is it possible this partly explains what's happening in Silicon Valley?

The odds of success in venture capital are often said to be 1 in 10—that one huge success makes up for the nine costly disasters that didn't survive. What if the long-odds nature of technology ventures looks like a bad risk to most women? To be a tech entrepreneur, you have to burn to be the next big thing. You have to focus on the win. It takes blatant overconfidence and willful ignorance of the odds. And ignoring the odds is something fewer women tend to do.

Yet, some do—and then succeed despite those odds. Is there anything special about them? Are they different?

Well, a major Italian insurance company was recently interested in that very question. The company's executives wanted to know what entrepreneurs were made of, and they decided to put up the money to fund a study. They contacted economists Aldo Rustichini and Luigi Guiso who, with the insurance company's money, hired a survey firm with an army of 200 interviewers to go out and meet with over 2,000 small-company founders all over Italy. The entrepreneurs were interviewed face-to-face, answering computer-assisted questions.

In the middle of the interviews, the entrepreneurs were asked to hold out their right hand, palm up, so a photograph could be taken of it.

Yes, Rustichini and Guiso were looking for the origin of entrepreneurs' competitive fire...in their hands.

It wasn't palm reading, but it doesn't sound much different from palm reading: specifically, the scholars were getting a measure of the ring finger relative to the index finger.

Sure enough, when the Italian scholars analyzed the photos of the entrepreneurs' hands, they found that the more successful the entrepreneur, the longer the ring finger compared to the index finger. The most successful entrepreneurs had ring fingers 10% to 20% longer than their index fingers.

As you hold up your hand to examine your own two fingers, this finding probably sounds downright absurd to you. For decades, people have speculated about what made Steve Jobs special, what set apart the Richard Bransons and Larry Ellisons and Mark Zuckerbergs from everybody else—what character traits facilitated their success, or what in their childhoods drove them to build their empires—and here comes two Italian economists to argue it's all about *the length of their fingers!*

Well, it's not really about the length of their fingers. Finger length is actually just a marker, a sign of what was going on when these entrepreneurs were in their mothers' wombs.

A couple of months into gestation, the fingers sprout and elongate, and, also during that time, the early limbic brain gets organized. Both of these are affected by the prevalence of the hormones testosterone and estrogen, which come both from the fetus's own sex glands and the mother's bloodstream (though the testosterone in the mother's bloodstream affects fetal girls more than fetal boys, because even fetal boys already are producing plenty of their own testosterone).

The fetal ring finger has many receptors for both hormones on it, and the index finger has fewer receptors. Testosterone lengthens the fetal fingers, while estrogen stops their growth, and thus the balance of the two hormones can affect the ring finger and index finger differently. The two hormones simultaneously shape the development of the brain.

All the ways the brain is affected aren't yet known—so far, the research has focused on how testosterone and estrogen alter cell migration in the hypothalamus gland. The hypothalamus is a tiny region in the middle of the base of the brain that regulates an immense number of bodily functions. Just as all roads lead back to Rome, the hypothalamus is the origin point for the entire, cascading hormone system. What seems to happen is this: higher levels of prenatal testosterone wire you to be permanently more *sensitive* to testosterone, forever on. It's not that you have *more* testosterone; it's that your body reacts more strongly to daily, even moment-to-moment, fluctuations in bloodstream testosterone. Whether the same happens for estrogen is thus far unclear.

All of which is a very technical way to explain that the length of the ring finger is a marker for fundamental—but not entirely known—brain system differences.

As strange as it may sound, the ratio of index to ring finger has been shown to correlate with traits such as spatial ability, risk taking, and assertiveness. It explains why some people focus on what they'll win, while others are so sensitive to the odds. Research has also connected finger ratio to success in competitive sports such as soccer and skiing. Rustichini's own work has connected it to real-life success, such as the profitability of high-frequency financial traders.

When the two Italian economists saw this same pattern repeated in their survey of the entrepreneurs, they decided to run the numbers again, this time comparing men against women. There were 780 female entrepreneurs in their survey—with a 2 to 1 ratio of men to women. Normally, men's ring fingers are a tad longer than their index fingers, and women's index fingers are a tiny bit longer than their ring fingers. But the researchers found that the Italian female entrepreneurs actually had more of a male pattern: their ring fingers were longer. In fact, not only was their digit ratio inverted, but it was more pronounced in that direction than the men's. On average, the women ran bigger companies, with higher growth rates. They also had greater ability to withstand enormous workloads.

This suggests that entrepreneurs *are* special, wired that way from the fetal stages of development. More men might be wired this way than women, but if you *are* wired this way, it transcends gender.

If you're wondering whether venture capital firms should just throw out the business plans and take photos of entrepreneurs' hands, that's the wrong idea. It's not *all* biology. Rustichini notes that some scientists believe that all the biological components of competitiveness, taken together, comprise 40% of the explanation. Others argue it's more like 60%. "So there's a big debate, but it's always been 40% on one end and 60% on the other," said Rustichini. "Let's call it a tie and say 50%. That is roughly what's at stake. I'm not afraid of determinist biology. It's half of it. The other half is influenced heavily by what you do with your child."

Remember that in the Italian study, the subjects were already entrepreneurs of ongoing companies. Millions of Italians (not in the study) have long ring fingers, and thus possibly are natural risk takers—but they're missing all the other necessary ingredients to be entrepreneurial, from cognitive ability to creativity to competitiveness. Everything in this chapter about group play, sibling competition, and roughhousing still applies. Indeed, they are directly connected. One of the first correlations found for finger length was to rough-and-tumble play. It's probable that natural biology and childhood psychology interact to form the psyche of tough competitors.

Ultimately, if people's childhoods don't cultivate the competitive psyche, they're never going to succeed as entrepreneurs, no matter how long their ring fingers are.

Nor are they going to succeed if society discriminates against them. Plenty of women do have the biological wiring and the psychological grit, but extremely few are going to break through. That's exactly what Rustichini and Guiso found.

They divided their results by region of Italy, from the tolerant northeast to the less-emancipated south and Isles. "The regional differences are so large, it's a culture shock that you couldn't measure in a more homogenous country," Rustichini told us. Not only did the scholars find more female entrepreneurs concentrated in the more tolerant regions, but they saw the same finger-length pattern again: in the south of Italy, women had to have ring fingers at the very top of the charts for them to be entrepreneurs. Only the most naturally gifted women made it. The rest, Rustichini felt safe to conclude, had been filtered out—in ways that men are not. If entrepreneurs are special, then female entrepreneurs have to be superspecial.

Importing this science back to Silicon Valley, what are we to conclude? It's clear the number of women-run venture start-ups is too low, and it's shameful for a system that aspires to be a meritocracy. But the biggest mistake might be using gender in any way to count, sort, or even think about entrepreneurs. The sex of a person turns out to be a distraction—mere noise. Finger-length tells you far more than gender does. Brain differences, combined with psychological differences, interact to forge the rare kind of risk ignorer who is competitive enough to succeed.

PART III

Individuals

"The credit belongs to the man who is actually in the arena, whose face is marred by dust and sweat and blood; who strives valiantly; who errs, and comes short again and again, because there is no effort without error and short-coming; but who ... spends himself in a worthy cause; who, at the best knows in the end the triumph of high achievement, and who at the worst, if he fails, at least fails while daring greatly, so that his place shall never be with those cold and timid souls who know neither victory nor defeat."

—Theodore Roosevelt

CHAPTER SEVEN

The Difference between Winning and Not Losing

1

During the 1960s, half the watches in the world were made in Switzerland—almost all of them mechanical. But throughout the 1970s, the Swiss watchmakers were undercut by Timex and Citizen, using new quartz and LED technology. The Swiss stood by as their market share slowly dwindled to 15%. They laid off employees, lowered prices, and, for a while, resigned themselves to their luxury niche. But in the early 1980s, a number of Swiss companies—including Omega, Tissot, and Longines—decided to fight back.

They did something very risky: they formed a new company, invested a fortune in it, hired tons of employees, and took a gamble. They decided to undercut the watchmakers who had undercut them.

Their idea was that you should always have a Swiss chronograph. It was a mark of adulthood—that serious gold or leather-banded timepiece you perhaps got at college graduation and would one day give to your grandkids. But you could also have a "second watch." That watch could be fun, fashionable, and so cheap as to be almost disposable. The new company began to manufacture these watches, with cut-rate electronics but dazzling to the eye. For the first time, watches were made with bright colors and bold graphics. The down-market Swatch was born.

Swatch wasn't just a defender of the Swiss luxury brands. Swatch became a phenomenon in its own right—100 million were sold within the first ten years. Rather than just protecting their profits on their luxury watches, Swatch became extremely profitable itself. At an auction, a one-off Swatch sold for $20,500. It was likely a publicity stunt (the company's own dealers were alleged to be the buyers), but it successfully portrayed Swatch as a kind of luxury item available to the masses.

Swatch, according to the work of German researcher Peter-J. Jost, is a prototypical example of a *fighter brand*. Ever since, when upmarket companies get undercut by new market entrants, they face the question of whether to do what Omega, Longines, and Tissot did. However, researchers such as Jost say that Swatch's success made it look deceptively simple. As Professor Mark Ritson has explored for *Harvard Business Review*, most examples fail—such as when Kodak launched Funtime film to stop the growth of Fujifilm, or United Airlines launched Ted to compete with Southwest Airlines, or General Motors created Saturn to compete with Honda and Toyota. It's enormously expensive, time consuming, and risky.

Risk taking is necessary in business, and heralded, but more risk is not always better. Risk taking is bounded by its own effectiveness. When it pays off, everyone looks like heroes; when it fails, you look stupid. The trick is, the longer a company waits it out, the less likely its fighter brand will be able to knock off the low-priced competitors, who gain traction and build loyalty month by month.

The last chapter introduced the idea that when people focus on the upside, they take risks that can defy the odds. When they focus on the odds, they tend not to take risks. Corporate culture, and management ethos, have a big impact on business strategy. Some are playing to win. They go for it. Challenged, they double up on their effort level, reinvest, and go on the attack. Others try to limit their losses, protect profits, and hope the new market entrants eventually pass, like a bad storm. When challenged, they slash costs, shrink investment in their future, stick to what they know, and hope to survive. They're playing not to lose.

The hallmark characteristics of playing to win are an intensification of effort and continuous risk taking. The equivalent for playing not to lose is conservatism and trying to avoid costly mistakes.

Under intense pressure, though, having a strategy of avoiding mistakes leads, by itself, to more mistakes. This is the paradox of playing not to lose.

The 2006 Wimbledon women's singles final was the first since 1999 not to feature either of the Williams sisters from the United States. Instead, the door opened for Amélie Mauresmo of France or Justine Henin of Belgium to take the title. The winner was to take home $1,016,620—and the runner-up half of that. It became a famous match, because the women played very aggressively, coming to the net on 89 of the 180 points played. (In other Grand Slam matches, only a quarter to a third of the points are at the net.)

In the first set, Henin was playing to win. In tennis, points are scored on winners, forced errors, or unforced errors. On average, it's about one-third of each. But in that first set at Wimbledon in the summer of 2006, Henin hit twice as many winners as unforced errors. She won the first set 6 to 2.

Talking to reporters after the match, Mauresmo described what she'd been thinking in the next moment: "You're 6-2 down against Justine in the final of a Grand Slam. You [are] not in such a great position at the time," she smiled. "You feel like, 'Okay, what do I need to do?...How am I gonna just make it go my way?' Again, I really felt

I pumped myself up. I let it out a little bit. I yelled a little bit. I was much more aggressive right from the beginning of that second set."

Now it was Mauresmo who was playing to win, and Henin just trying not to lose.

Henin was serving the second game of that second set. Her first serve had started to miss, and she now tried to compensate with more conservative serves and playing from the back line. This backfired; Mauresmo pounced on the soft shots and hit winners. Then Henin double-faulted with two awkwardly struck serves, the second of which bounced on her own side before catching the bottom of the net. A drop shot on the next point kept her in the game, and, at 40–30, she finally attacked the net. She cut off the ball, had the angle, but just tried not to miss. It went long. Serve was broken.

"I wasn't aggressive enough, and the match turned completely," Henin recalled in her postgame press conference. "There is nothing to say. She took more opportunities than me." By the final set, the BBC described Henin as merely "a shadow of the player who bossed the opener." Trying to avoid mistakes, she repeatedly put her forehand into the net, giving Mauresmo the lead. It was a vicious circle—the more safely she tried to locate her shots, the more unforced errors she made. But without an accurate first serve, she couldn't come to the net and force herself into aggressive situations.

In retrospect, Henin didn't hit that many unforced errors—only 22. But they always seemed to come on important points with the game on the line. At critical moments, her mental attitude ("just don't lose this one") led to an adoption of failed playing strategies (overcompensation and shorting her shots).

A Boston University researcher looked at nine Grand Slam tournaments from 2005 to 2007, doing a point-by-point analysis of errors and winners. He concluded that women, more so than men, make the mistake of becoming more conservative at critical points in matches. They've come so far—now they just don't want to screw up. Rallies become longer, but then end in unforced errors 40% of the time—errors for which the women have only themselves to blame. Both men and women are hoping to end up holding the trophy, but their orientation leads them to play different styles. One is trying to get the trophy; the other is trying to not lose it.

By no means are men immune: one study of every single pitch thrown during the 2005/2006 Major League Baseball season—some 1,374,923 pitches—showed that most MLB pitchers are secretly prevention-focused. As they get closer to finishing out innings, their pitch locations become more conservative. A similar study of over 2 million PGA tour putts showed that pro golfers tend to leave it short as the stakes and pressure rise.

"Playing to Win" and "Playing Not to Lose" are ubiquitous sports metaphors, thrown around to describe everything from business situations and military strategies to dating—pretty much wherever risk taking is involved.

But Playing to Win and Playing Not to Lose are more than just descriptive metaphors. They are diametrically opposing strategies, triggered by different psychological and physiological mechanisms. And they have real consequences—especially during competition.

Researchers have long held that the fundamental will of humans is to seek pleasure and avoid pain. But we are all shaded a little to one side or the other—we seek pleasure a little more than we avoid pain, or vice versa. Under the pressure of competition, our orientation may shift even further. We may be pleasure-seekers right up until the competition begins, or right up to critical points in the competition—but in those defining moments, we start playing not to lose.

There's a long history to the twinning of pleasure and pain, and many scholars have developed terms to further illuminate aspects of these psychological states. In 1935, psychologist Kurt Lewin wrote of people who are motivated by feelings of approach or feelings of avoidance. By the mid-1950s, John W. Atkinson was classifying people by their motivational leanings as either "success oriented" or "failure avoidant." Individuals motivated to succeed chose risky paths that could maximize their success, while individuals motivated to avoid failure withdrew from those risks. In the late 1990s, two New Yorkers were trying their own spins on the idea: University of Rochester's Andrew Elliot applied approach and avoidance specifically to performance and competition, while Columbia University's E. Tory Higgins was using "promotion-focused" and "prevention-focused." Higgins concluded that these two psychological impulses were so fundamentally different that the brain needed two separate neural systems to manage them.

In the last decade, neuroscience and physiological science have put seventy years of theory to the test. Higgins's thesis was not exactly right, but it was on track. The brain does indeed have separate systems, electrically and chemically distinct. One neural system is waiting for something to get excited about, at which point it cranks up and drives you to action. The other system is monitoring everything you do like a hovering parent. It's ready to jump in and stop you from taking a risk or making a careless mistake.

In light of this neurological support, we can consolidate all the historical terms into an idea that we are either "gain-oriented" or "prevention-oriented."

Gain-orientation pushes you to take risks to get something you don't already have. Prevention-orientation pushes you to avoid danger. It's the desire to freeze or flee when a saber-toothed tiger or disapproving manager approaches.

Both of these systems—the gain-oriented and prevention-oriented—are operating at all times, almost in equilibrium. But at a given moment, one or the other could be slightly more active—and that slight difference can result in very different mental states and attitudes. When someone is prevention-oriented, he adopts strategies we describe as "Playing Not to Lose." When someone is gain-oriented during a competition, he is using strategies that are "Playing to Win."

The question then becomes, during a competition, how do we stay in the gain-oriented mental state, and not slip up and switch into the prevention-oriented mental state? How do we keep the gain-system in control?

2

The closer you get to the end—as the goal looms larger—the stronger the tendency to shift into prevention-orientation. In one example of how this relates to the school setting, students at the University of Texas were given a series of GRE problems at the beginning and the end of a semester. Early in the semester, the students were gain-oriented. They did best on the GRE sets if they *gained points for every correct answer*. But late in the semester, their mindset was different; their mental focus was no longer on soaking up new material. Now they were just trying not to forget what they'd learned. They were prevention-oriented, trying to avoid careless mistakes. On similar GRE problems as before, this time, they performed best if *they lost points for every wrong answer*.

You would think this semantic difference in scoring method would not have mattered. Gaining points for right answers and losing points for wrong answers should, in a rational world, lead to the same score. If you can get 16 out of 20 questions correct, it shouldn't make a difference if you gain 16 points or if you start with 20 and subtract 4. But in this way, the average person is not quite rational. The scoring method—the framing of the contest—works with or against people's orientation. Early in a semester, the focus is on gaining knowledge. A scoring system that highlights gains induces best performance. Late in a semester, students' focus is on not losing knowledge. A scoring system that aligns with their focus—by deducting points for mistakes—induces the best performance.

Most of the time, though, people are more comfortable in a gain situation than a loss situation. A vivid example of this—which works somewhat as a universal moment—is the showdown when soccer players take penalty kicks to settle a tie. From a spot twelve yards away, the ball is struck at a speed of between 60 to 80 miles per hour at the goal, which spans 24 feet wide and 8 feet high. The goalkeeper is not allowed to move until the ball is struck, and making a save is next to impossible if the kick is placed within a yard of a post. Under this circumstance, the goalkeeper is not expected to save penalties. The expectation and pressure is all on the kicker, who is expected to make it every time. The true odds of making a penalty kick are 85%, but the goalkeeper can be a hero, and the kicker can only be the goat.

This psychology intensifies as you go deeper and deeper into a penalty round. Let's imagine you had to take the fifth penalty for a professional soccer team. Which situation would you rather be in?

- Your team is down by one, and you *have* to make it to tie; if you miss, your team will lose.
- Your team is tied, and you *don't* have to make it, but if you do make it, you'll win.

Most people would rather be in the latter situation. While both are high pressure, actual performance differs drastically in the two situations. Remember the paradox of playing not to lose: trying not to make a mistake often leads to mistakes. According to researchers Geir Jordet and Esther Hartman, when missing the kick will cause the kicker's team to lose, professional kickers succeed on those shots only 62% of the time. When making the goal will result in a win, kickers go for it—and they find the net 92% of the time. It's the same kick, the same twelve yards every time. The ball is still struck at 60 miles per hour and the goal is still a 72-square-foot target. But a 30% gap in the success rate results from the different psychological circumstances.

Another way to describe the difference between the two kicker scenarios is to label the first as a *threat* and the second as a *challenge*.

In a threat situation, the expectations are very high. You know you're being judged, and you feel you can't make a single mistake. Despite the intensity of the competition, the fear of mistakes invokes that prevention-orientation: you're trying to prevent catastrophe rather than initiate a success. Competitors feel more anxious, less energetic, and avoidant.

Heightened awareness that others are judging you is manifested in the "mentalizing system"—increased neural activity in four discrete regions of the brain. One of those regions is the medial prefrontal cortex, which signals that decision making has become more conscious and slower, less automatic. Another region is the left temporoparietal junction (l-TPJ). Constantly scanning for the unfamiliar to be guarded against, this region flashes brightly, indicating increased wariness. Additionally, the anterior cingulate cortex—the ACC—is constantly on the watch for errors in judgment.

A threat situation alters the way the brain sensitizes to risk and reward. The amygdala, deep in the limbic system, is highly attuned to fearful stimuli. The risks of a situation become prominent in the mind. Meanwhile, the brain's reward center—though activated by the opportunity—is still the lesser partner.

All this changes in a challenge frame of mind. In a challenge state, you're not expected to be perfect, and not expected to win, but you have a fighting chance to rise to the occasion. You're free to take risks and go for it, which activates the gain-orientation system. A cascade of hormones is released that suppresses l-TPJ activity, and the brain gets comfortable, as if everything is familiar. Decision making shifts back to automatic mode. The hormones dampen the amygdala, making you fearless, and they juice up the reward networks, making you highly attuned to the spoils of victory. Competitors breathe freely, feel energized, and approach opportunities.

While top competitors do need to learn to perform in threat situations—because they are sometimes unavoidable—most competitors will perform better in a challenge situation.

And in many situations, changing the framing of a task from threat to challenge is all it may take for success.

Earlier in this book, we wrote about Alter and Aronson's work with Princeton undergrads. The researchers presented the students with a test of GRE questions. For half the students, the questions were presented in a threat context—they were a test of the students' ability, a judgment on whether they truly belonged at Princeton. The other students got the same questions, but in a challenge context. That test was titled "Intellectual Challenge Questionnaire," and the questions were construed as brainteasers. Nobody was expected to solve them all. In the threat context, the Princeton undergrads got 72% correct. In the challenge context, they got 90% correct.

Anson Dorrance, the North Carolina soccer coach, knew his players were constantly living under threat: his program was so successful for so long that—from the players' perspective—everyone was just waiting for them to lose. To take the expectation of perfection off his girls, Dorrance rearranged his team's schedule. The team would go on long road trips, playing back-to-back games, in different cities, on consecutive nights—all against nationally ranked teams. Because no one could expect a team to win every game under such demanding conditions, the threat was transformed into a challenge—allowing the team to play looser and better. They won every time. But now each win was considered a hard-fought achievement, instead of a foregone conclusion.

One of the great mysteries of coaching children is how some kids can be fearlessly competitive during practice—but timid and nervous when competing against strangers. The reason may be that competing against strangers is a threat situation; practicing doesn't threaten their place on the team. At practice, no ultimate judgment of them is being made. They know this is a ritual that will repeat itself continuously. The familiarity of friends' tendencies makes them feel safe. But against strangers, knowing so little about their opponents, they fill the gap with fear. It's a situation they can't control. "Better" and "worse," "winner" and "loser" are truly on the line—their status is being threatened. They feel they *have* to do well. In the face of all that, kids can become reticent and conservative. You want them to fight, but, instead, they freeze.

3

We all make mistakes, but we need to learn from them and move on. You can own a mistake, or the mistake will own you.

How, then, are some people able to learn from mistakes while others crumble after making an error? Why are some mistakes even repeated by one person after another, as if mistakes were contagious?

As we discussed earlier, expectations play into this. An unexpected loss is far more upsetting than an expected loss, an expected win is far less glorious than an unexpected win. Same goes for the unexpected mistake.

Let's return to the setting of a tennis match, as a competitor abruptly stops taking risks, shifting from playing to win to playing not to lose. Prior to the switch, the player wasn't perfect; she missed shots, but they didn't rattle her. Then one mistake catches her off guard, and she dwells on it too long. Doubt sets in, and she can't get back to her aggressive mindset. Why does trying not to make a mistake so often lead to more mistakes?

We're all familiar with that drop in the pit of the stomach when we've been called out for a mistake, whether it's a line judge yelling from the sideline, a computer flashing a red light, or a supervisor calling, "My office!" But most of us don't need anyone to tell us when we've screwed up. We don't have to wait for the feedback, because we've already detected our mistake in some not-yet-conscious way.

Between 50 and 70 milliseconds after making an error—before you even understand what's happened—there's a drop in voltage in the brain's ACC, the anterior cingulate cortex.

Normal brain function in the ACC is enough to produce a minute electrical charge—around 7 to 10 microvolts. The ACC functions as an early warning system, a discrepancy detector. Any time something unexpected happens, such as making a mistake, the ACC's perception of that surprising anomaly triggers an instantaneous pulse in the voltage.

Researchers have conducted dozens of experiments to decipher what these pulses mean and what they foretell. To do this, in most experiments, subjects wear skullcaps with electrodes that detect brainwaves, then they play difficult games where mistakes are likely. Whenever subjects make mistakes, the researchers track how the brain responds, down to the millisecond.

First, there's the drop in voltage—then recovering from the mistake is marked by a return to the normal voltage. The more shocking or surprising the mistake, the bigger this pulse. (Picture something like the readings you've seen in a heart-rhythm monitor: the stronger an error, the bigger the spike pattern.)

This entire drop/recovery process all occurs within the first 50 to 500 milliseconds following the mistake.

You might think you don't want any drop in voltage at all—but that would mean you were truly oblivious to the mistake. And if that's the case, your brain wouldn't learn to correct the error or prevent it in the future.

Ideally, you want a moderate voltage drop, with more time spent in the recovery period. Although we're still talking in terms of milliseconds, that longer period of time is a sign of a heightened awareness of the task before you. During recovery, the brain's plasticity changes, ensuring that the neurons process a new correct response. Once the ACC's aware of the mistake, it's looking into the near future. Its job isn't to dwell on the mistake; its focus is on error-prevention. This pattern of drop/recovery then leads to making fewer repeated mistakes, while being comfortable taking risks.

Of course, it's much easier to learn from mistakes—without dwelling on them—outside of a competitive context. Once the stakes are increased, the drop in voltage can become much more pronounced. It's why a minor mistake you'd normally be able to shrug off suddenly seems catastrophic.

If this larger drop is followed by a shorter, or less strong, recovery, that's a sign the brain's becoming overwhelmed by the negative turn of events. There's less neural plasticity, so there's less learning and more mental paralysis. Stuck in shock, the brain isn't taking in new ways to handle the situation—which is when mistakes just lead to more mistakes. Your brain isn't learning how to fix the situation. It just keeps replaying the errors, so you keep making new ones.

In figure skating, a single mistake can knock someone out of the running for a medal. Since even one error can be so determinative, when a mistake has been made, it's incredibly difficult for a skater to recover. A skater often doesn't fall just once; she falls again and again.

In competition, the stakes are high enough that even watching opponents make a mistake can trigger a strong change in the brain's voltage. Your brain processes the other person's mistake as if it were your own. The better competitor is able to suppress this mirroring process, but it's incredibly difficult. Especially if the mistake is made by someone who's your friend or teammate. That's when mistakes become contagious—not just between teammates, but between competitors.

The 2007 World Figure Skating Championships in Tokyo were to be the final skate for the retiring pair of Poles, Mariusz and Dorota Siudek. The beloved couple placed ninth after the short program and were ready for a long, sentimental farewell. It didn't go as planned.

During the warm-up for their grouping, Mariusz's back spasmed during a routine throw. They left the ice with Dorota in tears. While no one was sure of the extent of his injury, it was time for Dan and Hao Zhang to take the ice. On their very first combination jump—side-by-side double Axel, double toe loop—Dan fell.

Back in the dressing room, Mariusz was doubled over in pain as medics attended to him. It sent the backstage area at Tokyo Metropolitan Gymnasium into emotional chaos. The couple argued over Mariusz's desire to still compete. Dorota convinced Mariusz to withdraw, and the Siudeks went to the ice to take their final bows.

Having trained near Montreal, under the tutelage of Canadian coaches, the Siudeks were very close with the three Canadian pairs in the competition, including the next pair, Valerie Marcoux and Craig Buntin. Marcoux and Buntin knew they weren't ready to skate, but they didn't have a choice. They endured errors on their side-by-side jumps and their throws. On their very first sequence, they lost points. Three jumps later, they were penalized again on a double Axel. When it came time for their throw into a triple toe loop, they couldn't hold it together.

At that point, mistakes passed down like a contagion, as one pair after another watched what came before: activity in their ACCs spiked, and they all started dwelling on the mistakes they'd seen. The next Canadian pair, skating immediately after, fell twice. Then the American pair did even worse—with Rena Inoue falling on a solo jump and then twice more when thrown—and receiving a time penalty, too.

There was a break, and a warm-up period for the final group, the favorites of the night. This final group was better, but still error-prone. The Germans and Russians both had unison problems and came out early on jumps. Chinese pairs took well-deserved first and second places, on a night when the rest of the field gave them little competition.

Most competitions, though, are not like ice-skating. If you make a mistake, you have the rest of the competition to recover and make up for it. In a basketball game, an early mistake can cost you a basket, but it doesn't cost you the game. As long as you learn from it, you can still win.

Is calling out someone's mistakes a good thing or a bad thing? The conventional wisdom is it's a bad thing, because it oversensitizes competitors and stresses them out. It makes them so afraid to make a mistake they can't stay loose and don't take risk.

While that's mostly true, it's not the rule. Remember that some people's ACC response is too low; they don't even notice their mistakes. Pointing out their mistakes, and forcing them to care, is one way to get their ACC working and helping. People can't learn from their mistakes if they don't even know they've made one.

On the other hand, too strong a reaction can lead to anxiously dwelling on the mistake. The prevention system goes on high alert.

4

Given that we have two neural systems inside us, it makes sense that there are two distinct competitive styles, depending on which system is in control.

When you're gain-oriented, you brush off details. You are confident that you will succeed. Getting more information would only make you guarded and unwilling to take risks. You're eager and work fast, and you excel under time pressure. You perceive the competition as arousing and animating, and ultimately a thrill. You respond to (and learn most from) praise and feedback that highlights what you've done well.

When you're prevention-oriented, you absorb all the details, since focusing on details cuts down mistakes. You like to resolve ambiguities before moving on: it helps to have as much information as possible about the opponent. You are often underconfident. You're vigilant and work meticulously, avoiding risks. You work best without time pressure. You perceive the competition inherently as a threat and, ultimately, a great stress. You learn the most from feedback on your mistakes.

When gain-oriented, you're driven by a desire to succeed; when prevention-oriented, you're driven by a fear of failure. When playing to win, you perceive ties as a loss; when playing not to lose, ties are satiating.

Overall, a gain-orientation—playing to win—sustains those during competition. Gain-oriented people are more likely to persevere: as long as they have a fighting chance, they are never willing to admit defeat.

The prevention-focused, however, are more likely to lose their motivation to compete along the way. Instead of persevering, they are *perseverating*—obsessing on their mistakes until they wonder if it's worth continuing on.

For the most part, when one considers the list of traits that define playing to win and playing not to lose, there's no doubt that playing to win comes across as the cool, sexy option of the two. If you could choose one personality over the other—if you could manually control the neural systems inside you—you'd choose to be gain-oriented.

Here's the catch. Look at this short list of common careers on the following page. Which personality type is best suited for each job? Is it the personality that goes for the big score, on little information? Or is it the personality that is meticulous, avoids mistakes, and gathers all available information?

Accountant	Lawyer
Air traffic controller	Loan officer
Automotive mechanic	Nurse
Chef	Pilot
Chemist	Police officer
Childcare worker	Psychologist
Computer engineer	Reporter
Designer	Social worker
Entrepreneur	Surgeon
Environmental scientist	Teacher
Firefighter	Webmaster

Instantly, it's clear that most adult work is predicated on the expectation that employees should be thorough, careful, and mistake-free. There are times when playing not to lose is the optimal strategy. Even if you're a chef who's a restaurateur, or a computer engineer who's also an entrepreneur, planning and forecasting are essential.

There's a sort of inherent irony in this dichotomy. On one hand, new ideas and new ventures are going to come from gain-oriented personalities, yet everyday dutiful work trains people to be prevention-oriented. A reporter very much might need to go with her instinct, but that doesn't mean she can play loose with the facts. An environmental scientist might need to be very creative to solve problems, but those solutions need to be measurable and sound. The kind of labor that feeds the economy requires *both* neural systems to be highly trained.

In the short term, an astute manager might take advantage of employees' orientation by structuring and rewarding their work in a way that aligns with their daily motivation. The common structure of reward pay is, "I'm going to pay you this base amount, plus a bonus of a certain amount if you get up to 95% done." But a number of experiments have shown that, for many employees, they're more productive when their reward pay is structured in the negative: "I'm going to pay you this entire bonus, but I'll deduct a certain amount if you don't get at least 95% done."

Also, someone's orientation can help others understand what kind of role models make the biggest impact. A prototypical role model is a rags-to-riches, hard-work-pays-off success story. But a role model can also be a cautionary tale, of a success story gone off track. Prevention-oriented individuals are most impacted by the latter—real-life examples of someone who made the mistake of not working hard enough. That message has a bigger impact.

But in the long run, employees need to have gain-orientation to sustain growth.

In the mid-2000s, Westinghouse Electric's nuclear plant division realized it had a deep-seated culture problem. Their engineers had spent years absorbing a management strategy called Six Sigma, which has as its goal the eradication of errors from industrial processes. A Six Sigma process is one in which 99.99966% of the products manufactured are statistically expected to be free of defects. With this strategy firmly in place, Westinghouse had never bid on jobs unless its engineers already knew exactly what they'd be doing: they had to have proven, mistake-free expertise before even considering a new contract. And even when the engineers were willing to go to a potential new customer, they came in with a "Here's what we can do for you," and never asked, "What do you need?"

Such a prevention-orientation is unsurprising in the nuclear industry, since if there's ever a problem, nuclear fuel has to be discharged. These incidents are called a "failure case," and a failure case takes seven years to understand, correct, and set right.

"Nuclear engineers treat *everything* as if it were a nuclear power emergency that would threaten the lives of a community," explained Jeanne Liedtka, a researcher at the University of Virginia's Darden School of Business.

But Westinghouse executives knew that the nuclear industry was about to see huge growth. With concern over climate change, coal-fired power plants were falling out of favor. There were over 400 nuclear reactors already in the world, and plenty of them needed refurbishing.

At first glance, Westinghouse's repair of these aging plants would have seemed to be a natural fit, but many of the reactors used different pressurizing technologies, turbines, generators, and metal alloys than the Westinghouse engineers were used to. If it wanted to keep up with its competitors, Westinghouse would need nine new business lines, and their engineers would just have to figure things out as they went along. It had to train its nuclear engineers to take risks and be gain-oriented.

Hard-wired to be "the ultimate in risk-averse," just hearing the phrase "new business" had the engineers immediately worrying about the people who might die because of their work, says Liedtka.

Given the market-pressure to innovate and the staff's equal resistance to it, in 2006, Westinghouse flew its senior staff and 45 top managers to the University of Virginia for a week-long seminar with Liedtka and her colleagues, Robert Rosen and Robert Wiltbank.

Liedtka's team reassured the engineers that when they were servicing power plants, the goal of 100% safety wasn't going to change. No one was asking them to put the public at risk. But, Liedtka's team continued, the engineers didn't need to use this prevention-oriented approach in every context. Just going to a meeting was not a threat to public safety. It was all right to ask what the customer needed, instead of solely discussing what they had to offer. They would have to accept some small risks that would come along with innovation. They had to brace themselves for the fact that they might even fail sometimes.

By definition, new ideas can't come from a playing-not-to-lose mindset, where the inhibition system is hyperactive. Creativity requires disinhibition: it requires turning off the internal censors in order to allow brainstorming and idea generation. Neuroscience has shown that in the very moment when a new idea sparks to life in the brain, the prevention system is turned off.

While the engineers agreed in spirit to accept failure in these new settings, it was harder done than said. As Liedtka's team described in their book, *The Catalyst*, when Westinghouse's employees first began seeking new deals, they often came back empty-handed, and they were still surprised and disappointed at their failures.

But a Westinghouse senior executive, Nick Liparulo, expected these early missteps. He knew that they would be pitching businesses that they wouldn't get. But he saw the value in having the team learn from the process. He expected mistakes to be made—and accepted them as part of an institutional learning curve.

And over time, the Westinghouse managers learned how to listen to customers. They listed every obstacle to growth inside their company, and they decided to eradicate those obstacles, like they had once eradicated errors. They vowed to compete in worldwide regions they had once ceded, and they recognized that speed of implementation would be the best way to beat the competition.

What does all this have to do with competitive fire? In a way, the Westinghouse Electric case is a parable for competitiveness that fits both individually and society-wide. If we want to compete harder, if we want to show more competitive fire, that means playing to win. And that might mean having to overcome the way we've been trained to think: to overcome the loss-avoidant orientation that our daily work puts us in.

Think back to the college students in Texas, taking those GRE test questions. When they first arrived on campus as freshmen, they wanted to get an education that would last them a lifetime. But by the end of the semester, they were fixated on learning just what they would need to get through final exams.

Competitive fire will never ignite, or be expressed, when our orientation is just to get through the day. Competitive fire will flourish when long-term goals are high, and when it's accepted that risks and mistakes go hand-in-hand, and we are free to let ambition reign.

CHAPTER EIGHT

How One Night of Blackjack Sped Up the World Economy

1

One Friday in July of 1973, Fred Smith, then a 28-year-old head-strong entrepreneur, was sitting at the Chicago airport, waiting for a flight home to Memphis, Tennessee. He'd just come from a failed meeting with General Dynamics, who had turned him down for a loan. He had only $5,000 left in the bank.

While everyone else in the airport lounge was thinking about their planes about to take off, Smith was consumed by the thought of planes about to be grounded. His own.

Smith's four-month-old fledgling delivery service had a small fleet of eight jets. On Monday, Smith had to write a check for $24,000, to pay for the jet fuel needed for the week ahead. One missed fuel bill risked taking down the entire company.

Going home empty-handed was not an option. Smith traded in his plane ticket to Memphis for a flight to Las Vegas. Over the weekend, he played blackjack until his winnings totaled $32,000—his original

$5,000 plus $27,000 in winnings. Later that week, Smith's staff secured another round of financing. Within six months, the company, now known as FedEx, was flying in twenty-five cities across the country.

It's impossible to hear this story without thinking, *What if he hadn't gone to Vegas?* and *What if he'd lost? FedEx would have been ruined.*

It's a story that portrays the company as vulnerable, desperate, and a little bit crazy. You might think the top executives at the company would have kept hush-hush about this critical weekend in its history, when it survived its near-miss. If you were a pilot looking for a good, stable job, would you want to work for a company that flirted with disaster? If you were a truck driver, would you work for someone who couldn't pay you?

But as the near-disaster story got out, it had an interesting effect on FedEx employees. First, the story had the effect of deepening their loyalty to the firm, say Northwestern University researchers, who have since retested stories like these in experiments. Also, the employees began to make riskier and riskier decisions, often putting themselves into situations akin to Fred Smith that weekend. When a pilot learned about the company's unpaid airport fees, he paid the bill with his own credit card. Drivers trained their wives on delivery routes, so their families could help with deliveries if needed. When money was still tight, employees would agree not to deposit their paychecks. Playing to win quickly became part of FedEx corporate culture: everyone was taking a chance.

"Near-miss bias" is the tendency to take *more* risk after an event in which luck played a critical role in deciding the event's outcome. Despite the fact that luck just as easily could have turned against them, near-misses trigger, in effect, streaks of overoptimism. People don't perceive that the outcome was merely lucky—they begin to believe that *they* are lucky.

Unless challenged to think otherwise, people quickly move from "Phew! Dodged a bullet on that one!" to "I'm a great bullet-dodger."

A couple of years ago, a German researcher brought college students into her lab, where a green turf golf putting mat had been set up. For half the students, when she handed them the ball, she told them, "This is the ball everyone has used so far." The other half were told, "Here is your ball. So far it has turned out to be a lucky ball." The first group made, on average, 4.75 putts out of 10. The group told they had a hot ball sank, on average, 6.42 putts out of 10. The conclusion: believing your luck is good *works*, because it boosts your confidence and optimism, which, in turn, benefits performance.

The same idea might be at work in baseball players, who are famously superstitious; their good-luck charms and rituals work because the players *believe* they work. As long as their belief gives them the illusion of having some control over the role of chance, then it's beneficial.

But before you try to employ this idea, keep this in mind: Dr. Neil Lutsky, the head of the psychology department at Minnesota's Carleton College, spotted a problem in the German putting study. When subjects heard, "So far this has turned out to be a lucky ball," there were really two messages in the line. The first was that the ball was lucky. The second, implicit message was that "Many other people doing the experiment before you sank a lot of putts." This informed the subjects that they were being compared with others—and that good scores had been posted.

Lutsky recreated the experiment. This time, he added a third group, who was told, "Here is your ball. So far, people are doing pretty well on this task." This group sank the most putts by far. Lutsky's conclusion is that luck is no match for the power of social comparison. Nobody wants to be the one guy who can't do well.

Luck plays a role in all competitions. In a close contest, the role of chance is demotivating—it reminds players that no matter how hard they work, the outcome might still be decided by random luck. But in a contest between unequal competitors, the role of luck helps both teams stay motivated. The stronger team knows that just because they're favored, they can't slack off, because this might be the day they have to overcome both the opponent *and* some bad luck.

Meanwhile, the weaker team is often wondering why even to play the game; on paper, they're expected to lose. But the fact that this could be their lucky day—random moments could help them—gives them the fighting chance they need to put the effort into the game. Thus, in unequal contests, it's valuable to strategically remind yourself of the role of luck—and even to embrace it.

While we can see how luck may affect a win, belief in luck can hide a related problem. We naturally examine our *losses* for what went wrong, and we try to learn from them, but we don't do the same for our successes. Our near-misses are left unexamined. In the case of FedEx, it all worked out. The company's near-misses didn't cost it. In the case of NASA, it was a different story.

In 2003, the space shuttle *Columbia* disintegrated over Texas and Louisiana during reentry into the earth's atmosphere. During launch, briefcase-size pieces of foam fell off the shuttle's external tank, hitting the orbital wing and damaging its thermal protection system. In the aftermath, the public learned that this was not a one-time problem; foam had fallen off the tanks in almost every prior shuttle launch. There are photographs of it having happened in 65 out of the 79 prior launches. NASA officials knew it was damaging the orbitals: orbitals would return home riddled with dents from the foam hits (an average of 143 divots per flight). At first, NASA engineers were concerned, but they very quickly fell prey to near-miss bias. They stopped examining it. They came to accept that foam would hit the orbiter during launch, but it would never hit anything important.

You might think NASA engineers are the very people who'd be able to resist near-miss bias. But there was enormous institutional momentum behind the space shuttle voyages, and billions of dollars invested in the venture, all of which biased them to see what they were expecting to see.

NASA engineers would probably object to any comparison between the *Columbia* accident and Fred Smith's trip to Vegas. The NASA staff would insist that they aren't gambling when they work on a mission. However, what they had done was rely on small risks that accumulated over time.

"And if you take on more and more risk, and if you don't really know what risk you're taking, then you are gambling," opined Edward Rogers.

Shortly after the *Columbia* disaster, Rogers began work as the chief knowledge officer for the Goddard Space Flight Center. Goddard is the research base for 9,000 NASA employees charged with unmanned space missions and related research. Rogers was tasked to look at how Goddard managed its institutional knowledge.

While Rogers was still settling into his new post, he received two reports on recent satellite missions. In one, a piece of equipment had malfunctioned: they couldn't get any of the scientific data they had planned for the mission, so the mission was reported to have been a failure. In the other, the satellite had an error in its orbit, but by hook and by crook, they were able to rescue it. The mission had been just a hair's breadth away from being a total loss, but this mission was described as a success. Rogers went to both teams to talk about the missions. He found that the members of the second team were steadfast in their belief that theirs had been a successful mission: they didn't see that they'd just gotten lucky. They saw successes and failures as a zero-sum game: the other guys had lost, and they'd won.

With the tragedy of *Columbia* still fresh in everyone's mind, Rogers took the briefing reports to his bosses at Goddard, suggesting they conduct a study to determine how near-miss bias might affect NASA decision making. They agreed, but they didn't even know who could run such a study. NASA officials knew everyone at the major engineering universities, but they didn't have a single business school contact. Rogers essentially cold-called the dean of Georgetown University's business school, who put him in touch with a couple of professors, Robin Dillon and Catherine Tinsley.

Based on reports given them by Rogers, the professors wrote lengthy after-action reports about fictional lunar missions. Some of these reports were clear successes or failures. Still others had near-misses in them; luck had played a hand in the missions getting completed. The professors then asked college students to read the reports and rate the performance of the missions' managers. The students rated the managers just about as successful when they were lucky as when the managers had made good decisions. They didn't see the mistakes being made. Instead, the near-miss bias was in full force.

Rogers brought the data to his Goddard higher-ups, but they were unconvinced. Those were college students. NASA engineers wouldn't fall prey to the near-miss bias. Skeptically, Rogers arranged for the researchers to replicate the experiment by adding it to existing NASA conference schedules.

The researchers ended up with a sample of highly experienced NASA managers: on average, they'd been at NASA for 14 years. But they were just as prone to the near-miss bias as the undergrads. The NASA engineers also gave positive ratings to the managers whose success was reliant upon a lucky break. Furthermore, when the engineers were asked what they would do, if they were in charge of a subsequent stage of the same mission, they adopted the same risky strategy that had been used before. Unwittingly, they were now relying on luck as the standard operating procedure.

Based on these findings, NASA changed how it does business.

While NASA engineers had always been very good at figuring out their errors (they don't repeat the same mistake twice), its leadership conceded that they weren't good at looking at the ten thousand decisions that may have led up to a mistake.

And they had even less understanding of their successes: they just did things again, in the exact same way, counting on the same result. It was a true case of "If it ain't broke, don't fix it."

At Goddard, Rogers uses a version of the fictional landing reports experiment in employee training. Yet again, the managers fall for the near-miss bias. But when he debriefs them, "People are shocked. They almost feel violated." They can't believe that they've let their decision making be so easily misled.

Before, NASA employees filed required reports, but no one read them. Now, reports are read, and it's expected that the lessons learned will be put into action. Team members have to be unafraid to speak up, but Rogers says that's often difficult to put into practice.

Picture an engineer in his office, wondering if a gear needs to be tested. There's no evidence that it's broken, but he realizes that it was sitting on a shelf for a while: perhaps it's not as strong as it once was. "Can we run a test on this?" he asks. Sure, it's $500, and his team's work will be delayed a few hours, but it's not really a problem.

Compare that to two weeks later. Same situation—the same engineer. But now he is on the launchpad. The rocket's engines are roaring to life; the sound of the countdown echoes through the air. If he asks, "Can we run a test on this?" that same exact test will now cost $5,000,000. They'll have to stop the launch; it could be months before a new launch can be rescheduled. There's still no evidence that the part's broken: it's just his gut feeling. So he dismisses his concern, and the mission goes forward.

That kind of pressure pervades NASA's halls before a mission: it's called "launch fever."

According to the Georgetown research, one of the best ways to eliminate near-miss bias is specifically to stop and think about the risks at issue. Therefore, Rogers initiated a program called "Pause and Reflect." Every few months, teams are asked to assess their progress on a mission, including an analysis of their risk decisions. It's like an after-action report—except they aren't waiting for the action to have happened.

It also helps for NASA engineers to understand the entire mission, so they can see how risks they take may affect the larger whole.

"We are in a risky business, but risk shouldn't be in the way we make decisions," Rogers explained. Risks are constantly reassessed, reanalyzed. You won't hear a NASA manager say, "We talked about that last week, so let's move on." Instead, issues of risk are always on the table. Risk taking is something they will *decide* to do. The fate of a mission is no longer going to be determined by unnecessary risks that crept in from inattention or biased thinking.

They now understand that those fooled into thinking they are great bullet-dodgers eventually get hit.

2

You might have noticed that the human brain spends a lot of time occupied with thoughts of things that didn't actually happen and things that probably never will happen. But the mere fact they *almost* happened (or could happen) brings them into our conscious awareness, and we deliberate on them with the same kind of fervor we give to something real.

Researchers at the University of Illinois have found that, for an average person on an average day, 3% of all human thoughts are devoted to contemplating these near realities and alternative scenarios. They are called counterfactuals, because they are conditional thoughts in which the opening clause premises something contrary to fact: "If I had only done it the other way...," or "If I hadn't made that mistake..." These stray thoughts are somewhat inescapable, compulsive, and usually feel like an unproductive distraction.

We then devote another 6% of our thoughts to temporal comparisons, contrasting the present against the past, or the present against the future. We devote a lot of mental power to errors and misjudgments, even though they are behind us—and we get worked up over what might go wrong next time. We also get lost in our idyllic dreams of how it might unfold if all goes well.

Then we spend yet another 3% of our thoughts comparing ourselves to others and evaluating ourselves negatively or positively.

All told, it adds up: 12% of our thoughts are devoted to self-evaluation through comparison. *And that's on an average day.* The number of these thoughts soars before and after competitions, especially after bouts that were difficult or leading up to those we anticipate will be difficult.

The conventional wisdom is that we should eliminate this constant stream of self-comparison in order to curtail anxiety, basically because anxiousness leads to making mistakes.

We take it as a given that positive feelings—such as happiness—are beneficial for performance, while negative affects—anxiety and anger—are debilitating for performance. The early decades of psychology were built on this idea; the only problem was there was a significant amount of evidence that went against this premise.

The belief that anxiety must hurt performance was so ingrained and deeply entrenched that the contrary data were deeply controversial. Some scholars decided to disentangle *somatic anxiety* from *cognitive anxiety*. Somatic anxiety is the physiological state—the faster heart rate, clammy hands, raised blood pressure, dry throat, hot face, and tense muscles. Cognitive anxiety is the mental state—the inability to control one's thoughts, anticipating and agonizing over problems, and the fear of disapproval. Cognitive anxiety, it was postulated, surely would have an inverse relation to competitive performance.

Except it didn't. Again, the data were very mixed, and, in many studies, cognitive anxiety went hand in hand with performance. As one went up, so did the other. And the theory that somatic anxiety would top out—that very high levels of physiological arousal would hurt performance—also didn't hold up in the lab or in the field.

Researchers quantify anxiety levels during an event, with a scale spanning from a minimum score of 20 to a maximum score of 80. But lower anxiety scores don't automatically lead to better performance; it isn't as though the best performers were immune to the pressure. On the contrary, just prior to peak performances, elite athletes' anxiety levels tend to range from a low 26 all the way to 67. Film and stage star Bob Hope was always incredibly anxious before going onstage.

According to researcher Gordon Goodman, Hope told his writers that if he wasn't nervous, the show wouldn't go well.

While explanations were unsuccessfully proposed and dismissed, Russian psychologist Yuri Hanin proposed an idea for anxiety and athletic performance that has come to be broadly tested and accepted. Hanin postulated that everyone has an *Individual Zone of Optimal Functioning* (IZOF), a level of anxiousness beneficial to his performance. But some players need more anxiety to be at their best, while others need much less. Player A might need to be at an anxiety level of 30, while Player B might need to be at 60, but Player A will *always* play best at around 30, and Player B will always play best if near 60. Athletes in every sport—from the very physical to the not-so-physical—have been asked to complete anxiety inventories right before performance. Great performances are logged at almost every level of anxiety, across most of the anxiety spectrum. Since Hanin's theory was originally proposed, the IZOF has been applied in nonathletic contexts—from actors coping with stage fright to soldiers in military operations.

An individual's optimal level of anxiety for performance is not that far above his baseline level for normal life. A person who is normally relaxed will perform best if somewhat at ease. A person who is wound tight, or who is normally intense, will perform best at high levels of arousal.

The important thing to recognize is there's a difference between experiencing a stressful situation and being in distress. As we learned from the COMT-gene research, some people *need* pressure to perform their best. Reflecting once again about the Princeton students challenge experiment—the students weren't told, "Calm down." Instead, it was about how they *interpreted* the task.

Jeremy Jamieson, a Harvard researcher, has run two similar experiments with undergraduates who were prepping to take the GRE. He had them take a practice exam, and before and after the test the students gave saliva samples. On the cover page of the practice exam, they read:

The goal of this research is to examine how physiological arousal during a test correlates with performance. Because it is normal for people to feel anxious during standardized tests, saliva samples... will be analyzed for hormones that indicate your arousal level.

For half the students, that's all they saw. But the other half also learned:

People think that feeling anxious while taking a standardized test will make them do poorly on the test. However, recent research suggests that arousal doesn't hurt performance on these tests and can even help performance... people who feel anxious during a test might actually do better. This means that you shouldn't feel concerned if you do feel anxious while taking today's GRE test. If you find yourself feeling anxious, simply remind yourself that your arousal could be helping you do well.

Reframing their nerves as a positive state of excitement enabled those in the second group to make fewer mistakes: they scored more than 50 points higher on the practice exam—even after controlling for their grade point average.

Just to be clear, this tidbit of wisdom didn't lower their physiological stress levels; their stress hormone levels were actually *higher*. Instead, it changed their perception and interpretation of the stress. They were able to harness that stress into superior focus and faster decision making. And they took the lesson to heart; on the actual GRE, they scored 65 points higher than the control group.

If you recall, at the very beginning of this book, we learned that ballroom dancers in Germany were *all* stressed by performing in front of judges. Even dancers with over ten years of competitive experience get slammed with the physiological components of stress. But they don't all interpret that stress the same way.

The real distinction between amateur competitors and professionals is how they interpret anxiety. Whether it's male rugby players, female volleyball players, or concert pianists, the amateurs view anxiety as detrimental, while the professionals tend to view it as beneficial. They recognize that they're anxious, but they also remain confident that they're still in control and well prepared, and that their goals are attainable. They're stressed, but not threatened. In this state of mind, higher levels of arousal help them perform their best.

The goal, then, is not necessarily to calm competitors to the point of being relaxed. Rather, it's to help them get into their optimal zone, be that at 30 or 60.

3

Where does this leave the idea that our thoughts need to be affirming and positive?

The positive thinking movement originated in religious ideology in the 1880s. Positive thinking was prescribed as a way to get closer to God and to do God's work. Even when minister Norman Vincent Peale penned his 1952 self-help classic *The Power of Positive Thinking*, he was evangelizing Christian notions of seeing God's grace at work in the world.

But somewhere between Peale and today, threads of science slowly replaced the threads of religion, and the tapestry of positive thinking got repurposed as a means to well-being.

People are advised to block out the blunders and failures in their past—to *not go there* in the mind. They're also warned to avoid thinking about anything that could go wrong in their future. The concern is that negativity inherently leads to anxiety and fear. The best-case scenario is that negativity pushes you into a prevention-orientation: the worst case is that you're in a perpetual state of threat. The antidote, then, is to train the mind to think positively, never letting negative thoughts or emotions drag you down. Otherwise, negative thoughts have a tendency to be self-fulfilling, as surely as saying, "Don't think about pink elephants" triggers images in the mind of pink elephants. Negativity bias causes the brain to look for confirmation, to look for the worst in everything, to affirm its conclusion about the worthless self.

Given all that, the promises of positive-thinking psychology are no longer limited to promises of happiness and general well-being. In the last fifteen years, the doctrine has been expanded into a technique to "get results." It's now purported to help us succeed in our life's varied ambitions, from achieving career dreams to meeting corporate sales quotas.

The problem is that what's good for your well-being is not necessarily going to be effective in a competitive context, or help you sustain the drive to achieve your goals. In the well-being realm, traits such as ambition, dominance, and perfectionism are considered psychological maladies that need to be treated. But during a performance, or when striving to achieve goals, they can all be adaptive. It bears repeating: the mental states needed to compete are not always socially palatable.

When the object is to compete, positive psychology becomes a handicap. Its Panglossian ban on negative thought denies the value of critical thinking about past performance, which is necessary in order to learn from one's mistakes and alter strategy going forward.

Positive pep talks don't necessarily lead to sincere positive belief; often they're just unconvincing talk. But even when they lead to sincere belief in your own self-efficacy, it's not predictive of much. Self-efficacy certainly gets people to choose to compete, but it doesn't correlate much with actual performance, and the higher the level of competition, the weaker and weaker the correlation. At a certain point, those with seeds of doubt actually do best. Having a little doubt in the mind leads you to not underestimate your opponents, and it ensures that you truly push yourself.

When it comes to "getting results," the science says it isn't the *power* of positive thinking but the *perils* of positive thinking. Anticipating mistakes can help you win. Imagining yourself on the podium may, in actuality, undermine your attempts to get there.

Students who visualize doing really well in class actually have lower final grades—even accounting for their performances on the midterm. Those who think about "all they are going to get done this week" don't really get much done.

There's no clear evidence that reassuring yourself "You're great!" promotes better outcomes during competition. A number of studies have found that more negative self-talk is associated with more successful performance. Athletes who chided themselves on their mistakes, then moved on, became Olympians. Those who spent meets telling themselves they were wonderful didn't make the squad.

In longitudinal studies, Gabriele Oettingen, professor at New York University and the University of Hamburg, concluded that when jobseekers spend time visualizing their dream job, two years later they are less likely to have found employment in any job. (If they someday do find a job, it will be for lower pay and lower recognition than the jobs held by those who had spent less time daydreaming about their careers.) Women who fantasize about a secret crush never date him; in fact, five months later, they are less likely to be dating anyone at all.

In Oettingen's study of patients who needed hip replacement surgery, the patients were about evenly split in their prehospitalization mindset. About half were predominantly thinking about the benefits they'd have from the surgery: they envisioned themselves dancing and running marathons. They were sure they'd be better than ever. The others were consumed with fears about the pain and difficulties they might endure during rehab. They fretted about how long it would take before they could navigate a hallway without crutches; they anxiously wondered if postsurgery life was worse than anything they'd already experienced.

Weeks after surgery, those who had dreaded their rehab had more mobility and less pain than those who had been sure they'd be dancing in no time.

The problem with all those positive images and fantasies is that you aren't as motivated to work toward your goal because you're taking success for granted. "You can seduce yourself into thinking that you've already achieved your dream, and that can prevent you from doing what you actually need to attain it," explained Oettingen. Always staying positive means that setbacks are unanticipated: they are more upsetting and demoralizing, which leads to perseveration, like the tennis player constantly replaying her miss in her mind.

Is there really no place here for positive thinking? Well, there is—but its real benefit is boosting and reviving motivation. Dr. Paul Dennis is a University of Toronto sports psychologist who also works with the NHL's Toronto Maple Leafs. During the off-season, when there's a lot of training and not much payoff, he has players visualize a peak moment in their careers—"It's very important that it be based on what really happened, not a naïve, delusional vision," he said. "I have them visualize the game, visualize the crowd, celebrating with teammates afterward, and being with their family after the game. The visualization gives them hope. If it happened once, it can happen again." He does this to reinvigorate their drive and persistence.

But not for one second does he believe this kind of visualization makes them better hockey players; it doesn't replace the hard work of training. Nor does he try to get hockey players to express an upbeat, sunny, positive demeanor. "Many of them play best when they are intense, moody, or irritated. I don't take them away from what got them there in the first place."

We all need a toolbox to deal with setbacks. But the correct variable to focus on is not the positivity-negativity spectrum. Just as the IZOF research recognizes that not everyone competes best when calm, not everyone competes best when he's optimistic and cheery. Instead, the factor that determines whether we recover is whether our thinking is additive or subtractive. What matters is not Positive Thinking vs. Negative Thinking, it's Additive Thinking vs. Subtractive Thinking.

Explained University of California, Berkeley, professor Laura Kray, "Additive counterfactuals are what we might have done—but it didn't occur in reality. Subtractive counterfactuals are things that actually occurred in the past, that we'd subtract—thinking of how things would be different if it hadn't really happened." An additive counterfactual is, "If only I had driven toward the hoop…," while a subtractive counterfactual is like, "If only I hadn't missed the shot…"

A subtractive counterfactual usually expresses regret over a mistake or a failed strategy. An additive counterfactual sees new strategies and options—it adds to the choices available if the situation happens again.

Researchers—including Kray, Keith Markman, and Adam Galinsky—have tested the efficacy of counterfactuals in various scenarios, such as sales pitches, negotiations, flight training, and athletic tasks. People who look back on their performance with subtractive counterfactuals perform worse the next time. Those who employ additive counterfactuals perform better over time. This is true both in experimental studies (where subjects are told to reflect in one style or the other) and in naturalistic studies (looking at what people actually do).

By thinking through different versions of "If only this had happened instead," you can avoid some of the blind spots due to overconfidence. You can predict problems that may arise, and then rerun the scenarios in your head until you've figured out a solution.

In effect, additive counterfactuals trigger a problem-solving mindset. Additive counterfactuals activate regions of the brain that would otherwise be deactivated during positive thinking, or even experiential learning. When engaged in counterfactual thinking, the lateral frontal polar cortex, dorsomedial frontal cortex, and posteromedial cortex seem to operate as a network. Through this interaction, the brain identifies the best road not taken and retains this information until the next time you have to make a similar decision.

The benefit of activating this network exists *even if you can't spot the solution right away.* Counterfactual thinking seems to prime the brain to think more creatively; it readies the creative neural net-works. Research has shown that people do better on creative-thinking tasks after having been asked to mentalize a series of counterfactual thoughts. When faced with a unique problem, a scenario that wasn't previously anticipated or considered, they're better at finding solutions.

Oettingen once went to a school where German children were about to start learning English. She asked them to write an essay, fantasizing about the most wonderful thing that could possibly happen once they'd mastered the new language. (The responses ranged from "Make my father proud!" to "Talk to the members of my favorite American band!") Then she asked one group of the children to write about what obstacles they might face while learning English; the others just kept riffing on how great fluency would be.

After the kids had had three months of English lessons, Oettingen returned to the schools and gathered up the children's grades. Oettingen's task had had a remarkable effect. Of the children who had only fantasized about English fluency, their average grade was roughly a "C." For the group who had written about both their fantasy and the obstacles they'd face, their average grade was an "A." A few minutes of critical thought had resulted in an entire semester of improvement. And it wasn't as if those children were just better handling the problems they'd anticipated: they were more motivated and worked harder from the very first.

Oettingen believes that a bit of fantasy at the outset can be productive, because it helps you envision all that you could achieve. But it takes thinking about the obstacles in your way to turn those lofty aspirations into a binding goal.

Once people consciously identify those obstacles, Oettingen says she can see the relief on their faces. They sit back with a relaxed sigh. Because now people can decide if their goal is truly worth it or not. If it isn't, they can move on with their lives. If the goal *is* worth it, from then on, figuring a way to working through those obstacles becomes part and parcel with the goal itself. I will work through the pain of my hip rehab exercises so that I can walk on my own. I will play fewer video games so that I can practice my English. I will keep hitting deep shots and continue going to the net. And so on. Rather than wishing away any difficulties, overcoming the obstacles is now the goal.

4

In a series of studies, Japanese researcher Michiko Yoshie investigated professional pianists in practice and during competitions. Yoshie audiotaped their rehearsals and their performances, and she measured their heart rates and self-reported anxiety and several other physiological levels. She staged competitions with prestigious judges, cash prizes, and sizable audiences. On average, these pianists had been training continuously for over twenty years.

Nevertheless, Yoshie found that the stress of the competition came through their performances. Most pianists played *worse* in contests than in rehearsal: they made more subtle errors. It is quite rare to find someone who performs as well or better in a competition than at practice. What's more is that their psychological state was manifested in their physiology. Their heart rates went up an average of 34 beats per minute, and they were sweating. They had more muscle tension in their shoulders and arms, and that alone hurt the quality of their performances. They played the notes faster, and they hit the keys harder.

What separated the winners from the also-rans was not how great they sounded in rehearsal. It was whether they could perform in the competition at the same level as their rehearsal.

As with the anxious pianists and stressed-out ballroom dancers— in a recent study of professional actors, almost 70% of them reported that they had been grappling with stage fright during their most recent roles, and the amount of experience they had didn't protect them from worry.

Practice, it seems, doesn't make perfect. Even "practicing perfect" doesn't make perfect. To compete at the highest levels requires something more; it requires taking control of the body's physiology.

As we mentioned before, the stress of competition triggers responses in the brain, but that's just the beginning. According to researchers Wendy Berry Mendes and Jim Blascovich, the threat state has other, very real physiological consequences—a cascade of other biological responses.

In a threat condition, the heart rate increases, while heart rate variability decreases—when your heart's pounding so hard you can hear it, even if you're just standing still. All our blood vessels are lined with smooth muscle, which works either to constrict or relax the vessels. In a threat state, blood vessels constrict: all that blood basically has nowhere to go, and blood pressure shoots up. The lungs mirror the blood vessels—also constricting, so there is less oxygen coursing through them, and you tire more easily. There's a short burst of energy, from burning stored glucose in your cells, but it quickly gets sapped, and you don't feel that you can get the energy back. Trying to compete in the threat condition is close to impossible, whether you're a gymnast or a pianist or a student taking a final exam.

In a challenge state, as Berry Mendes and Blascovich explain, the stress is still there, but it has a different underlying physiology. As heart rate goes up, the veins dilate, so that blood flow improves: there's an invigorating rush of oxygen throughout the body. The body turns to blood glucose and more free fatty acids for an instant boost in energy. The blood even thickens with platelets—if injury occurs, the body's ready to bandage itself up and keep fighting. The physiology helps the psychology play to win.

In both states, all these changes are the result of noradrenaline and adrenaline. These two chemicals drive vasodilation/vasoconstriction, the production of glucose, and lung function. The two are so often found in tandem that they are commonly, and inaccurately, described as working in much the same way. Noradrenaline actually converts into adrenaline. During the rush of competition, your body floods with four times as much adrenaline as noradrenaline. The chemical mix is what's determinative. Nerves that control vasodilation and vasoconstriction run straight up through the spinal cord. When someone is afraid or threatened, more noradrenaline gets into the mix, and vasoconstriction is triggered. But when the brain reads a situation as challenging-yet-doable, it supplies adrenaline in the right proportion, resulting in the all-important vasodilation of the blood vessels and lungs. Adrenaline also facilitates glucose production in the liver.

The physiological effects of performance anxiety are so severe that 27% of professional musicians regularly use beta-blockers—prescription drugs that block noradrenaline and adrenaline—when they perform. Most opera principals also use these drugs.

But pharmaceutical interventions are not the only answer. Professional sports teams around the world are hiring psychologists to teach their athletes to willfully control their physical responses to stress—consciously ensuring that they are in a challenge, not threat, state.

For example, the athletes watch videos of their game performances, while wearing a cap with electrodes that measures every spike in brain activity. They aren't watching their successes to load up on positive imagery. Instead, they're watching their mistakes—over and over again. They aren't supposed to analyze and critique their technique. They're just learning to keep the mind steady, without feeling the sense of dread at the errors they made.

In theory, if a player does this enough, he will be better trained to do the same in a live game. He's trying to teach his amygdala and ACC not to overreact when he's made a mistake. He's working to stay in the relaxed focus defined by the brain's alpha waves, and avoid the busy, panicky beta waves. He's learning to consciously slow his breathing, which will, in turn, regulate his heart rate and vasodilation. The

Italian national soccer team started doing this training before its 2006 World Cup victory, and the technique has since spread throughout professional sports.

Staying calm is one way to try to maintain optimal physiology and avoid vasoconstriction. But as we've noted, many athletes don't perform best at low levels of arousal.

To find an athlete's Individual Zone of Optimal Functioning, sports psychologists typically ask athletes to recall their emotional states during their best performances ever and their worst performances ever. In these interviews—often compiled for scholarly analysis—it's intriguing how frequently athletes report that their best performances were produced when athletes were feeling angry, vengeful, or resentful.

When talking about anger, it's necessary to distinguish between "trait" anger and "situational" anger. The former is when someone is prone to anger all the time—definitely unhealthy. But situational anger is quite different. People who respond with anger to a confrontation have higher emotional intelligence scores while ranking higher in life satisfaction and greater well-being.

Situational anger is triggered by a disconnect between what ought to happen and what has happened; it's what you feel when your goals are blocked by someone who has improperly thwarted you. There's a sense of injustice in the ingredients for anger. The other crucial ingredient that sparks anger is that you feel you can do something about the injustice: there's a sliver of empowerment, a sense that you still have a fighting chance to change the situation, right the wrong. Without that chance, you're blocked, which leads to despair, not anger.

Just as people have for too long connected anxiety with weak performance, people have thought that anger was synonymous with aggression. But researchers have found that—compared with those who are hopeful or fearful—angry people are more likely to seek a compromise. Aggression is a strategy for the angry, but it's not the only one: they'll be nonaggressive and prosocial if it solves the underlying problem.

Of course, when anger is too hot, there's no doubt it's debilitating. It causes people to lose focus, find fault with others, and violate the rules of the competition. That level of anger, to the point of rage, though, is not what people are describing when they talk about their peak performances. They sometimes name what they felt as "controlled anger" or "channeled anger." This kind of anger pushes someone into a sense of determination.

It's not really a surprise that 75% of national karate team members feel that anger helps them; nor is it surprising that rugby players feel the same way. But the feeling is also reported by figure skaters, gymnasts, rowers, and long-distance runners—athletes who never come into physical contact with opponents. And anger has been found to have benefits in purely cognitive settings as well: angry college students taking a exam did better than peers who were happy as they entered the test room.

Anger is used in military psychological operations: officers are taught to develop an "anger architecture" and "rage control"—mental processes they can use to steel themselves through difficult missions.

In negotiations, anger is often used as an attempt to intimidate the other side. And there is sizable evidence to show that such a strategy is somewhat successful. (At least in the first few rounds of the negotiations.) But anger can also help the negotiator's own performance. In lab experiments, angry negotiators are more focused on the terms at issue. They are more optimistic about the success of a deal, and they get more of what they want. The key there—Dutch researchers warn—is that anger only works if people believe they are in control of the situation. Again, anger is about being able to remove an obstacle that stands in your way. If someone walks into a meeting desperate to make a deal, then anger only weakens his ability to negotiate: he pays too much attention to being angry and forgets to look at the bigger picture.

All this is also mirrored in the brain, neurologically. While fear and anxiety trigger the brain's prevention-system—leading to withdrawal and risk aversion—when someone shifts into anger, he shifts neurological systems, like a train jumping the tracks. The gain-oriented system activates. The prevention system downregulates, allowing someone to be less inhibited, to act, and take risks.

By tamping down inhibitions, anger thus frees up desire—desire is no longer restrained. It's often when people are angry that they finally recognize what they want, and the intensity of their desire surges. Anger doesn't cloud the picture: it clarifies it.

Angry people become more intense, and they pursue the rewards harder. Attention narrows, distractions disappear. Anger makes them want it more. They are faster in making a response. Thomas Denson's team of neuroscientists at the University of New South Wales in Australia discovered that the anger leading to meaningful action lights up the brain's dorsal anterior cingulate cortex—that part of the brain heavily involved in conflict resolution.

Getting calm is perhaps the more socially acceptable route to peak performance. But if you're full of anxiety and you can't calm down, find out what is holding you back. Then try getting angry about it. And channel that anger into *doing something productive.*

Think of the entrepreneur, driven by rejection, on a mission to prove the world wrong. Think of the young author, defending her talent, motivated to overcome waves of rejection letters. Think of anyone trying to lose weight, or trying to learn guitar, or any other goal-directed behavior—how he gets mad at himself for failing to make progress, and uses that to push himself harder. Think of the rap artist, who puts the struggles of urban life to music. Think of the young mother, upset about the quality of local schools, who decides to run for the school board.

In each case, despair is the other option; anger is a negative emotion that's a positive force—motivating people to go farther.

CHAPTER NINE

The 'Roid Rage
of Chess

1

Twenty years ago, a University of Nebraska professor went to a prominent chess club in Lincoln and asked the members if he could track their testosterone levels during upcoming tournaments. All they needed to do was frequently spit in a cup.

At the time, the hormone testosterone had a reputation for being linked to physical and behavioral aggression. Those with high baseline testosterone were more likely to be arrested, more likely to see military combat, and more likely to divorce. Testosterone, it was believed, made you into the Incredible Hulk.

There was no reason to think testosterone would improve performance in a strategic game that relied on cognitive brainpower and rational decision making. If anything, one might expect testosterone to make a chess player perform worse.

But the professor, Alan Booth, was curious. Several studies had shown that athletes in physically taxing sports saw their testosterone significantly rise *prior* to an event—their bodies were anticipating the contest by altering their chemistry. Booth was interested in this pregame boost. Would it also be the case in a nonphysical competition?

"I'd been told that chess players were a real competitive bunch, and they are," Booth recalled.

Nine of the players from the chess club went to a prestigious regional tournament held in a Lincoln hotel ballroom. The tournament drew players from Iowa, Kansas, and South Dakota, as well as from Omaha and other cities in Nebraska. "These tournaments were very important to the players," Booth explained. The players' results would be reported to the World Chess Federation, thus "Their record at the tournament was made public and significantly affected their overall standing."

There were four rounds of competition over the course of the day. Each game had a time limit, and players had to decide how aggressively or cautiously to play to engineer a win. They had to be very calculated in looking quickly for their chance to make a killer move; they couldn't waste too much time looking for the best chess move in every position, or they would end up rushing to make their last ten or fifteen moves in just a few minutes.

Booth had the nine players from the local club spit in a cup before and between every match.

Some surprises happened at the tournament. The club's top player crashed out early. Four players from the club made it to the final round; one of those players was a long-shot underdog going in. Even though he was the second-worst of the nine club players at the tourney, on that day, he rose to the occasion and played superbly.

To Booth's surprise, all this was foretold by the players' prematch testosterone levels. When he processed the saliva and reconstructed the timelines, Booth could see that the top player hadn't gotten a boost in testosterone before his first match. Perhaps overconfident, his body hadn't readied itself, and he'd lost as a result. Meanwhile, his lower-ranked teammate had anticipated the challenge. He had a much bigger pregame boost, and he continued to get more pumped up with every round, with every successive win. Testosterone didn't make chess players worse; it made them *better*.

As a result of Booth's chess study, two intriguing questions needed further investigation.

The first was why a hormone notorious for physical aggression helped chess players outsmart opponents.

The second was a tantalizing possibility—how the psychoendocrine cocktail present in our bodies could foretell who would win and who would lose *before an event had even begun*.

Competing changes the body's chemistry. The more intense the competition, the greater the change.

There are hundreds of hormones in our bodies, but what's important to know is that most of them are slight variations on one another, descendants in a chain of enzymatic processes. Tyrosine turns into l-dopa, which turns into dopamine, which turns into noradrenaline, which turns into adrenaline. Testosterone, progesterone, and cortisol all are downstream conversions of cholesterol. DHEA turns into testosterone, which may turn into estradiol and dihydrotestosterone, a kind of turbo-testosterone five times stronger than its precursor. Similarly, oxytocin can convert into a hexapeptide that is 100 times more potent than its precursor.

Because these hormones are such close cousins, their jobs often overlap; several different hormones can bind to the same receptors. Substance P regulates pain, but so does oxytocin. Oxytocin and serotonin both elevate moods. One hormone might work instantaneously, while another hormone might do much the same thing, over a longer period. Also, when one hormone is already bound to the receptor, it blocks other hormones out, and it may do this partially or fully, depending on how strongly it binds.

While there are hundreds of hormones, they come together to do a few basic tasks in competition: to make us more or less ready to act;

be more or less interested in winning a challenge; become more or less afraid; be more or less emotional; be more or less sensitive to pain; be more or less offended by injustice; and become more or less attuned to the feelings of others around us.

What we want to do in this chapter is look more closely at a few key hormones, and—as we get to know their real effects—this will help us better understand what truly happens in competition.

2

Twenty years after Booth's chess study, a British study of surgeons showed the same anticipation effect of testosterone. Scholars took blood samples of maxillofacial surgeons on mornings before they were to perform complicated cancer and postcancer facial reconstruction surgeries. These procedures would require the surgeons to cut out cancerous bone tumors, graft bone from the pelvis into the face, and reconstruct the nerves and facial muscles to restore patients' ability to express themselves.

As in the chess study, the scholars found that the surgeons' bodies had anticipated the arduous challenge. The more complicated the surgery, and the bigger the tumor they had to remove, the greater the boost in testosterone in the surgeon's bloodstream the morning of the surgery. These were expert surgeons, between the ages of 42 and 60. Baseline testosterone peaks in early adulthood and then drops consistently as one ages—but that doesn't mean older adults can't *respond* to an imminent challenge. For the most demanding surgeries, the surgeons' anticipatory boost was gigantic, producing a 500% increase in testosterone.

That testosterone boosts performance for elite surgeons and chess masters every bit as much as it does for weightlifters and home run hitters is radically changing how science has regarded the steroid.

"I like to think of testosterone as *intensity*, not as aggression," Booth says, when considering the last twenty years of research into the hormone. "It increases the intensity with which someone approaches an activity—it increases their response to challenge."

"Testosterone *is* motivation," said Dr. Jack van Honk, in a presentation to his colleagues. Van Honk, an experimental psychologist at Utrecht University, has done many experiments where subjects are given a dose of testosterone under the tongue. "Without testosterone, there is no motivation at all. When you take some testosterone sublingually, you're ready to go, you're up for it, there's no fear, no hesitation."

This ability to get "up for it" is partially set by prenatal brain development in the womb (which we wrote about several chapters ago) and it's partially *also* a trained response. Competitors learn to recognize a future contest, and their minds need to mark it as a salient challenge in order for the testosterone response to kick in.

For instance, Booth's chess club members also played in a city tournament that was far less prestigious and far less meaningful to the players. In that case, very few of the players got the anticipatory response—almost none of them were taking it seriously and so their testosterone levels didn't predict performance.

This could be one reason why positive thinking can backfire, as seen in the last chapter. If you envision yourself cruising to victory, false overconfidence fails to trigger the testosterone response. If you envision a close, contested race where every bit of *aretas* will be needed to win, the mind will mark the event as salient, and your body will start producing the needed testosterone.

If adrenaline is the body's instantaneous response to challenge—pulsing and burning up in 30 to 40 seconds—testosterone is more of a medium-term response; most of the extra testosterone is burned up in about 90 minutes. Adrenaline has instantaneous effects because it triggers the nerves that run through the spinal cord. Testosterone is not quite as fast, since it travels through the bloodstream. The hormone's effects are vast, throughout the body, producing anabolic energy and increasing the size of cells, but for our purposes—where we are interested in its effect on the mind—there's a dual mechanism of action.

Testosterone is a small enough steroid to cross from the bloodstream through the blood-brain barrier. It enters into the cytoplasm of brain cells, where androgen receptors let it pass right into the nucleus. There, it binds to DNA. This causes the DNA to change its transcription rate, markedly increasing the production of vital neurotransmitters. In this way, testosterone builds up an extra supply of the neurotransmitters that will be needed in the competition. That's the important reason to have testosterone going *before* a competition—it stocks up the war chest.

There are androgen receptors on the *outside* of brain cells, too—not everywhere in the brain, but prominently in a network that connects the amygdala, hypothalamus, and brainstem. By binding to the outside of nerve cells in this network, testosterone has a more immediate effect on perception, emotion, cognition, and behavior.

Success in competition requires taking risks that are normally constrained by fear. This is one way testosterone works, by acting on the amygdala and dampening the fear response. At the same time, it binds to androgen receptors in the brain's reward system, making the brain more responsive to the rewards of competition, helping it mount enough desire to overcome inhibitions. The result: less fear of risk, more drive for reward. The risk-reward calculation changes.

Even though testosterone makes you take more risks, it doesn't cause you to take *stupid* risks. The studies of chess and face surgeons—and financial traders and others as well—illustrate how testosterone helps you recognize smart risks and take them. This chemical, originally assumed to make people irrational and primitive, actually helps you be more rational.

It removes the emotional wariness we have toward uncertainty.

Testosterone uncouples the delta brainwaves of emotion from the beta brainwaves of cognitive thought. Though we often become very emotional during a competition, testosterone keeps those emotions from interfering with cognitive processing.

A recent study of competitors playing Shogi, the Japanese version of chess, zeroed in on exactly this. During the tournament, competitors were rated as playing emotionally or playing cognitively. Those with higher testosterone boosts were playing cognitively.

Probably the most noteworthy proof of this was when Jack van Honk gave subjects testosterone and then had them take a math-ability test. Their scores shot up 9%.

Under the spell of testosterone, you think more analytically, almost hyperrationally. This is a somewhat shocking idea.

Hyperrationality has its downside, however: argumentativeness. When an opponent breaks the rules, high-testosterone people *react* more strongly. Their sense of right and wrong intensifies into fury. If they take on an aggressive demeanor, it's only in retaliation. They don't start it, but when someone else starts it, they become the rule enforcers. This has been confirmed in studies of those with naturally responsive testosterone and in studies where testosterone is administered orally.

In the previous chapter, we teased out how anger is the result of a sense of injustice. Many competitive people will no doubt identify with this portrait; they think of themselves as being competitive, but also as rule-abiders. It's when someone else breaks the rules that they get enraged.

If you go back and think about the Incredible Hulk analogy, it's not totally wrong, after all. You just have to remember that the Hulk was in a long line of Marvel superheroes. When he wasn't the green monster, he was the brilliant nuclear scientist, Bruce Banner. As the green monster, he fought the bad guys. *They* started it.

The Incredible Hulk's creator, Stan Lee, had the thought, "Wouldn't it be fun to create a monster and make him the good guy?" Lee also was inspired by Jewish myths of the Golem, who protected the Jews in Prague from attacks by the Holy Roman emperor Rudolf II. At first the Hulk wanted to get rid of his powers so he wouldn't hurt people, but he was forced to use them to protect his girlfriend. Eventually, he gained some control over his powers and took on villains such as Bi-Beast, Zzzax, the Abomination, and General "Thunderbolt" Ross.

Much like the Hulk, testosterone isn't the bad guy; it has just been misunderstood.

3

Dog shows are a surprising part of American cultural history: the famed Westminster competition has been around longer than the electric lightbulb. Dog shows are a small but highly competitive niche industry: owners spend around $330 million a year in show-related expenses. A champion dog's expenses can run up to $200,000 annually. One of the most popular forms of dog competition are "agility" contests. A canine version of the decathlon, an agility contest involves a dog racing as fast as possible around a track, jumping over hurdles, climbing up and down seesaws, crawling through tunnels, and weaving between 10 poles (like a miniature ski slalom). Dogs must navigate through as many as 22 different obstacles within as little as 40 seconds. Fast-enough qualifying times are deemed "wins" because they get the dog an entrée into increasingly prestigious competitions.

At the most competitive levels, often it isn't the dog's owner who is sprinting around with the dog. Instead, the dog is spurred on by a professional dog handler. The dog world equivalent of jockeys, handlers are trained experts brought in to train the dog and run it through the competition. Working in as many as 150 competitions a year, accomplished handlers can command fees as high as $2,500 a day per dog (plus travel and expenses). At every race, their reputation is on the line.

Drs. Pranjal Mehta and Amanda Jones decided to go to one such competition in San Antonio, to record the hormones of 140 dog handlers. One of the reasons they chose dog handlers was because men and women handlers compete side by side, and men show no advantage over women.

Women's bodies have far lower baseline testosterone than men's. On average, they have only one-seventh as much as men. But as the face surgeons showed, baseline levels aren't determinative. Testosterone can respond to a challenge. Whether this happens in women had been unclear for quite some time. Many early studies were inconclusive.

The 83 male dog handlers showed the usual pattern: testosterone rising before the competition and continuing to rise during the competition. If they won, they got an even bigger boost, and if they lost, testosterone fell. But the 57 women didn't show this pattern: consistent with many other studies, the female handlers' testosterone didn't rise during the competition, and they didn't get a boost or a drop after winning and losing.

Even though the findings were consistent with prior studies, Mehta still questioned the data. Backstage at the dog competition, female dog handlers made friends with one another and chatted a lot with dog owners.

According to the "tend-and-befriend" theory, when women experience a stressful situation, they seek out others' companionship to alleviate their tension. They are still playing by the rules of the dyad, learned in early childhood, in which dominance is forbidden and equality is prized.

Mehta knew that testosterone doesn't respond when two friends compete, or when one teammate beats the other in practice. When you have to go up against someone you care for, your concern for his regard defuses the testosterone response. In fact, often the opposite happens after a contest between friends—the winner's testosterone goes *down*.

Mehta wondered if the female handlers had defused their own testosterone response by making friends backstage.

Setting up a laboratory experiment in Austin to test this, Mehta and Jones created a competitive paradigm where women could not tend and befriend one another.

When a pair of female study participants arrived at the lab, they were given a short task to get to know each other. Then the researchers informed the women that they'd be competing against each other in the next task, a computerized version of an intelligence test. The researchers then escorted the two to computers they'd placed on adjacent sides of the room. Once seated, the women were far enough away from each other that they couldn't see what was on the other's screen, but close enough that they could hear the other working. The researchers insisted the women not interact during the task, because it was highly predictive of the women's cognitive abilities. One of Mehta's assistants hovered nearby, to make sure there was no more chitchat. The test itself was a series of puzzles. Whenever she solved one, each woman was to announce, "Done," loud enough so that the other could hear her.

However, the test was rigged. One woman got much easier puzzles to solve: she was saying "Done" and finishing twice as many puzzles as the other. As expected, this completely upset the loser.

With the women separated by distance and unable to chat, their testosterone responded just as it did in all the studies of men's.

In the last couple of years, it has been established that women's testosterone responds just as it does for men. Studies of female tennis players, volleyball players, professional soccer players, and even women's badminton players have all confirmed this. The key is that they have to be serious competitors and really care about the outcome.

When someone doesn't care that much about the outcome—regardless of gender—then testosterone doesn't respond. Chatting up opponents, making friends with them, can defuse the testosterone response for everyone.

A savvy competitor may even take advantage of this mechanism, by knowing when to distance himself from his rivals and when intentionally to befriend opponents.

At a job interview, should you talk to the other applicants who are waiting? When a batter reaches first and must decide if he should steal second, what's the effect of his chatting up the first baseman? Is an NBA final less of a game because the opposing superstars greet each other like best friends instead of bitter rivals?

4

Let's spend a little time with two other hormones that are involved in competition: cortisol and oxytocin. Just as we are learning that testosterone is not what we always thought, cortisol and oxytocin are also proving to be chemicals we've long gotten wrong.

For decades, cortisol has been synonymous with stress. Long-term elevated cortisol levels meant chronic distress, and short-term increases in cortisol meant acute stress. Stress was bad for you, cortisol was bad for you. It weakens the immune system; impairs learning; damages the hippocampus, where long-term memories are stored; and is associated with depression.

There was only one thing wrong with this portrait: our bodies *need* cortisol. It's what our bodies use to metabolize food and produce energy and keep blood sugar levels up. At the very least, in physical competitions, cortisol is necessary to maintain a constant supply of energy.

It was less clear what effect cortisol had on the mind during competition.

The first clue came a couple of years ago, when researchers started administering subjects cortisol orally. They found that when they gave cortisol to phobic patients, the patients became less anxious. And when the researchers dared to stress these phobic patients, they were okay; it didn't crush them.

This was followed up by studies where normal subjects were given cortisol and then shown angry faces while their brains were being scanned. Cortisol softened their response in the amygdala, making people less reactive to the angry faces. In effect, the cortisol calmed them.

What the researchers realized is that cortisol is not causing stress, but rather the body is producing cortisol *in response* to stress. It's the body's remedy for stress.

Chronically high levels of cortisol can signal that there's too much constant stress in someone's life: that's a problem. But spikes in cortisol following an acute stressor—such as a competition—are a *healthy* response. If someone has high levels of cortisol when competing, it isn't an automatic sign of trouble. It could be that the cortisol is working, effectively doing its job. The cortisol helps her manage.

Cortisol is not stress—it is repair. It's the balancing hormone: it returns the body to homeostasis.

Cortisol is so omnipresent in stressful situations that science long misunderstood its role. It's like noticing that ambulances are always found at car wrecks; one might draw the wrong conclusion, thinking that ambulances cause car wrecks. Instead, they've come to help.

For those championship ballroom dancers in Germany at the beginning of the book, regardless of how much experience they had, all of them had that large increase of cortisol before and during the dance contest. Again—that didn't necessarily mean they were in *dis*tress. For successful competitors, the rise in cortisol was managing the stress for them, just enough for them to do well.

How does it work? Dampening the amygdala and reducing fear is one way. Cortisol is also the secret factor in the adrenaline-to-noradrenaline ratio we wrote about in the last chapter. If you recall, noradrenaline causes vasoconstriction (bad), while adrenaline is vasodilating (good). Cortisol upregulates the enzyme that converts noradrenaline into adrenaline. Cortisol increases the conversion rate: the ratio between the two hormones improves.

All that said, we shouldn't be left with the impression that cortisol is a procompetition hormone. It's not. If anything, cortisol defuses the competitive desire. It makes you care less about the outcome. Cortisol and testosterone regulate each other; one tries to stop the other and vice versa. It's very common for both to shoot up during a competition, because that's very much how we feel during a competition. For a second, we are energized and confident. The next moment, our enthusiasm wanes and we drift a bit; we don't work quite as hard; and back and forth.

When someone loses a contest, afterward the body usually produces a last blast of cortisol. This, too, is adaptive: it helps the psyche begin to restore and regenerate. The cortisol makes you care less about the outcome. It helps you put it in the past and move on. It allows you to tune out and forget the loss.

Now take a good look into the eyes of this man:

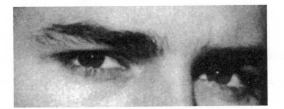

Would you say he was concerned? Or would you say that was a look of guilt? Or would you say he was embarrassed?

The set of eyes is one pair among 36 in a test called *Reading the Mind in the Eyes*, created by Cambridge psychologist Simon Baron-Cohen. It measures a person's ability to accurately read the subtle emotional expressions of others. While this one is comparatively easy (he's guilty), the test is very difficult, overall.

What if you were confronted by a man with this expression in his eyes? What should you do? Once again, the trait of successful aggression—developed during roughhousing—becomes the critical factor for knowing what he's thinking and knowing how to respond.

When subjects are administered a dose of the hormone oxytocin, they score higher on the *Reading the Mind in the Eyes* test. They also score higher on the *Interpersonal Perception Task*, a video test that requires subjects to watch two people's body language and then infer the relationship between them from their interaction.

Oxytocin is famously known as the "love hormone." It's triggered in mothers by breastfeeding infants. It's released during orgasm. It's the chemical that forges a deep and enduring bond, even though it lasts only a few minutes in the brain before disintegrating. All it takes to get a little spritz is a good hug. But the very newest science is revealing that this hug hormone has an important role in challenge contests, too.

It helps you recognize the enemy. It helps you see the intent in his eyes.

Previously, scientists had known that oxytocin made you trust other humans. But when they administered oxytocin to patients with borderline personality disorder—hoping it would help them trust people more—they were surprised to see that it had the opposite effect. It made their patients even more distrustful. Oxytocin helps a breastfeeding mother bond to her baby, but it also makes her into a mama bear, ready to defend her child. Breastfeeding women are twice as aggressive as bottle-feeding moms.

In another study by Dr. Wendy Berry Mendes, women were given oxytocin and then put through a social stress paradigm, where they were rejected and ostracized by others. The oxytocin didn't calm them; it made them really angry. Oxytocin takes some of the restraint off our feelings. If what you feel is love, the love can be intense. But if what you feel is anger, then oxytocin unleashes that anger.

The University of Amsterdam's Dr. Carsten De Dreu also gives people oxytocin to study its role. "Oxytocin's real effect is marking other people as your in-group or your out-group," he says. It drives the brain to determine if someone is friend or foe. If the brain decides "friend," then it triggers friendly behavior. But if it decides "foe," then wariness, vigilance, and aggression are stirred. In a recent study, De Dreu gave subjects oxytocin and then had them choose from an array of faces. They had to pick people they would ally with, or have on their team. Under the influence of oxytocin, they chose much scarier-looking, physically intimidating teammates.

We have to keep in mind that the hormones of competition didn't evolve to help us do better on the SAT, or to move chess pieces around, or to be careful surgeons. The hormones evolved to help us in face-to-face threats.

In the movie adaptation of *The Blind Side*, based on the high school years of NFL tackle Michael Oher, Sandra Bullock plays Leigh Anne Tuohy, the wealthy mother who adopts the impoverished Oher. At practice one day, Oher can't block anyone. Defenders easily get around him and tackle the running back and quarterback. Oher is massive, but he hasn't learned to bring any passion or purpose to his blocking. His coaches describe him as soft as a marshmallow. Tuohy comes down out of the stands and pulls Oher aside.

Tuohy reminds him of how he was ready to ferociously protect her when they went to a bad side of town. She reminds him how he stopped the blow of a car airbag from hurting her younger son, S. J. She tells Oher, "This team is your family.... Tony is your quarter-back...when you look at him, think of me. How you have my back.... When you look at him think of S. J. and how you'd never let anything or anyone hurt him."

She teaches Oher how to think like a mama bear and tap into his protective instincts. Oher immediately begins flattening defensive linemen on play after play.

Leigh Anne Tuohy in that scene is what oxytocin is in the brain. Love and aggression find themselves intertwined.

This new understanding of oxytocin says something philosophically important about the true nature of competition. Some people think that competing is the opposite of nurturing, that fighting is the opposite of loving. But in fact one is at the core of the other, and they are forces in parallel. We compete our hardest to protect our team. We fight hardest for those we love.

5

Here's a stark example of how wrong the folk understanding of testosterone is. Dr. Christoph Eisenegger, an experimental psychologist at Cambridge, had 120 women play three rounds of a money game: each round, they could share the pot with their opponent, or steal it from their opponent. The women then got to take their winnings home. Before the game, Eisenegger gave all of them a substance to be placed under their tongue. He told them that it was either testosterone or a placebo, but he wouldn't tell them which.

After they had played the game, he asked the women whether they thought they had gotten the testosterone or the placebo.

Women who played selfishly believed they had been given testosterone. Women who played unselfishly thought they had been given the placebo.

But the exact opposite was the case. It was women who had been given testosterone who shared the pot far more often with their opponents.

The *idea* of testosterone directly contradicts the *truth* of testosterone.

The folk wisdom of testosterone is that it makes you selfish—it makes you not care about what others think of you. The truth about testosterone is that it makes you care more that others hold you in high regard. In Eisenegger's money game, going home with the cash wasn't as important as making sure other women liked you. And the way to make them like you was to share the pot, even if it cost you money.

Behavioral neuroscientist David Edwards, of Emory University, had a similar result with college soccer players.

During the season, Edwards and the Emory coaching staff came up with a 15-item player-rating scale. This was not a scale that rated how good a player was overall. It was 100% devoted to the very small nuances of teamwork. In soccer, players continuously have to reposition themselves, even if they don't get the ball; they have to make runs to drag marking defenders out of spaces, in order for a teammate to get the ball in the space left behind. On defense, they have to provide support for teammates. They have to work very hard, and run long distances, without being rewarded. They also have to coordinate with teammates using facial expressions, gestures, and a moderated tone of voice that doesn't make teammates feel bossed around. When their teammates use deception to fool the opposing team, players need to be able to see through the disguise and read their teammate's true intentions. The 15-question player-rating scale got at the core of what team play really involves.

A month before the end of the season, every one of the 22 players on the men's team rated their teammates. So for each player, there were 21 evaluations. In each player's cumulative score was what his team truly thought of him.

Edwards did not share the rating results with the players; he did not want to disrupt the team, which was ranked in the Top 10 nationally. In the last week of the regular season, the team had a big home game that would impact its seeding in the national tournament. While everyone at Emory was rooting hard for their team, Edwards and his grad student watched the game with special interest. They had taken saliva samples before the game, to measure the players' hormones, and they would do so again immediately after.

The men dug out a 1–0 victory in double overtime.

Edwards was surprised to see that, once analyzed, the samples revealed a very strong pattern. The more a player's testosterone rose during the game, the higher his teamwork rating. Those most highly rated as team players had testosterone boosts of almost 60% during the game. The players with low ratings—the selfish players—didn't get the testosterone boost. They didn't care what their teammates thought of them; they didn't share the ball, didn't make runs, didn't communicate.

Testosterone wasn't making the better team players pass the ball more. What it did was make them care more about the regard of their teammates and do the hard work to get their respect.

In this sense, testosterone adjusts to the social circumstance. Whatever it takes to earn the high regard of others, testosterone will increase that behavior.

Among firefighters, those with high testosterone exhibit a lot of fearlessness. They run into more burning buildings and attempt daring rescues. But that same hormone has a different effect in paramedics. They exhibit the trait of conscientiousness, caring for patients under duress, communicating well with doctors at the hospital, and meticulously delivering triage treatment.

This is an extremely valuable insight. Whenever biological factors are at work, there's a tendency to assume that biology drives psychology, and that we are all at the whim of the biological lottery. If you're one of the lucky ones whose testosterone responds to challenge, then you've won the lottery. But that's not actually how the scholars see it. Testosterone and motivation are locked in a chicken-and-egg cycle. Testosterone increases motivation, but it's equally true that motivation increases testosterone. When you care—really care—testosterone responds.

More important, testosterone doesn't drive a certain type of behavior. It will induce the behavior that the social situation deems as important. If you want to harness the power of testosterone—if you want to change the behavior it expresses—then change the rules of what earns social regard. In soccer, ball hogs need to know that dribbling the opponent won't earn them social status, not from the team, not from coaches or parents, not from fans. In the lunchrooms of high schools, students need to know that social dominance won't earn high regard. If you change the culture around high-testosterone competitive people, you'll change what they do to earn respect. This is true in the boardrooms of corporations, in the halls of government, in the ranks of rescue personnel, and in the platoons of soldiers.

PART IV

Collective

"An artist is somebody who enters into competition with God."

—Patti Smith

CHAPTER TEN

The Hierarchy of Teams

1

Jason Lezak was not a nationally ranked swimmer in high school or during the first two years of college. He'd never completely dedicated himself to the sport. At Irvine High School, he was the point guard for the basketball team and an All-American water polo player. "I'd never given swimming my all," he said. At the University of California, Santa Barbara, he began to train harder and more intensely study his stroke technique. "My junior year of college, I made a breakthrough at the World University Games." The next year, he won the national collegiate title.

Most swimmers don't compete long after college, but Lezak had just broken into the elite ranks. From 1999 to 2002, he was the fastest American in the 100 freestyle, so he was made the relay anchorman. That's what swim teams traditionally do: they put the fastest guy last. But Lezak was different. He held onto the anchorman job for a decade because his relay times were always faster than his solo times. "That always gave the other guys confidence. I was always nine-tenths of a second faster in a relay." The relay start cuts about 0.6 or 0.7 off your time, but even accounting for that, he was reliably 2 or 3 tenths of a second faster swimming for a team than for himself.

What could explain this?

Being on a team is a chance to belong to something greater than yourself. Even the barest suggestion of a shared identity can trigger an esprit de corps. Researchers have found that just telling people that they shared the same birthday with a lab partner made them work harder on a shared task: they were more motivated and more persistent.

This effect is magnified as a shared identity grows by layer upon layer. A communal history, a team color and mascot, opposition from rivals and obstacles—the more ways a team is genuinely connected, the deeper the commitment.

Despite Lezak's speed as the American anchorman, his tenure was stained by losing. The Americans had the fastest swimmers; however, for an eight-year stretch, they no longer won as a team. "Prior to Sydney in 2000, we had dominated the event for thirteen straight Olympics. It was *our* event," said Lezak. The team had the fastest four swimmers at the Sydney Olympics, but they all faded in their legs and lost to the Australians. "We really felt like we'd let down our country." In Athens, in 2004, they also came in as the favorites, but lost again.

But Lezak learned something that last week at Athens. One of the final races was the 4 × 100 medley relay, and Lezak swam the freestyle. "There was great camaraderie among those guys. All the other three had attended the University of Texas, and had that in common; they pumped each other up, and I fit in well with them. You could feel it. Those guys wanted the race for all the right reasons, for themselves, for the team, for our country." He was certain that made a difference in the pool. "We went out and dominated, breaking the world record by *three seconds*."

"I knew we needed that in the freestyle relay." The sense of connection had been missing. He used to feel it as a basketball player and water polo player, but it had been missing from his swimming experience. He realized they'd stood there at the podium holding hands,

looking like a team, but not really being one. They were just the four
fastest American guys.

The difference between relay swimming and solo swimming is
very thin, almost invisible. The only mechanical difference is the relay
start, but the distance is the same, the strokes are the same. The only
other difference is psychological. This makes swimming a unique
paradigm of team energy, but not teamwork per se. It's not like basketball, where players share a ball, set picks, and play zone defense.
Swimming faster or slower is entirely about what the relay swimmers
feel toward each other, and what that does to performance.

At the Water Cube in Beijing, Lezak and his teammates were in
the Ready Area, about to walk out and swim. Thirty-two different men from eight countries were there. Some guys paced to control their nerves. Others had their heads down, listening to music
on headphones. Others were staring at competitors, trying to psyche
them out. Normally, Lezak liked to quietly sit and relax before a race.
But on that day, he decided to forgo his usual routine, and, instead, he
brought the American team together.

He reminded his teammates that this event had been the United
States' for thirteen straight Olympics. It belonged to them; it was theirs.
"I wanted us to get it back. I told them, 'We're a team. We're one unit.
Let's go swim *together*. Let's make this a 400, not a 4 by 100.'" Five minutes before their swim, they marched from the Ready Area out to the
pool. "I can't remember the exact words the others said, but I remember
the look in the others' eyes. I could tell each swimmer was focused and
ready to go, and my words had made an impact—they felt it. I could feel
that we cared about each other. I could feel the chemistry was there."

If you can't see it, and can't describe it, but you can still *feel* it—
what is this invisible element?

Researchers have put participants in fMRIs to see if being on
a team changes brain function. They found that it does, even if you
are just a spectator. If you're a Red Sox fan, watching a Sox game, you're

using a different region of the brain to judge if a runner is safe than you would if you were watching a game between two teams you didn't care about. When it's neutral teams, you are a rational being, using the decision-making parts of the brain. When it's your team, obviously emotional parts of the brain are active. But those neutral decision-making areas disengage and, instead, you're using the inferior parietal lobe (IPL), which governs "mirror processing." Your brain is functioning as if it were you doing the action. On a neurological level, it isn't your teammate but you yourself who is sliding into home.

Mirror processing is why one person's yawning triggers another's yawn, or why when one person in a meeting crosses his legs, others will follow. But mirroring isn't limited to motor movement—it's *ideo-motor* mirroring. We automatically mirror attitudes, biases, stress levels, and goal activation.

Mirror processing is one of the ways people on teams unconsciously influence one another through nonverbal cues. Moods and energy levels are contagious, and you can "catch" a sense of urgency from teammates. It's an automatic process, not something you control. Teams have vibes; everyone can feel when a team is gaining confidence, or when a team is turning indifferent and passive.

As they moved toward the starting blocks, the Americans were gaining confidence from Lezak. Lezak knew that the French team had the fastest swimmers. But at two prior Olympics, he'd seen that the fastest swimmers don't automatically win. "I believed we could take it. I thought we had a great chance to win."

2

In the 1970s and 1980s, the American automobile industry was getting clobbered by its Japanese competitors. Japanese cars were more technologically advanced; they were safer and cheaper. The explanation for how they could do it—so much better than we could—was that the Japanese had a profoundly different kind of corporate culture. Japanese companies were team-based: individuals set aside their needs and agendas for the good of the company. Teams were more efficient, more driven, more innovative.

American auto manufacturers began to adopt team-based manufacturing. Gradually, companies in all industries transformed. According to a multiyear study of Fortune 1000 companies, working on a team—and being paid for how your team performs—is the name of the game now. In 1980, just 20% of firms were using team-based pay. Twenty years later, this had jumped to 80% of firms. Teams have become so ubiquitous that American education is increasingly using team-based learning in classrooms—the belief being that this is the inexorable environment of children's future workplaces.

Several scholars have noted that teams have "an irresistible social appeal," because they are seen as a democratizing structure that empowers workers who would otherwise feel buried in a hierarchy. Teams, theoretically, increase participation and the sense of responsibility.

When at their best, teams are better than the sum of their parts. 1 + 1 = 3. In the National Basketball Association, great team chemistry is worth six more wins a year, above what would be predicted from players' individual contributions. In pharmaceutical sales, better teamwork explains 13% of the variance in revenue among sales teams.

But teams are not *automatically* better than the sum of their parts. They are often worse. This is termed "collaborative inhibition" or "process loss."

Sixty-two percent of software projects are delivered late. Forty-nine percent are over budget. People have a bias to romanticize the benefits of team productivity, while underestimating just how much time is wasted by teams. According to University of North Carolina professor Bradley Staats, productivity per person can drop 40% even on a small team. It eats up a lot of time to coordinate a team's efforts—making sure everyone has replaced the April 10, 5:00 P.M., draft with the April 10, 6:00 P.M—no, wait—*6:15* draft.

Magic is supposed to happen when a group of people are united in their dedication to a singular purpose. But modern, corporate teams aren't remotely like that: estimates are that up to 90% of knowledge workers are on *multiple* teams, each team fighting for its members' time and attention. No project gets singular devotion. And with the rise of technology-assisted "virtual teams," where coworkers are spread around the country or world, people may have no real relationship with teammates; often, they don't even meet.

In studies of thousands of companies that have implemented teamwork, there's no firm evidence that, on average, they make any more money, or are even more productive, after instituting a team-based structure. But the CEO still gets a pay raise: to adopt a team-based structure signals to the rest of the world that you are a forward-thinking innovator.

There's a "halo effect" around teams—when they do well, the whole team is assigned the credit. But when they do poorly, an individual gets the blame. People think, *If only he hadn't fumbled that ball*, or *If only she hadn't insisted on using that iffy technology*. The team structure itself never gets blamed. Teams are always seen as the panacea and never the problem.

Successful teams are as small as possible to get the job done. In a small team, people feel responsible for the project and have a sense of what everyone else is doing. But this becomes incredibly difficult as the team size grows. In a team of six, there are 15 connections to manage. Just adding two more people to that team almost doubles its complexity—now there are 28 connections to keep track of.

In great teams, teammates anticipate the others' moves and needs: they don't need to be told what should be done. Teams that struggle have meetings. Lots of meetings. And in those meetings, they talk a lot.

Successful teams communicate in short, clear sentences, and communication is reciprocal. Requests are made, and then there's a confirmation that a request has been received, understood, and will be acted upon. On struggling teams, communication is dominated by fewer people, making longer soliloquies.

In great teams, team members trust that each teammate will do his best. In struggling teams, team members worry that teammates are riding on others' coattails, not working hard enough, or stealing credit for others' work—which leads them to work less hard themselves.

One of the most important lessons the science has to offer: the most indispensable elements of teamwork happen before any work is done at all.

3

In a post-9/11 world, the U.S. intelligence community knew that it needed to pool its efforts in order to combat terrorism. Compartmentalization has been one of the long-held rubrics of the spy business: "need to know" means that even members on a single team don't share access to the same information.

Perplexed how to go forward with a more team-based approach, officials from the Central Intelligence Agency turned to researchers at Harvard University.

The researchers, led by Professor J. Richard Hackman, were invited to observe "Project Looking Glass." Held at a secure location, Project Looking Glass would be a modified version of the military's war games, but, instead of wars, these spy-game simulations would center around potential terrorist attacks.

For each week-long simulation, the CIA formed two teams: a Red Team and a Blue Team. Each time, the Red Team's job was to think like terrorists, spending the week planning an attack. The Blue Team—always made up of intelligence specialists and law enforcement officials from a number of federal agencies—was supposed to figure out what the Red Team was plotting and then foil the plan. To do so, Blue Team members could use small-scale versions of the real-world methods they'd normally use to track terrorists, such as hacking into the Red Team's computers and electronically eavesdropping on some conversations.

All the data being used was real: the material was so classified that no one was allowed to discuss anything after hours, and no work could be removed from the buildings.

During the initial sessions of the very first Looking Glass simulation, Hackman and his colleague Anita Woolley immediately noticed a difference between the teams. The Red Team members were scientists and other experts from outside the intelligence agencies. Since they'd never met before, Red Team members introduced themselves by talking about their specific areas of expertise—what they had studied and what they were working on. And they talked about how their knowledge might be relevant to their mission.

A typical Red Team identification might have gone something like: "I'm a chemist, and I'm interested in how you can weaponize commercially available chemicals, so I could come up with a list of things like that we could use in an explosive device." Then the others in the room asked her follow-up questions, to determine the strengths and weaknesses in her knowledge.

When the members of the Blue Team first met, a typical Blue Team introduction was something more like: "I'm an agent at the FBI, working for the Assistant Director on Counterintelligence." Blue Team members stood behind their titles and departments, not their subject expertise. And they never suggested how their experience could be beneficial to the group.

The consequences of this difference played out repeatedly over the course of the week, according to Woolley. "Playing the offense," the Red Team had the luxury of a choosing their strategy. But their experience-based introductions helped the Red Team become more outcome-focused from the very first. On the Blue Team, the introductions didn't help them envision their goal. Instead, the Blue Team got bogged down in agency stereotypes and argued over which agency's protocol to use. It never allocated work based on expertise. Blue Team members didn't realize until the second-to-last meeting that they had a physicist in the room, who knew most of the information they'd been searching for. At one point, a computer scientist was ignored when she guessed (correctly) that some pornographic images in Red Team e-mails actually held secret code.

The researchers observed that the teams' introduction-style differences repeated themselves week after week, with brand new people taking on the Red and Blue roles. And each time, the researchers were amazed at how dramatically these introductions affected both teams' performance.

Eventually, the researchers persuaded the CIA to let them experiment a little bit with the next simulation. To prevent the next Blue Team from doing the ordinary, title-based round of introductions, the researchers instructed the team members to interview each other about what exactly they did and knew. The teammates were so excited by the conversations that they ran out of time to complete the introductions. That particular Blue Team was the most successful by far. That Blue Team used its own expertise more, and the members had fewer arguments over procedure.

It is remarkable that something as small as a change in an introduction can influence a team's entire process; however, this is by no means atypical. Instead, it's consistent with what Hackman calls the "60/30/10 Rule."

Having studied teams in many settings, from airplane cockpits to symphony orchestras, Hackman believes that 60% of a team's fate has been written before the team members even meet. Its destiny is decided by a combination of the team leader's efficacy, whether the team's goal is challenging yet attainable, and the ability level of the people recruited to the team.

Thirty percent of a team's fate is sealed with the initial launch of the team—how the teammates meet and, in those initial exchanges, how they split up the responsibilities and tasks before them. They need to agree on common codes of conduct and shared expectations.

All told, 90% of a team's fate has been decided before the team ever begins its real work.

Hackman likens a team to a rocket. Most of the work has to happen beforehand—in the initial design, the structure, and the building of the team. Because once it launches, it takes on a set trajectory, and it is incredibly difficult to change course mid-flight.

When teams aren't working well, rather than making small changes, sometimes the best thing to do is to relaunch the teams entirely, as they did at one Dallas hospital.

A Harvard Business School doctoral student, Melissa Valentine, and her professor, Amy Edmondson, were studying the hospital's administration procedures, when Valentine learned that the Emergency Department was about to undergo a top-to-bottom reorganization.

Part of a large urban teaching hospital, the Emergency Department received more than 130,000 patients every year. Most patients coming into the hospital were uninsured: they came for everything from minor cases of the flu to life-threatening injuries. To manage the load, on any given day, around 80 physicians, residents, and nurses rotated in staggered shifts, treating about 250 patients a day. Still, the work always backed up—because of the long waiting time, 30% of the patients coming in left without ever being seen. On average, a treated patient spent over 8 hours in the ER.

Prior to the reorganization, the 30 or so hospital staff on duty at any one time had been operating in large, loosely defined teams organized around their functions. On one side of the floor was the team for the surgical patients, and on the other side of the floor was the team for the nonsurgical patients. Within each side, there was one workstation for doctors and a separate workstation for nurses. During a typical shift, each staff person had to coordinate with, or work with, an average of 17 other staff people.

With the reorganization, the hospital reassigned supply closets, crash rooms, and computers, until the Emergency Department was divided into five self-sufficient pods. Each pod had six well-defined roles—one attending physician, two residents, a nurse designated the "Pod Lead," and two additional nurses. The doctors and nurses in a pod shared the same workstation, facilitating their communication. When employees came on duty, they were assigned to a pod for the duration of their shift. Because duty periods were staggered, the same six people didn't work together for an entire shift; podmates would repeatedly change, but the roles stayed defined.

When a patient came in, she would be assigned to a pod. Each pod was automatically assigned every fifth patient. The patient-to-pod information was tracked on computer screens everyone could see.

A curious thing spontaneously happened when the staff began working in these pods. Competition between the five pods broke out, which they dubbed "the Pod Wars." As one pod would treat and release patients, its patient load would go down, and this was visible on every computer. Pod 3 might still have 25 patients in the ER, while Pod 1 had gotten its number of patients down to 9. Soon, the Pod 3 staff would be grumbling, "Pod 1 is killing us today!" Then everyone would pick up the pace. People hated to be in a losing pod. They wanted to win.

This went on continuously; the Pod Wars had no end to them, no finish line—24 hours a day, 7 days a week. Pods were only ahead or behind at any one time. And the competition endured even though no staff person was ever permanently assigned to one pod or another; on any shift, hospital staff could get assigned to any pod. A resident in Pod 1 would compete against Pod 2 as hard as he could—then, the next day, he'd be in Pod 2, competing as hard as he could against Pod 1.

Before the reorganization, nurses wandered the halls, trying to figure out who was supposed to help them with a given patient. Once the pods were in place, staff members always knew who their teammates were and could be more focused on their shared mission: treating the patient. People had a sense of belonging and claimed ownership of each other during their shift. Describing it, Valentine wrote:

> The doctors will say, "Where are my three nurses, who do I have today?" People rarely, if ever, claimed each other in this way before the pods were implemented even if they were working together on many shared cases. A resident might have said, "Who is this patient's nurse?" rather than, "These orders aren't done, where are *my* nurses?"

Between the pods' role clarification and the pods' competition, patients were seen faster, and more patients were seen every day. The average time a patient spent in the Dallas emergency department dropped from eight hours to five. The number of patients treated every day jumped from 250 to 321, an increase of nearly 30%. And the competition improved the quality of care the patients received. Staff were more motivated, and there was a sense of urgency, which meant that people communicated more. They just enjoyed going to work. Their faces lit up as they asked Valentine, "Have you heard about the Pod Wars?"

Clarifying who is going to do what—identifying distinct roles—is one of the most proven ways to increase the quality of teamwork. The egalitarian notion that team members should be equal in status and interchangeable in their roles is erroneous. Teams work best when participants know their roles, but not every role needs to be equal.

Dr. Eduardo Salas, at the University of Central Florida, is one of the most widely cited scholars studying team efficiency. He has devoted his life to understanding the vast sea of team-building and team-training processes—analyzing teams used in the military, law enforcement, NASA, and numerous corporate settings. The only strategies that consistently deliver results are those that focus on role clarification: who's going to do what when the pressure gets intense.

As we've said, the most effective use of role definitions happens at the leadership level, before the team is ever formed. But when teams lose their way, role clarification can help them renew their focus.

4

One fallacy about teams is that, to be successful, everyone must be friends.

The research says it's the other way around: team performance drives the quality of relationships.

When teams are failing, this poor performance upsets their members—and they take their frustration out on one another.

When a team is doing well, the team isn't bothered by friction within the group. Teammates will even say that their success was due to the cooperative style of the team... even when independent observers report that the team was quarreling most of the time.

Some of the greatest teams in history were equally well known for the hostility among the collaborators. Abraham Lincoln's "Team of Rivals," the geniuses at the Manhattan Project, and the Mercury astronauts were all famously at one another's throats.

Constant harmony may even be cause for alarm. A conflict-free team means no one is bringing anything to the table that might engender controversy. The team members aren't focused on the team's purpose; instead, they are focused on protecting the group's relationships. It's one of the ways teams can be less than the sum of their parts: fear of offending anybody.

Most research on teams has been done in Western, individualist societies—where you might think that teams are a sort of inherent anachronism. But researchers compared the performance of U.S.

negotiators with negotiators from Taiwan—a collectivist culture. U.S. negotiating teams outperformed those who negotiated alone. But in Taiwan, solo negotiators did better than those negotiating in teams. The reason being that the Taiwanese were more interested in maintaining harmony within their teams—they wouldn't risk shaming a teammate for making a mistake—than getting their team the best outcome.

For a team to work well under pressure, individuals need to be assertive; someone needs to speak up. And when a team is doing poorly and losing its will, someone needs to turn things around.

Dr. Pontus Leander studies the way moods and energy levels become contagious within a team through mirror processing. Not everyone is vulnerable to it, though—some people are what he terms "reactives." Reactives have a very strong subconscious urge to not be controlled by others. And when they sense their team is growing indifferent to its goal, no longer trying, reactives resist this influence, and rebel by turning up their energy level. They play a key role on a team, instigating the turnarounds and great comebacks that teams become famous for. Listless teammates are infected with this rebellious energy, and the team rights itself.

There is an argument to be made that not everyone on a team should be a classic "team player."

In a study of 78 European and American orchestras, Harvard's Hackman arrived at a counterintuitive conclusion: the better an orchestra sounded, the more likely there was rivalry, quarreling, and discord behind the scenes. The only times they were in harmony was onstage.

The musicians had begun their careers dreaming of being star soloists. In rounds of auditions, they'd beaten hundreds of other musicians to earn their spot; they'd proven that they were among their nation's best. But—as a matter of course—their greatest contribution to the orchestra would be that they never stood out from the rest.

In performance, they should be indistinguishable from musicians on either side of them. Their sounds should blend into one; their physical movements would be in perfect unison. Even their clothes would be identical. And that was how it was going to be . . . for the rest of their professional lives.

Having begun their musical training with such high ambitions and high hopes, the musicians were often miserable. Seen as stars from an early age, it wasn't so easy for them to now blend in.

An orchestra setting may seem exceptional, but the reality is that all teams face similar issues. You want a team to be filled with the best possible talent. You want the stars—but stars want to stand out. They don't want to be lost in the darkness. From the star's perspective, shining above the rest is his *job*.

While we might think of teams as a constellation of talented individuals, for stars, a team can seem more like a black hole—a place where their brightness utterly disappears. Thus teams, like black holes, are to be avoided. At all costs.

Professor Agnes Stribeck surveyed 1,824 students attending nine different colleges and universities. She asked them for their majors and average GPAs: they came from a number of fields, but the majority were pursuing a graduate degree of some kind. Stribeck asked the students to read a series of mock job descriptions, then rank which jobs interested them—the kinds of positions they'd look for after graduation.

Stribeck found that when the ad mentioned "teamwork," the very best students had no interest whatsoever in that position. The idea of forced collaboration drove them away. They believed that a team environment wouldn't be personally challenging—there would be little opportunity to grow, learn, and develop new skills.

The effect was so strong that Stribeck issued a warning to employers: even a mere mention of "teamwork" in a job advertisement likely lowers the quality of the entire pool of job applicants. The best aren't going to apply. They'll look for opportunities where they can shine— where they feel responsible for their destiny.

To get a star on a team, convince him the team's collective achievement will be greater than anything he could do by himself—but he'll still need the assurance that his contribution will be recognized as his own.

When you do manage to get a star on your team, the question still remains, should stars be treated differently from everyone else? Doesn't giving stars special treatment undermine the motivation of the rest of the team?

Researchers have looked at the pay of NBA stars, compared with that of their lesser-famous teammates. On average, if certain teammates are getting what is perceived to be an *unjustified* windfall, that hurts performance: team members won't work as hard to grab what they see as the short end of the stick. But as long the star treatment is warranted, it doesn't hurt performance. In some ways, it's just further role clarification: who is responsible for what. Teammates who spend most of the time on the bench would like to get more playing time, but they understand why the starters get paid more than they do. Rookies don't slack off if they're getting less money or recognition. They understand this is their time to learn from those with more experience and to prove themselves when given the opportunity.

Stars *aren't* the same. Stars face elevated levels of scrutiny: the expectations for their performances are much higher.

That's true, even within the team itself. No one is fighting for a spot on the bottom rung, but people will constantly challenge the star for her top spot. The stars aren't intimidated by such threats. Fierce competitors, they are determined to meet these challenges and secure their stature on the team. But then they may become ever more isolated. In an interview with Professor Hackman, famed basketball coach Mike Krzyzewski spoke about his concern for his star players. Said Krzyzewski, "When I am coaching my Duke team, I need to be the best player's best friend. Being the best player is a lonely position. Even though you get accolades, no matter how good of a team you have, there is always some level of jealousy. Always."

Despite the increased pressure facing stars, in some ways, coaches, managers, and teachers often all leave the best performers alone. They focus on the low performers, taking for granted the continued excellence of the high-achievers. That is a mistake, according to Krzyzewski.

Krzyzewski was head coach for the 2008 U.S. Olympic Men's Basketball team—which included stellar athletes such as LeBron James, Jason Kidd, and Kobe Bryant. Bryant was delighted the coach took interest in his motivation level at the Olympics. Bryant was surprised that Krzyzewski didn't take his desire for a gold medal for granted: "Since I was in high school, nobody has tried to motivate me, they just pay me."

Krzyzewski explained to Hackman that "Leadership is not just to let the star produce, but to be a friend of the star, to motivate the star. Your team is going to go a lot further if your stars push ahead, and everybody else has to work to catch up."

Study after study confirms this: the value in stars isn't just in their performance alone. It's also in how they can motivate their teammates to excel. The top 6% of physicists are responsible for 50% of all physics papers published. All-star immunologists boost their colleagues' research productivity by 35%. And this isn't just the amount of research—the research done when working under all-star scientists is qualitatively better as well.

In the idealized notion of a team, everyone is equal and interchangeable, and this equality drives commitment to the team effort. But the science argues that the ideal is, if anything, a distraction. The goal is not to live up to the ideal, but to perform. In real life, teammates are rarely true equals, and they don't always get along. Having a hierarchy, with its clear divisions of responsibility, is most often the solution to team performance.

CHAPTER ELEVEN

Michelangelo Had an Agent

1

In 1991, college student Linus Torvalds was participating in an online e-mail group, and he posted some related queries. A few months later, he let the group know that he'd written some source code, and he invited people to poke around it, send him ideas for improving it as they wished.

The ideas began pouring in. And they have never stopped.

The code eventually became known as Linux. Since its creation more than 20 years ago, Linux, now with 15,000,000 lines of code, has become the world's most ubiquitous operating system, powering Android phones, eight out of ten financial trades, and the likes of Amazon, Facebook, Google, and Twitter.

The promise of open source innovation is that you reach far beyond your team for ideas—beyond the walls of your company to the community at large. By harvesting tiny bits of ideas from thousands of different altruistic contributors, the result is something far beyond anything that one person could ever have imagined, let alone created.

The way the open source story is told, collaboration is the secret to creative innovation. Competition—between teams, between companies, and between people—is so last century. "Collaboration is the New Revolution," announced the editors of the *Guardian*, the British newspaper. "The key to solving any problem is collaboration, not competition," opined *USA Today*. Supposedly gone from the creative process are concepts such as property and authorship: nobody owns the jointly created project, and nobody gets to take credit, but everyone can benefit from the result.

But is this characterization accurate?

One of the amusing things about Linux is that because it's open source, all the LISTSERV e-mails are online. We can read the flurry of e-mails—such as in 2007, when one developer got angry that his code wasn't chosen to be included. Another coder's design was preferred. Eventually, Linus Torvalds himself defended the process:

Does this mean that there will be tension and rivalry? Hell yes. But that's kind of the point. Life is a game, and if you aren't in it to win, what the heck are you still doing here?

We don't want to play politics. But encouraging people's competitive feelings? Oh, yes.

A research team at the University of Toulouse studied the Linux development process and concluded that it was a "winner-take-all game." Hackers, disseminated around the world, work on the same part of code, and there's a single winner at the end of the race. They don't collaborate; they compete—on speed and utility. And as with any other competition, sometimes the losers gripe. Only one person, in the end, can claim to have solved the problem.

The Linux development method might be a grand collaboration, but any one programmer is not collaborating. He is writing code, alone, hoping to beat other programmers.

Claiming credit is a huge deal in the Linux community. About

13,000 people submitted e-mails to the Linux LISTSERV between 1995 and 2000, but only 350 of them were eventually credited as Linux contributors.

Here's Torvalds again:

> One of the most motivating things there *is* in open source is "personal pride."

If you look over the entire history of Linux, a few thousand have since been given credit as Linux developers. Coders put it on their résumés, and companies troll the code to spot top programmers to hire.

But the widely told story that Linux has been built by a worldwide movement of coders coming together is just about as real as Tom Sawyer's fence-painting. Of those credited for their contribution, many coders suggested a single change, and that was it. During that same time, a single programmer, David S. Miller, contributed 3,258 changes, and Al Viro made 2,840. Out of the 15,000,000 lines of code written, just ten developers have been responsible for over 60% of all its changes.

Furthermore, many programmers are getting a salary to work on Linux. They aren't being paid by Linux itself; rather, their employers use the family of Linux products and see a direct benefit from these contributions. The Linux Foundation has concluded that at least 75% of all Linux development has been done by people being paid for their work. In a 2011 version of Linux, 226 companies were listed as active developers. Microsoft was one of the Top 20 contributors.

So much for the claim that the open source movement is driven by altruistic volunteers.

Since its inception, Linux has been a very public contest between a handful of gladiators in front of an audience of thousands of spectators.

"If you aren't in it to win it, what are you doing here?" If you can't handle the brutality of competition, you don't belong here. The open

source community is not for everyone, notes programmer and author Eric Raymond; it's for the most talented 5%. The stars. It's an open competition where anyone can try her hand, but only the best stick around.

Is it collaboration that's driving innovation, or is it competition?

Harvard Business School professor Karim Lakhani has been researching how innovation occurs in open source projects such as Linux and another software development site, TopCoder.

Lakhani tells the story of how Jack Hughes came up with a solution to an intractable problem: how to find, recruit, and retain the best computer programmers. In 2000, Hughes persuaded Sun Microsystems and Google to put up significant prize money for open contests he called TopCoder. Any programmer around the world could log on and attempt to solve the challenges inside the time limit. Hughes's hunch was that the good coders couldn't resist a challenge; they'd come out of the woodwork to compete.

From 2001 to 2003, TopCoder held contests to build up its fame in the global coder community. By 2004, 50,000 programmers from around the world were registered, though only a fifth of them had dared enter a competition. Those who were brave enough to compete received an objective ability/performance ranking, much like a chess ranking. The other 40,000 were effectively the audience.

Hughes hired as many of the contest-winning programmers as he could, and he put them to work on a variety of corporate projects. His employees were billed out to clients on an hourly basis. But again, he had trouble hanging on to his best coders. There was something dull about working that way. The programmers attracted to his contests seemed bored once they were within a traditional work environment.

Hughes started to wonder: what if he never hired the programmers at all? What if the corporate projects were construed as contests? What if the corporate payments were instead posted as prize money?

When Hughes bet his company on this idea, TopCoder had $20

million in annual revenue, mostly billing clients by the hour. Hughes designed a system where up to 20 coders could sign up to compete on a discrete job, which might take a couple of hours. Once the contestants had read the specs in detail, and looked at the other competitors' rankings, almost all of them would decide it wasn't worth the effort. They dropped out before they invested too much time in what they saw as a losing proposition. But two or three contestants liked their chances. They'd duke it out, each coding their solution—and then only *one* of them would get paid.

The premise that a couple of programmers would do all the work—yet not get paid one cent—contradicts the normal assumptions about labor contracts. But Hughes gambled that good coders and bad coders are different. Bad coders would get discouraged and quit. Good coders should try harder next time and push themselves to get better.

It worked so well that his operation quickly began to grow. Hughes soon ran into a problem: cleaving a corporate project into discrete weekly contests took a lot of work. His project managers were overwhelmed. He doubled-down on his idea; dividing up the project into tasks just became another phase of the contest. Soon every stage of software development—from conceptualization to specification to architecture to assembly, all the way to deployment and debugging—was a contest.

TopCoder looks more overtly competitive than Linux, and the programmers attracted to one are not necessarily attracted to the other. But Harvard's Lakhani has found that both rely on cycles of competition and collaboration. For each weekly TopCoder contest, each of the contestant's codes is visible to all the contestants. As the next slice of the project is teed up for a new contest, competitors can borrow from ideas they've seen in earlier rounds. Collaboration and competition are not at odds; they are the twin stages of idea generation.

By 2008, *Inc.* magazine had crowned TopCoder as one of the fastest-growing private companies in the United States, with $200 million in revenue. TopCoder now produces software solutions for dozens of clients, including Facebook, Google, Intel, the U.S. Defense Advanced Research Projects Agency (DARPA), ESPN, GEICO, and Pfizer. A project may be broken up into several dozen discrete contests, each of which can be completed in a night of programming.

By 2012, TopCoder had 400,000 programmers in its community, but a great number of them are understudies, just watchers, who learn from seeing the best code get created. As with Linux, TopCoder's contests are dominated by stars. The top 5% of prize earners received approximately 80% of the total prize pool.

Fundamentally, Lakhani has found that the presence of competitors doesn't decrease effort and intrinsic motivation—it increases both. It's more fun to match wits and compete with money on the line than it is to take a job for a paycheck.

As TopCoder six-year veteran Michael Paweska told Lakhani: "To be successful at TopCoder, you must ask yourself, 'Are you a competitor?' You need to be able to thrive on competition; you can't be scared of it."

There's value in collaboration, no doubt—but there's danger in taking it too far, or demanding that every creative effort be "open source," or expecting every student to be a collaborator.

The Director of Admissions for the Massachusetts Institute of Technology posted a list of the top qualities he was looking for in future MIT students. Number two on his priority list? Those who were able to work collaboratively and cooperatively. He wrote that collaboration was an intrinsic part of the MIT experience—students should expect mandatory group homework and other required team-based activity.

This goes against 50 years of research. Most elite, creative scientists are highly ambitious and highly achievement-focused, but also asocial, arrogant, and introverted. That's hardly a surprise—geeks are famous for their introversion—but has MIT hastily forgotten from whence it came?

Introverts do best when working alone. Performance plummets when they are forced to work on a team. And while one might presume introverts don't like the social nature of competition, the truth is that introverts' performance improves significantly in a competition. (Extroverts improve in a collaborative setting, but perform worse in a competitive one.)

In its commitment to evangelize collaboration, MIT may be inadvertently scaring off the very students who could become the elite of science.

2

Society readily accepts that market competition and product innovation go hand in hand. But for some reason, it's often assumed this same dynamic doesn't drive creativity in the fine arts. There is a noble mythos around painters, writers, and musicians—they are idealized for creative purity, for being untainted by the lowly forces of money, competition, and direct comparison. But this noble mythos flies directly in the face of history.

In her book *Renaissance Rivals*, art historian Rona Goffen explained how one of the engines of the Italian Renaissance was the concept of *paragone*—placing creative endeavors right next to one another, in a head-to-head competition. The belief was that only through *paragone* could you see works' real significance. *Paragone* began as a way to ascertain the merit of entire fields of art. You could have walked into a salon to find Leonardo da Vinci participating in a public debate on which was a more worthwhile endeavor, poetry, painting, or sculpture.

The nature of the *paragone* gradually shifted into competitions between specific works of art. There were patron-sponsored contests for commissions. (Lorenzo Ghiberti's famed Florentine bronze doors were the winning design from one such competition.) In Medici palaces, salons were built so that one set of paintings would directly face another. The whole intent was that salon visitors would come to opine on which were the better paintings. It was through these competitions that artists became known as individuals who should be recognized and celebrated. Before *paragone*, the focus was on art's subjects—not its creators. But if one painting was manifestly superior to another, then you needed to know who was the person responsible for that piece, in order to hire him again.

The *paragone* was part of all artists' training during the Renaissance: a roomful of young artist-apprentices would all tackle the same assignment, vying for their master's approval.

Da Vinci believed artists thrived under the pressure of such a competitive environment. He encouraged young artists to paint in the same room as other artists. Da Vinci once wrote:

> You will be ashamed to be counted among draughtsmen if your work is inadequate, and this disgrace must motivate you to profitable study. Secondly a healthy envy will stimulate you to become one of those who are praised more than yourself, for the praises of others will spur you on.

Da Vinci regularly invited artists to come to his studio to see his works-in-progress; in this way, he could begin to make his works famous when they were still just preliminary sketches. Word would spread, and competing artists had already heard about da Vinci's newest masterpiece years before it was finished and on display.

Artists were even commissioned to paint works in direct competition with one another. On one such occasion, da Vinci and Michelangelo were both hired to paint murals of battles on opposite walls in the Sala del Gran Consiglio of Florence's Palazzo Vecchio. (Some reports suggest that the artists were even informed that only one of the murals would be kept.)

Michelangelo was miserable working alongside da Vinci. Less

than three months after accepting the challenge, he abandoned the mural and fled to Rome. But it wasn't that Michelangelo disliked competition—in fact, Goffen concluded that it was probably his hypercompetitiveness that drove him out of the Florence salon.

Michelangelo didn't really consider himself a painter; instead, he thought of himself as a sculptor. But quarrying large blocks of marble was incredibly expensive, and the only way Michelangelo could work in his medium of choice was to persuade people to give him commissions—regardless of the media. To do that, he had an agent. All the major Renaissance artists had them; the agents brokered the contracts between artists and patrons. In the contract for Michelangelo to sculpt his masterpiece *Pietà*, it was promised that the *Pietà* "will be the most beautiful work of marble that exists in Rome today, and that no master trader could do the work better." It bears repeating: it was a contractual provision that Michelangelo's sculpture would surpass all of Roman antiquity and his modern competitors. If he'd failed to do so, his patron would not have had to pay him. But Michelangelo did get paid, because he had created one of the greatest sculptures of all time.

According to Goffen, it was standard in Renaissance art contracts for artists to agree to outdo another artist's work. Raphael made a career out of improving upon competitors' paintings. In one contract, he agreed to create an altarpiece that was better than a work by Perugino (Raphael's own mentor). Later, Perugino retaliated by contracting to build an altarpiece that would surpass Raphael's.

When Michelangelo was asked to paint the Sistine Chapel, he first turned the request down. But he'd lost the sculpting commission he had coveted, so, politically and financially, he felt obligated to accept Pope Julius's offer.

To make matters worse, the artists who had recommended Michelangelo for the post intended for him to fail. Their hope was that his ceiling design would be a disaster, and that Raphael—who was painting *School of Athens* in a room down the hall from the Sistine—would come in as the project's savior. Instead, when Raphael saw Michelangelo's murals, Raphael decided that his own work wasn't good enough. He changed his paintings—even copying Michelangelo's image of God into one of his own Vatican murals.

Michelangelo and Raphael continued to rival each other in person and on canvas until their deaths.

While Italian Renaissance competitions had forever changed the visual arts, according to Dr. Roland Vaubel, University of Mannheim professor of economics, Western classical music also arose out of competitions during the Renaissance and Baroque periods. Individual musicians were competing, and there was also enormous rivalry between royal families, driving musical innovation. But the real competition that transformed Western musical tradition was the fight between the Catholic and Protestant churches.

In the medieval era, there was the occasional strolling troubadour, or someone playing the flute at a village dance, but most major musical works were commissioned by the Catholic Church. Much of what people heard was up to the church fathers. For almost a thousand years, Gregorian chant was the hallmark of religious music. And the church officials regularly quashed attempted musical innovations as being insufficiently holy and reverent.

Then came Martin Luther and the Reformation. Luther wanted his congregations to be more involved in the church service. One way to do this was to have them participate through music. Drawing on folk music, he wrote hymns to be sung by the entire congregation in their native German. Luther created the first songs with verses and a chorus. And he had hymnals prepared and sent home with people, for them to sing on their own.

The Catholics met Luther's challenge, argues Vaubel. The Council of Trent decreed that songs used in Catholic services also needed to be intelligible to the congregation's ears. Many of the new Protestant sects allowed singing, but they banned musical instruments. The

Catholics seized on this split within the Protestant sects by welcoming larger and larger ensembles into Catholic services. The advent of Italian opera pushed the churches further. The congregations expected music similar to opera's beautiful lyricism: they wanted ornate music that matched the elaborateness of the Renaissance cathedrals and palaces. The Catholics didn't satisfy this need only in Italy. A new Catholic religious order, the Jesuits, understood the appeal of a more ornate style of music: they became worldwide exporters of what would become the Baroque orchestral style.

As both churches and their musicians constantly tried to outdo each other, music became more intricate—even the music itself reflected the competing social movements of the day. Choral arrangements began to include competing harmonies and counterpoint to musicians' varying rhythms. The basic musical unit of the chord took hold. Gradually, people started listening to the instrumentals of music: it wasn't just seen as background for singing or dancing.

In a world fragmented by warring churches and actual wars, music became a symbol of political, religious, and financial authority. Music told you whether you were in a Protestant or Catholic land. Nowhere was this truer than in Germany. Following the Thirty Years' War, there were nearly 300 different principalities. Each prince needed his own court composers and musicians.

With pieces such as Bach's *Mass in B Minor*, Beethoven's *Missa Solemnis*, and Mozart's *Requiem Mass* regularly heard in concert halls, it's difficult to remember that pieces such as these were written to be performed in churches during religious services. But cathedrals had become large enough that they had full-time orchestras playing for Masses and other services. Even small villages required a small orchestra for an important-enough feast day.

Vaubel explains that the inter-church-and-prince competition was enough that musicians could demand ever higher salaries and commissions. Composers would negotiate how many new songs they would write each year: typically they wrote dozens, if not hundreds, of compositions a year. And it was a point of contention if they were under an exclusive contract or not. Johann Sebastian Bach held a number of court appointments, and he apparently bristled when employers wouldn't let him occasionally pen a freelance sonata for a rival duke or prince. At a certain point, mere money just wasn't enough to keep an ambitious musician such as Bach at court.

In 1717, Prince Leopold of Cöthen offered the young Bach the position of Kapellmeister—court music director. At the time, Bach was a court composer in Weimar, for Duke Wilhelm Ernst, a relative of the prince. It might seem as if the family connection would make such a move easy, but the Weimar and Cöthen courts hated each other. Wilhelm repeatedly refused Bach's requests to leave the Weimar court.

With the result of Bach's defection still unclear, Bach went on a trip to Dresden. The French musician Louis Marchand had challenged Bach to the musical equivalent of a duel, and Bach responded, basically, "Anytime, anywhere, any instrument." So in Dresden they were going to play each other in a harpsichord tournament. It would be a personal challenge for pride, but there was national reputation on the line as well: it would be a test of German versus French musical superiority. If that weren't enough, Handel also was in Dresden at the time, and there is a possibility that all three men were secretly vying for a Dresden court appointment. But the night before the competition, Marchand ran away—presumably because he knew he'd lose to Bach.

All this must have been hollow when Bach returned to Weimar: Wilhelm promptly threw the composer in prison for disloyalty. Bach was jailed for almost a month before finally being freed and allowed to join Leopold's court. When he arrived, his salary reflected his status: Bach was paid as much as the second-highest figure in Leopold's government.

All that commotion didn't seem to stifle Bach's creativity. Some historians believe that he began his masterpiece, *The Well-Tempered Clavier*, while in the Weimar prison.

Far from competition limiting the creativity of its musicians, the vast number of churches and royal courts fighting over talent meant that Germany became a worldwide force in musical composition for the next two hundred years. The innovations made by Bach and Handel led to the music of Mozart and Beethoven—and the influence of the Germans can still be heard in music written today.

3

Sadly, the innovation and competitiveness that marked the Baroque history of Cöthen and Dresden had largely vanished in the modern era. That's because Cöthen and Dresden were part of the Soviet-run East Germany. The Western Allies had poured Marshall Plan money and development into building a vibrant West Germany, which became a world leader in innovation and growth. But in that same time, East Germany's postwar fate was dictated by the Soviet Union. And East Germany's hallmark was stagnation.

Following the fall of the Berlin Wall in 1989, East Germany was reunited with West Germany. Instantly, the entire nation was forced to wonder: can you teach an entire people how to compete, when they've never competed before?

For the previous 40 years, every aspect of Eastern life had been dictated by the Soviet "planned economy." The Soviet government determined the needs of the entire Communist bloc, and it then allocated responsibility for fulfilling those needs throughout the Soviet states. Everyone was expected to play a part in keeping the Soviet system running. (Unemployment was at zero percent.) This was in keeping with the socialist principles of division of labor, but it was also politically pragmatic: if people had jobs, they were too busy to revolt.

Keeping the Soviet system operational did not mean it was an efficient machine. If anything, efficiency was anathema, because if fewer people needed to work on something, you'd have to figure out something else to keep them busy. Similarly, there was just no room for spontaneous improvement in the plan. Even innovation—research and development—was planned in advance. For as long as anyone could remember, maintenance had been the order of the day.

Knowing all that, the Western Germans had always expected East Germany would need a Marshall Plan redux. They knew the taken-for-granted Soviet market for East German products would dry up overnight. The challenge would be to find new places to sell Eastern goods and services. However, as the responsibilities transferred from the Politburo to the Bundestag, the Westerners were stunned to realize just how badly their Eastern counterparts had been doing. None of the Eastern products were Western market–worthy. Factories were so old and decrepit, it was usually cheaper to raze and rebuild them than to repair or retrofit them. The East German high-tech field was 15 years behind the West—essentially pirated technology from IBM computing.

Even if, on the rare occasion, the quality of the manufacturing was sufficient, the costs of production were unsustainable. Companies that needed only 1,000 employees were staffed with 10,000. For example, one firm, Jenoptik, was purportedly a high-technology manufacturer of optics and lenses, but, of its 27,000 employees, 3,000 of them had been working in the company's canteens. Jenoptik began rebuilding by laying off 17,500 employees. In a place where there had been no such thing as unemployment, the layoffs hit every single household in the city of Jena. Employment had been a civic duty for the East Germans—and they were grief-stricken and terrified to suddenly learn they were dispensable. They didn't understand why efficiency was now more important than their livelihoods.

Western managers were moved in to run the few companies worth saving. (Jenoptik brought in a team of 15 Berlin executives. They all shared a single rooming house, because there were no hotels or decent houses in all of Jena.) Again, East Germans couldn't figure out why new factories were needed. They'd never worried about addressing customer preferences or complaints before. Since the Eastern sole focus had been to fulfill orders, they had no experience developing or improving products. There was no such thing as customization. Having lived with stores that had 150 products for sale, in total, they were overwhelmed at the idea that their product was now competing with 1,500 other options. They had no experience whatsoever in marketing. They had lost even basic industrial skills. (After 40 years of Soviet cement-slab housing, no one in the East knew anything about bricklaying.)

The West Germans complained that the Easterners—derisively called "Ossies"—were unreliable workers. If something in a factory broke, it was said that Ossies would just wait for a supervisor to arrive to report it; it never occurred to them to find a supervisor. Ossie secretaries would just stop working if they had a wrong phone number: they didn't seek the correct one. Ossies left work at 1:45 P.M.—if they'd bothered to come back from lunch at all. While some of the complaints were unfounded, there was a serious problem with Eastern productivity. The Germans—famous for running their trains on time—had to have workshops to teach Ossies about punctuality. One study found that at least 50% of East German factories were sending their employees to the West for training or flying in Western employees to train staffs on site: banks had more than 5,000 Western managers training their new Eastern employees how to work in their branches.

Bright spots encouraged everyone. Jenoptik—the lone East German high-tech firm to survive after reunification—was on its way to becoming an international conglomerate, specializing in high-quality lenses for lasers and other photographic equipment. And Jenoptik's managers weren't just interested in resuscitating the factory: they wanted to rebuild the entire community. They encouraged their newly unemployed technicians to use the vacant facilities to develop new technology start-ups. When the German government wanted to increase the nation's biotech industry, the Jena community began one from scratch. And Jena's leading employer became the local university; the push for mastering new fields and technology was omnipresent.

Still, even in its initial prosperity, Jenoptik struggled—and it needed yet more cash. It was finally able to stand on its own, but its experience was a pattern seen throughout the East. Initial spurts of growth would soon flounder; billions were poured into the East only to evaporate. East German productivity rose for a few years, but then plateaued—remaining about half that of its Western counterparts. Eastern wages were lower, but worker productivity was still so low that it cost more to do less.

As rebuilding efforts stalled, Western Germans started coming to the conclusion that progress would only be generational. Younger East Germans were able to embrace the changes. But East Germans over 35 were said to be too invested in security over innovation. Not until the next generation took over would the new *Länder* really take off.

On an individual level, social psychologists found the transition to be a fascinating laboratory for discovering and predicting who would thrive amid the change, and who would struggle. There were studies of Easterners who'd escaped to the West (before the Wall fell). Likewise, there were longitudinal studies of workers in Dresden and Jena, to discern the personality traits that determined whether an individual could and would transform with the times. One economic incongruity the researchers had observed: most highly educated East Germans did not pursue new careers in engineering or technology, despite being qualified to do so. Instead, they took low-paying jobs in the construction industry, as laborers. This perpetuated the productivity gap between East and West, because so many college grads in the East took jobs beneath their intellectual capabilities. They had the education of a modern knowledge worker, but not the mindset.

Over time, researchers started to see a pattern. Those who succeeded—those who became competitive and innovative—were higher in *agency*.

Agency is the capacity to act independently, to make one's own free choices, and to make decisions quickly. Agency is the core inside self-starters, the trait that grows into personal initiative. Those low in agency don't trust themselves, and they are more reliant on others' leadership. They give up easily.

Those who were struggling—the factory workers waiting to be laid off, or the educated construction workers who took the sure thing—were low in agency.

Those succeeding in the new East didn't need to wait for approval to move forward. They believed they could put their ideas into practice. These were the men and women who overcame the layoffs and began the Jena start-ups.

Around the same time, scholars were studying the children of former East Germany. These children would be the next generation, but they would also be raised during an era of unemployment and price instability. In these studies, too, the variable of agency popped out as a predictor of postunification success.

East German schools had been very rigorous but had provided little outlet for individualism. All the children had the same exact books and assignments. Children were on the same schedule, no matter what. Those who did well in their education were not rewarded or accelerated. Children who struggled were not accommodated. They were just told to stand in front of the class and apologize to their classmates, since their poor performance had let the rest of the students down. They'd been taught to wait for someone else to tell them what to do, when, and how much effort to put in it.

In former East Germany, the only kids who had agency were the ones who got great grades. They were the only ones who felt somewhat in control of their lives. In West Germany, agency was not strictly associated with, or ruled by, school grades. In the Western schools, children could play to their strengths and pursue their own interests, and their education was somewhat customized according to their abilities. Kids had all sorts of ways to develop agency, not just through academic performance.

4

Just as Germany has had to train an entire country of 16 million to compete and innovate, we all have to nurture our children to become the kind of people who will, one day, be innovators. This is asking of them more than just creativity—to have not just original ideas of their own, but also the courage to risk rejection and put their ideas out into the world.

The gold standard in creativity assessment is the Torrance Tests of Creative Thinking (TTCT), which were put together by University of Minnesota professor of education E. Paul Torrance in the 1950s. His 50-year longitudinal study of nearly 400 people—starting in elementary school and following them far into adulthood—showed that his creativity tasks were three times better at predicting adult creative achievement than was IQ.

Back in the 1960s, Torrance warned of those who ignored the value of competition for kids, especially as it related to nurturing creative psychology. Creative people, he noted, are comfortable with ambiguity and are able to accept conflict and tension between contradicting ideas. They are not afraid of opposition, criticism, or competition, and all these may stimulate their creativity. Competition breeds the creative mindset.

In a recent experiment, trained musicians were asked to improvise a short piece on an electronic keyboard. Half were told it was a competition, with prizes and public rankings, while others were told it was a straightforward exploration of how pianists improvised. Those who were in the competition reported higher levels of stress and more intrinsic motivation than the others. Examining the improvs' sophistication, judges then determined that those in the competition had been more creative than those who had been playing with no risk.

University of Calgary professor Jock Abra concluded that, during the self-esteem movement, competition had been unfairly vilified for its effect on children's creativity. He wrote: "The realities of creative work and evidence from past creators indicate that talented youngsters must learn to handle intimidating experiences, including competition. Because competition provides a major energy source and incentive for creating, its curtailment, even if possible, would be undesirable."

A few years ago, Colgate University's Regina Conti decided to test the effect of competition on children's artistic creativity. She conducted an experiment under the guise of "art parties" at a Boston day camp and a local Catholic school. The kids who participated were six to eleven years old. They were given lots of colored paper and other arts supplies, and they were asked to use the supplies to make a creative collage.

At half of the parties, the kids were told it was a contest, that the collages would be judged by adults, and that the three best collages would win nifty prizes.

The rest of the kids were given no such competitive framing, and no rewards were promised. Those kids were, in theory, just doing the collages for the love of it.

Afterward, five trained artists rated all the children's collages on overall creativity and technical quality. Conti compared the creativity ratings of the work produced in the contest condition against the work produced in the noncompetitive condition.

On the whole, Conti found that the contest made the kids *more* creative: the judges rated their work as superior. But as with Norman Triplett's kids on the Competition Machine, this wasn't true of all children. There were two kinds of kids: those who seemed to be more creative when going for a prize, and those who were less creative and didn't like having their work judged.

What separated the kids? Conti's results showed that this difference hinged on a particular character trait—the same trait that mattered in East German schoolchildren: agency.

The kids high in agency loved the collage competition and were more creative. The kids low in agency didn't like being judged or compared, and they became less creative.

A strong sense of agency, once again, seems paramount.

We cultivate agency in children by allowing them freedom to make choices, and by encouraging them to trust the decisions they make. We must let them have opinions, feel their needs, and act to satisfy those needs. This also means allowing them the chance to make mistakes.

Agency doesn't lead to creativity per se, but it builds a psychology that leads, down the road, to flexibility, adaptivity, and creative problem-solving capacity.

As a society, we make a mistake about cultivating creativity. We focus only on the outputs—the art projects, science fairs, dramatic performances, and music recitals. Sure, we need to encourage those, and praise those efforts, but that's not the whole answer. We also need to build up kids' sense of agency, so that competition doesn't threaten them, but rather, challenges them to improve and makes them confident enough to put their work forward. That's the real lesson that has descended from Paul Torrance down through Regina Conti.

The truth is that many highly creative adults never had significant art training as children. What they had instead were childhoods where they learned to trust their own judgment without anyone's input. They grew up learning to be comfortable with conflict, contradiction, and opposition. Eventually, as adults, this enabled them to put their ideas out into the world, despite the risk of rejection or criticism.

Paragone—that Italian word for competitive debate—has come down to modern English and understanding as "paragon," often to describe something without peer, and in particular, diamonds. We can't forget that diamonds become peerless because they've withstood centuries of heat and pressure. That's what kids need to have: clarity and strength of vision built up over time—a brilliance that can withstand enormous pressure.

CHAPTER TWELVE

How the Black Sox Cleaned Up Wall Street

1

Which came first? Democracy or the Olympics?

The Olympics, by about 200 years.

Both the Olympics and democracy are considered legacies of Ancient Greece, but rarely does anyone discuss a relationship between these two events. It may seem as if there were no connection between them, but actually there's a strong relationship. The evidence suggests that the Olympic Games were *the precursor* for democracy.

Traditionally, the honor of lighting a temple's sacrificial flame was given to the highest member of the political hierarchy present—kings, oligarchs, or military leaders. However, the temples of Zeus and Hera at Olympia drew faithful from throughout Asia Minor. And it would be difficult—even dangerous—to assert anyone's superiority over another in such a sanctified setting. Thus, at some point in the eighth century B.C., the Greeks decided to have a 200-yard footrace: the winner would light the flame. A race was impartial to all—with everyone able to witness and accept the result. And, in keeping with the religious setting, the race was an opportunity to prove racers' worthiness of the honor: to win would demonstrate the gods' favor.

Over time, the Greeks added other events to what became a quadrennial festival: the first historic record of the Olympics is from 776 B.C.

While there were frequent local competitions, the Olympics were the centerpiece of Grecian life. The event was calendared years in advance so that everyone in the Hellenic world could attend.

There was a widespread truce during the Olympic festival: warring peoples could set down their weapons and travel unharmed through enemy territory to go to the Games. Athletes often came representing a city-state or a powerful tribe, but they could also compete themselves, if they could pass the initial inspection of fitness. For a month preceding the games, all athletes had to live in Olympia: they had to train together, even eating the same meals.

For the duration of the festival, warring Spartans and Athenians had to constrain themselves to a friendly rivalry, marked by rules and impartial judges (nowhere to be found on a real battlefield). The Games began with a ceremony, during which the athletes swore oaths to Zeus: they promised to conduct themselves according to the rules and to abide by the judges' decisions. The events—races, wrestling, boxing—all had clear-cut winners: everyone in the stadium audience of 40,000 knew who had won.

Olympic winners were given money and, more important, social status and honor. They were celebrated by poets; statues were erected in tribute to their achievements.

The competitive atmosphere of the Olympics was not limited to the athletes. In the audiences were politicians, philosophers, aristocrats, poets. As boxers took their shots, diplomats knocked back and forth terms of agreement; merchants bartered over imported wares. A culture of debate took hold. Orators gave public speeches about the importance of Panhellenic union, while philosophers debated ideas about how to change the world.

As in many other societies, Greek status was traditionally conferred by birth. But the athletes showed everyone that a person of low status who trained hard enough could best someone of a higher caste. Over time, the orators and philosophers adopted the same attitude: watching athletes improve with practice led people to believe that you could train one's mind as well.

After two centuries of the Olympics, the tradition of rules-based competitions and public debates slowly became part of the Athenian government. There were smaller fora for local problems. For larger issues, citizens would all come to Athens, to gather in a huge public arena. There were impartial juries and rules of conduct for civil discourse. Men would come forward to stand before 5,000 of their fellow citizens and argue why their course of action would be best for the populace. When the debate had ended, every citizen would vote, and the majority ruled. Men were chosen as leaders, but only for limited periods of time.

Aretas—the virtue of excellence found through competition—was something you had to develop, prove you had, and then use for the good of all.

The historians' work on Grecian democracy parallels research being done by Robert Washington, a Bryn Mawr sociologist. Washington is considering the possibility that, in countries without institutionalized sports, there is more corruption. In countries with more organized sports, there's less corruption. And these honest sporting events don't merely reflect the more ethical approach of the nation. Instead, the organized sports might be the actual *cause* of the countries' honesty.

Admittedly, this is just a theory at this point, but here are the broad strokes of Washington's premise.

Most people don't have access to the information needed to

thoroughly understand how Wall Street is performing or to assess the efficacy of a Pentagon operation. On the other hand, sporting events are unique among institutions: all the relevant records are available to the public. When the St. Louis Cardinals play a baseball game, 40,000 people can be there in the stadium, witnessing every move they make. The game is heard on the radio, seen on television. The box scores for every player come out in real time, and they're widely disseminated after the game.

Additionally, people don't need any special training to understand how the Cardinals scored their runs, and the count of home runs is easily tallied. When we see an aberration from the historical pattern, we get suspicious—and we root out the source.

Furthermore, people have an emotional connection to their teams. When corruption in sports does occur, it has a more tangible, immediate effect on their lives (compared to a scandal involving a defense contractor or Wall Street analyst).

Washington's team is looking at the infamous 1919 "Black Sox Scandal," when members of the Chicago White Sox admitted to having fixed the World Series. Before the Black Sox, baseball players gambled, but there was no established sense of what was right or wrong. After the Black Sox players were expelled from baseball, the rules were crystal clear—as were the penalties.

The reform spirit of the Progressive Era had already begun prior to the Black Sox—with regulations on adulterated food and drugs, then child labor laws—and the reformers had touted baseball as a model of fair play. At baseball parks, people from all strata of society came together with a sense of shared values: respect for man's individualism, intelligence, athleticism, and competitive spirit.

The White Sox players had been national heroes—but the heartless team owner regarded the players as just another set of workers who should be mistreated. Underpaid and denied bonuses for years, forced to wash their own uniforms, the players responded in turn, hatching a plan to even the score. The Black Sox scandal recast base-ball from a Progressive dream into a nightmare.

At the center of the scandal: Arnold Rothstein, a New York gambler who was equally at the center of New York's corrupt Tam-many Hall. The connection between Rothstein, Tammany, and the scandal was indelible. (F. Scott Fitzgerald included a reference to it in *The Great Gatsby*; Henry Ford publicly excoriated Rothstein in a newspaper editorial.)

From the corrupted players to the gamblers who corrupted them, everyone involved had turned their backs on American values of hon-esty, trustworthiness, and hard work. That the World Series could be fixed became a warning sign of how the industrial system could collapse.

To salvage the sport, the baseball team owners created a Commis-sioner of Baseball, whose job would be to police the teams, giving the public confidence that such corruption wouldn't happen again. It would take almost 14 years and a stock market crash before Wall Street had its own top cop—also given the title of commissioner.

Washington argues that when so much of our lives is predictable—scripted, even—sporting events provide a community with a shared sense of suspense and excitement that can't easily be found anywhere else. Therefore, the idea that a game would be rigged is intolerable.

Over time, Washington argues, people start wondering why other institutions aren't as transparent as sports events. They start asking why box scores aren't as widely available and easily understood for CEOs, companies, and government officials.

Washington points out that it's through sports terms that Ameri-cans frequently define fairness. We invoke sports metaphors such as "wanting a level playing field" and "a clean game." To act unfairly is to "hit below the belt" or "deliver a low blow." During his confirmation hearing for Supreme Court chief justice, John Roberts explained his understanding of his role in sports terms: "Judges are like umpires. Umpires don't make the rules; they apply them. The role of an umpire and a judge is critical. They make sure everybody plays by the rules."

India is a comparatively new democracy, saddled by a centuries-old culture of corruption. In studies, half of Indians admit they've bribed a public official, for everything from getting a birth certificate to filing their taxes on time. In a 2009 general election, 222 of the 1,400 candidates weren't just campaigning; they were also awaiting criminal trial. Truckers pay an estimated $5 billion in bribes each a year. Yet efforts to clean up Indian politics have met with little success.

While cricket is a national sport, it was only in 2007 that an Indian professional league was formed, using a shorter, television-friendly format—intended to be the cricket version of the NBA. But repeated allegations of corruption in the new league have triggered national outrage. In 2010, a foreign minister had a succession of public relations disasters and intimations of misuse of public funds—but it was when he was alleged to be in a cricket scheme that he was forced to resign. As one reporter was told, "You can steal land, take bribes, avoid paying taxes, and no one will really care. But don't screw with cricket."

After a second round of allegations in May of 2012—that yet more cricket players were accepting bribes to fix games—a politician went even further: "Whatever is happening is neither cricket nor is it our culture." There are public outcries for transparency in cricket—and arguments are made that the continued corruption in the game is proof that the Indian government doesn't care about its people.

If Washington's hypothesis is correct, outrage over cricket corruption will concretize the country's feelings about fairness, which will lead to a more robust effort to root out corruption in politics and business affairs. Sports scandals are the leading edge of broader reform.

2

During an Olympic game in the fourth century B.C., a boxer, Eupolos, was caught bribing three opponents. It was the first-known instance of cheating during the Games, according to historian Nigel Spivey. The guilty athletes were fined as punishment, and the money was used to commission ten life-size statues, each portraying an angry Zeus. At the base of each statue was inscribed a culprit's name and his offense. The bronze statues were placed immediately outside the entrance to the Olympic stadium—a permanent source of shame for the athletes and the cities they represented.

"Victory is to be achieved by speed of feet and strength of body, not with cash," warned Pausanias.

Over the years, there were a few more incidents of cheating, but, on balance, the Olympians of Ancient Greece seem to have played by the rules. That strong sense of fairness is probably why the Games survived for so long.

According to research done by Hungarian Academy of Sciences professor Márta Fülöp, it's fairness above all else that determines how we respond to competitions.

Maladaptive responses are usually the result not of individual character failings, but of a competition being unfair. When treated unjustly, even good people start doing bad things.

Winners in an unfair contest feel shame, fear, or malicious joy, which result in an emotional distance from the loser. Likewise, those who are the victims of an unfair competition can't be happy for the winner. They can't accept their defeat and move on. Instead, they feel anger and hatred—or sometimes helplessness, which turns them off entirely.

When competition is fair, both winning and losing trigger adaptive responses. In a fair contest, winners are able to feel sympathy for the losers: they feel an emotional connection. And the losers can accept the outcome; they can be happy for the winner's success. The result isn't just victory. It's about mutual respect for the effort.

The emotional responses we have to winning and losing are universal. Fülöp has studied winning and losing in traditionally collectivist cultures (such as Japan and China) or individualist "competitive" Western cultures (e.g., Canada). And she's found that the most common reactions to a victory are joy and satisfaction at one's competence. Three-fourths of the time, that's how people respond to victory, in her sample.

However, according to Fülöp, there are four reactions to winning.

1) Joy: gleeful enthusiasm and activation;
2) Satisfaction at one's competence;
3) Denial of win: having guilt and fear over triggering others' retaliation, they feel a strong need to mask the inner joy; and
4) Narcissistic self-enhancement: a malicious feeling of superiority over the loser.

There are also, according to Fülöp, four reactions to losing:

1) Sadness and disappointment leading to a graceful acceptance of the loss without ill will or blame;
2) Denial of loss: doesn't care, tired, bored affect, emotional divestment;
3) Self-devaluation: I'm no good, I'm a liability to my team, hatred of self, extreme embarrassment; and
4) Aggression toward the winner: envy, anger, hatred of the winner.

Again, as seen in her research, the first category of responses is by far the most common: the last three are much rarer.

How you respond to a win is highly predictive of how you will respond to a loss, and vice versa. For example, Fülöp has found that those who respond to a win with narcissistic superiority are likely to be the same ones who, after a loss, aggressively strike back at the winner.

Those who are likely to deny the importance of a win are also similarly likely to deny the significance of a loss, or they'll berate themselves for their failure. Win or lose, they temper their responses in accordance with what they feel are the likely reactions of others.

The maladaptive responses are demotivating. The narcissistic competitor doesn't feel a need to work harder in the next round. Instead, he believes that victories are his entitlement. As such, fairness isn't important: narcissists are more likely to cheat their way to a victory.

The maladaptive competitor's reaction is just as wrongheaded in a win as in a loss.

Contrast that to the adaptive responses seen in fair competitions. Winners who feel joy or satisfaction at a positive outcome are more likely to accept a loss gracefully. Yes, they are sad: they may be upset. But they channel those emotions into a commitment to work harder the next time. Both their joy and their frustration become motivators—fuel for the next competition.

Too often we use the old adage, "It's not if you win or lose, but how you played the game" as trite consolation to the loser. (When was the last time anyone said it to the winner?) But it shouldn't be thought of as a consolation prize. It's about building the groundwork for understanding one's self, one's competition, and how to play better the next time.

3

To compete requires that we embrace uncertainty—that we instinctively recognize that the suspense of an unscripted outcome, even if we lose, is more rewarding than a life preplanned.

We've seen that, in politics, to run for elected office requires a willingness to defy odds. We've seen that, in Olympic swimming, the uncertainty of the outcome leads to historic performances. We've seen that, with face surgeons, worrying over the complexity and uncertainty of the procedure triggers the vital hormone response to be truly up for the challenge. Playing to Win requires continuing to take risks; it's when we stop taking risks that we're Playing Not to Lose. And it's the uncertainty of a competition that gives underdogs a narrow chance, just as it's the overconfidence of favorites that makes them beatable.

We need to be ready for a change in circumstance. We need to acknowledge that a competitor may be just as skilled and prepared. It's uncertainty that keeps the mind active.

If competition is wearing you down, use the science to help diagnose why, and what can be done to improve your performance in competition.

Is the competition unfair? Is it an infinite competition, rather than a finite one? Are you competing against too many others, rather than just a few respected rivals? When you lose, do you feel anger, or helplessness and despair?

Learning how to frame competitions as a challenge, not a threat, can help overcome early timidity. Over time, people's minds—even their physiology—can acclimate to the stress of competing. People can learn to recognize when their effort level might be sagging and why that might be. Discovering an Individual Zone of Optimal Functioning—whether it's calm or arousal—can also help people become Top Dog. There's a mental edge that comes from recognizing which self-evaluation thoughts are productive and which are unproductive. Teams can identify when being too big, or lacking a hierarchy, is undermining their performance.

With experience, people learn that winning and losing are just short-term consequences to the long-term goal: improvement.

Some argue that our daily lives are already burdened by too much competition, that everything from cradle to grave is a race. Remember that the very definition of maladaptive competitiveness is a compulsion to compete in every aspect of life—it's not having an "off" switch. Healthy, successful, adaptive competitiveness is choosing what matters to you and fighting for it, while letting the other challenges pass. Choosing when not to compete is essential to sustaining the energy for the battles that matter most.

This book began by talking about skydiving—how astonishingly rapidly we can become accustomed to hurtling toward the earth. Psychologist Paul Rozin puts parachuting in the same class of activities as riding roller coasters, watching tragedies, and eating chili peppers. Rozin has found that most people enjoy the dare of testing themselves. The scariest roller coaster is their favorite one; similarly, they like chili peppers that are just below the experience of real pain. They get pleasure from experiencing small amounts of danger.

We want to know how much we can take, and then we want to go even further. According to Rozin, pushing ourselves to the brink is our preferred state.

We like competition for exactly that reason. It's dangerous, and we want to be tested—to prove ourselves. We want that thrill ride, beyond the limit of our fears.

SELECTED SOURCES AND REFERENCES

Authors' Note:

To make the references manageable, we've organized sources by chapter and further divided citations by the major subjects discussed within each chapter. Relevant notes—e.g., additional facts that might be helpful, a particular reference for a quote—can be found immediately following the relevant subject heading.

There is only one full citation per reference, included in the section where the study most directly relates to the text. (Some citations include a note to highlight a report's particular influence on the text.) On occasion, when research in one section is vital to our understanding of other material, we've also included pointers to those related references in the subsection notes.

PART I

The "Size of the Dog" Quote:

President Eisenhower made the "size of the dog" quote famous during a speech on January 21, 1958, and it appears that he used it at least once prior to that, in 1957. The quote has also been attributed to a number of individuals, including Mark Twain. However, it appears nowhere in Twain's published work, and it's probably not one of his quips. A popular expression throughout the 1930s, the earliest published use we could find dated from a 1928 appearance in *MacLean's Weekly*. However, the expression likely goes back further. A 1933 South Dakota publication describes it as "an Old Black Hills saying."

American Assn. of Port Authorities, *World Ports*, vol. 20–21, pp. 16 (1957)

Eisenhower, Dwight D., "Excerpts from Remarks at Republican National Committee Breakfast," Washington, DC (1958)

Kenner, Samantha, Correspondence with Author (2012)

Schmidt, Barbara, Correspondence with Author (2012)

State Bar of South Dakota, *South Dakota Bar Journal*, vol. 2, pp. 53 et seq. (1933)

Word Study, vol. 1–15, p. 34, Springfield, MA: G. & C. Merriam Co. (1968)

Ovid quote:

Collins English Language, Dictionary Entry for "Competition," http://bit.ly/NA8WZh

Chapter 1—Introduction / Parachutists and Ballroom Dancers

1.

Parachutes:

"Cortisol Luminescence Immunoassay (RE62019)," vers. 2009_09, IBL International, Hamburg (2009)

Deinzer, R., C. Kirschbaum, C. Gresele, & D. H. Hellhammer, "Adrenocortical Responses to Repeated Parachute Jumping and Subsequent h-CRH Challenge in Inexperienced Healthy Subjects," *Physiology & Behavior*, vol. 61(4), pp. 507–511 (1997)

Deinzer, Renate, Correspondence with Author (2012)

Deinzer, Renate, Interview with Author (2011)

"FAQ's," Georgia Tech Sport Parachute Club, http://bit.ly/MSFdap (2011)

"Frequently Asked Questions," U.S. Parachute Assn., http://bit.ly/LZrD2z (2008)

Kalman, Brian A., & Ruth E. Grahn, "Measuring Salivary Cortisol in the Behavioral Neuroscience Laboratory," *Journal of Undergraduate Neuroscience Education*, vol. 2(2), pp. A41–A49 (2004)

Lyng, Stephen, "Edgework: A Social Psychology Analysis of Voluntary Risktaking," *American Journal of Sociology*, vol. 95(4), pp. 851–886 (1990)

Meyer, James, "Syncope and Hypoxia," *Toggle Times*, Parachute Assn. of South Africa, http://bit.ly/Qwlr4i (1/27/2011)

Ryan, Allan J., & Clayton L. Thomas, "Sport Parachuting and Sky Diving," *JAMA*, vol. 194(3), pp. 259–263 (1965)

Strahler, Katharina, Felix Ehrlenspiel, Moritz Heene, & Ralf Brand, "Competitive Anxiety and Cortisol Awakening Response in the Week Leading Up to a Competition," *Psychology of Sport & Exercise*, vol. 11(2), pp. 148–154 (2010)

United States Parachute Assn., *2012–2013 Skydiver's Information Manual* (Sept. 2011)

2.

And Ballroom Dancers:

The irony that you can habituate to parachuting within a day, but not years of competitive ballroom dancing, first came to our attention via Strahler et al.'s 2010 paper.

Kalman, Brian A., & Ruth E. Grahn, "Measuring Salivary Cortisol in the Behavioral Neuroscience Laboratory," *Journal of Undergraduate Neuroscience Education*, vol. 2(2), pp. A41–A49 (2004)

Rohleder, Nicolas, Silke E. Beulen, Edith Chen, Jutta M. Wolf, & Clemens Kirschbaum, "Stress on the Dance Floor: The Cortisol Stress Response to Social-Evaluative Threat in Competitive Ballroom Dancers," *Personality & Social Psychology Bulletin*, vol. 33(1), pp. 69–84 (2007)

Rohleder, Nicolas, Correspondence with Author

Rohleder, Nicolas, Interview with Author

Strahler, et al. (2010) *supra*

Expertise and 10,000 Hours:

Adler, Amy, Interview with Author (2011)

Ericsson, K. Andres, "The Influence of Experience and Deliberate Practice on the Development of Superior Expert Performance," In: K. Anders Ericsson, Neil Charness, Paul J. Feltovich, & Robert R. Hoffman (Eds.), *Cambridge Handbook of Expertise and Expert Performance*, ch. 38, pp. 683–703, New York: Cambridge University Press (2006)

Ericsson, K. Andres, Ralf Th. Krampe, & Clemens Tesch-Römer, "The Role of Deliberate Practice in the Acquisition of Expert Performance," *Psychological Review*, vol. 100(3), pp. 363–406 (1993)

Gladwell, Malcolm, *Outliers: The Story of Success*, New York: Little, Brown & Co. (2008)

Syed, Matthew, *Bounce: Mozart, Federer, Picasso, Beckham & The Science of Success*, New York: Harper (2010)

3.
On the Morality of Competition/Competitiveness as a Personality/Character Trait:

Bergin, D., & C. Tsai, "A Taxonomy for Categorizing Research on Competition," Paper Presentation at Annual Meeting of the MWERA, St. Louis, MO, http://bit.ly/UffPis (2009)

Bergin, David, Correspondence with Author (2011)

Bullinger, Angelika C., Anne-Katrin Neyer, Matthias Rass, & Kathrin M. Moeslein, "Community-Based Innovation Contests: Where Competition Meets Cooperation," *Creativity and Innovation Management*, vol. 19(3), pp. 290–303 (2010)

Chance, Zoë, "A Temporal View of Self-Deception," Paper Presentation at Annual Convention for the Society for Personality and Social Psychology, San Diego (2011)

Chance, Zoë, Michael I. Norton, Francesca Gino, & Dan Ariely, "Temporal View of the Costs and Benefits of Self-Deception," *Proceedings of the National Academy of Sciences*, vol. 108(supp. 3), pp. 15655–15659 (2011)

Collier, A. Shawn, Richard M. Ryckman, Bill Thornton, & Joel A. Gold, "Competitive Personality Attitudes and Forgiveness of Others," *Journal of Psychology: Interdisciplinary & Applied*, vol. 144(6), pp. 535–543 (2010)

Connell, Joseph H., "On the Prevalence and Relative Importance of Interspecific Competition: Evidence from Field Experiments," *American Naturalist*, vol. 122(5), pp. 661–696 (1983)

Green, Vanessa A., & Ruth Rechis, "Children's Cooperative and Competitive Interactions in Limited Resource Situations: A Literature Review," *Applied Developmental Psychology*, vol. 27, pp. 42–59 (2006)

Kwateng, Danielle, "Decoding the Business of Earvin," *Black Enterprise*, http://bit.ly/McSy14 (2012)

Lallemand, Thierry, Robert Plasman, & François Rycx, "Intra-Firm Wage Dispersion and Firm Performance: Evidence from Linked Employer-Employee Data," *KYKLOS*, vol. 57(Fasc. 4), pp. 541–566 (2004)

Morey, Nadege, & Gwendolyn L. Gerber, "Two Types of Competitiveness: Their Impact on the Perceived Interpersonal Attractiveness of Women and Men," *Journal of Applied Social Psychology*, vol. 25(3), pp. 210–222 (2006)

Ryckman, Richard M., Bill Thornton, & J. Corey Butler, "Personality Correlates of the Hypercompetitive Attitude Scale: Validity Test of Horney's Theory of Neurosis," *Journal of Personality Assessment*, vol. 2(1), pp. 84–94 (1994)

Ryckman, Richard M., Bill Thornton, & Joel A. Gold, "Assessing Competition Avoidance as a Basic Personality Dimension," *Journal of Psychology*, vol. 143(2), pp. 175–192 (2009)

Shleifer, Andrei, "Does Competition Destroy Ethical Behavior?" *American Economic Review*, Papers & Proceedings of the One Hundred Sixteenth Annual Meeting of the American Economic Assn., San Diego, vol. 94(2), pp. 414–418 (2004)

Tauer, John M., & Judith M. Harackiewicz, "The Effects of Cooperation and Competition on Intrinsic Motivation and Performance," *Journal of Personality & Social Psychology*, vol. 86(6), pp. 849–861 (2004)

Tjosvold, Dean, David W. Johnson, Roger T. Johnson, & Haifa Sun, "Competitive Motives and Strategies: Understanding Constructive Competition," *Group Dynamics: Theory, Research, & Practice*, vol. 10(2), pp. 87–99 (2006)

"Weekly Address: To Win the Future, America Must Win the Global Competition in Education," Remarks by President Barack Obama, http://1.usa.gov/gCuCaK (2/19/2011)

Aretas and the Ancient Greek Olympics:

Note that while some scholars use *aretē*, we chose to use the conjugation of *aretas*, following discussions with Greek friends, regarding which form they would use in casual conversation. For additional sources regarding the Olympics, see Chapter 12 sources.

Hamilton, Edith, *The Greek Way*, New York: W. W. Norton (1930)

Hansen, William (Ed.), "The Oracles of Astrampsychus," In *Anthology of Ancient Greek Popular Literature* (Randall Stewart & Kenneth Morrell, Trans.), pp. 285–326 (1998)

Harris, William, *The Intelligent Person's Guide to Greek*, http://bit.ly/MSFha1 (u.d.)

Lendon, J. E., *Soldiers & Ghosts: A History of Battle in Classical Antiquity*, New Haven: Yale University Press (2005)

Littlewood, A. R., "Games and Sports," In: Nigel Guy Wilson (Ed.), *Encyclopedia of Ancient Greece*, New York: Routledge (2006)

Miller, Stephen G., *Arete: Greek Sports from Ancient Sources*, Berkeley, CA: University of California Press (1991)

Porter, David T., "The Pursuit of Arete," David O. McKay Lecture, Brigham Young University–Hawaii, http://bit.ly/McSCh8 (2007)

Rostkowska, Elżbieta, "Women and Sport: A Historical Outline and Contemporary Social and Physiological Issues," *Studies in Physical Culture & Tourism*, vol. 14(2), pp. 169–175 (2007)

4.

Jason Lezak at the 2008 Olympics:

Our primary sources for our account of the 2008 Olympics swim are our interview with Lezak and video footage of the race. However, a number of published accounts were also helpful in fleshing out the details.

"Beijing: Lezak, U.S. Make History in 4×100m Freestyle" (video), NBCOlympics.com, http://bit.ly/IEZSxB (8/2008)

Crouse, Karen, "Lezak, Not Phelps, Puts on a Show," *New York Times*, p. D1, http://nyti.ms/N2yxJA (8/10/2008)

"First-Ever Mutual of Omaha's Duel in the Pool to Settle Rivalry Between Powerhouse U.S. and Australian Swim Teams," Mutual of Omaha Press Release, http://prn.to/MSFeeA (8/7/2002)

Forde, Pat, "'No Way' Turns into 'No Quit' for Lezak, Men's Relay Team," ESPN.com, http://es.pn/N3Tujb (8/11/2008)

Henderson, John, "Bernard Holds Off Lezak in 100 Free," *Denver Post*, http://bit.ly/Q5ZWtY (8/14/2008)

Jenkins, Sally, "Getting By with a Little Help from His Friends," *Washington Post*, http://wapo.st/PWbnVj (9/12/2008)

Lezak, Jason, Interview with Author (2012)

Paxinos, Stathi, "Rivalry to Fire Phelps," *The Age*, http://bit.ly/olfSbu (7/16/2011)

Steele, David, "Deep Pool of Talent Fuels Rivalry," *San Francisco Chronicle*, p. D2, http://bit.ly/MLUa1z (9/14/2000)

Voepel, Mechelle, "At 32, Lezak Keeps Phelps' Dream Alive," *Kansas City Star*, http://bit. ly/LZshxb (8/11/2008)

5.

Competition as a Motivating Force:

These are just a fraction of the studies used to discuss competition as a source of motivation. For competition as a motivator in a specific context that is addressed later in the book (e.g., competition and creativity), see that specific topic's sources.

Carse, James P., *Finite and Infinite Games: A Vision of Life as Play and Possibility*, New York: The Free Press/Macmillan (1986)

Duplinsky, Michelle S., & Robert L. Woolfolk, "Motivation Styles, Attribution Styles, and Goal Orientations in Triathletes," Poster Presentation at Annual Convention of the American Psychological Assn. Washington, DC (2011)

Erev, Ido, Gary Bornstein, & Rachely Galili, "Constructive Intergroup Competition as a Solution to the Rider Problem: A Field Experiment," *Journal of Experimental Social Psychology*, vol. 29(6), pp. 463–478 (1993)

Myers, Albert, "Team Competition, Success, and the Adjustment of Group Members," *Journal of Abnormal & Social Psychology*, vol. 65(5), pp. 325–332 (1962)

Schapiro, Michelle, Barry H. Schneider, Bruce M. Shore, Judith A. Margison, & Stephen J. Udvari, "Competitive Goal Orientations, Quality, and Stability in Gifted and Other Adolescents' Friendships," *Gifted Child Quarterly*, vol. 53(2), pp. 71–88 (2009)

Schneider, Barry H., Joyce Benenson, Márta Fülöp, Mihaly Berkics, & Mónika Sándor, "Cooperation and Competition," In: P. K. Smith & C. H. Hart (Eds.), *The Wiley-Blackwell Handbook of Childhood Social Development*, 2nd Ed., ch. 25, pp. 472–490 (2011) (literature review of studies relating to children and competition)

Chapter 2—The Competition Machine

1.

Triplett and Kids in Competition:

For additional sources relating to competition and children beyond those included for this chapter, please see Schneider et al. (*supra*), Schapiro et al. (*supra*), and sources for Chapters 6, 7, and 11.

Bergin, David, "Use and Misuse of Incentives in School Settings," Paper Presentation at Annual Convention of the American Psychological Assn., Washington, DC (2011)

Bergin, David A., Correspondence with Author (2011)

Bergin, David A., & Helen C. Cooks, "Academic Competition among Students of Color: An Interview Study," *Urban Education*, vol. 35(4), pp. 442–472 (2000)

Bergin, David A., & Chia-Lin Tsai, "A Taxonomy for Categorizing Research on Competition," Paper Presentation at Mid-Western Educational Research Assn., St. Louis, MO (2009)

Davis, Stephen F., Matthew T. Huss, & Angela H. Becker, "Norman Triplett: Recognizing the Importance of Competition," In: Christopher D. Green, & Ludy T. Benjamin, Jr., *Psychology Gets in the Game: Sport, Mind, and Behavior, 1880–1960*, ch. 3, pp. 98–115, Lincoln, NE: University of Nebraska Press (2009)

Shermer, Michael, "Psyched Up, Psyched Out," *Scientific American*, vol. 11(3), pp. 36–43 (2000)

Triplett, Norman, "The Dynamogenic Factors in Pacemaking and Competition," *American Journal of Psychology*, vol. 9, pp. 507–533 (1898)

Vaughan, Graham, & Bernard Guerin, "A Neglected Innovator in Sports Psychology: Norman Triplett and the Early History of Competitive Performance," *International Journal of the History of Sport*, vol. 14(2), pp. 82–99 (1997)

2.

Air Force Academy Cadets / Effects of Peers on Success:

See also sources for Chapter 6, relating to participation in groups, Jackson's work on elite students, et cetera.

"America's Top Colleges," *Forbes*, http://onforb.es/oq7T4t (June 2011)

Azmat, Ghazala, & Nagore Iriberri, "The Importance of Relative Performance Feedback Information: Evidence from a Natural Experiment Using High School Students," *Journal of Public Economics*, vol. 94(7–8), pp. 435–452 (2010)

Bandiera, Oriana, Iwan Barankay, & Imran Rasul, "Social Incentives in the Workplace," *Review of Economic Studies*, vol. 77(2), pp. 417–458 (2010)

Bono, James W., "Sales Contests, Promotion Decisions and Heterogeneous Risk," *Managerial & Decision Economics*, vol. 29(4), pp. 371–382 (2008)

Carrell, Scott, Correspondence with Author (2011)

Carrell, Scott, Interview with Author (2011)

Carrell, Scott E., "Does Your Cohort Matter? Measuring Peer Effects in College Achievement," *Journal of Labor Economics*, vol. 27(3), pp. 439–464 (2009)

Carrell, Scott E., Robert N. Gilchrist, Richard L. Fullerton, & James E. West, "Peer Leadership Effects in Academic and Athletic Performance," Working Paper (2007)

Carrell, Scott E., Teny Maghakian, & James E. West, "A's From Zzzz's? The Causal Effect of School Start Time on the Academic Achievement of Adolescents," *American Economic Journal: Economic Policy*, vol. 3, pp. 62–81 (2011)

Carrell, Scott E., Bruce I. Sacerdote, & James E. West, "Beware of Economists Bearing Reduced Forms? An Experiment in How Not to Improve Student Outcomes," Working Paper (2010)

Carrell, Scott E., Bruce I. Sacerdote, & James E. West, "From Natural Variation to Optimal Policy? The Lucas Critique Meets Peer Effects," Working Paper, National Bureau of Economic Research, Cambridge, MA (7/5/2011)

De Giorgi, Giacomo, Michele Pellizzari, & William Gui Woolston, "Class Size and Class Heterogeneity," National Bureau of Economic Research, Cambridge, MA (2010)

Delfgaauw, Josse, Robert Dur, Arjan Non, & Willem Verbeke, "Dynamic Incentive Effects of Relative Performance Pay: A Field Experiment," Paper Presentation at Tournaments, Contests, and Relative Performance Evaluation Conference, Raleigh, NC (2011)

Delfgaauw, Josse, Robert Dur, Arjan Non, & Willem Verbeke, "The Effects of Prize Spread and Noise in Elimination Tournaments: A Natural Field Experiment," Working Paper TI 2011–120/1, Tinbergen Institute (2011)

Dur, Robert, Correspondence with Authors (2011)

"Fast Facts," Air Force Academy, http://bit.ly/QSxgGh (u.d.)

Frank, Douglas, & Tomasz Obloj, "Reference Points and Organization Performance from Retail Banking," Paper Presentation at Tournaments, Contests, and Relative Performance Evaluation Conference, Raleigh, NC, http://bit.ly/PWe3lT (2011)

Kruczek, Theodore, "A Cadet's Life: United States Air Force Academy," http://bit.ly/7rKIEH (1/12/2010)

"List of Acronyms and Explanations of Terms Used at the USAFA," United States Air Force Academy Parents Club of Central Florida, http://bit.ly/O6xVlE (u.d.)

Murphy, William H., & Peter A. Dacin, "Sales Contest Research: Business and Individual Difference Factors Affecting Intentions to Pursue Contest Goals," *Industrial Marketing Management,* vol. 38(1), pp. 109–118 (2009)

Poujol, F. Juliet, Christophe Fournier, & John F. Tanner Jr., "Compliance versus Preference: Understanding Salesperson Response to Contests," *Journal of Business Research,* vol. 64(7), pp. 664–671 (2011)

Sacerdote, Bruce, "Peer Effects with Random Association Results for Dartmouth Roommates," *Quarterly Journal of Economics,* vol. 116(2), pp. 681–704 (2001)

U.S. Air Force Academy Catalogue, http://1.usa.gov/QSz16m (2008)

3.

SATs / The N-Effect:

Garcia, Stephen, Correspondence with Authors (2009, 2011)

Garcia, Stephen, Interviews with Authors (2009, 2011)

Garcia, Stephen M., & Avishalom Tor, "The N-Effect: More Competitors, Less Competition," *Psychological Science,* vol. 20(7), pp. 871–877 (2009)

"State Profile Report: Alabama," College Board (2011)

"State Profile Report: Alaska," College Board (2011)

"State Profile Report: Arkansas," College Board (2011)

"State Profile Report: California," College Board (2011)

"State Profile Report: Massachusetts," College Board (2011)

"State Profile Report: New York," College Board (2011)

Tor, Avishalom, & Stephen M. Garcia, "The N-Effect: Beyond Probability Judgments," *Psychological Science,* vol. 21(5), pp. 748–749 (2010)

4.

Harvard/Yale and Other College Rivalries:

Bensch, Bob, "Harvard Defeats Yale 45–7 to Extend Domination of 'The Game'," *Bloomberg Business Week,* http://buswk.co/s8pqXO (11/19/2011)

Cohn, Steve, & Bob Barton, *Yale Football 2009,* http://bit.ly/PPozui (2009)

Conroy, Tom, "Investment Return of 21.9% Brings Yale Endowment Value to $19.4 Billion," *Yale News,* http://bit.ly/wGZYi8 (9/28/2011)

"Financial Aid," Yale University, http://bit.ly/eXcxhK (u.d.)

"Football by Year," http://bit.ly/O6wgwo (u.d.)

"Harvard University Endowment Earns 21.4 Percent Return for Fiscal Year," *Harvard Gazette,* http://hvrd.me/oyh9ZS (9/22/2011)

"Harvard-Yale Grid Contests Feature Upsets, Stars in 75 Year History," *Harvard Crimson,* http://bit.ly/OvgwTf (11/25/1950)

"The Harvard-Yale Rivalry," GoCrimson.com, http://bit.ly/OmNGWF (2010)

"Heads of State," Harvard University, http://hvrd.me/OvgBWV (2012)

Kilduff, Gavin J., Hillary Anger Elfenbein, & Barry M. Staw, "The Psychology of Rivalry: A Relationally Dependent Analysis of Competition," *Academy of Management Journal,* vol. 53(5), pp. 943–969 (2010)

Lakin, Tom, "Harvard-Yale Brings History to Life," ESPNBoston.com, http://es.pn/MLVphm (11/20/2009)

Mathews, Jay, "The 12 Top Rivals," *Newsweek,* http://bit.ly/O9kBu0 (8/8/2008)

"Nobel Laureates," Yale University, http://bit.ly/O9kIFM (2011)

"Nobel Laureates at Harvard University," Harvard University, http://hvrd.me/rhFnp6 (2012)

Pisner, Noah B., "The Name of the Game," *Harvard Crimson*, http://bit.ly/uiyw7F (11/17/2011)

"Record for Financial Aid," *Harvard Gazette*, http://hvrd.me/GWf8X1 (3/26/2012)

Wanger, Emily, "Yale Redistributes Financial Aid," *Yale Daily News*, http://bit.ly/gQ6AWc (2/18/2011)

"Welcome to the Harvard Financial Aid Office," Harvard University, http://bit.ly/oTJE7 (2009)

"Yale Alumni in U.S. Politics," *Yale News*, http://bit.ly/O6ybRJ (3/27/2009)

Packaging Valley / Rivalries in Business Contexts:

"ACMA Group: Company Profile" http://bit.ly/P0TlfW

Alpern, Peter, "Italian Packaging Machinery Industry Proves Resilient," *Industry Week*, http://bit.ly/LV33Vn (11/17/2009)

"Are You Ready for Track&Trace???" Marchesini.com, http://bit.ly/NA9Ch5 (11/25/2011)

Barnett, William P., "The Red Queen: History-Dependent Competition among Organizations," In: Barry M. Staw & Roderick Moreland Kramer (Eds.), *Research In Organizational Behavior: An Annual Series Of Analytical Essays & Critical Reviews*, vol. 26, pp. 351–371, Oxford: Elsevier (2005)

Barnett, William P., & Olav Sorenson, "The Red Queen in Organizational Development," *Industrial & Corporate Change*, vol. 11(2), pp. 289–325 (2002)

Belussi, Fiorenza, "The Generation of Contextual Knowledge through Communication Processes: The Case of the Packaging Machinery Industry in the Bologna District," In: Fiorenza Belussi, Giorgio Gottardi, & Enzo Rullani (Eds.), *The Technological Evolution of Industrial Districts (Economics of Science, Technology & Innovation)*, ch. 15, pp. 341–366, Norwell, MA: Kluwer Academic Press (2003)

Belussi, Fiorenza, Alessia Sammarra, & Silvia Rita Sedita, "Entrepreneurship and Innovation—Organization Systems and Regions," Paper Presentation for 25th Celebration Conference, DRUID, Copenhagen (2005)

Boari, Cristina, "Industrial Clusters, Focal Firms, and Economic Dynamism: A Perspective from Italy," Paper No. 37186, Washington, DC: World Bank Institute (2001)

Boari, Cristina, Guido Fioretti, & Vincenza Odorici, "Rivalry and Learning among Clustered and Isolated Firms," In: Edoardo Mollona (Ed.), *Computational Analysis of Firms' Organization and Strategic Behaviour*, ch. 8, pp. 171–192, New York: Routledge (2010)

Boari, Cristina, & Andrea Lipparini, "Networks within Industrial Districts: Organising Knowledge Creation and Transfer by Means of Moderate Hierarchies," *Journal of Management & Governance*, vol. 3(4), pp. 339–360 (1999)

Boari, Cristina, Vincenza Odoricia, & Marco Zamarian, "Clusters and Rivalry: Does Localization Really Matter?" *Scandinavian Journal of Management*, vol. 19(4), pp. 467–489 (2003)

Camuffoa, Arnaldo, & Roberto Grandinetti, "Italian Industrial Districts as Cognitive Systems: Are They Still Reproducible?," *Entrepreneurship & Regional Development*, vol. 23 (9–10), pp. 815–852 (2011)

D'Agostino, Giorgio, & Margherita Scarlato, "Innovation, Growth, and Quality of Life: A Theoretical Model and an Estimate for the Italian Regions," Working Paper No. 138, Dipartimento di Economia, Università degli Studi Roma Tre (2011)

Eriksson, Tor, Sabrina Teyssier, & Marie-Claire Villeval, "Self-Selection and the Efficiency of Tournaments," *Economic Inquiry*, vol. 47(3), pp. 530–548 (2009)

Goldoni, Manuela, "Marchesini Group at Pack Expo: In the Limelight, 'Track & Trace' and Counting Solutions," Press Release, Marchesini Group (Sept. 2011)

González-Moreno, Angela, & Francisco J. Sáez-Martínez, "Rivalry and Strategic Groups: What Makes a Company a Rival?," *Journal of Management & Governance*, vol. 12, pp. 261–285 (2008)

Gripsrud, Geir, & Kjell Grønhaug, "Structure and Strategy in Grocery Retailing: A Sociometric Approach," *Journal of Industrial Economics*, vol. 33(3), pp. 339–347 (1985)

Grohsjean, Thorsten, & Tobias Kretschmer, "Product Line Extension in Hypercompetitive Environments—Evidence from the US Video Game Industry," Paper Presentation for Summer Conference, Copenhagen Business School (2009)

"Interpreting the Competition: Italy and Germany: Behind Their Success in World Export Markets for Packaging Machinery," Packaging Machinery Manufacturers Institute (2004)

Lorenzoni, Gianni, & Andrea Lipparini, "The Leveraging of Interfirm Relationships as a Distinctive Organizational Capability: A Longitudinal Study," *Strategic Management Journal*, vol. 20(4), pp. 317–338 (1999)

Malipiero, A., F. Munari, & M. Sobrero, "Focal Firms as Technological Gatekeepers within Industrial Districts: Knowledge Creation and Dissemination in the Italian Packaging Machinery Industry," Communication to the DRUID Winter Conference, DRUID Working Paper No. 05–05 (2005)

McTigue Pierce, Lisa, "Pent-Up Manufacturing Demand Plus Growing Consumer Confidence Bodes Well for Machinery Sales," *Packaging Digest*, http://bit.ly/hg2zYe (4/1/2011)

Munari, Federico, Maurizio Sobrero, & Alessandro Malipieroy, "Absorptive Capacity and Localized Spillovers: Focal Firms as Technological Gatekeepers in Industrial Districts," *Industrial & Corporate Change*, vol. 21(2), pp. 429–462 (2012)

"Packaging Machinery Industry," Invest in Bologna, http://bit.ly/Mrju8J (u.d.)

Porac, Joseph F., Howard Thomas, Fiona Wilson, Douglas Paton, & Alaina Kanfer, "Rivalry and the Industry Model of Scottish Knitwear Producers," *Administrative Science Quarterly*, vol. 40(2), pp. 203–227 (1995)

Promo Bologna, "Packaging Valley," Discover Bologna: Where Quality of Life, Entrepreneurship and Culture Meet, http://bit.ly/NAb2sb (u.d.)

Quatraro, Franceso, "Innovation, Structural Change and Productivity Growth: Evidence from Italian Regions, 1980–2003," *Cambridge Journal of Economics*, vol. 33(5), pp. 1001–1022 (2009)

Ruys, Kirsten I., & Henk Aarts, "When Competition Merges People's Behavior: Interdependency Activates Shared Action Representations," *Journal of Experimental Social Psychology*, vol. 46(6), pp. 1130–1133 (2010)

Sorkin, Aaron (scr.), David Fincher (dir.), *The Social Network*, Columbia Pictures, Film (2010)

UCIMA Book 2010, Unione Costruttori Italiani, Macchine Automatiche per il Confezionamento e l'Imballaggio/ Italian Packaging Machinery Manufacturers Assn., Italy (2010)

Zucchini, Leon, & Tobias Kretschmer, "Competitive Pressure: Competitive Dynamics as Reactions to Multiple Rivals," Discussion Paper 2011–03 (2011)

Matthew Effect versus Mark Effect:

Bothner, Matthew S., Joel M. Podolny, & Edward Bishop Smith, "Organizing Contests for Status: The Matthew Effect vs. the Mark Effect," *Management Science*, vol. 57(3), pp. 439–457 (2011)

Gospel According to Matthew 25:29, *New American Bible/Catholic Study Bible*, New York: Oxford University Press (1991)

Gospel According to Mark 10:31, *New American Bible/Catholic Study Bible*, New York: Oxford University Press (1991)

Merton, Robert K., "The Matthew Effect in Science," *Science*, vol. 159(3810), pp. 56–63 (1968)

Chapter 3—What Goes Down When the Stakes Go Up

1.

Kirk Hanlin and the 1996 Presidential Trip to Japan:

Our primary source for this account comes from Kirk Hanlin; additional reports added to our understanding of the political facets of the trip. Hanlin's concern about the White House press pool making a conspiracy story out of an exclusion from the motorcade shouldn't be taken as hyperbole. During President Barack Obama's 2012 trip to South Korea, the White House press pool covering the trip was temporarily, accidentally excluded from a presidential event. The Associated Press filed a story on the reporters' exclusion, portraying a lack of commitment to free speech and a free press in South Korea—and by implication, the AP called into question the wisdom of the U.S.'s alliance with the nation. See Gearan 2012.

Chronicle New Services, "Clinton Gives Japan Stern Lecture / He Says Nation Must Open its Markets," *San Francisco Chronicle* (11/20/1998)

"Clinton Visit Scheduled to Begin Thursday," *Japan Times* (11/13/1998)

Edwards III, George C., & Stephen J. Vayne, *Presidential Leadership: Politics and Policy Making*, 8th Ed., Boston: Wadsworth Publishing (2010)

Gearan, Anne, "Obama Press Corps Temporarily Blocked Out in South Korea," *Huffington Post*, http://huff.to/H5TL48 (3/25/2012)

Hanlin, Kirk, Correspondence with Author (2011, 2012)

Hanlin, Kirk, Interviews with Author (2011, 2012)

Hodgson, James D., Yoshihiro Sano, & John L. Graham, *Doing Business with the New Japan*, Lanham, MD: Rowman & Littlefield (2008)

Hunt, Terence, "Clinton, Obuchi Conclude Talks," AP News Archive (11/20/1998)

Knowlton, Brian, "He Calls Japan Key to Recovery: Clinton Exhorts Asia to Pursue Reforms," *New York Times* (11/19/1998)

McPherson, James Brian, *Journalism at the End of the American Century, 1965–Present*, Westport, CT: Praeger Publishers (2006)

Meyrowitz, Joshua, "Displaying the Body Politic: Televisual Exposures and Concealments," Lawrence J. Prelli (Ed.), *Rhetorics of Display*, Columbia, SC: University of South Carolina Press (2006)

Nelson, Michael, "Why the Media Love Presidents and Presidents Hate the Media," *Virginia Quarterly Review*, vol. 76(2), pp. 255–268 (2000)

"President Clinton Lauds Japan's Efforts to Stem Economic Woes and Cites 'Best Days Lay Ahead for Both US and Japan,'" Ministry of Foreign Affairs of Japan (11/1998)

"Remarks by the President and Prime Minister Obuchi in Exchange of Toasts," Office of the Press Secretary, The White House, Washington, DC (11/19/1998)

Shipman, Claire, "Clinton's Absence at Summit Could Hurt U.S.-Japan Ties," CNN, http://bit.ly/S3Nhv4 (11/17/1995) (mentioning polls finding the Japanese wanted the U.S. out of Okinawa)

"Significance of the Japan-U.S. Relationship—President Clinton's Visit to Japan," Ministry of Foreign Affairs of Japan (11/30/1998)

"Today's U.S. Military Bases in Okinawa," Okinawa G8 Summit Host Preparation Council, http://bit.ly/elsexW (u.d.)

Home Field Advantage:

Additional sources on biochemical aspects of home field advantage can be found in the Chapter 10 notes; see Carré and Fuxjager's research referenced therein.

Amenta, Carlo, & Paolo Di Betta, "You Can Even Walk Alone: Stadium Attendance and Professional Soccer Clubs' Social Role," *International Business & Management*, vol. 1(1), pp. 69–79 (2010)

Balmer, N. J., A. M. Nevill, & A. M. Lane, "Do Judges Enhance Home Advantage in European Championship Boxing?," *Journal of Sports Sciences*, vol. 23(4), pp. 409–416 (2005)

Balmer, Nigel J., Alan M. Nevill, Andrew M. Lane, Paul Ward, Mark A. Williams, & Stephen Fairclough, "Influence of Crowd Noise on Soccer Refereeing Consistency in Soccer," *Journal of Sport Behavior*, vol. 30(2), pp. 130–145 (2007)

Berger, Jonah A., Marc Meredith, & S. Christian Wheeler, "Can Where People Vote Influence How They Vote? The Influence of Polling Location Type on Voting Behavior," Working Paper, Stanford GSB Research Paper No. 1926 (2006)

Blumenthal, Jeremy A., & Terry L. Turnipseed, "Is Voting in Churches (or Anywhere Else) Unconstitutional? The Polling Place Priming (PPP) Effect," *Boston University Law Review*, vol. 91, pp. 1–43 (2011)

Brown, Graham, "Claiming a Corner at Work: Measuring Employee Territoriality in Their Workspaces," *Journal of Environmental Psychology*, vol. 29(1), pp. 44–52 (2009)

Brown, Graham, "Setting (and Choosing) the Table: The Influence of the Physical Environment in Negotiation," In: Michael Benoliel (Ed.), *Negotiation Excellence: Successful Deal Making*, Singapore: World Scientific Publishing Co. Pte. Ltd., ch. 2, pp. 39–56 (2011)

Brown, Graham, & Markus Baer, "Location in Negotiation: Is There a Home Field Advantage?" *Organizational Behavior & Human Decision Processes*, vol. 114(2), pp. 190–200 (2011)

Brown, Graham, Thomas B. Lawrence, & Sandra L. Robinson, "Territoriality in Organizations," *Academy of Management Review*, vol. 30(3), pp. 577–594 (2005)

Buraimo, Babatunde, David Forrest, & Robert Simmons, "The 12th Man?: Refereeing Bias in English and German Soccer," *Journal of the Royal Statistical Society: Series A*, vol. 173(2), pp. 431–449 (2010)

Costa, Marco, "Territorial Behavior in Public Settings," *Environment & Behavior*, vol. 44 (5), pp. 713–721 (2012)

Cox, B., R. Raper, & W. Langston, "Male Territoriality When Choosing Pornographic Videos," Poster Presentation at Annual Meeting of the Society for Personality & Social Psychology, Nashville (2000)

DeScioli, Peter, & Bart J. Wilson, "The Territorial Foundations of Human Property," *Evolution & Human Behavior*, vol. 32(5), pp. 297–304 (2011)

Fuxjager, Matthew J., Jon L. Montgomery, Elizabeth A. Becker, & Catherine A. Marler, "Deciding to Win: Interactive Effects of Residency, Resources and 'Boldness' on Contest Outcome in White-Footed Mice," *Animal Behaviour*, vol. 80(5), pp. 921–927 (2010)

Gomez, Miguel A., Sergio J. Ibáñez, Enrique Ortega, Nuno Leite, & Jaime Sampaio, "An Analysis of Defensive Strategies Used by Home and Away Basketball Teams," *Perceptual & Motor Skills*, vol. 110(1), pp. 159–166 (2010)

Han, Ru, Shu Li, & Jian-Nong Shi, "The Territorial Prior-Residence Effect and Children's Behavior in Social Dilemmas," *Environment & Behavior*, vol. 41(5), pp. 644–657 (2009)

Hansen, Darah, "How the Right Seat Can Reduce Office Stress," Staff Blog, *Vancouver Sun*, http://bit.ly/pnxrnn (9/19/2011)

Hirst, Alison, "Settlers, Vagrants and Mutual Indifference: Unintended Consequences of Hot-Desking," *Journal of Organizational Change Management*, vol. 24(6), pp. 767–788 (2011)

Ibáñez, Sergio J., Javier García, Sebastian Feu, Alberto Lorenzo, & Jaime Sampaio, "Effects of Consecutive Basketball Games on the Game-Related Statistics that Discriminate Winner and Losing Teams," *Journal of Sports Science & Medicine*, vol. 8(3), pp. 458–462 (2009)

Jamieson, Jeremy P., "The Home Field Advantage in Athletics: A Meta-Analysis," *Journal of Applied Social Psychology*, vol. 40(7), pp. 1819–1848 (2010)

Jansen, Friederike, Rebecca S. Heiming, Vanessa Kloke, Sylvia Kaiser, Rupert Palme, Klaus-Peter Lesch, & Norbert Sachser, "Away Game or Home Match: The Influence of Venue and Serotonin Transporter Genotype on the Display of Offensive Aggression," *Behavioural Brain Research*, vol. 219(2), pp. 291–301 (2011)

Jones, Marshall B., "Home Advantage in the NBA as a Game-Long Process," *Journal of Quantitative Analysis in Sports*, vol. 3(4), art. 2 (2007)

Koning, Ruud H., "Home Advantage in Speed Skating: Evidence from Individual Data," *Journal of Sports Sciences*, vol. 23(4), pp. 417–427 (2005)

Koyama, Mark, & J. James Reade, "Playing Like the Home Team: An Economic Investigation into Home Advantage in Football," *International Journal of Sports Finance*, vol. 4(1), pp. 16–41 (2009)

Lane, Andrew M., Alan M. Nevill, Nahid S. Ahmad, & Nigel Balmer, "Soccer Referee Decision-Making: Shall I Blow the Whistle?" *Journal of Sports Science & Medicine*, vol. 5(2), pp. 243–453 (2006)

Li, Hong-chen, Xu Shui-sheng, & Chen Qian-shan, "Investigation on the Preparation for the Curling Match in 2009 Winter Universiade," (English abstract) doi:CNKI:SUN:BXYD.0.2008-06-014 (2008)

Marcelino, Rui, Isabel Mesquita, José Manuel Palao, & Jaime Sampaio, "Home Advantage in High-Level Volleyball Varies According to Set Number," *Journal of Sports Science & Medicine*, vol. 8(3), pp. 352–356 (2009)

Morton, Hugh, "Home Advantage in Southern Hemisphere Rugby Union: National and International," *Journal of Sports Sciences*, vol. 24(5), pp. 495–499 (2006)

Page, Lionel, & Katie Page, "The Second Leg Home Advantage: Evidence from European Football Cup Competitions," *Journal of Sports Sciences*, vol. 25(14), pp. 1547–1556 (2007)

Pollard, R., & G. Pollard, "Long-Term Trends in Home Advantage in Professional Sports in North America and England (1876–2003)," *Journal of Sports Sciences*, vol. 23(4), pp. 337–350 (2005)

Pollard, Richard, "Evidence of a Reduced Home Advantage When a Team Moves to a New Stadium," *Journal of Sports Sciences*, vol. 20(12), pp. 969–973 (2002)

Pollard, Richard, "Home Advantage in Football: A Current Review of an Unsolved Puzzle," *Open Sports Sciences Journal*, vol. 1, pp. 12–14 (2008)

Rahnama, N., E. Bambaeichi, & M. Zarei, "The Comparison of Performance and Injury Incidence Rate in Home and Away Games in Iran Premier League Teams," *World Journal of Sports Sciences*, vol. 2, pp. 89–94 (2009)

Ruback, R. Barry, "Deserted (and Nondeserted) Aisles: Territorial Intrustion Can Produce Persistence, Not Flight," *Social Psychology Quarterly*, vol. 50(3), pp. 270–276 (1987)

Ruback, R. Barry, & Daniel Juieng, "Territorial Defense in Parking Lots: Retaliation against Waiting Drivers," *Journal of Applied Social Psychology*, vol. 27(9), pp. 821–834 (1997)

Ruback, R. Barry, Karen D. Pape, & Philip Doriot, "Waiting for a Phone: Intrusion on Callers Leads to Territorial Defense," *Social Psychology Quarterly*, vol. 52(3), pp. 232–241 (1989)

Rutchick, Abraham M., "Deus ex Machina: The Influence of Polling Place on Voting Behavior," *Political Psychology*, vol. 31(2), pp. 209–225 (2010)

Ryall, Richard, & Anthony Bedford, "The Intra-Match Home Advantage in Australian Rules Football," *Journal of Quantitative Analysis in Sports*, vol. 7(2), ISSN (Online) 1559–0410, doi:10.2202/1559-0410.1314 (2011)

Salacuse, Jeswald W., & Jeffrey Z. Rubin, "Your Place or Mine? Site Location and Negotiation," *Negotiation Journal*, vol. 6(1), pp. 3–10 (1990)

Sampaio, Jaime, Sergio Jose Ibáñez, Miguel Angel Gomez, Alberto Lorenzo, & Enrique Ortega, "Game Location Influences Basketball Players' Performance across Playing Positions," *International Journal of Sport Psychology*, vol. 39(3), pp. 205–216 (2008)

Smith, D. Randall, "The Home Advantage Revisited Winning and Crowd Support in an Era of National Publics," *Journal of Sport & Social Issues*, vol. 27(4), pp. 346–371 (2003)

Sutter, Matthias, & Martin G. Kocher, "Favoritism of Agents—The Case of Referees' Home Bias," *Journal of Economic Psychology*, vol. 25(4), pp. 461–469 (2004)

Taylor, Ralph B., & Debra Kaye Brooks, "Temporary Territories? Responses to Intrusions in a Public Setting," *Population & Environment*, vol. 3(2), pp. 135–145 (1980)

Taylor, Ralph B., & Joseph C. Lanni, "Territorial Dominance: The Influence of the Resident Advantage in Triadic Decision Making," *Journal of Personality & Social Psychology*, vol. 41(5), pp. 909–915 (1981)

Terry, Peter C., Nicholas Walrond, & Albert V. Carron, "The Influence of Game Location on Athletes' Psychological States," *Journal of Science & Medicine in Sport*, vol. 1(1), pp. 29–37 (1998)

van de Ven, Niels, "Supporters Are Not Necessary for the Home Advantage: Evidence from Same-Stadium Derbies and Games without an Audience," *Journal of Applied Social Psychology*, vol. 41(12), pp. 2785–2792 (2011)

Van Dyne, Linn, & Jon L. Pierce, "Psychological Ownership and Feelings of Possession: Three Field Studies Predicting Employee Attitudes and Organizational Citizenship Behavior," *Journal of Organizational Behavior*, vol. 25(4), pp. 439–459 (2004)

Waters, Anna, & Geoff Lovell, "An Examination of the Homefield Advantage in a Professional English Soccer Team from a Psychological Standpoint," *Football Studies*, vol. 1(5), pp. 46–59 (2002)

Wheeler, S. Christian, Jonah A. Berger, & Marc Meredith, "Where You Vote Affects How You Vote," Presentation at Annual Meeting of the Society for Personality & Social Psychology, Tampa, FL (2004)

Zengaro, F., & S. Zengaro, "Fouls, Penalties, and Aggression: The Psychology of the Home Field Advantage in Italian Professional Soccer," Paper Presentation at Annual Convention of the American Psychological Assn., Washington, DC (2011)

2.

The Impact of an Audience upon Performance:

Aiello, John R., "Benefits of Distraction Above and Mere Presence," Paper Presentation at Annual Convention of the American Psychological Assn., Washington, DC (2011)

Aiello, John R., & Elizabeth A. Douthitt, "Social Facilitation from Triplett to Electronic Performance Monitoring," *Group Dynamics: Theory, Research, & Practice*, vol. 5(3), pp. 163–180 (2001)

Aiello, John R., & Carol M. Svec, "Computer Monitoring of Work Performance: Extending the Social Facilitation Framework to Electronic Presence," *Journal of Applied Social Psychology*, vol. 23(7), pp. 499–507 (1993)

Bergum, Bruce O., & Donald J. Lehr, "Vigilance Performance as a Function of Task and Environmental Variables," Washington, DC, Human Resources Research Office, HRRC Rep. 11 (1963)

DeCaro, Marci S., Robin D. Thomas, Neil B. Albert, & Sian L. Beilock, "Choking under Pressure: Multiple Routes to Skill Failure," *Journal of Experimental Psychology: General*, vol. 140(3), pp. 390–406 (2011)

Dedovic, Katarina, Annie Duchesne, Julie Andrews, Veronika Engert, & Jens C. Preussner, "The Brain and the Stress Axis: The Neural Correlates of Cortisol Regulation in Response to Stress," *NeuroImage*, vol. 47(3), p. 864–871 (2009)

Feinberg, Joshua M., & John R. Aiello, "The Effect of Challenge and Threat Appraisals under Evaluative Presence," *Journal of Applied Social Psychology*, vol. 40(8), pp. 2071–2104 (2010)

Finkelstein, Stacey R., & Ayelet Fishbach, "Tell Me What I Did Wrong: Experts Seek and Respond to Negative Feedback," *Journal of Consumer Research*, vol. 39(1), pp. 22–38 (2012)

"Hey, Mom. Stop Coaching from the Stands," Icemom.net, http://bit.ly/TCcrff (10/5/2009)

Kirschbaum, Clemens, Thomas Klauer, Sigrun-Heide Filipp, & Dirk Helmut Hellhammer, "Sex-Specific Effects of Social Support on Cortisol and Subjective Responses to Acute Psychological Stress," *Psychosomatic Medicine*, vol. 57(1), pp. 23–31 (1995)

Pessin, Joseph, "The Comparative Effects of Social and Mechanical Stimulation on Memorizing," *American Journal of Psychology*, vol. 45(2), pp. 263–270 (1933)

Pessin, Joseph, & Richard W. Husband, "Effects of Social Stimulation on Human Maze Learning," *Journal of Abnormal & Social Psychology*, vol. 28(2), pp. 148–154 (1933)

"Responsibilities of a Skating Parent," San Diego Figure Skating Communications, http://bit.ly/PRhRVP (u.d.)

Stein, Lyra, "Individual Differences in Task Performance," Paper Presentation at Annual Convention of American Psychological Assn., Washington, DC (2011)

Travis, Lee Edward, "The Effect of a Small Audience upon Eye-Hand Coordination," *Journal of Abnormal & Social Psychology*, vol. 20(2), pp. 142–146 (1925)

Zajonc, Robert B., "Social Facilitation," *Science, New Series*, vol. 149(3681), pp. 269–274 (1965)

3.

NASCAR Race of 1979 and NASCAR Prize Structures:

Becker, Brian E., & Mark A. Huselid, "The Incentive Effects of Tournament Compensation Systems," *Administrative Science Quarterly*, vol. 37(2), pp. 336–350 (1992)

Caldwell, Dave, "Recalling a Fight, and Titles," *New York Times*, p. SP3 (10/25/2009)

Dole, C.A., "Risk Taking in NASCAR: An Examination of Compensating Behavior and Tournament Theory in Racing," *Journal of Economics & Economic Education Research*, vol. 8(2), pp. 47–64 (2007)

"Each State's Low Temperature Record," *USA Today*, http://usat.ly/c29cPK (2006)

Frick, Bernd, & Brad R. Humphreys, "Prize Structure and Performance: Evidence from NASCAR," Working Paper 2011–12 (2011)

Groothuis, Peter A., Jana D. Groothuis, & Kurt W. Rotthoff, "Time on Camera: An Additional Explanation of NASCAR Tournaments," *Journal of Sports Economics*, vol. 12(5), pp. 561–570 (2011)

King, Michael, "Atlanta Snow Storm: Atlanta's Worst Snowfall Amounts," 11Alive.com, http://on.11alive.com/ybPwST (1/7/2011)

McGee, Ryan, "Dramatic '79 Daytona 500 Put NASCAR on the Worldwide Map," *ESPN The Magazine*, http://es.pn/PvKLru (1/14/2008)

Miller, David, "Cale Yarborough & Bobby Allison—On-Track Feuds—Inside Racing Who Wins and Loses," *Circle Track* (2000)

"NASCAR Sprint Cup Series Schedule, Results & Tickets," http://bit.ly/R06Ltk (2012)

Scolnik, Steve, "Huge Snowfall Shuts Down DC Area," *Washington Post*, http://wapo.st/ODDHfa (2/19/2008)

Smith, Marty, "Cale vs. Bobby: Fight of the Century," ESPN.com, http://es.pn/O09zMD (8/6/2010)

von Allmen, Peter, "Is the Reward System in NASCAR Efficient?" *Journal of Sports Economics*, vol. 2(1), pp. 62–79 (2001)

Prize Spreads / The Effect of Awards, Rewards on Motivation:

"2012 Tournaments," PGA Tour, http://bit.ly/EeiR (2012)

Baldwin, Alec (perf.), David Mamet (scr.), James Foley (dir.), *Glengarry Glen Ross*, New Line Cinema, Film (1992)

Bijleveld, Erik, Ruud Custers, & Henk Aarts, "Once the Money is in Sight: Distinctive Effects of Conscious and Unconscious Rewards on Task Performance," *Journal of Experimental Social Psychology*, vol. 47(4), pp. 865–869 (2011)

Bijleveld, Erik, Ruud Custers, & Henk Aarts, "Unconscious Reward Cues Increase Invested Effort, but Do Not Change Speed–Accuracy Tradeoffs," *Cognition*, vol. 115(2), pp. 330–335 (2010)

Brown, Jennifer, "Quitters Never Win: The (Adverse) Incentive Effects of Competing with Superstars," *Journal of Political Economy*, vol. 119(5), pp. 982–1013 (2011)

"The Business of Golf," *The Economist*, http://econ.st/jMOQs5 (6/9/2011)

Cason, Timothy N., William A. Masters, & Roman N. Sheremata, "Entry into Winner-Take-All and Proportional-Prize Contests: An Experimental Study," *Journal of Public Economics*, vol. 94(9–10), pp. 604–611 (2010)

"CME Group Titleholders: Full Results," LPGA, http://bit.ly/Q637Se (u.d.)

"CME Group Titleholders Info," LPGA, http://bit.ly/TCdjk6 (u.d.)

Custers, Ruud, & Henk Aarts, "The Unconscious Will: How the Pursuit of Goals Operates Outside of Conscious Awareness," *Science*, vol. 329(5987), pp. 47–50 (2010)

Deci, Edward L., Richard Koestner, & Richard M. Ryan, "A Meta-Analytic Review of Experiments Examining the Effects of Extrinsic Rewards on Intrinsic Motivation," *Psychological Bulletin*, vol. 125(6), pp. 627–668 (1999)

Ehrenberg, Ronald G., & Michael L. Bognanno, "Do Tournaments Have Incentive Effects?" *Journal of Political Economy*, vol. 98(6), pp. 1307–1324 (1990)

Franke, Jörg, "The Incentive Effects of Leveling the Playing Field—An Empirical Analysis of Amateur Golf Tournaments," *Applied Economics*, vol. 44(9), pp. 1193–1200 (2012)

Frick, Bernd, & Rob Simmons, "The Allocation of Rewards in Athletic Contests," In: Brad R. Humphreys & Dennis Ramsay Howard (Eds.), *The Business of Sports*, Westport, CT: Praeger (2008)

Harbring, Christine, & Bernd Irlenbusch, "How Many Winners are Good to Have?: On Tournaments with Sabotage," *Journal of Economic Behavior & Organization*, vol. 65(3–4), pp. 682–702 (2008)

Harbaugh, Rick, & Robert Ridlon, "Handicapping and Reverse Handicapping under Uncertainty in an All-Pay Auction," Working Paper (2010)

Höchtl, Wolfgang, Rudolf Kerschbamer, Rudi Stracke, & Uwe Sunde, "Incentives vs. Selection in Promotion Tournaments: Can a Designer Kill Two Birds with One Stone?," IZA Discussion Paper No. 5755, http://bit.ly/O09IiW (2011)

Kohn, Alfie, "Why Incentive Plans Cannot Work," *Harvard Business Review*, vol. 71(5), pp. 54–61 (Sept./Oct. 1993)

Kosfeld, Michael, & Susanne Neckermann, "Getting More Work for Nothing? Symbolic Awards and Worker Performance," *American Economic Journal: Microeconomics*, vol. 3(3), pp. 86–99 (2011)

Lallemand, Thierry, Robert Plasman, & François Rycx, "Women and Competition in Elimination Tournaments," *Journal of Sports Economics*, vol. 9(1), pp. 3–19 (2008)

Leuven, Edwin, Hessel Oosterbeek, J. H. Sonnemans, & Bas Van der Klaauw, "Incentives versus Sorting in Tournaments: Evidence from a Field Experiment," CEPR Discussion Paper No. DP6670, http://bit.ly/TCdzQ2 (2008)

Lim, Noah, Michael J. Ahearne, & Sung H. Ham, "Designing Sales Contests: Does the Prize Structure Matter?" *Journal of Marketing Research*, vol. 46(3), pp. 356–371 (2009)

"LPGA Tour Schedule," LPGA.com, http://bit.ly/PDdidk (2012)

Mantrala, Murali K., Sönke Albers, Fabio Caldierar, Ove Jensen, Kissan Joseph, Manfred Krafft, Chakravarthi Narasimhan, Srinath Gopalakrishna, Andris Zoltners, Rajiv Lal, & Leonard Lodish, "Sales Force Modeling: State of the Field and Research Agenda," *Marketing Letters*, vol. 21(3), pp. 255–272 (2010)

"Maria Hjorth Wins LPGA Tour Championship," GOLF.com, http://bit.ly/RvzM4P (12/5/2010)

Matthews, Peter Hans, Paul M. Sommers, & Francisco J. Peschiera, "Incentives and Superstars on the LPGA Tour," *Applied Economics*, vol. 39(1), pp. 87–94 (2007)

Melton, Michael, & Thomas S. Zorn, "An Empirical Test of Tournament Theory: The Senior PGA Tour," *Managerial Finance*, vol. 26(7), pp. 16–32 (2000)

Naimah, Jabali-Nash, "LPGA Tour Championship Underway," CBSNews.com, http://cbsn.ws/gxCVVR (12/4/2010)

Neckermann, Susanne, Reto Cueni, & Bruno S. Frey, "What Is an Award Worth?: An Econometric Assessment of the Impact of Awards on Employee Performance" CESInfo Working Paper (2009)

Pan, Xiaofei Sophia, & Daniel Houser, "Competition for Trophies Triggers Male Generosity," *PLoS ONE*, vol. 6(4), e18050 (2011)

Pink, Daniel H., *Drive: The Surprising Truth about What Motivates Us*, New York: Riverhead Books (2009)

Prendergast, Canice, "The Provision of Incentives in Firms," *Journal of Economic Literature*, vol. 37(1), pp. 7–63 (1999)

Szymanski, Stefan, "The Economic Design of Sporting Contests," *Journal of Economic Literature*, vol. 41, pp. 1137–1187 (2003)

Zedelius, Claire M., Harm Veling, & Henk Aarts, "Boosting or Choking—How Conscious and Unconscious Reward Processing Modulate the Active Maintenance of Goal-Relevant Information," *Consciousness & Cognition*, vol. 20(2), pp. 355–362 (2011)

PART II

The Walt Disney quote can be found in Disney, Walt, In: Dave Smith (Ed.), *The Quotable Walt Disney*, New York: Disney Enterprises/Disney Editions (2001)

Chapter 4—How the Worriers Can Beat the Warriors

1.

The Polygenic Nature of Physical Traits:

Bouchard, Claude, "Genomic Predictors of Trainability," *Experimental Physiology*, vol. 97, pp. 347–352 (2012)

Bouchard, Claude, Mark A. Sarzynski, Treva K. Rice, William E. Kraus, Timothy S. Church, Yun Ju Sung, D. C. Rao, & Tuomo Rankinen, "Genomic Predictors of the Maximal O2 Uptake Response to Standardized Exercise Training Programs," *Journal of Applied Physiology*, vol. 110(5), pp. 1160–1170 (2011)

Huang, Kenneth G., & Fiona E. Murray, "Entrepreneurial Experiments in Science Policy: Analyzing the Human Genome Project," *Research Policy*, vol. 39(5), pp. 567–582 (2010)

Rankinen, Tuomo, & Claude Bouchard, "Genetic Predictors of Exercise Training Response," *Current Cardiovascular Risk Reports*, vol. 5(4), pp. 368–372 (2011)

Tucker, Ross, "Genes and Performances: Why Some Are More Equal than Others," *The Science of Sport*, http://bit.ly/po6PT0 (8/11/2011)

Tucker, Ross, & Malcolm Collins, "What Makes Champions? A Review of the Relative Contributions of Genes and Training to Sports Success," *British Journal of Sports Medicine*, vol. 46, pp. 555–561 (2012)

Yang, Jian, Beben Benyamin, Brian P. McEvoy, Scott Gordon, Anjali K. Henders, Dale R. Nyholt, Pamela A. Madden, Andrew C. Heath, Nicholas G. Martin, Grant W. Montgomery, Michael E. Goddard, & Peter M. Visscher, "Common SNPs Explain a Large Proportion of the Heritability for Human Height," *Nature Genetics*, vol. 42(7), pp. 565–569 (2010)

2.

Julius Axelrod's Work and Other Foundational Research in COMT:

To give a more quantifiable perspective on COMT's significance in the brain: COMT enzymes are responsible for 15% of the dopamine clearance in the ventral striatum. However, COMT is responsible for clearing *60%* of the dopamine clearance within the prefrontal cortex (PFC).

Axelrod, Julius, "Banquet Speech," Nobel Banquet, Stockholm, Sweden, http://bit.ly/NFF7kY (12/10/1970)

Axelrod, Julius, "Julius Axelrod," In: Larry R. Squire (Ed.), *The History of Neuroscience in Autobiography*, vol. 1, pp. 50–78, Washington, DC: Society for Neuroscience (1996)

Axelrod, Julius, "Noradrenaline: Fate and Control of Its Biosynthesis," Nobel Lecture, http://bit.ly/PDdKIP (12/12/1970)

Connors, Barry W., & Michael A. Long, "Electrical Synapses in the Mammalian Brain," *Annual Review of Neuroscience*, vol. 27, pp. 393–418 (2004)

Diamond, Adele, "Consequences of Variations in Genes that Affect Dopamine in Prefrontal Cortex," *Cerebral Cortex*, vol. 17(supp. 1), pp. 161–170 (2007)

Hariri, Ahmad R., "The What, Where, and When of Catechol-O-Methyltransferase," *Biological Psychiatry*, vol. 70(3), pp. 214–215 (2011)

Tunbridge, Elizabeth M., "The Catechol-O-Methyltransferase Gene: Its Regulation and Polymorphisms," In: Erkki Nissinen & Alireza Minagar (Eds.), *Basic Aspects of Catechol-O-Methyltransferase and the Clinical Applications, International Review of Neurobiology*, vol. 95, pp. 7–27, New York: Academic Press (2010)

Yavich, Leonid, Markus M. Forsberg, Maria Karayiorgou, Joseph A. Gogos, & Pekka T. Mannisto, "Site-Specific Role of Catechol-O-Methyltransferase in Dopamine Overflow within Prefrontal Cortex and Dorsal Striatum," *Journal of Neuroscience*, vol. 27(38), pp. 10196–10202 (2007)

3.

Findings Relating to Genetic Variations of COMT and Cognitive Functioning:

In the scientific literature, the genetic variations of COMT are typically referred to as "met-met," "val-val," and "val-met," referring the possible allele combinations. Someone with two methionine ("met") instructions—the slower enzyme—would be "met-met." Having two valine ("val"), and thus the faster enzyme processing, would be "val-val." And val-met is naturally someone with one of each.

Barnett, J. H., P. B. Jones, T. W. Robbins, & U. Müller, "Effects of the Catechol-O-Methyltransferase Val 158Met Polymorphism on Executive Function: A Meta-Analysis of the Wisconsin Card Sort Test in Schizophrenia and Healthy Controls," *Molecular Psychiatry*, vol. 12(5), pp. 502–509 (2007)

Barnett, Jennifer H., Jon Heron, Susan M. Ring, Jean Golding, David Goldman, Ke Xu, & Peter B. Jones, "Gender-Specific Effects of the Catechol-O-Methyltransferase Val108/158Met Polymorphism on Cognitive Function in Children," *American Journal of Psychiatry*, vol. 164(1), pp. 142–149 (2007)

Blasi, Giuseppe, Venkata S. Mattay, Alessandro Bertolino, Brita Elvevåg, Joseph H. Callicott, Saumitra Das, Bhaskar S. Kolachana, Michael F. Egan, Terry E. Goldberg, & Daniel R. Weinberger, "Effect of Catechol-O-Methyltransferase Val158Met Genotype on Attentional Control," *Journal of Neuroscience*, vol. 25(20), pp. 5038–5045 (2005)

Colzato, Lorenz, Florian Waszak, Sander Nieuwenhuis, Danielle Posthuma, & Bernhard Hommel, "The Flexible Mind Is Associated with the Catechol-O-Methyltransferase (COMT) Val158Met Polymorphism: Evidence for a Role of Dopamine in the Control of Task-Switching," *Neuropsychologia*, vol. 48(9), pp. 2764–2768 (2010)

Diamond, Adele, "Biological and Social Influences on Cognitive Control Processes Dependent on Prefrontal Cortex," In: O. Braddick, J. Atkinson, & G. Innocenti (Eds.), *Progress in Brain Research*, ch. 18, pp. 319–339 (2011)

Diamond, Adele, Lisa Briand, John Fossella, & Lorrie Gehlbach, "Genetic and Neurochemical Modulation of Prefrontal Cognitive Functions in Children," *American Journal of Psychiatry*, vol. 161(1), pp. 125–132 (2004)

Doll, Bradley B., Kent E. Hutchison, & Michael J. Frank, "Dopaminergic Genes Predict Individual Differences in Susceptibility to Confirmation Bias," *Journal of Neuroscience*, vol. 31(16), pp. 6188–6198 (2011)

Farrell, Sarah M., Elizabeth M. Tunbridge, Sven Braeutigam, & Paul J. Harrison, "COMT Val158Met Genotype Determines the Direction of Cognitive Effects Produced by Catechol-O-Methyltransferase Inhibition," *Biological Psychiatry*, vol. 71(6), pp. 538–544 (2012)

Frank, Michael J., "Cross-Talk Individual Differences in Error Processing: Neural, Electrophysiological, and Genetic Components," *Cognitive, Affective & Behavioral Neuroscience*, vol. 7(4), pp. 297–308 (2007)

Frank, Michael J., Bradley B. Doll, Jen Oas-Terpstra, & Francisco Moreno, "Prefrontal and Striatal Dopaminergic Genes Predict Individual Differences in Exploration and Exploitation," *Nature Neuroscience*, vol. 12(8), pp. 1062–1068 (2009)

Herrmann, Martin J., Heidi Würflein, Theresa Schreppel, Saskia Koehler, Andreas Mühl-berger, Andreas Reif, Turhan Canli Marcel Romanos, Christian P. Jacob, Klaus-Peter Lesch, & Andreas J. Fallgatter, "Catechol-*O*-methyltransferase Val158Met Genotype Affects Neural Correlates of Aversive Stimuli Processing," *Cognitive, Affective, & Behavioral Neuroscience*, vol. 9(2), pp. 168–172 (2009)

Lachman, Herbert M., Demitri F. Papolos, Takuya Saito, Yue-Min Yu, Carol L. Szum-lanski, & Richard M. Weinshilboum, "Human Catechol-O-Methyltransferase Pharma-cogenetics: Description of a Functional Polymorphism and Its Potential Application to Neuropsychiatric Disorders," *Pharmacogenetics*, vol. 6(3), pp. 243–250 (1996)

Marco-Pallarés, Josep, Wido Nager, Ulrike M. Krämer, Toni Cunillera, Estela Càmara, David Cucureil, Rebecca Schüle, Ludger Schöls, Antoni Rodriguez-Fornells, & Thomas F. Münte, "Neurophysiological Markers of Novelty Processing Are Modulated by COMT and DRD4 Genotypes," *NeuroImage*, vol. 52(3), pp. 962–969 (2010)

Munakata, Yuko, B. J. Casey, & Adele Diamond, "Developmental Cognitive Neuroscience: Progress and Potential," *Trends in Cognitive Sciences*, vol. 8(3), pp. 122–128 (2004)

Palmatier, Meg A., A. Min Kang, & Kenneth K. Kidd, "Global Variation in the Frequencies of Functionally Different Catechol-O-Methyltransferase Alleles," *Biological Psychiatry*, vol. 46(4), pp. 557–567 (1999)

Tang, Yong, Jens. R. Nyengaard, Didima M. G. De Groot, & Hans Jørgen G. Gundersen, "Total Regional and Global Number of Synapses in the Human Brain Neocortex," *Synapse*, vol. 41(3), pp. 258–273 (2001)

Ursini, Gianluca, Valentina Bollati, Leonardo Fazio, Annamaria Porcelli, Luisa Iacovelli, Assia Catalani, Lorenzo Sinibaldi, Barbara Gelao, Raffaella Romano, Antonio Rampino, Paolo Taurisano, Marina Mancini, Annabella Di Giorgio, Teresa Popolizio, Andrea Baccarelli, Antonio De Blasi, Giuseppe Blasi, & Alessandro Bertolino, "Stress-Related Methylation of the Catechol-*O*-Methyltransferase Val158 Allele Predicts Human Pre-frontal Cognition and Activity," *Journal of Neuroscience*, vol. 31(18), pp. 6692–6698 (2011)

Findings Relating to the Valine and Met Variations of COMT and Social and Emotional Functioning:

Goldman et al. were the first to use the "Warriors" and "Worriers" analogy relating to COMT. Since then, others have adopted the terms as well. As described in the preceding section notes, the fast enzyme carrier—the "val-val"—is described as having the "Warrior" gene, while the "met-met" is described as the "Worrier." A "val-met" would be roughly in the middle of the spectrum.

Similar to the findings of the Rwandan PTSD study (done by Kolassa et al.), Brazilian researchers found a similar increased vulnerability to PTSD for the Worrier/met-met—met-mets were more sensitive to exposure to incidents of urban violence (Valente et al.).

Additionally, met-met carriers have been found to be more aggressive than val-vals; met-met adolescent girls struggle more with social relationships and end up more unsuccessfully aggressive. (See, e.g., Volavka et al., Waugh et al., and Albaugh et al.) And on the flip side—those with the Warrior gene—the val-vals—have been found to be more altruistic (Reuter et al.).

Albaugh, Matthew D., Valerie S. Harder, Robert R. Althoff, David C. Rettew, Erik A. Ehli, Timea Lengyel-Nelson, Gareth E. Davies, Lynsay Ayer, Julie Sulman, Catherine Stanger, & James J. Hudziak, "COMT Val158Met Genotype as a Risk Factor for Prob-lem Behaviors in Youth," *Journal of the American Academy of Child & Adolescent Psychiatry*, vol. 49(8), pp. 841–849 (2010)

Bishop, Sonia J., Jonathan D. Cohen, John Fossella, B. J. Casey, & Martha J. Farah, "COMT Genotype Influences Prefrontal Response to Emotional Distraction," *Cognitive, Affective & Behavioral Neuroscience*, vol. 6(1), pp. 62–70 (2006)

Caspi, Avshalom, Terrie E. Moffitt, Mary Cannon, Joseph McClay, Robin Murray, Hona-Lee Harrington, Alan Taylor, Louise Arseneault, Ben Williams, Antony Braithwaite, Richie Poulton, & Ian W. Craig, "Moderation of the Effect of Adolescent-Onset Cannabis Use on Adult Psychosis by a Functional Polymorphism in the Catechol-O-Methyltransferase Gene: Longitudinal Evidence of a Gene X Environment Interaction," *Biological Psychiatry*, vol. 57(10), pp. 1117–1127 (2005)

Egan, Michael F., Terry E. Goldberg, Bhaskar S. Kolachana, Joseph H. Callicott, Chiara M. Mazzanti, Richard E. Straub, David Goldman, & Daniel R. Weinberger, "Effect of COMT Val108/158 Met Genotype on Frontal Lobe Function and Risk for Schizophrenia," *Proceedings of the National Academy of Sciences*, vol. 98(12), pp. 6917–6922 (2001)

Goldman, David, Gabor Oroszi, & Francesca Ducci, "The Genetics of Addiction: Uncovering the Genes," *Nature Reviews Genetics*, vol. 6, pp. 521–532 (2005)

Kolassa, Iris-Tatjana, Verena Ertl, Cindy Eckart, Lamaro P. Onyut, Stephan Kolassa, & Thomas Elbert, "Spontaneous Remission from PTSD Depends on the Number of Traumatic Event Types Experienced," *Psychological Trauma: Theory, Research, Practice, & Policy 2*, vol. 3, pp. 169–174 (2010)

Kolassa, Iris-Tatjana, Stephan Kolassa, Verena Ertl, Andreas Papassotiropoulos, & Dominique J.-F. De Quervain, "The Risk of Posttraumatic Stress Disorder after Trauma Depends on Traumatic Load and the Catechol-O-Methyltransferase Val158Met Polymorphism," *Biological Psychiatry*, vol. 67(4), pp. 304–308 (2010)

Lachman, Herbert, "Does COMT Val158Met Affect Behavioral Phenotypes: Yes, No, Maybe?," *Neuropsychopharmacology*, vol. 33(13), pp. 3027–3029 (2008)

Lonsdorf, Tina B., Christian Rück, Jan Bergström, Gerhard Andersson, Arne Öhman, Nils Lindefors, & Martin Schalling, "The COMT Val158Met Polymorphism Is Associated with Symptom Relief During Exposure-Based Cognitive-Behavioral Treatment in Panic Disorder" *BMC Psychiatry*, vol. 10, pp. 99 et seq. (2010)

Reuter, Martin, Clemens Frenzel, Nora T. Walter, & Sebastian Markett, "Investigating the Genetic Basis of Altruism: The Role of the COMT Val158Met Polymorphism," *Social Cognitive & Affective Neuroscience*, vol. 6(5), pp. 662–668 (2011)

Rujescu, Dan, Ina Giegling, Anton Gietl, Annette M. Hartmann, & Hans-Jürgen Möller, "A Functional Single Nucleotide Polymorphism (V158M) in the COMT Gene is Associated with Aggressive Personality Traits," *Biological Psychiatry*, vol. 54(1), pp. 34–39 (2003)

Stein, Dan J., Timothy K. Newman, Jonathan Savitz, & Rajkumar Ramesar, "Warriors versus Worriers: The Role of COMT Gene Variants," *CNS Spectrums / Pearls in Clinical Neuroscience*, vol. 11(10), pp. 745–748 (2006)

Tiihonen, J., T. Hallikainen, H. Lachman, T. Saito, J. Volavka, J. Kauhanen, J. T. Salonen, O-P Ryynänen, M. Koulu, M. K. Karvonen, T. Phojalainen, E. Syvälahti, & J. Hietala, "Association between the Functional Variant of the Catechol-O-Methyltransferase (COMT) Gene and Type 1 Alcoholism," *Molecular Psychiatry*, vol. 4, pp. 286–289 (1999)

Valente, Nina Leão Marques, Homero Vallada, Quirino Cordeiro, Rodrigo Affonseca Bressan, Sergio Baxter Andreoli, Jair Jesus Mari, & Marcelo Feijó Mello, "Catechol-O-Methyltransferase (COMT) Val158Met Polymorphism as a Risk Factor for PTSD After Urban Violence," *Journal of Molecular Neuroscience*, vol. 43(3), pp. 516–523 (2011)

Volavka, Jan, Robert Bilder, & Karen Nolan, "Catecholamines and Aggression: The Role of COMT and MAO Polymorphisms," *Annals of the New York Academy of Sciences*, vol. 1036, pp. 393–398 (2004)

Waugh, Christian E., Karen F. Dearing, Jutta Joormann, & Ian H. Gotlib, "Association between the Catechol-O-Methyltransferase Val158Met Polymorphism and Self-Perceived Social Acceptance in Adolescent Girls," *Journal of Child and Adolescent Psychopharmacology*, vol. 19(4), pp. 395–401 (2009)

Wichers, Marieke, Mari Aguilera, Gunter Kenis, Lydia Krabbendam, Inez Myin-Germeys, Nele Jacobs, Frenk Peeters, Catherine Derom, Robert Vlietinck, Ron Mengelers, Philippe Delespaul, & Jim van Os, "The Catechol-O-Methyl Transferase Val158Met Polymorphism and Experience of Reward in the Flow of Daily Life," *Neuropsychopharmacology*, vol. 33(13), pp. 3030–3036 (2008)

4.

COMT's Effects on Learning / Succeeding in Stressful Conditions:
See also the earlier citations relating to COMT and cognitive function.

Alexander, Nina, Roman Osinsky, Eva Mueller, Anja Schmitz, Sarah Guenthert, Yvonne Kuepper, & Juergen Hennig, "Genetic Variants within the Dopaminergic System Interact to Modulate Endocrine Stress Reactivity and Recovery," *Behavioural Brain Research*, vol. 216(1), pp. 53–58 (2011)

Alter, Adam L., Joshua Aronson, John M. Darley, Cordaro Rodriguez, & Diane N. Ruble, "Rising to the Threat: Reducing Stereotype Threat by Reframing the Threat as a Challenge," *Journal of Experimental Social Psychology*, vol. 46(1), pp. 166–171 (2010)

Aronson, Joshua, Correspondence with Author (2012)

Blair, Clancy, & Adele Diamond, "Biological Processes in Prevention and Intervention: The Promotion of Self-Regulation as a Means of Preventing School Failure," *Development & Psychopathology*, vol. 20(3), pp. 899–911 (2008)

Chang, Chun-Yen, Correspondence with Author (2012)

Enoch, M.-A., J. F. Waheed, C. R. Harris, B. Albaugh, & D. Goldman, "COMT Val158Met and Cognition: Main Effects and Interaction with Educational Attainment," *Genes, Brain & Behavior*, vol. 8(1), pp. 36–42 (2009)

Frank, Michael J., & John A. Fosella, "Neurogenetics and Pharmacology of Learning, Motivation, and Cognition," *Neuropsychopharmacology*, vol. 36, pp. 133–152 (2011)

Frank, Michael J., Ahmed A. Moustafa, Heather M. Haughey, Tim Curran, & Kent E. Hutchinson, "Genetic Triple Dissociation Reveals Multiple Roles for Dopamine in Reinforcement Learning," *Proceedings of the National Academy of Sciences*, vol. 104(41), pp. 16311–16316 (2007)

Kennedy, Q., J. L. Taylor, A. Noda, M. Adamson, G. M. Murphy, J. M. Zeitzer, & J. A. Yesavage, "The Roles of COMT Val158Met Status and Aviation Expertise in Flight Simulator Performance and Cognitive Ability," *Behavior Genetics*, vol. 41(5), pp. 700–708 (2011)

Kennedy, Quinn, Interview with Author (2011)

Krugel, Lea K., Guido Biele, Peter N. C. Mohr, Shu-Chen Li, & Hauke R. Heekeren, "Genetic Variation in Dopaminergic Neuromodulation Influences the Ability to Rapidly and Flexibly Adapt Decisions," *Proceedings of the National Academy of Sciences*, vol. 106(42), pp. 17951–17956 (2009)

Malhotra, Anil K., Lisa J. Kestler, Chiara Mazzanti, John A. Bates, Terry Goldberg, & David Goldman, "A Functional Polymorphism in the COMT Gene and Performance on a Test of Prefrontal Cognition," *American Journal of Psychiatry*, vol. 159(4), pp. 652–654 (2002)

Yeh, Ting-Kuang, Chun-Yen Chang, Chung-Yi Hu, Ting-Chi Yeh, & Ming-Yeh Lin, "Association of Catechol-O-Methyltransferase (COMT) Polymorphism and Academic Achievement in a Chinese Cohort," *Brain & Cognition*, vol. 71(3), pp. 300–305 (2009)

5.

Estrogen's Effect on COMT / Gender Differences in Response to Stress:

For additional information on gender differences in stress, see references for Chapter 9.

Brizendine, Louann, *The Female Brain*, New York: Three Rivers Press (2006)

Chen, Jingshan, Barbara K. Lipska, Nader Halim, Quang D. Ma, Mitsuyuki Matsumoto, Samer Melhem, Bhaskar S. Kolachana, Thomas M. Hyde, Mary M. Herman, Jose Apud, Michael F. Egan, Joel E. Kleinman, & Daniel R. Weinberger, "Functional Analysis of Genetic Variation in Catechol-O-Methyltransferase (COMT): Effects on mRNA, Protein, and Enzyme Activity in Postmortem Human Brain," *American Journal of Human Genetics*, vol. 75(5), pp. 807–821 (2004)

Cohn, Cal R., & Julius Axelrod, "The Effect of Estradiol on Catechol-O-Methyltransferase Activity in Rat Liver," *Life Sciences*, vol. 10(1), pp. 1351–1354 (1971)

Comasco, Erika, Charlotte Hellgren, & Inger Sundström-Poromaa, "Influence of Catechol-O-Methyltransferase Val158Met Polymorphism on Startle Response in the Presence of High Estradiol Levels," *European Neuropsychopharmacology* (in press) (2012)

Dedovic, Katarina, Mehereen Wadiwalla, Veronika Engert, & Jens C. Pruessner, "The Role of Sex and Gender Socialization in Stress Reactivity," *Developmental Psychology*, vol. 45(1), pp. 45–55 (2009)

Desbonnet, Lieve, Oma Tighe, Maria Karayiorgou, Joseph A. Gogos, John L. Waddington, & Colm M.P. O'Tuathaigh, "Physiological and Behavioural Responsivity to Stress and Anxiogenic Stimuli in COMT-Deficient Mice," *Behavioural Brain Research*, vol. 228(2), pp. 351–358 (2012)

Diamond, Adele, "Developmental Change in, and Environmental Modulation of, Cognitive Control: Differences by Gender and Genetics," Paper Presentation at U.C. Berkeley Conference on the Developing Brain, Berkeley, CA (2009)

Diamond, Adele, Interview with Authors (2011)

Harrison, Paul J., & Elizabeth M. Tunbridge, "Catechol-O-Methyltransferase (COMT): A Gene Contributing to Sex Differences in Brain Function, and to Sexual Dimorphism in the Predisposition to Psychiatric Disorders," *Neuropsychopharmacology*, vol. 33(13), pp. 3037–3045 (2008)

Jacobs, Emily, & Mark D'Esposito, "Estrogen Shapes Dopamine-Dependent Cognitive Processes: Implications for Women's Health," *Journal of Neuroscience*, vol. 31(14), pp. 5286–5293 (2011)

Lighthall, N. R., M. Sakaki, S. Vasunilashorn, L. Nga, M. A. Gorlick, S. Somayajula, & M. Mather, "Stress Effects on Risk- and Reward-Related Decision Processing are Modulated by Sex," Paper Presentation at Annual Convention for Assn. for Psychological Science, Boston (2010)

Lighthall, Nichole R., & Mara Mather, "Risk and Reward Are Processed Differently in Decisions Made under Stress," *Current Directions in Psychological Science*, vol. 21(1), pp. 36–41 (2012)

Lighthall, Nichole R., Mara Mather, & Marissa A. Gorlick, "Acute Stress Increases Sex Differences in Risk Seeking in the Balloon Analogue Risk Task," *PLoS ONE*, vol. 4(7), e6002, doi:10.1371/journal.pone.0006002 (2009)

Lighthall, Nichole R., Michiko Sakaki, Sarinnapha Vasunilashorn, Lin Nga, Sangeetha Somayajula, Eric Y. Chen, Nicole Samii, & Mara Mather, "Gender Differences in Reward-Related Processing under Stress," *Social Cognitive & Affective Neuroscience*, vol. 7(4), pp. 476–484 (2012)

Lin, Chin-Yo, Anders Ström, Vinsensius Berlian Vega, Say Li Kong, Ai Li Yeo, Jane S. Thomsen, Wan Ching Chan, Balraj Doray, Dhinoth K. Bangarusamy, Adaikalavan Ramasamy, Liza A. Vergara, Suisheng Tang, Allen Chong, Vladimir B. Bajic, Lance D. Miller, Jan-Åke Gustafsson, & Edison T. Liu, "Discovery of Estrogen Receptor α Target Genes and Response Elements in Breast Tumor Cells," *Genome Biology*, vol. 5(9), pp. R66 et al. (2004)

Mather, M., N. R. Lighthall, L. Nga, L, & M. A. Gorlick, "Sex Differences in How Stress Affects Brain Activity during Face Viewing," *NeuroReport*, vol. 21(14), pp. 933–937 (2010)

Smeets, Tom, Isabel Dziobek, & Oliver T. Wolf, "Social Cognition under Stress: Differential Effects of Stress-Induced Cortisol Elevations in Healthy Young Men and Women," *Hormones & Behavior*, vol. 55(4), pp. 507–513 (2009)

Tang, S., H. Han, & V. B. Bajic, "ERGDB: Estrogen Responsive Genes Database," *Nucleic Acids Research*, vol. 32, pp. D533–D536 (2004)

Worda, C., M. O. Sator, C. Schneeberger, T. Jantschev, K. Ferlitsch, & J. C. Huber, "Influence of the *Catechol-O-Methyltransferase* (COMT) Codon 158 Polymorphism on Estrogen Levels in Women," *Human Reproduction*, vol. 18(2), pp. 262–266 (2003)

Anson Dorrance's Development of the UNC Soccer Teams:

Crothers, Tim, *The Man Watching: Anson Dorrance and the University of North Carolina Women's Soccer Dynasty*, New York: Thomas Dunne Books (2010)

DiCicco, Tony, Colleen Hacker, & Charles Salzberg, *Catch Them Being Good: Everything You Need to Know to Successfully Coach Girls*, New York: Penguin Books (2003)

Dorrance, Anson, Interview with Author (2012)

Dorrance, Anson, & Gloria Averbuch, *The Vision of a Champion: Advice and Inspiration from the World's Most Successful Women's Soccer Coach*, Ann Arbor, MI: Huron River Press (2005)

Price, S. L., "Anson Dorrance," *Sports Illustrated*, pp. 86–125 (12/7/1998)

Wahl, Grant, "Dateline: Greensboro, N.C., December 7, 1997," *Sports Illustrated*, p. 34 (12/15/1997)

Chapter 5—Even Odds: Why Women Need Them and Men Don't

1.
Male and Female Participation in Political Office:

Adams, Brian E., & Ronnee Schreiber, "Gender, Campaign Finance, and Electoral Success in Municipal Elections," *Journal of Urban Affairs*, vol. 33(1), pp. 83–97 (2011)

Anzia, Sarah F., & Christopher R. Berry, "The Jackie (and Jill) Robinson Effect: Why Do Congresswomen Outperform Congressmen?" *American Journal of Political Science*, vol. 55(3), pp. 478–493 (2011)

"Beck Again Calls Sen. Landrieu a Prostitute: 'So We Know You're Hookin', but You're Just Not Cheap,'" *Media Matters*, http://bit.ly/9oqkRW (11/23/2009)

"Beck on Landrieu: "We're with a High-Class Prostitute," *Media Matters*, http://bit.ly/6NyzzV (11/23/2009)

Begala, Paul, Interview with Author (2011)

Begala, Paul, "A Warrior on a Mission in Rush Limbaugh's Home District," *Huffington Post*, http://huff.to/2Z3RaS (11/10/2009)

Bureau of Labor Statistics, U.S. Department of Labor, Occupational Outlook Handbook, 2012–13 Edition, Computer Programmers, http://1.usa.gov/Lc3sCX

Bureau of Labor Statistics, U.S. Department of Labor, Occupational Outlook Handbook, 2012–13 Edition, Data for Occupations Not Covered in Detail, http://1.usa.gov/PRj1AF

Catanese, David, "GOP Poll: Emerson Dominant," *Politico*, http://bit.ly/T0q0Yt (4/22/2010)

"City Councils," National League of Cities, http://bit.ly/KqWUNS (u.d.)

Conway, M. Margaret, "Women's Political Participation at the State and Local Level in the United States," *Political Science & Politics*, vol. 37(1), pp. 60–61 (2004)

Deckman, Melissa, "Gender Differences in the Decision to Run for School Board," *American Politics Research*, vol. 35(4), pp. 541–563 (2007)

"Echoing Beck, Limbaugh Claims Landrieu 'May Be the Most Expensive Prostitute in the History of Prostitution,'" *Media Matters*, http://bit.ly/PDenSA (11/23/2009)

Eller, Jeffrey, Interview with Author (2011)

"Fast Facts," Center for American Women and Politics, http://bit.ly/hKFGRb (2012)

Fox, Richard L., & Jennifer L. Lawless, "Entering the Arena? Gender and the Decision to Run for Office," *American Journal of Political Science*, vol. 48(2), pp. 264–280 (2004)

Fox, Richard L., & Jennifer L. Lawless, "To Run or Not to Run for Office: Explaining Nascent Political Ambition," *American Journal of Political Science*, vol. 49(3), pp. 642–659 (2005)

"Full and Part-Time Legislators," National Conference of State Legislatures, http://bit.ly/4n2oBC (2009)

Fulton, Sarah, Correspondence with Author (2011)

Fulton, Sarah, Interview with Author (2011)

Fulton, Sarah A., "Running Backwards and in High Heels: The Gendered Quality Gap and Incumbent Electoral Success," *Political Research Quarterly*, vol. 65(2), pp. 303–314 (2012)

Fulton, Sarah A., Cherie D. Maestas, L. Sandy Maisel, & Walter J. Stone, "The Sense of a Woman: Gender, Ambition, and the Decision to Run for Congress," *Political Research Quarterly*, vol. 59(2), pp. 235–248 (2006)

Hess, Frederick M., & Olivia Meeks, "School Boards Circa 2010: Governance in the Accountability Era," National School Boards Assn., http://bit.ly/RvAb7a (2011)

"I'm No Lady; I'm a Member of Congress," Office of History and Preservation, Office of the Clerk, Women in Congress, 1917–2006, Washington, DC: U.S. Government Printing Office, http://1.usa.gov/O9nvZ (2007)

"Jeannette Rankin," Office of History and Preservation, Office of the Clerk, Women in Congress, 1917–2006, Washington, DC: U.S. Government Printing Office, http://1.usa.gov/O9nvZ (2007)

Jensen, Jennifer M., & Wendy L. Martinek, "The Effects of Race and Gender on the Judicial Ambitions of State Trial Court Judges," *Political Research Quarterly*, vol. 62(2), pp. 379–392 (2009)

Keller, Rudi, "Emerson, Sowers Reach $1 Million in Campaign Funding," *Southeast Missourian*, http://bit.ly/ODFCQV (7/18/2010)

Keller, Rudi, "Sowers Shrinking Fundraising Gap with Emerson," *Southeast Missourian*, http://bit.ly/dkQxOx (4/18/2010)

Krupnick, Ellie, & Jessica Misener, "Hillary Clinton Wore a Scrunchie AGAIN," *Huffington Post*, http://huff.to/uUzzYr (10/25/2011)

Lake, Celinda, "Gender Gap in Politics Is Invite for More to Run," *Women's E-News*, http://bit.ly/cwAGNw (3/4/2009)

Lawless, Jennifer, Interview with Author (2011)

Lawless, Jennifer L., & Richard L. Fox, *It Still Takes a Candidate: Why Women Don't Run for Office* (Rev. Ed.), New York: Cambridge University Press (2010)

Lawless, Jennifer L., & Richard L. Fox, "Men Rule: The Continued Under-Representation of Women in U.S. Politics," Washington, DC: Women & Politics Institute (2012)

Lawless, Jennifer L., & Richard L. Fox, "Why Are Women Still Not Running for Public Office?" *Issues in Governance*, no. 16, pp. 1–20 (2008)

Linthicum, Kate, "When It's Time to Run for Office, Fewer Women Stand Up," *Los Angeles Times*, http://lat.ms/RvAm2k (5/23/2011)

Maestas, Cherie D., Sarah Fulton, Sandy Maisel, & Walter J. Stone, "When to Risk It? Institutions, Ambitions, and the Decision to Run for the US House," *American Political Science Review*, vol. 100(2), pp. 195–208 (2006)

"Map: States Grant the Right to Vote," National Constitution Center, http://bit.ly/kHY-CjZ (u.d.)

"Men or Women: Who's the Better Leader?" Pew Center Publications, http://bit.ly/3U7XQO (8/25/2008)

Morales, Gilda, Center for American Women and Politics, Correspondence with Author (2012)

Moyers, Scott, "Poll Says Emerson Beating Sowers," *Southeast Missourian*, http://bit.ly/aijnND (9/23/2010)

Palmer, Barbara, & Dennis Simon, "Political Ambition and Women in the U.S. House of Representatives, 1916–2000," *Political Research Quarterly*, vol. 56(2), pp. 127–138 (2003)

Pesta, Abigail, "Why Kirsten Gillibrand Wants You to Run for Office," *Marie Claire*, http://bit.ly/nyWtwo (Jul. 2011) (reporting on significance of Emily's List in getting her elected)

"Savage Dubs Sen. Snowe 'Jezebel' for Finance Committee Health Care Vote," *Media Matters*, http://bit.ly/OMWCTa (10/13/2009)

Smith, Adrienne R., Beth Reingold, & Michael Leo Owens, "The Political Determinants of Women's Descriptive Representation in Cities," *Political Research Quarterly*, vol. 65(2), pp. 315–329 (2012)

SowersforCongress.com

Taylor, Paul, Rich Morin, D'Vera Cohn, April Clark, & Wendy Wang, "A Paradox in Public Attitudes," Pew Social Trends, http://bit.ly/O7OwDh (2008)

Tumulty, Karen, "Twenty Years On, 'Year of the Woman' Fades," *Washington Post*, http://wapo.st/H2A5y3 (3/21/2012)

"U.S. House Missouri, District 8," MSNBC.com, http://on-msn.com/OMWJ19 (8/31/2012)

Williams, Margaret S., "Ambition, Gender, and the Judiciary," *Political Research Quarterly*, vol. 61(1), pp. 68–78 (2008)

2.

Gender Differences in Competitiveness on Context:

Adler, Amy B., Ann H. Huffman, Paul D. Bliese, & Carl Andrew Castro, "The Impact of Deployment Length and Experience on the Well-Being of Male and Female Soldiers," *Journal of Occupational Health Psychology*, vol. 10(2), pp. 121–137 (2005)

Bajtelsmit, Vickie L., & Jack L. VanDernei, "Risk Aversion and Pension Investment Choices," In: Michael S. Gordon, Olivia S. Mitchell, & Marc M. Twinney (Eds.), *Positioning Pensions for the Twenty-First Century*, ch. 4, pp. 47–66, Philadelphia: University of Pennsylvania Press (1997)

Bertrand, Marianne, "New Perspectives on Gender," *Handbook of Labor Economics*, ch. 17, vol. 4(B), pp. 1543–1590 (2011)

Blanes i Vidal, Jordi, & Mareike Nossol, "Evidence from Personnel Records," *Management Science*, vol. 57(10), pp. 1721–1735 (2011)

Booth, Alison L., & Patrick Nolen, "Choosing to Compete: How Different Are Girls and Boys?" *Journal of Economic Behavior & Organization*, vol. 81(2), pp. 542–555 (2012)

Booth, Alison L., & Patrick Nolen, "Gender Difference in Risk Behaviour: Does Nurture Matter?" *Economic Journal*, vol. 122(558), pp. F56–F78 (2012)

Brownlow, Shelia, Rebecca Whitener, & Janet M. Rupert, "'I'll Take Gender Differences for $1000!' Domain-Specific Intellectual Success on 'Jeopardy,'" *Sex Roles*, vol. 38(314), pp. 269-285 (1998)

Cadsby, Charles Bram, Maroš Serváa, & Fei Song, "How Competitive Are Female Professionals? A Tale of Identity Conflict," http://d.doiorg/102139/ssrn1907727 (2012)

Cárdenas, Juan-Camilo, Anna Dreber, Emma von Essen, & Eva Ranehill, "Gender Differences in Competitiveness and Risk Taking: Comparing Children in Colombia and Sweden," *Journal of Economic Behavior & Organization*, vol. 83(1), pp. 11–23 (2012)

Casari, Marco, John C. Ham, & John H. Kagel, "Selection Bias, Demographic Effects, and Ability Effects in Common Value Auction Experiments," *American Economic Review*, vol. 97(4), pp. 1278–1304 (2007)

Cotton, Christopher, Frank McIntyre, & Joseph Price, "Gender Differences in Competition: A Theoretical Assessment of the Evidence," *The Selected Works of Christopher Cotton*, http://bit.ly/Q654OM (2011)

Dargnies, Marie-Pierre, "Men Too Sometimes Shy Away from Competition: The Case of Team Competition," http://d.doiorg/102139/ssrn1814989 (2011)

Dreber, Anna, Interview with Author (2011)

Dreber, Anna, Christer Gerdes, & Patrik Gränsmark, "Beauty Queens and Battling Knights: Risk Taking and Attractiveness in Chess," IZA Discussion Paper No. 5314, Institute for the Study of Labor (2010)

Dreber, Anna, Emma von Essen, & Eva Ranehill, "Outrunning the Gender Gap—Boys and Girls Compete Equally," *Experimental Economics*, vol. 14(4), pp. 567–582 (2011)

Eckel, Catherine C., & Philip J. Grossman, "Men, Women and Risk Aversion: Experimental Evidence," In: Charles R. Plott & Vernon L. Smith (Eds.). *Handbook of Experimental Economics Results*, ch. 113, pp. 1061–1073 (2008)

Franken, Robert E., & Douglas J. Brown, "Why Do People Like Competition? The Motivation for Winning, Putting Forth Effort, Improving One's Performance, Performing Well, Being Instrumental, and Expressing Forceful/Aggressive Behavior," *Personality & Individual Differences*, vol. 19(2), pp. 175–184 (1995)

Frick, Bernd, "Gender Differences in Competitiveness: Empirical Evidence from Professional Distance Running," *Labour Economics*, vol. 18(3), pp. 389–398 (2011)

Frick, Bernd, "Gender Differences in Competitive Orientations: Empirical Evidence from Ultramarathon Running," *Journal of Sports Economics*, vol. 12(3), pp. 317–340 (2011)

Garza, R. T., & J. E. Borchert, "Maintaining Social Identity in a Mixed-Gender Setting: Minority/Majority Status and Cooperative/Competitive Feedback," *Sex Roles: A Journal of Research*, vol. 22(11/12), pp. 679–691 (1990)

Gerdes, Christer, & Patrik Gränsmark, "Strategic Behavior across Gender: A Comparison of Female and Male Expert Chess Players," *Labor Economics*, vol. 17(5), pp.766–775 (2010)

Gervais, S., & T. Odean, "Learning to Be Overconfident," *Review of Financial Studies*, vol. 14(1), pp. 1–27 (2001)

Gill, David, & Victoria Prowse, "Gender Differences and Dynamics in Competition: The Role of Luck," MPRA Paper No. 38220 (2012)

Gneezy, Uri, Kenneth L. Leonard, & John A. List, "Gender Differences in Competition: Evidence from a Matrilineal and a Patriarchal Society," *Econometrica*, vol. 77(5), pp. 1637–1664 (2009)

Gneezy, Uri, Muriel Niederle, & Aldo Rustichini, "Performance in Competitive Environments: Gender Differences," *Quarterly Journal of Economics*, vol. 118(3), pp. 1049–1074 (2003)

Gneezy, Uri, & Aldo Rustichini, "Gender and Competition at a Young Age," *American Economic Review Papers & Proceedings*, vol. 94(2), pp. 377–81 (2004)

Gränsmark, Patrik, Correspondence with Author (2011)

Gränsmark, Patrik, "Strategic Learning in Repeated Chess Games," *Essays on Economic Behavior, Gender and Strategic Learning*, Stockholm: The Swedish Institute for Social Research (SOFI), Stockholm University (2010)

Günther, Christina, Neslihan Arslan Ekinci, Christiane Schwieren, & Martin Strobel, "Women Can't Jump?—An Experiment on Competitive Attitudes and Stereotype Threat," *Journal of Economic Behavior & Organization*, vol. 75(3), pp. 395–401 (2010)

Heffner, Tonia, Len White, & Robert Kilchullen, "Screening for Attrition and Performance with Non-Cognitive Measures," Presentation for Military Operations Research Society Workshop, http://1.usa.gov/O7OOdl (2010)

Hoffman, Moshe, Uri Gneezy, & John A. List, "Nurture Affects Gender Differences in Spatial Abilities," *Proceedings of the National Academy of Sciences*, vol. 108(36), pp. 14786–14788 (2011)

Houser, Daniel, "Rewarding Generosity," Paper Presentation at Interdisciplinary Center for Economic Science, Fairfax, VA (2010)

Huffman, Ann H., Amy B. Adler, & Carl Andrew Castro, "The Impact of Deployment History on the Well-Being of Military Personnel," Walter Reed Hospital–Europe (1999)

Johnson, Daniel K. N. Johnson, & Tracy Gleason, "Who REALLY Wants to be a Millionaire? Gender Differences in Game Show Contestant Behavior under Risk," *Social Science Quarterly*, vol. 90(20), pp. 243-261 (2009) (finding that winning women won about $10,000 less than winning men)

Johnson, J. E. V., & P. L. Powell, "Decision Making, Risk and Gender: Are Managers Different?," *British Journal of Management*, vol. 5(2), pp. 123–138 (2005)

Kling, Jeffrey R., Jens Ludwig, & Lawrence F. Katz, "Neighborhood Effects of Crime for Female and Male Youth: Evidence from a Randomized Housing Voucher Experiment," *Quarterly Journal of Economics*, vol. 120(1), pp. 87–130 (2005)

Lavy, Victor, "Gender Differences in Market Competitiveness in a Real Workplace: Evidence from Performance-Based Pay Tournaments among Teachers," Working Paper No. 14338, National Bureau of Economic Research, Cambridge, MA (2008)

Lindquist, Sjögren, Gabriella, & Jenny Säve-Söderbergh, "'Girls Will Be Girls', Especially among Boys: Risk-Taking in the 'Daily Double' on Jeopardy," *Economic Letters*, vol. 112(2), pp. 158–160 (2011)

MacLean, Vicky M., & Carolyn Rozier, "From Sport Culture to the Social World of the 'Good PT': Masculinities and the Career Development of Physical Therapists," *Men & Masculinity*, vol. 11(3), pp. 286–306 (2009)

Matsa, David A., & Amalia R. Miller, "A Female Style in Corporate Leadership? Evidence from Quotas," http://ssrn.com/abstract=1636047 (2011)

Müller, Helge, Christoph Schumacher, & Eberhard Feess, "Gender Behavior in Betting Markets," Beiträge zur Jahrestagung des Vereins für Socialpolitik 2011: Die Ordnung der Welfwirtschaft: Lektionen aus der Krise-Session: Gender Economics, No. D13-V2, http://hdlhandlenet/10419/48697 (2011)

Niederle, Muriel, Interview with Author (2011)

Niederle, Muriel, & Lise Vesterlund, "Do Women Shy Away From Competition? Do Men Compete Too Much?," *Quarterly Journal of Economics*, vol. 122(3), pp. 1067–1101 (2007)

Niederle, Muriel, & Lise Vesterlund, "Explaining the Gender Gap in Math Test Scores: The Role of Competition," *Journal of Economic Perspectives*, vol. 24(2), pp. 129–144 (2010)

Niederle, Muriel, & Lise Vesterlund, "Gender and Competition," *Annual Review of Economics*, vol. 3, pp. 601–630 (2011)

Niederle, Muriel, & Lise Vesterlund, "Gender Differences in Competition," *Negotiation Journal*, vol. 24(4), pp. 447–463 (2008)

Reback, Charles, & Kristin Stowe, "Unnatural Experiments: The Case of the Television Game Show," *Applied Economic Letters*, vol. 18(10), pp. 919-923 (2011) (finding that winning women leave *Jeopardy!* with about $1,000 less than the men, but arguing this could be because the women aren't as strong contestants)

Reuben, Ernesto, Pedro Rey-Biel, Paolo Sapienza, & Luigi Zingales, "The Emergence of Male Leadership in Competitive Environments," *Journal of Economic Behavior & Organization*, vol. 83(1), pp. 111–117 (2012)

Sasson-Levy, Orna, & Sarit Amram-Katz, "Gender Integration in Israeli Officer Training: Degendering and Regendering the Military," *Signs*, vol. 33(1), pp. 105–133 (2007)

Shurchkov, Olga, "Under Pressure: Gender Differences in Output Quality and Quantity under Competition and Time Constraints," *Journal of the European Economic Association*, vol. 10(5), pp. 1189-1213 (2012)

Sutter, Matthias, & Daniela Rützler, "Gender Differences in Competition Emerge Early in Life," IZA Discussion Paper No. 5015, http://ssrncom/abstract=1631480 (2010)

3.

Gender Differences in Responding to Competitive Academic Environments:

Angrist, Joshua, & Victor Lavy, "The Effects of High Stakes High School Achievement Awards: Evidence from a Randomized Trial," *American Economic Review*, vol. 99(4), pp. 1384–1414 (2009)

Barankay, Iwan, "Gender Differences in Productivity Responses to Performance Rankings: Evidence from a Randomized Workplace Experiment," Working Paper, Wharton School of Business, University of Pennsylvania (2011)

Cotton, Christopher, Frank McIntyre, & Joseph Price, "The Gender Gap Cracks under Pressure: A Detailed Look at Male and Female Performance Differences during Competitions" (2010)

Deming, David J., Justine S. Hastings, Thomas Kane, & Douglas Staiger, "School Choice and College Attendance: Evidence from Randomized Lotteries," DHKS Draft (2009)

Deming, David J., Justine S. Hastings, Thomas J. Kane, & Douglas O. Staiger, "School Choice, School Quality, and Postsecondary Attainment," *American Economic Review* (forthcoming) (July 2012)

Dobbie, Will, & Ronald G. Fryer Jr., "Are High-Quality Schools Enough to Increase Achievement Among the Poor? Evidence from the Harlem Children's Zone," *American Economic Journal: Applied Economics*, vol. 3(3), pp. 158–187 (2011)

Guggenheim, Davis (dir.), *Waiting for Superman*, Participant Productions / Walden Media / Paramount, Film (2010)

Han, Li, & Tao Li, "The Gender Difference of Peer Influence in Higher Education," *Economics of Education Review*, vol. 28(1), pp. 129–134 (2009) (quoting their conclusion that female roommates serve as a "shining star")

Hastings, Justine S., Thomas Kane, & Douglas O. Staiger, "Gender and Performance: Evidence from School Assignment by Randomized Lottery," *American Economic Review*, vol. 96(2), pp. 232–236 (2006b)

Hastings, Justine S., Thomas Kane, & Douglas O. Staiger, "Gender, Performance and Preferences: Do Girls and Boys Respond Differently to School Environment? Evidence from School Assignment by Randomized Lottery," *American Economic Review Papers & Proceedings*, vol. 96(2), pp. 232–236 (2006)

Jackson, C. Kirabo, "Do Students Benefit from Attending Better Schools? Evidence from Rule-Based Student Assignments in Trinidad and Tobago," *Economic Journal*, vol. 120(549), pp. 1399–1429 (2010)

Jackson, C. Kirabo, Interview with Author (2011)

Jackson, C. Kirabo, "Single-Sex Schools, Student Achievement, and Course Selection: Evidence from Rule-Based Student Assignments in Trinidad and Tobago," *Journal of Public Economics*, vol. 96(1–2), pp. 173–187 (2012)

Lavy, Victor, Olmo Silva, & Felix Weinhardt, "The Good, the Bad and the Average: Evidence on the Scale and Nature of Ability Peer Effects in Schools," Working Paper, No. 15600, National Bureau of Economic Research, Cambridge, MA (2009)

4.

Gender on Wall Street, and Taking the One-in-a-Million Shot:

Begala, Paul, Interview with Author (2011)

Bosquet, Katrien, Peter de Goeij, & Kristien Smedts, "Trading on Gender Heterogeneity in Analyst Recommendations: A Profitable Investment Strategy?" Paper Presentation at Annual Meeting of Financial Management Assn., Denver (2011)

Caliendo, Marco, Frank Fossen, & Alexander Kritikos, "The Impact of Risk Attitudes on Entrepreneurial Survival," *Journal of Economic Behavior & Organization*, vol. 76(1), pp. 45–63 (2010)

Calvo, Dana, "WGA Puts Writers One Click Closer," *Los Angeles Times*, http://lat.ms/16hImL (10/3/2002)

Carrey, Jim, Lauren Holly (perfs.), Farrelly, Peter (dir.), Bennett Yellin, Bobby Farrelly, Peter Farrelly (scrs.), *Dumb and Dumber*, New Line Cinema, Film (1994)

Harvey, Campbell R., Khalil Mohammed, & Sandy Rattray, "Do Analyst Experience, Location and Gender Affect the Performance of Broker Recommendations in Europe?" http://dx.doi.org/10.2139/ssrn.1850672 (2011)

Higgins, Michael, "Police Beating of 'Girl in the Blue Bra' Becomes New Rallying Call for Egyptians," *National Post*, http://natpo.st/tVhpP6 (12/20/2011)

Huang, Hua-Wei, Yun-Chia Yan, James M. Fornaro, & Ahmed Elshahat, "Market Reactions to Audit Committee Director's Gender: Evidence from U.S.-Traded Foreign Firms," *International Journal of Banking & Finance*, vol. 8(1), art. 4 (2011)

Ittonen, Kim, Johanna Miettinen, & Sami Vähämaa, "Does Female Representation on Audit Committees Affect Audit Fees?" *Quarterly Journal of Finance and Accounting*, vol. 49(3–4), pp. 113–139 (2010)

Kumar, Alok, Correspondence with Author (2011)

Kumar, Alok, Interview with Author (2011)

Kumar, Alok, "Self-Selection and the Forecasting Abilities of Female Equity Analysts," *Journal of Accounting*, vol. 48(3), pp. 393–435 (Supp. 2010)

Levi, Maurice, Kai Li, & Feng Zhang, "Men Are from Mars, Women Are from Venus: Gender and Mergers and Acquisitions," Presentation at Annual Meeting of the Academy of Behavioral Finance & Economics, San Diego (2011)

Michalaszek, Agata, & Joanna Sokolowska, "The Relative Input of Payoffs and Probabilities into Risk Judgment," *Polish Psychological Bulletin*, vol. 41(2), pp. 46–51 (2010)

Myers, Scott, "2011 Spec Script Sales Analysis: Genres," *Go into the Story*, http://bit.ly/ADn0ua (1/30/2012)

Peltz, Michael, "All-America Research Team—Four Decades of Excellence," *Institutional Investor*, http://bit.ly/QGN4fx (10/13/2011)

Sapienza, Paola, "Discussion of Self-Selection and the Forecasting Abilities of Female Equity Analysts," *Journal of Accounting Research*, vol. 48(2), pp. 437–443 (2010)

Short, Jeremy C., G. Tyge Payne, Keith H. Brigham, G. T. Lumpkin, & J. Christian Broberg, "Family Firms and Entrepreneurial Orientation in Publicly Traded Firms: A Comparative Analysis of the S&P 500," *Family Business Review*, vol. 22(1), pp. 9–24 (2009)

Thiruvadi, Sheela, & Hua-Wei Huang, "Audit Committee Gender Differences and Earnings Management," *Gender in Management: An International Journal*, vol. 26(7), pp. 483–498 (2011)

"Welcome to Powerball—Prizes and Odds," http://bit.ly/18fEl (u.d.)

Chapter 6—The Utter Importance of Pillow Fights

1.

Sherif's "Robbers Cave" Experiment:

Billig, Michael (Ed.), *Social Psychology and Intergroup Relations*, London: Academic Press, Inc. (1976)

Gaertner, Samuel L., John Dovidio, Brenda S. Banker, Missy Houlette, Kelly M. Johnson, & Elizabeth A. McGlynn, "Reducing Intergroup Conflict: From Superordinate Goals to Decategorization, Recategorization, and Mutual Differentiation," *Group Dynamics: Theory, Research, & Practice*, vol. 4(1), pp. 98–114 (2000)

Garup, Gian, Correspondence with Author (2011)

Golding, William, *Lord of the Flies*, London: Faber & Faber (1954)

Granberg, Donald, Correspondence with Author (2011)

Granberg, Donald, Interview with Author (2011)

Granberg, Donald, & Gian Sarup (Eds.), *Social Judgment and Intergroup Relations: Essays in Honor of Muzafer Sherif*, New York: Springer-Verlag (1992)

"Muzafer Sherif," Obituaries, *New York Times*, http://nyti.ms/RsrG8S (10/27/1988)

Rohrer, John H., & Muzafer Sherif (Eds.), *Social Psychology at the Crossroads*, New York: Harper & Bros. (1951)

Sherif, Joan, Correspondence with Author (2011)

Sherif, Sue, Correspondence with Author (2011)

Sherif, Muzafer, "Conformity-Deviation, Norms, and Group Relations," In: Irwin A. Berg & Bernard M. Bass (Eds.), *Conformity & Deviation*, ch. 5, pp. 159–198, New York: Harper & Row (1961)

Sherif, Muzafer, "Experiments in Group Conflict," *Scientific American*, vol. 195, pp. 54–59 (1956)

Sherif, Muzafer, "On the Relevance of Social Psychology," *American Psychologist*, vol. 25(2), pp. 144–156 (1970)

Sherif, Muzafer, "Superordinate Goals in the Reduction of Intergroup Conflict," *American Journal of Sociology*, vol. 63(4), pp. 349–356 (1958)

Sherif, Muzafer, O. J. Harvey, B. Jack White, William R. Hood, & Carolyn W. Sherif, *The Robbers Cave Experiment: Intergroup Conflict and Cooperation*, Middletown, CT: Wesleyan University Press (1988)

Sherif, Muzafer, B. Jack White, & O. J. Harvey, "Status in Experimentally Produced Groups," *American Journal of Sociology*, vol. 60(4), pp. 370–379 (1955)

Sherif, Muzafer, & Carolyn W. Sherif, "Ingroup and Intergroup Relations," In: James O. Whittaker (Ed.), *Introduction to Psychology*, ch. 19, Philadelphia: Saunders (1965)

Sherif, Muzafer, & Carolyn W. Sherif, *An Outline of Social Psychology* (Rev. Ed), New York: Harper & Brothers (1956)

Sherif, Muzafer, & M. O. Wilson (Eds.), *Group Relations at the Crossroads*, New York: Harper & Bros. (1953)

Tyerman, Andrew, & Christopher Spencer, "A Critical Test of the Sherifs' Robber's Cave Experiments," *Small Group Behavior*, vol. 14(4), pp. 515–531 (1983)

Wood Sherif, Carolyn, *Orientation in Social Psychology*, New York: Harper & Row (1976)

2.

Growing Up in Groups versus Growing Up in Dyads:

Baumeister, Roy F., & Kristin L. Sommer, "What Do Men Want? Gender Differences and Two Spheres of Belongness: Comment on Cross and Madson," *Psychological Bulletin*, vol. 122(1), pp. 38–44 (1997)

Benenson, Joyce, Interview with Author (2012)

Benenson, Joyce F., & Kiran Alavi, "Sex Differences in Children's Investment in Same-Sex Peers," *Evolution & Human Behavior*, vol. 25(4), pp. 258–266 (2004)

Benenson, Joyce F., Timothy J. Antonellis, Benjamin J. Cotton, Kathleen E. Noddin, & Kristin A. Campbell, "Sex Differences in Children's Formation of Exclusionary Alliances under Scarce Resource Conditions," *Animal Behavior*, vol. 76(2), pp. 497–505 (2008)

Benenson, Joyce F., Nicolas H. Apostoleris, & Jodi Parnass, "Age and Sex Differences in Dyadic and Group Interaction," *Developmental Psychology*, vol. 33(3), pp. 538–543 (1997)

Benenson, Joyce F., & Deborah Benarroch, "Gender Differences in Responses to Friends' Hypothetical Greater Success," *Journal of Early Adolescence*, vol. 18(2), pp. 192–208 (1998)

Benenson, Joyce F., Hassina P. Carder, & Sarah J. Geib-Cole, "The Development of Boys' Preferential Pleasure in Physical Aggression," *Aggressive Behavior*, vol. 34(2), pp. 154–166 (2008)

Benenson, Joyce F., & Athena Christakos, "The Greater Fragility of Females' versus Males' Closest Same-Sex Friendships," *Child Development*, vol. 74(4), pp. 1123–1129 (2003)

Benenson, Joyce F., Vanessa Duggan, & Henry Markovits, "Sex Differences in Infants' Attraction to Group versus Individual Stimuli," *Infant Behavior & Development*, vol. 27(2), pp. 173–180 (2004)

Benenson, Joyce F., Alana J. Gordon, & Rosanne Roy, "Children's Evaluative Appraisals of Competition in Tetrads versus Dyads," *Small Group Research*, vol. 31(6), pp. 635–652 (2000)

Benenson, Joyce F., & Anna Heath, "Boys Withdraw More in One-on-One Interactions, Whereas Girls Withdraw More in Groups," *Developmental Psychology*, vol. 42(2), pp. 272–282 (2006)

Benenson, Joyce F., Lindsay Hodgson, Sarah Heath, & Patrick J. Welch, "Human Sexual Differences in the Use of Social Ostracism as a Competitive Tactic," *International Journal of Primatology*, vol. 29(4), pp. 1019–1035 (2008)

Benenson, Joyce F., Rebecca Maiese, Eva Dolensky, Nicole Dolensky, Nancy Sinclair, & Anna Simpson, "Group Size Regulates Self-Assertive versus Self-Deprecating Responses to Interpersonal Competition," *Child Development*, vol. 73(6), pp. 1818–1829 (2002)

Benenson, Joyce F., Henry Markovits, Caitlin Fitzgerald, Diana Geoffroy, Julianne Flemming, Sonya M. Kahlenberg, & Richard W. Wrangham, "Males' Great Tolerance of Same-Sex Peers," *Psychological Science*, vol. 20(2), pp. 184–190 (2009)

Benenson, Joyce F., Henry Markovits, Ingrid Muller, Andrew Challen, & Hassina P. Carder, "Explaining Sex Differences in Infants' Preferences for Groups," *Infant Behavior & Development*, vol. 30(4), pp. 587–595 (2007)

Benenson, Joyce F., Henry Markovits, Rosanne Roy, & Paul Denko, "Behavioural Rules Underlying Learning to Share: Effects of Development and Context," *International Journal of Behavioral Development*, vol. 27(2), pp. 116–121 (2003)

Benenson, Joyce F., Henry Markovits, Melissa Emery Thompson, & Richard W. Wrangham, "Under Threat of Social Exclusion, Females Exclude More Than Males," *Psychological Science*, vol. 22(4), pp. 538–544 (2011)

Benenson, Joyce F., Catherine Nicholson, Angela Waite, Rosanne Roy, & Anna Simpson, "The Influence of Group Size on Children's Competitive Behavior," *Child Development*, vol. 72(3), pp. 921–928 (2001)

Benenson, Joyce F., Rosanne Roy, Angela Waite, Suzanne Goldbaum, Lisa Linders, & Anna Simpson, "Greater Discomfort as a Proximate Cause of Sex Differences in Competition," *Merrill-Palmer Quarterly*, vol. 48(3), pp. 225–247 (2002)

Benenson, Joyce F., & Joy Schinazi, "Sex Differences in Reactions to Outperforming Same-Sex Friends," *British Journal of Developmental Psychology*, vol. 22(3), pp. 317–333 (2004)

Benenson, Joyce F., Nancy Sinclair, & Eva Dolenszky, "Children's and Adolescents' Expectations of Aggressive Responses to Provocation: Females Predict More Hostile Reactions in Compatible Dyadic Relationships," *Social Development*, vol. 15(1), pp. 65–81 (2006)

Colarelli, Stephen M., Jennifer L. Spranger, & Ma Regina Hechanova, "Women, Power, and Sex Composition in Small Groups: An Evolutionary Perspective," *Journal of Organizational Behavior*, vol. 27(2), pp. 163–184 (2006)

Fabes, Richard A., Carol Lynn Martin, & Laura D. Hanish, "Young Children's Play Qualities in Same-, Other-, and Mixed-Sex Peer Groups," *Child Development*, vol. 74(3), pp. 921–932 (2003)

Lee, I-Ching, Felicia Pratto, & Blair T. Johnson, "Intergroup Consensus/Disagreement in Support of Group-Based Hierarchy: An Examination of Socio-Structural and Psycho-Cultural Factors," *Psychological Bulletin*, vol. 137(6), pp. 1029–1064 (2011)

Maccoby, Eleanor E., "Gender and Group Process: A Developmental Perspective," *Current Directions in Psychological Science*, vol. 11(2), pp. 54–58 (2002)

MacEvoy, Julie Paquette, & Steven R. Asher, "When Friends Disappoint: Boys' and Girls' Responses to Transgressions of Friendship Expectations," *Child Development*, vol. 83(1), pp. 104–119 (2012)

Markovits, Henry, & Joyce F. Benenson, "Males Outperform Females in Translating Social Relations into Spatial Positions," *Cognition*, vol. 117(3), pp. 332–340 (2010)

Markovits, Henry, Joyce Benenson, & Susan White, "Gender and Priming Differences in Speed of Processing of Information Relating to Social Structure," *Journal of Experimental Social Psychology*, vol. 42(5), pp. 662–667 (2006)

Schneider, Barry H., Kristopher Dixon, & Stephen Udvari, "Closeness and Competition in the Inter-Ethnic and Co-Ethnic Friendships of Early Adolescents in Toronto and Montreal," *Journal of Early Adolescence*, vol. 27(1), pp. 115–138 (2007)

3.

Honus Wagner and Siblings in Sports:

Barrow, Edward Grant, with James M. Kahn, *My Fifty Years in Baseball*, New York: Coward-McCann, Inc. (1951)

Carmichael, Evan, Correspondence with Author (2011)

Carmichael, Evan, Honus-Wagner.org (u.d.)

Collier, Gene, "Too Many Cheaters and Not Enough Thieves," *Pittsburgh Post-Gazette*, http://bit.ly/ODHyIU (3/15/2012)

Finoli, David, & Bill Rainer, "Top 100 Pirates Players," *Pittsburgh Pirates Encyclopedia*, ch. 3, USA: Sports Publishing, LLC (2003)

Hageman, William, *Honus: The Life and Times of a Baseball Hero*, Champaign, IL: Sagamore Pub. (1996)

Hittner, Arthur D., *Honus Wagner: The Life of Baseball's "Flying Dutchman,"* Jefferson, NC: McFarland & Co. (1996)

Mendelson, Abby, "Honus Wagner," Pittsburgh Pirates, http://atmlb.com/PDax1p (2012)

Society for American Baseball Research, *The SABR Baseball List & Record Book: Baseball's Most Fascinating Records*, New York: Simon & Schuster (2007)

"Statistics," Major League Baseball, MLB.com, http://atmlb.com/Q65Z1w (2012)

"Stealing Second → Stealing Third → Stealing Home," *Baseball Almanac*, http://bit.ly/q2BoIm (2012)

Sulloway, Frank J., *Born to Rebel*, New York: Vintage (1997)

Sulloway, Frank, Interview with Author (2011)

Sulloway, Frank J., & Richard L. Zweigenhaft, "Birth Order and Risk Taking in Athletics: A Meta-Analysis and Study of Major League Baseball," *Personality & Social Psychology Review*, vol. 14(4), pp. 402–416 (2010)

4.

Sibling Conflict:

We dedicated an entire chapter of our book, *NurtureShock*, to sibling conflict. We invite you to look there for a fuller discussion of the nature of sibling arguments, research on how to respond to sibling quarreling, et cetera. (A couple of the studies briefly mentioned in this book, regarding the frequency of sibling quarrels, are addressed more fully in its pages, as well.)

Bartling, Björn, Ernst Fehr, Michel André Maréchal, & Daniel Schunk, "Egalitarianism and Competitiveness," *American Economic Review*, vol. 99(2), pp. 93–98 (2009)

Fehr, Ernst, Helen Bernhard, & Bettina Rockenbach, "Egalitarianism in Young Children," *Nature*, vol. 454, pp. 1079–1083 (2008)

Holmes, Robyn, "Young Children's Emotional Responses to Cheating in Game Play," In: Eva E. Nwokah (Ed.), *Play as Engagement and Communication*, pp. 100–119, Lanham, MD: University Press of America, Inc. (2010)

Kramer, Laurie, Lisa A. Perozynski, & Tsai-Yen Chung, "Parental Responses to Sibling Conflict: The Effects of Development and Parent Gender," *Child Development*, vol. 70(6), pp. 1401–1414 (1999)

Perlman, Michal, Daniel A. Garfinkel, & Sheri L. Turrell, "Parent and Sibling Influences on the Quality of Children's Conflict Behaviours across the Preschool Period," *Social Development*, vol. 16(4), pp. 619–641 (2007)

Punch, Samantha, "'You Can Do Nasty Things to Your Brothers and Sisters without a Reason': Siblings' Backstage Behaviors," *Children & Society*, vol. 22(5), pp. 333–344 (2007)

Ram, Avigail, & Hildy S. Ross, "Problem Solving, Contention, and Struggle: How Siblings Resolve a Conflict of Interests," *Child Development*, vol. 72(6), pp. 1710–1722 (2001)

Ross, Hildy, Michael Ross, Nancy Stein, & Tom Trabasso, "How Siblings Resolve Their Conflicts: The Importance of First Offers, Planning, and Limited Opposition," *Child Development*, vol. 77(6), pp. 1730–1745 (2006)

The Value of Roughhousing:

Flanders, Joseph L., Vanessa Leo, Daniel Paquette, Robert O. Pihl, & Jean R. Séguin, "Rough-and-Tumble Play and the Regulation of Aggression: An Observational Study of Father–Child Play Dyads," *Aggressive Behavior*, vol. 35(4), pp. 285–295 (2009)

Flanders, Joseph L., Melissa Simard, Daniel Paquette, Sophie Parent, Frank Vitaro, Robert O. Pihl, & Jean R. Séguin, "Rough-and-Tumble Play and the Development of Physical Aggression and Emotional Regulation: A Five-Year Follow-Up Study," *Journal of Family Violence*, vol. 25(4), pp. 357–367 (2010)

Paquette, Daniel, "Dichotomizing Paternal and Maternal Functions as a Means to Better Understand Their Primary Contribution," *Human Development*, vol. 47(4), pp. 237–238 (2004)

Paquette, Daniel, "Theorizing the Father-Child Relationship: Mechanisms and Developmental Outcomes," *Human Development*, vol. 47(4), pp. 193–219 (2004)

Paquette, Daniel, & Marc Bigras, "The Risky Situation: A Procedure for Assessing the Father-Child Activation Relationship," *Early Child Development & Care*, vol. 180(1–2), pp. 33–50 (2010)

Paquette, Daniel, René Carbonneau, Diane Dubeau, Marc Bigras, & Richard E. Tremblay, "Prevalence of Father-Child Rough-and-Tumble Play and Physical Aggression of Preschool Children," *European Journal of Psychology of Education*, vol. 18(2), pp. 171–189 (2003)

Schore, Allan, & Jennifer McIntosh, "Family Law and the Neuroscience of Attachment," *Family Court Review*, vol. 49(3), pp. 501–512 (2011)

5.

Sandra Lerner; Women in Silicon Valley:

Boyd, E. B., "Where is the Female Mark Zuckerberg?," *San Francisco*, pp. 82–93, 106–114 (Dec. 2011)

Brush, Candida, Nancy Carter, Elizabeth Gatewood, Patricia Greene, & Myra Hart, "The Diana Project: Women Business Owners and Equity Capital, the Myths Dispelled," Kansas City, MO: Kauffman Center for Entrepreneurial Leadership, (2001)

Coleman, Susan, & Alicia Robb, "A Comparison of New Firm Financing by Gender: Evidence from the Kauffman Firm Survey Data," *Small Business Economics*, vol. 33(4), pp. 397–411 (2009)

Crets, Douglas, "Recruiting Women to the Burgeoning (But Mostly Male) Host of Angel Investors," *Fast Company*, http://bit.ly/odqVEn (8/1/2011)

Flynn, F. J., C. Anderson, & S. Brion, "Too Tough, Too Soon: The Impact of Familiarity on the Backlash Effect," Working Paper (u.d.)

Flynn, Frank, "Gender-Related Material in the New Core Curriculum," Remarks at WIM Banquet, Stanford, CA (2007)

Geller, Dan, & Danya Goldfine, Interviews with Author (2011)

Kerr, William, "Venture Financing and Entrepreneurial Success," *Harvard Business Review* Blog Network, http://bit.ly/duHBUw (5/12/2010)

Lerner, Sandra (subj.), Dan Geller, Dayna Goldfine (dirs.), *Something Ventured*, Miralan Productions, Film (2011)

Reuben, Ernesto, Pedro Rey-Biel, Paolo Sapienza, & Luigi Zingales, "The Emergence of Male Leadership in Competitive Environments," *Journal of Economic Behavior & Organization*, vol. 83(1), pp. 111–117 (2012)

Schade, Christian, & Sabrina Boewe, "Characterizing the Female Entrepreneur: Comparing Behavior in a Market Entry Experiment with Other Groups of Individuals," *Frontiers of Entrepreneurship Research*, vol. 30(8), art. 8. (2010)

"Women 2.0's Female Founder Successes of 2010," Women 2.0, http://bit.ly/S3R0IS (12/18/2010)

Zider, Bob, "How Venture Capital Works," *Harvard Business Review*, pp. 113–139 (Nov–Dec. 1998)

Prenatal Testosterone / Digit Ratio as Predictors of Development and Behavior:

Brañas-Garza, Pablo, & Aldo Rustichini, "Organizing Effects of Testosterone and Economic Behavior: Not Just Risk Taking," *PLoS ONE*, vol. 6(12), e29842, doi:10.1371/journal.pone.0029842 (2011)

Coates, J. M., & J. Herbert, "Endogenous Steroids and Financial Risk Taking on a London Trading Floor," *Proceedings of the National Academy of Science*, vol. 105(16), pp. 6167–6172 (2008)

Coates, John M., Mark Gurnell, & Aldo Rustichini, "Second-to-Fourth Digit Ratio Predicts Success among High-Frequency Financial Traders," *Proceedings of the National Academy of Sciences*, vol. 106(2), pp. 623–628 (2009)

Collaer, Marcia L., & Melissa Hines, "Human Behavioral Sex Differences: A Role for Gonadal Hormones during Early Development?" *Psychological Bulletin*, vol. 118(1), pp. 55–107 (1995)

Dreber, Anna, & Moshe Hoffman, "Biological Basis of Sex Differences in Risk Aversion and Competitiveness," Working Paper, http://bit.ly/OMXrLL (u.d.)

Golby, Jim, & Jennifer Meggs, "Exploring the Organizational Effect of Prenatal Testosterone upon the Sporting Brain," *Journal of Sports Science & Medicine*, vol. 10(3), pp. 445–451 (2011)

Guiso, Luigi, & Aldo Rustichini, "What Drives Women Out of Entrepreneurship: The Joint Role of Testosterone and Culture," European University Institute & EIEF Working Paper, ECO 2011/2012 (2011)

Hines, Melissa, "Gender Development and the Human Brain," *Annual Reviews of Neuroscience*, vol. 34, pp. 69–88 (2011)

Malas, Mehmet Ali, Sevkinaz Dogan, E. Hilal Evcil, & Kadir Desdicioglu, "Fetal Development of the Hand, Digits and Digit Ratio (2D:4D)," *Early Human Development*, vol. 82(7), pp. 469—475 (2006)

Manning, J. T., D. Scutt, J.Wilson, & D. I. Lewis-Jones, "The Ratio of 2nd to 4th Digit Length: A Predictor of Sperm Numbers and Concentrations of Testosterone, Luteinizing Hormone and Oestrogen," *Human Reproduction*, vol. 13(11), pp. 3000–3004 (1998)

Manning, John T., "Resolving the Role of Prenatal Sex Steroids in the Development of Digit Ratio," *Proceedings of the National Academy of Sciences*, vol. 108(39), pp. 16143–16144 (2011)

Manning, John T., & Rogan P. Taylor, "Second to Fourth Digit Ratio and Male Ability in Sport: Implications for Sexual Selection in Humans," *Evolution & Human Behavior*, vol. 22(1), pp. 61–69 (2001)

Millet, Kobe, & Siegfried Dewitte, "A Subordinate Status Position Increases the Present Value of Financial Resources for Low 2D:4D Men," *American Journal of Human Biology*, vol. 20(1), pp. 110–115 (2008)

Neave, Nick, Sarah Laing, Bernhard Fink, & John T. Manning, "Second to Fourth Digit Ratio, Testosterone, and Perceived Dominance," *Proceedings of the Royal Society, Biological Sciences B*, vol. 270, pp. 2167–2172 (2003)

Paul, S. N., B. S. Kato, J. L. Hunkin, S. Vivekanadndan, & T. D. Spector, "The Big Finger: The Second to Fourth Digit Ratio is a Predictor of Sporting Ability in Women," *British Journal of Sports Medicine*, vol. 40(12), pp. 981–983 (2006)

Pearson, Matthew, & Burkhard C. Shipper, "The Visible Hand: Finger Ratio (2d:4d) and Competitive Bidding," *Experimental Economics*, vol. 15(3), pp. 510–529 (2012)

Rustichini, Aldo, Interview with Author (2011)

Sandri, Serena, Christian Schade, Oliver Mußhoff, & Martin Odening, "Holding On for Too Long? An Experimental Study on Inertia in Entrepreneurs' and Non-Entrepreneurs Disinvestment Choices," SiAg-Working Paper, No. 02 (2009)

Schade, Christian, & Sabrina Boewe, "Characterizing the Female Entrepreneur: Comparing Behavior in a Market Entry Experiment with Other Groups of Individuals," *Frontiers of Entrepreneurship Research*, vol. 30(8), art. 8. (2010)

Stenstrom, Eric, Gad Saad, Marcelo V. Nepomuceno, & Zack Mendenhall, "Testosterone and Domain-Specific Risk: Digit Ratios (2D:4D and rel2) as Predictors of Recreational, Financial, and Social Risk-Taking Behaviors," *Personality & Individual Differences*, vol. 51(4), pp. 412–416 (2011)

Tobet, Stuart, J. Gabriel Knoll, Cheryl Hartshorn, Emily Aurand, Matthew Stratton, Pankaj Kumar, Brian Searcy, & Kristy McClellan, "Brain Sex Differences and Hormone Influences: A Moving Experience?," *Journal of Neuroendocrinology*, vol. 21(4), pp. 387–392 (2009)

Trahms, Cheryl A., "Does Biology Matter? How Prenatal Testosterone, Entrepreneurial Risk Propensity, Entrepreneur Risk Perception, Influence Venture Performance," *Frontiers of Entrepreneurship Research*, vol. 30(5), art. 4 (2010)

Unger, Jens M., Andreas Rauch, Jayanth Narayanan, Sophie Weis, & Michael Frese, "Does Prenatal Testosterone Predict Entrepreneurial Success? Relationships of 2d:4d and Business Success (Summary)," *Frontiers of Entrepreneurship Research*, vol. 29(5), art. 15 (2009)

Zheng, Zhengui, & Martin J. Cohn, "Developmental Basis of Sexually Dimorphic Digit Ratios," *Proceedings of the National Academy of Sciences*, vol. 108(39), pp. 16289–16294 (2011)

PART III

The Roosevelt quote has a number of circulating versions. This version is from *Respectfully Quoted: A Dictionary of Quotations from the Library of Congress*, edited by Suzy Platt, published by Congressional Quarterly, Inc., Washington, DC (1992). Another version, frequently used in speeches by President John F. Kennedy, appears in Kennedy, John F., & Edward M. Kennedy, *Words Jack Loved*, Private Printing (1977).

Chapter 7—The Difference between Winning and Not Losing

1.

Swatch, Fighter Brands, Entrepreneurial Approach:

"The Amazing Adventures of the 'Second Watch,'" Swatch Group, http://bit.ly/Rss6w2 (u.d.)

Barrett, M. Edgar, "Time Marches On: The Worldwide Watch Industry," *Thunderbird International Business Review*, vol. 42(3), pp. 349–373 (2000)

Burmeister, Katrin, & Christian Schade, "Are Entrepreneurs' Decisions More Biased? An Experimental Investigation of the Susceptibility to Status Quo Bias," *Journal of Business Venturing*, vol. 22(3), pp. 340–362 (2007)

Hyatt, Josh, "And in This Corner, the Price-Fighter," *CFO Magazine*, http://bit.ly/S3Ra3c (12/1/2008)

Jost, Peter-J., "The Use of Fighter Brands to Thwart New Entrants," GEABA Discussion Paper 10–3 (2010)

Ketchen, David J., Jr., Charles C. Snow, & Vera L. Hoover, "Research on Competitive Dynamics: Recent Accomplishments and Future Challenges," *Journal of Management*, vol. 30(6), pp. 779–804 (2004)

Long, Mary M., & Leon G. Schiffman, "Swatch Fever: An Allegory for Understanding the Paradox of Collecting," *Psychology & Marketing*, vol. 14(5), pp. 495–509 (1997)

Mattarella-Micke, Andrew, Jill Mateo, Megan N. Kozak, Katherine Foster, & Sian L. Beilock, "Choke or Thrive? The Relation between Salivary Cortisol and Math Performance Depends on Individual Differences in Working Memory and Math-Anxiety," *Emotion*, vol. 11(4), pp. 1000–1005 (2011)

Mudambi, Ram, "Branding Time: Swatch and Global Brand Management," *ICFAI Journal of Management*, vol. 2(2), pp. 39–54 (2005)

Raasch, Christina, "Launching a Fighter Brand to Cushion Patent Expiry: The Case of Zocor," *Journal of Medical Marketing: Device, Diagnostic & Pharmaceutical Marketing*, vol. 8, pp. 119–126 (2008)

Ritson, Mark, "Is Your Fighter Brand Strong Enough to Win the Battle?," *Advertising Age*, http://bit.ly/PTTkgi (10/13/2009)

Ritson, Mark, "One Fighter Brand Strategy that Just Might Work," *Branding Strategy Insider*, http://bit.ly/OwImgQ (12/1/2008)

Ritson, Mark, "Should You Launch a Fighter Brand?" *Harvard Business Review*, reprint R0910K (Oct. 2009)

"Swatch Group History (Yesterday)," Swatch Group, http://bit.ly/16lZW9 (u.d.)

Truong, Lynn, "5 Reasons Fighter Brands Fail," American Express OPEN Forum, http://amex.co/JU4y0T (2/11/2010)

Tutton, Mark, "Businesses Hit Back with 'Fighter Brands,'" CNN.com, http://bit.ly/14BDX3 (10/5/2009)

Wallace, J. Craig, Laura M. Little, Aaron D. Hill, & Jason W. Ridge, "CEO Regulatory Foci, Environmental Dynamism, and Small Firm Performance," *Journal of Small Business Management*, vol. 48(4), pp. 580–604 (2010)

Sports Examples of Playing to Win versus Playing Not to Lose:

A University of Ulster study found an interesting tennis parallel to Fulton's research on women running for politics. In Grand Slam tennis, women are more calculating about when they are going to go to the net—only going to the net when they believe they're going to win. Men go to the net more, and, because of that, they win more points during the game (O'Donoghue & Ingram).

"Amelie Mauresmo / Activity," Women's Tennis Assn. / WTATennis.com, http://bit.ly/N2CqhN (u.d.)

"Amelie Mauresmo, Wimbledon," ASAP Sports Transcripts, http://bit.ly/PTTvZ4 (7/8/2006)

"Combative Mauresmo Buries Demons to Prove Herself as World's Best," *Scotsman*, http://bit.ly/T0tKsV (7/10/2006)

Garber, Greg, "Exorcising Demons of Doubt," ESPN.com, http://es.pn/QGOWoD (7/13/2006)

Goff, J., J. D. Foster, M. S. Gordon, & C. S. Brown, "Regulatory Focus and the 'Goal Looms Larger' Effect in Major League Baseball," Paper Presentation at Annual Meeting of the Society for Personality and Social Psychology, Tampa, FL (2009)

Harlow, Phil, "Gamewatch: Mauresmo v. Henin-Hardenne," *BBC Sport*, http://bbc.in/RvBrr2 (7/8/2006)

"Highlights: Wimbledon Women's Final," *BBC Sport*, http://bbc.in/O7Qxzp (7/8/2006)

"Justine Henin / Activity," Women's Tennis Assn. / WTATennis.com, http://bit.ly/OAN5fU (2012)

"Justine Henin, Wimbledon," ASAP Sports Transcripts, http://bit.ly/PDccE3 (7/8/2006)

"Match Statistics," Archive of Wimbledon Official Site, http://bit.ly/R0cm30 (2007)

"Mauresmo Overcomes Nerves, Wins Wimbledon," AP via NBC Sports, http://on.msnbc.com/QGPkDL (7/9/2006)

"Mauresmo Wins Wimbledon for First Time," ESPN.com, http://es.pn/N2CDBx (7/8/2006)

O'Donoghue, Peter, *Research Methods for Sports Performance Analysis*, New York: Routledge (2010)

O'Donoghue, Peter, & Billy Ingram, "A Notational Analysis of Elite Tennis Strategy," *Journal of Sports Science*, vol. 19(2), pp. 107–115 (2001)

Paserman, M. Danielle, "Gender Differences in Performance in Competitive Environments: Evidence from Professional Tennis Players," IZA Discussion Paper No. 2834, http://bit.ly/PvNd12 (June 2007)

Paserman, M. Danielle, "Gender Differences in Performance in Competitive Environments: Evidence from Professional Tennis Players," http://bit.ly/TCgsQY (2010)

Pope, Devin G., & Maurice E. Schweitzer, "Is Tiger Woods Loss Averse? Persistent Bias in the Face of Experience, Competition, and High Stakes," *American Economic Review*, vol. 101(1), pp. 129–157 (2011)

"Rally Propels Mauresmo to First Fitle at Wimbledon," AP via *USA Today*, http://usat.ly/PDjLVP (7/14/2006)

"Tennis—List of Wimbledon Women's Singles Champions," Reuters UK, http://reut.rs/KPlZ8G (7/21/2012)

The Progression of Psychological Theories of Gain/Prevention Orientation:

Appelt, Kirstin C., & E. Tory Higgins, "My Way: How Strategic Preferences Vary by Negotiator Role and Regulatory Focus," *Journal of Experimental Social Psychology*, vol. 46(6), pp. 1138–1142 (2010)

Atkinson, John W., "The Achievement Motive and Recall of Interrupted and Completed Tasks," *Journal of Experimental Psychology*, vol. 46(6), pp. 381–390 (1953)

Atkinson, John W., "Motivational Determinants of Risk-Taking Behavior," *Psychological Review*, vol. 64(6), pp. 359–372 (1957)

Brockner, Joel, E. Tory Higgins, & Murray B. Low, "Regulatory Focus Theory and the Entrepreneurial Process," *Journal of Business Venturing*, vol. 19(2), pp. 203–220 (2004)

Crowe, Ellen, & E. Tory Higgins, "Regulatory Focus and Strategic Inclinations: Promotion and Prevention in Decision-Making," *Organizational Behavior & Human Decision Processes*, vol. 69(2), pp. 117–132 (1997)

Cunningham, William, "Motivation and the Amygdala: Goals Shape Activation," Paper Presentation at Annual Convention of Assn. for Psychological Science, San Francisco (2009)

Cunningham, William A., Carol L. Raye, & Marcia K. Johnson, "Neural Correlates of Evaluation Associated with Promotion and Prevention Regulatory Focus," *Cognitive, Affective, & Behavioral Neuroscience*, vol. 5(2), pp. 202–211 (2005)

Cunningham, William A., Jay J. Van Bavel, & Ingrid R. Johnsen, "Affective Flexibility: Evaluative Processing Goals Shape Amygdala Activity," *Psychological Science*, vol. 19(2), pp. 152-160 (2008)

Eddington, Kari M., Florin Dolcos, Amy Noll McLean, K. Ranga Krishman, Roberto Cabeza, & Timothy J. Strauman, "Neural Correlates of Idiographic Goal Priming in Depression: Goal-Specific Dysfunctions In the Orbitofrontal Cortex," *Social Cognitive and Affective Neuroscience*, vol. 4, pp. 238-246 (2009)

Elliot, Andrew J., "Approach and Avoidance Motivation and Achievement Goals," *Educational Psychologist*, vol. 34(3), pp. 169–189 (1999)

Elliot, Andrew J., & Marcy A. Church, "A Hierarchical Model of Approach and Avoidance Achievement Motivation," *Journal of Personality & Social Psychology*, vol. 72(1), pp. 218–232 (1997)

Elliot, Andrew J., & Martin V. Covington, "Approach and Avoidance Motivation," *Educational Psychology Review*, vol. 13(2), pp. 73–92 (2001)

Elliot, Andrew J., & Todd M. Thrash, "Approach-Avoidance Motivation in Personality: Approach and Avoidance Temperaments and Goals," *Journal of Personality & Social Psychology*, vol. 82(5), pp. 804–818 (2002)

Higgins, E. Tory, "Beyond Pleasure and Pain," *American Psychologist*, vol. 52(12), pp. 1280–1300 (1997)

Packer, Dominic J., & William A. Cunningham, "Neural Correlates of Reflection on Goal States: The Role of Regulatory Focus and Temporal Distance," *Social Neuroscience*, vol. 4(5), pp. 412-425 (2009)

Rutherford, Helena J. V., & Annukka K. Lindell, "Thriving and Surviving: Approach and Avoidance Motivation and Lateralization," *Emotion Review*, vol. 3(3), pp. 333-343 (2011)

Schlund, Michael W., Sandy Magee, & Caleb D. Hudgins, "Human Avoidance and Approach Learning: Evidence for Overlapping Neural Systems and Experiential Avoidance Modulation of Avoidance Neurocircuitry," *Behavioural Brain Research*, vol. 225(2), pp. 437-448 (2011)

Schmeichel, Brandon J., Cindy Harmon-Jones, & Eddie Harmon-Jones, "Exercising Self-Control Increases Approach Motivation," *Journal of Personality and Social Psychology*, vol. 99(1), pp. 162–173 (2010)

Scholer, Abigail A., Xi Zou, Kentaro Fujita, Steven J. Stroessner, & E. Tory Higgins, "When Risk Seeking Becomes a Motivational Necessity," *Journal of Personality & Social Psychology*, vol. 99(2), pp. 215–231 (2010)

Taylor Bianco, Amy, E. Tory Higgins, & Adena Klem, "How 'Fun/Importance' Fit Affects Performance: Relating Implicit Theories to Instructions," *Personality & Social Psychology Bulletin*, vol. 29(9), pp. 1091–1103 (2003)

Vickery, Timothy J., Marvin M. Chuh, & Daeyeol Lee, "Ubiquity and Specificity of Reinforcement Signals throughout the Human Brain," *Neuron*, vol. 72(1), pp. 166–177 (2011)

Zhang, Shu, E. Tory Higgins, & Guoquan Chen, "Managing Others Like You Were Managed: How Prevention Focus Motivates Copying Interpersonal Norms," *Journal of Personality & Social Psychology*, vol. 100(4), pp. 647–663 (2011)

2.

Threat versus Challenge:

For additional sources relating to the difference between a "threat" and a "challenge," see the work of Wendy Berry Mendes, Jim Blascovich and others in the Chapter 8 sources for the physiology of challenge and threat.

Connecting this to the earlier discussion of close races, Brown and Li (2010) have found that PGA players tend to take more risks in a close race. When there is little chance that the winner will be defeated, both those in the lead and those likely to lose play more conservatively. So when the verdict is uncertain, those in a close race perceive the competition as a challenge. However, if the game is uneven, then both those ahead and below may perceive themselves to be in a threat situation. That is, the leader believes that the win is his to lose (a threat), while those at the bottom are trying to prevent an embarrassing result (again, a threat).

Worthy et al. found an intriguing NBA equivalent to the soccer penalty scenario: NBA players do worse than their career average when at the freethrow line and their team is behind or ahead by one: they are better than their averages if their game is tied.

Aarts, Henk, Ruud Custers, & Rob W. Holland, "Nonconscious Cessation of Goal Pursuit: When Goals and Negative Affect Are Coactivated," *Journal of Personality and Social Psychology*, vol. 92(2), pp. 165–178 (2007)

Berndt, Thomas J., "Prosocial Behavior between Friends in Middle Childhood and Early Adolescence," *Journal of Early Adolescence*, vol. 5(3), pp. 307–317 (1985)

Berndt, Thomas J., T. Bridgett Perry, & Kristelle E. Miller, "Friends' and Classmates' Interactions on Academic Tasks," *Journal of Educational Psychology*, vol. 80(4), pp. 506–513 (1988)

Brown, Jennifer, & Jin Li, "Going for It: The Adoption of Risky Strategies in Tournaments," Working Paper (2010)

Chalabaev, Aïna, Brenda Major, Phillippe Sarrazin, & François Cury, "When Avoiding Failure Improves Performance: Stereotype Threat and the Impact of Performance Goals," *Motivation & Emotion*, vol. 36(2), pp. 130–142 (2012)

Gramzow, Richard H., Greg Willard, & Wendy Berry Mendes, "Big Tales and Cool Heads: Academic Exaggeration Is Related to Cardiac Vagal Reactivity," *Emotion*, vol. 8(1), pp. 138–144 (2008)

Grimm, Lisa R., Arthur B. Markman, & W. Todd Maddox, "End-of-Semester Syndrome: How Situational Regulatory Fit Affects Test Performance over an Academic Semester," *Basic & Applied Social Psychology*, vol. 34(4), pp. 376-385 (2012)

Halevy, Nir, Eileen Y. Chou, & Adam D. Galinsky, "Exhausting or Exhilarating? Conflict as Threat to Interests, Relationships and Identities," *Journal of Experimental Social Psychology*, vol. 48(2), pp. 530–537 (2012)

Halko, Marja-Liisa, Yevhen Hlushchuk, Riitta Hari, & Martin Schürmann, "Competing with Peers: Mentalizing-Related Brain Activity Reflects What Is at Stake," *NeuroImage*, vol. 46(2), pp. 542–548 (2009)

Jones, Marc, Carla Mijen, Paul Joseph McCarthy, & David Sheffield, "A Theory of Challenge and Threat States in Athletes," *International Review of Sport and Exercise Psychology*, vol. 2(2), pp. 1611–80 (2009)

Jordet, Geir, "When Superstars Flop: Public Status and Choking under Pressure in International Soccer Penalty Shootouts," *Journal of Applied Sports Psychology*, vol. 21(2), pp. 125–130 (2009)

Jordet, Geir, "Why Do English Players Fail in Soccer Penalty Shootouts? A Study of Team Status, Self-Regulation, and Choking under Pressure," *Journal of Sports Sciences*, vol. 27(2), pp. 97–106 (2009)

Jordet, Geir, & Esther Hartman, "Avoidance Motivation and Choking under Pressure in Soccer Penalty Shootouts," *Journal of Sport & Exercise Psychology*, vol. 30(4), pp. 450–457 (2008)

Jordet, Geir, Esther Hartman, & Einar Sigmundstad, "Temporal Links to Performing under Pressure in International Soccer Penalty Shootouts," *Psychology of Sport & Exercise*, vol. 10(6), pp. 621–627 (2009)

Jordet, Geir, Esther Hartman, & Pieter Jelle Vuijk, "Team History and Choking under Pressure in Major Soccer Penalty Shootouts," *British Journal of Psychology*, vol. 103(2), pp. 268–283 (2012)

Radke, Sina, F. P. de Lange, M. Ullsperger, & E. R. A. de Bruijn, "Mistakes that Affect Others: An fMRI Study on Processing of Own Errors in a Social Context," *Experimental Brain Research*, vol. 211(3–4), pp. 405–413 (2011)

Schapiro, Michelle, Barry H. Schneider, Bruce M. Shore, Judith A. Margison, & Stephen J. Udvari, "Competitive Goal Orientations, Quality, and Stability in Gifted and Other Adolescents' Friendships : A Test of Sullivan's Theory about the Harm Caused by Rivalry," *Gifted Child Quarterly*, vol. 53(2), pp. 71–88 (2009)

Schneider, Barry H., Joyce Benenson, Márta Fülöp, Mihaly Berkics, & Mónika Sándor, "Cooperation and Competition," In: P. K. Smith & C. H. Hart (Eds.), *The Wiley-Blackwell Handbook of Childhood Social Development*, 2nd Ed., ch. 25, pp. 472–490 (2011)

Williams, Jay, "Cutting Edge Research: PK Shootouts, Pressure, and Choking," *Science of Soccer Online*, http://bit.ly/OMY7Rq (9/4/2008)

Worthy, Darrell A., Arthur B. Markman, & W. Todd Maddox, "Choking and Excelling at the Free Throw Line," *International Journal of Creativity and Problem Solving*, vol. 19, pp. 53–58 (2009)

3.

Neuroscience of Mistakes:

While we've gone into detail about the ACC's role in monitoring, the subsequent response to the error involves a neural network. For example, one of the brain areas that activates following the ACC activation is the amygdala (See Pourtois et al., 2010), which may explain why fear is often connected to our comprehension of a mistake—perhaps the difficulty is in differentiating whether fear is the consequence of the mistake, or the cause of the mistake.

In a more technical parse, the drop in the brain's electrical response following a mistake is described in the scientific literature as Error-Related Negativity (ERN), followed by "Pe"—a positive increase after the ERN. And it's around this Pe that learning seems to occur. There's also "FRN"—Feedback Related Negativity—when you are told by an external source of the mistake—but what's more interesting to us is how often the brain's already perceived the mistake without this external alert.

Boksem, Maarten A. S., Evelien Kostermans, & David De Cremer, "Failing Where Others Have Succeeded: Medial Frontal Negativity Tracks Failure in a Social Context," *Psychophysiology*, vol. 48(7), pp. 973–979 (2011)

Boksem, Maarten A. S., Kirsten I. Ruys, & Henk Aarts, "Facing Disapproval: Performance Monitoring in a Social Context," *Social Neuroscience*, vol. 6(4), pp. 360–368 (2011)

Cavanaugh, James F., Michael J. Frank, & John J. B. Allen, "Social Stress Reactivity Alters Reward and Punishment Learning," *Social, Cognitive, & Affective Neuroscience*, vol. 6(3), pp. 311–320 (2011)

Cavanaugh, James F., Michael J. Frank, Theresa J. Klein, & John J. B. Allen, "Frontal Theta Links Prediction Errors to Behavioral Adaptation in Reinforcement Learning," *NeuroImage*, vol. 49(4), pp. 3198–3209 (2010)

Cavanaugh, James F., Laura Zambrano-Vazques, & John J. B. Allen, "Theta Lingua Franca: A Common Mid-Frontal Substrate for Action Monitoring Processes," *Psychophysiology*, vol. 49(2), pp. 220–238 (2012)

de Bruijn, Ellen R. A., Floris P. de Lange, D. Yves von Cramon, & Markus Ullsperger, "When Errors Are Rewarding," *Journal of Neuroscience*, vol. 29(39), pp. 12183–12186 (2009)

de Bruijn, Ellen R. A., Stephan F. Miedl, & Harold Bekkering, "Fast Responders Have Blinders On: ERP Correlates of Response Inhibition in Competition," *Cortex*, vol. 44(5), pp. 580–586 (2008) de Bruijn, Ellen R. A., Stephan F. Miedl, & Harold Bekkering, "How a Co-actor's Task Affects Monitoring of Own Errors," *Experimental Brain Research*, vol. 211(3–4), pp. 397–404 (2011)

de Bruijn, Ellen R. A., Rogler B. Mars, & Harold Bekkering, "Your Mistake Is My Mistake or Is It? Behavioural Adjustments Following Own and Observed Actions in Cooperative and Competitive Contexts," *Quarterly Journal of Experimental Psychology*, vol. 65(2), pp. 317–325 (2012)

Decenty, Jean, Philip L. Jackson, Jessica A. Sommerville, Thierry Chaminade, & Andrew N. Meltzoff, "The Neural Bases of Cooperation and Competition: An fMRI Investigation," *NeuroImage*, vol. 23(2), pp. 744–751 (2004)

Dhar, Monica, Jan Roelf Wiersema, & Gilles Pourtois, "Cascade of Neural Events Leading from Error Commission to Subsequent Awareness Revealed Using EEG Source Imaging," *PLoS ONE*, vol. 6(5), e19578, doi:10.1371/journalpone0019578

Frank, Michael J., Christopher D'Lauro, & Tim Curran, "Cross-Task Individual Differences in Error Processing: Neural, Electrophysiological, and Genetic Components," *Cognitive, Affective, & Behavioral Neuroscience*, vol. 7(4), pp. 297–308 (2007)

Frank, Michael J., Brion S. Woroch, & Tim Curran, "Error-Related Negativity Predicts Reinforcement Learning and Conflict Biases," *Neuron*, vol. 47(4), pp. 495–501 (2005)

Gu, Ruolei, Yue Ge, Yang Jiang, & Yue-Jia Luo, "Anxiety and Outcome Evaluation: The Good, the Bad and the Ambiguous," *Biological Psychology*, vol. 85(3), pp. 200–206 (2010)

Gu, Ruolei, Tingting Wu, Yang Jiang, & Yue-Jia Luo, "Woulda, Coulda, Shoulda: The Evaluation and the Impact of the Alternative Outcome," *Psychophysiology*, vol. 48(10), pp. 1354–1360 (2011)

Hajcak, Greg, & Dan Foti, "Errors Are Aversive Defensive Motivation and the Error-Related Negativity," *Psychological Science*, vol. 19(2), pp. 103–108 (2008)

Holroyd, Clay B., Kaivon L. Pakzad-Vaezi, & Olave E. Krigolson, "The Feedback Correct-Related Positivity: Sensitivity of the Event-Related Brain Potential to Unexpected Positive Feedback," *Psychophysiology*, vol. 45(5), pp. 688–697 (2008)

Hyman, James Michael, Michael Erik Hasselmo, & Jeremy Keith Seamans, "What Is the Functional Relevance of Prefrontal Cortex Entrainment to Hippocampal Theta Rhythms?," *Frontiers in Neuroscience*, vol. 5(24), pp. 1–13 (2011)

Kang, Sonia K., Jacob B. Hirsh, & Alison L. Chasteen, "Your Mistakes Are Mine: Self-Other Overlap Predicts Neural Response to Observed Errors," *Journal of Experimental Social Psychology*, vol. 46(1), pp. 229–232 (2010)

Meyer, Alexandria, Anna Weinberg, Daniel N. Klein, & Greg Hajcak, "The Development of the Error-Related Negativity (ERN) and Its Relationship with Anxiety: Evidence from 8 to 13 Year-Olds," *Developmental Cognitive Neuroscience*, vol. 2(1), pp. 152–161 (2012)

Moser, Jason S., Greg Hajcak, & Robert F. Simons, "The Effects of Fear on Performance Monitoring and Attentional Allocation," *Psychophysiology*, vol. 42(3), pp. 261–268 (2005)

Moser, Jason S., Hans S. Schroder, Carrie Heeter, Tim P. Moran, & Yu-Hao Lee, "Mind Your Errors: Evidence for a Neural Mechanism Linking Growth Mind-Set to Adaptive Posterror Adjustments," *Psychological Science*, vol. 22(12), pp. 1484–1489 (2011)

Mowrer, Samantha M., Andrew A. Jahn, Amir Abdulhalil, & William A. Cunningham, "The Value of Success: Acquiring Gains, Avoiding Losses, and Simply Being Successful," *PLoS ONE*, vol. 6(9), e25307, doi:10.1371/journal.pone.0025307

Petzold, Antje, Franziska Plessow, Thomas Goschke, & Clemens Kirschbaum, "Stress Reduces Use of Negative Feedback in a Feedback-Based Learning Task," *Behavioral Neuroscience*, vol. 124(2), pp. 248–255 (2010)

Potts, Geoffrey F., Laura E. Martin, Philip Burton, & P. Read Montague, "When Things Are Better or Worse Than Expected: The Medial Frontal Cortex and the Allocation of Processing Resources," *Journal of Cognitive Neuroscience*, vol. 18(7), pp. 1112–1119 (2006)

Pourtois, Gilles, Roland Vocat, Karin N'Diaye, Laurent Spinelli, Margitta Seeck, & Patrik Vuilleumier, "Errors Recruit Both Cognitive and Emotional Monitoring Systems: Simultaneous Intracranial Recordings in the Dorsal Anterior Cingulate Gyrus and Amygdala Combined with fMRI," *Neuropsychologia*, vol. 48(4), pp. 1144–1159 (2010)

Rigoni, Davide, David Polezzi, Rino Rumiati, Ramona Guarino, & Giuseppe Sartori, "When People Matter More Than Money: An ERPs Study," *Brain Research Bulletin*, vol. 81(4–5), pp. 445–452 (2010)

Sailer, Uta, Florian Ph S. Fischmeister, & Herbert Bauer, "Effects of Learning Feedback-Related Brain Potentials in a Decision-Making Task," *Brain Research*, vol. 1342, pp. 85–93 (2010)

Unger, Kerstin, Jutta Kray, & Axel Mecklinger, "Worse Than Feared? Failure Induction Modulates the Electrophysiological Signature of Error Monitoring during Subsequent Learning," *Cognitive, Affective & Behavioral Neuroscience*, vol. 12(1), pp. 34–55 (2012)

van der Helden, Jurjen, Maarten A. S. Boksem, & Jorian H. G. Blom, "The Importance of Failure: Feedback-Related Negativity Predicts Motor Learning Efficiency," *Cerebral Cortex*, vol. 20(7), pp. 1596–1603 (2010)

Van Meel, Catharina S., & Caroline A. A. Van Heijningen, "The Effect of Interpersonal Competition on Monitoring Internal and External Error Feedback," *Psychophysiology*, vol. 47(2), pp. 213–222 (2010)

Wilson, Timothy D., David B. Centerbar, Deborah A. Kermer, & Daniel T. Gilbert, "The Pleasures of Uncertainty: Prolonging Positive Moods in Ways People Do Not Anticipate," *Journal of Personality and Social Psychology*, vol. 88(1), pp. 5–21 (2005)

Zhou, Zhiheng, Rongjun Yu, & Xiaolin Zhou, "To Do or Not to Do? Action Enlarges the FRN and P300 Effects in Outcome Evaluation," *Neuropsychologia*, vol. 48(12), pp. 3606–3613 (2010)

2007 World Figure Skating Finals:

"Canadian Pairs Struggle in Tokyo," TSN, http://bit.ly/PDdajI (3/21/2007)

Kaye, Rosaleen, "Shen and Zhao Win Third World Title," GoldenSkate.com, http://bit.ly/IDoKCq (3/22/2007)

"Pairs Free Skating Judges Details per Skater," ISUResults.com, http://bit.ly/OMYf3o (2007)

"Poles' Mishap Contagious for Canadians," *Montreal Gazette*, http://bit.ly/RvBJOB (3/22/2007)

Smith, Beverley, "Pandemonium Rules in Pairs Final," *The Globe & Mail*, http://bit.ly/ODJAsA (3/21/2007)

"U.S. Skaters Stumble through Day to Forget," AP via ESPN, http://es.pn/NFHeoQ (3/21/2007)

4.

Traits of Gain-Orientation versus Prevention-Orientation:

Bjørnebekk, Gunnar, Torgrim Gjesme, & Robin Ulriksen, "Achievement Motives and Emotional Processes in Children during Problem-Solving: Two Experimental Studies of Their Relation to Performance in Different Achievement Goal Conditions," *Motivation & Emotion*, vol. 35(4), pp. 351–367 (2011)

Chiaburu, Dan S., "Chief Executives' Self-Regulation and Strategic Orientation: A Theoretical Model," *European Management Journal*, vol. 28(6), pp. 467–478 (2010)

Hertel, Guido, Henk Aarts, & Marcel Zeelenberg, "What Do You Think Is 'Fair'? Effects of Ingroup Norms and Outcome Control on Fairness Judgments," *European Journal of Social Psychology*, vol. 32(3), pp. 327–341 (2002)

Lee, Angela Y., Punam Anand Keller, & Brian Sternthal, "Value from Regulatory Construal Fit: The Persuasive Impact of Fit between Consumer Goals and Message Concreteness," *Journal of Consumer Research*, vol. 36(5), pp. 735–747 (2010)

McMullen, J. S., D. Shepherd, & S. Zahra, "Regulatory Focus and Executives' Intentions to Commit Their Firms to Entrepreneurial Action," In: A. Zacharakis et al. (Eds.), *Frontiers of Entrepreneurship Research*, pp. 661–74, Babson Park, MA: Babson College (2006)

Miele, David B., Daniel C. Molden, & Wendi L. Gardner, "Motivated Comprehension Regulation: Vigilant versus Eager Metacognitive Control," vol. 37(6), pp. 779–795 (2009)

Norem, Julie K., & Edward C. Chang, "The Positive Psychology of Negative Thinking," *Journal of Clinical Psychology*, vol. 58(9), pp. 993–1001 (2002)

Righetti, Francesca, Catrin Finkenauer, & Caryl Rusbult, "The Benefits of Interpersonal Regulatory Fit for Individual Goal Pursuit," *Journal of Personality and Social Psychology*, vol. 101(4), pp. 720–736 (2011)

Scholer, Abigail A., Xi Zou, Kentaro Fujita, Steven J. Stroessner, & E. Tory Higgins, "When Risk Seeking Becomes a Motivational Necessity," *Journal of Personality & Social Psychology*, vol. 99(2), pp. 215–231 (2010)

Shu, Tse-Mei, & Shui-fong Lam, "Are Success and Failure Experiences Equally Motivational? An Investigation of Regulatory Focus and Feedback," *Learning & Individual Differences*, vol. 21(6), pp. 724–727 (2011)

Smith, Jessi L., Jill Wagaman, & Ian M. Handley, "Keeping It Dull or Making It Fun: Task Variation as a Function of Promotion versus Prevention Focus," *Motivation and Emotion*, vol. 33(2), pp. 150–160 (2009)

Ten Velden, Femke S., Bianca Beersma, & Carsten K. W. De Dreu, "When Competition Breeds Equality: Effects of Appetitive versus Aversive Competition in Negotiation," *Journal of Experimental Social Psychology*, vol. 47(6), pp. 1127–1133 (2011)

Wan, Echo Wen, Jiewen Hong, & Brian Sternthal, "The Effect of Regulatory Orientation and Decision Strategy on Brand Judgments," *Journal of Consumer Research*, vol. 35(6), pp. 1026–1038 (2009)

Zhu, Rui, & Joan Meyers-Levy, "Exploring the Cognitive Mechanism that Underlies Regulatory Focus Effects," *Journal of Consumer Research*, vol. 34(1), pp. 89–96 (2007)

Westinghouse Electric:

Hindo, Brian, "Rewiring Westinghouse," *Business Week*, http://buswk.co/NAnF7s (5/8/2008)

Liedtka, Jeanne, Correspondence with Author (2012)

Liedtka, Jeanne, Interview with Author (2012)

Liedtka, Jeanne, Robert H. Rosen, & Robert Wiltbank, *The Catalyst: How You Can Become an Extraordinary Growth Leader*, New York: Crown Publishing (2009)

Spanjol, Jelena, & Leona Tam, "To Change or Not to Change: How Regulatory Focus Affects Change in Dyadic Decision-Making," *Creativity and Innovation Management*, vol. 19(4), pp. 346–363 (2010) (noting that Westinghouse had changed to a promotion orientation)

"Westinghouse Announces New Organizational Structure," Press Release, http://bit.ly/PDdJtR (2010)

"World View: Interview with Meena Mutyala," *Westinghouse World View*, pp. 10–13 (Oct. 2007)

Neuroscience in the Creative Process:

Benedek, Mathias, Sabine Bergner, Tajan Könen, Andreas Fink, & Ajoscha C. Neubauer, "EEG Alpha Synchronization is Related to Top-Down Processing in Convergent and Divergent Thinking," *Neuropsychologica*, vol. 49(12), pp. 3505-3511 (2011)

Berkowitz, Aaron L., & Daniel Ansari, "Expertise-Related Deactivation of the Right Temporoparietal Junction during Musical Improvisation," *NeuroImage*, vol. 49(1), pp. 712–719 (2010)

Chakravarty, Ambar, "The Creative Brain—Revisiting Concepts," *Medical Hypothesis*, vol. 74(3), pp. 606–612 (2010)

Fink, Andreas, Karl Koschutnig, Mathias Benedek, Gernot Reishofer, Anja Ischebeck, Elisabeth M. Weiss, & Franz Ebner, "Stimulating Creativity via the Expression to Other People's Ideas," *Human Brain Mapping*, vol. 33 (11), pp. 2603–2610 (2011)

Fink, Andreas, Daniela Schwab, & Ilona Papousek, "Sensitivity of EEG Upper Alpha Activity Creativity Interventions," *International Journal of Psychophysiology*, vol. 82(3), pp. 233-239 (2011)

Chapter 8—How One Night of Blackjack Sped Up the World Economy

1.

Fed-Ex, Luck, and the Value of Origin Stories:

Berger, Johannes, & Petra Nieken, "Heterogeneous Contestants and Effort Provision in Tournaments—An Empirical Investigation with Professional Sports Data," SFB/TR 15 Discussion Paper No. 325, http://bit.ly/Q67A7q (2010)

Damisch, Lysann, Barbara Stoberock, & Thomas Mussweiler, "Keep Your Fingers Crossed! How Superstition Improves Performance," *Psychological Science*, vol. 21(7), pp. 1014–1020 (2010)

Ersner-Hershfield, Hal, Adam D. Galinsky, Laura J. Kray, & Brayden G. King, "Company, Country, Connections: Counterfactual Origins Increase Organizational Commitment, Patriotism, and Social Investment," *Psychological Science*, vol. 21(10), pp. 1479–1486 (2010)

"Federal Express Honors 'Day One' Employees," FedEx Press Releases, http://at.fedex.com/NAnNDQ (9/22/98)

"Fred Smith: An Overnight Success," *Entrepreneur*, http://bit.ly/RstGhz (10/9/2008)

"Frederick W. Smith," About FedEx, FedEx, http://at.fedex.com/ODJYaw (2012)

"Frederick W. Smith: No Overnight Success," *Business Week*, http://buswk.co/OMGfs0 (9/20/2004)

Frock, Roger, *Changing How the World Does Business: FedEx's Incredible Journey to Success*, San Francisco: Berrett-Koehler Publishers, Inc. (2006)

Kopko, Ed, & Jeffrey Sonnenfeld, "What's in a Leader?" *Forbes*, http://onforb.es/NAoaOH (8/7/2007)

Kräkel, Matthias, "Optimal Risk Taking in an Uneven Tournament Game with Risk Averse Players," *Journal of Mathematical Economics*, vol. 44(11), pp. 1219–1231 (2008)

Lutsky, Neil S., "What's Luck Got to Do with It? Social Comparison May Account for Superstition's Effect on Performance," Poster Presentation at Annual Meeting of the Society for Personality & Social Psychology, San Diego (2012)

Smith, Fred, "How I Delivered the Goods," *Fortune Small Business* (Oct 2002/reprint)

Teigen, Karl Halvor, "Luck: The Art of a Near Miss," *Scandinavian Journal of Psychology*, vol. 37(2), pp. 156–171 (1996)

Wohl, Michael J. A., "Croyance en un Soi Chanceux: Effet de la Croyance en la Chance Personnelle sur l'Émergence et le Maintien des Conduites de Jeu de Hasard et d'Argent (Belief in a Lucky Self: The Role of Personal Luck in the Facilitation and Maintenance of Gambling Behavior)," *Psychologie Française*, vol. 53(1), pp. 7–23 (2008)

NASA and Near-Miss Bias:

Our interview with Ed Rogers was invaluable: not only did he explain the backstory of the Dillon and Tinsley study, but he also was helpful at depicting "launch fever" and other aspects of NASA procedure.

Columbia Accident Investigation Board Press Briefing, Transcript, Washington, DC, http://1.usa.gov/O7SLic (8/26/2003)

"Decision Making at NASA," *Columbia Accident Investigations Board Report*, vol. 1, ch. 6, http://1.usa.gov/57zF6i (2003)

Dillon, Robin L., & Catherine H. Tinsley, "How Near-Misses Influence Decision Making under Risk: A Missed Opportunity for Learning," *Management Science*, vol. 54(8), pp. 1425–1440 (2008)

Kunerth, Jeff, & Michael Cabbage, "NASA's Safety Culture Blamed," *Baltimore Sun*, http://bit.ly/OAPg3k (8/27/2003)

Madsen, Peter M., & Vint Desai, "Failing to Learn? The Effects of Failure and Success on Organizational Learning in the Global Orbital Launch Vehicle Industry," *Academy of Management Journal*, vol. 53(3), pp. 451–476 (2010)

Morris, Michael W., & Paul C. Moore, "The Lessons We (Don't) Learn: Counterfactual Thinking and Organizational Accountability after a Close Call," *Administrative Science Quarterly*, vol. 45(4), pp. 737–765 (2000)

Rogers, Edward, Interview with Author (2012)

Tinsley, Catherine H., Robin L. Dillon, & Peter M. Madsen, "How to Avoid Catastrophe," *Harvard Business Review* (Apr. 2011)

"Understanding Near-Misses at NASA," NASA Ask the Academy, http://1.usa.gov/PDf-CXz (8/17/2006)

Wohl, Michael J. A., & Michael E. Enzle, "The Effects of Near Wins and Near Losses on Self-Perceived Personal Luck and Subsequent Gambling Behavior," *Journal of Experimental Social Psychology*, vol. 39(2), pp. 184–191 (2003)

2.

Making Mental Comparisons:

Epstude, Kai, & Johanna Peetz, "Mental Time Travel: A Conceptual Overview of Social Psychological Perspectives on a Fundamental Human Capacity," *European Journal of Social Psychology*, vol. 42(3), pp. 269–275 (2012)

Summerville, Amy, & Neal J. Roese, "Dare to Compare: Fact-Based versus Simulation-Based Comparison in Daily Life," *Journal of Experimental Social Psychology*, vol. 44(3), pp. 664–671 (2008)

Anxiety—Physiology and the Individual Zone of Optimal Functioning:

Many of the researchers studying anxiety review anger's performance at the same time; therefore, look at the sources for the section on anger as well.

Aidman, Eugene, "Competitive Anxiety: From Coping to Harvesting the Power of Stress," *The Sporting Mind*, vol. 3(2), pp. 11–14 (2005)

Cerin, Ester, "Anxiety versus Fundamental Emotions as Predictors of Perceived Functionality of Pre-Competitive Emotional States, Threat, and Challenge in Individual Sports," *Journal of Applied Sports Psychology*, vol. 15(3), pp. 223–238 (2003)

Cerin, Ester, Attila Szabo, Nigel Hunt, & Clive Williams, "Temporal Patterning of Competitive Emotions: A Critical Review," *Journal of Sports Sciences*, vol. 18(8), pp. 605–626 (2000)

Esfahani, N., & H. Gheze Soflu, "The Comparison of Pre-Competitive Anxiety and State Anger between Female and Male Volleyball Players," *World Journal of Sport Sciences*, vol. 3(4), pp. 237–242 (2010)

Eubank, Martin, & Dave Collins, "Coping with Pre- and In-Event Fluctuations in Competitive State Anxiety: A Longitudinal Approach," *Journal of Sports Science*, vol. 18(2), pp. 121–131 (2000)

Fishbein, Martin, Susan E. Middlestadt, Victor Quatti, Susan Straus, & Alan Ellis, "Medical Problems among ICSOM Musicians: Overview of a National Survey," *Medical Problems of Performing Artists*, vol. 3, pp. 1–8 (1988)

Goodman, Gordon, "Actors and Fear: The Role of Stage Fright," unpublished dissertation (2011)

Goodman, Gordon, Correspondence with Author (2012)

Hagtveta, Knut A., & Yuri L. Hanin, "Consistency of Performance-Related Emotions in Elite Athletes: Generalizability Theory Applied to the IZOF Model," *Psychology of Sport & Exercise*, vol. 8(1), pp. 47–72 (2007)

Hanin, Yuri L., "Performance Related Emotional States in Sport: A Qualitative Analysis," *Qualitative Research*, vol. 4(1), art. 5 (2003)

Hanton, S., O. Thomas, & I. Maynard, "Competitive Anxiety Responses in the Week Leading Up to Competition: The Role of Intensity, Direction and Frequency Dimensions," *Psychology of Sport & Exercise*, vol. 5(2), pp. 169–181 (2004)

Hanton, Shelton, Richard Neil, Stephen D. Mellalieu, & David Fletcher, "Competitive Experience and Performance Status: An Investigation into Multidimensional Anxiety and Coping," *European Journal of Sport Science*, vol. 8(3), pp. 143–152 (2008)

Jamieson, Jeremy P., Wendy Berry Mendes, Eric Blackstock, & Tori Schmader, "Turning the Knots in Your Stomach into Bows: Reappraising Arousal Improves Performance on the GRE," *Journal of Experimental Social Psychology*, vol. 46(1), pp. 208–212 (2010)

Jones, Marc, & Mark Uphill, "Emotion in Sport," In: Joanne Thatcher, Marc Jones, & David Lavallee (Eds.), *Coping and Emotion in Sport*, 2nd Ed., ch. 2, pp. 33–61, New York: Routledge (2012)

Kane, Kristin Leigh, "An Examination into the Temporal Pattern of Emotions, Cognitions, and Coping Strategies of Instrumental Performers," unpublished dissertation (2008)

Lane, Andrew M., Gordon Bucknail, Paul A. Davis, & Christopher J. Beedle, "Emotions and Emotion Regulation among Novice Military Parachutists," *Military Psychology*, vol. 24(3), pp. 331–345 (2012)

Papageorgi, Ioulia, Andrea Creech, & Graham Welch, "Perceived Performance Anxiety in Advanced Musicians Specializing in Different Musical Genres," *Psychology of Music*, (in press) doi: 10.1177/0305735611408995 (2011)

Pellizzari, M., M. Bertollo, & C. Robazza, "Pre- and Post-Performance Emotions in Gymnastics Competitions," *International Journal of Sport Psychology*, vol. 42(3), pp. 278–302 (2011)

Raglin, James, & Yuri L. Hanin, "Competitive Anxiety," In: Yuri L. Hanin (Ed.), *Emotions in Sport*, ch. 4, pp. 93–112, Champaign, IL: Human Kinetics (2000)

Robazza, Claudio, Laura Bortoli, Filippo Nocini, Giovanna Moser, & Carlo Arslan, "Normative and Idiosyncratic Measures of Positive and Negative Affect in Sport," *Psychology of Sport & Exercise*, vol. 1(2), pp. 103–116 (2000)

Roland, David, "How Professional Performers Manage Performance Anxiety," *Research Studies in Music Education*, vol. 2(1), pp. 25–35 (1994)

Salminen, Simo, Jarmo Liukkonen, Yuri Hanin, & Ari Hyvönen, "Anxiety and Athletic Performance of Finnish Athletes: Application of the Zone of Optimal Functioning Model," *Personality & Individual Differences*, vol. 19(5), pp. 725–729 (1995)

Skinner, Natalie, & Neil Brewer, "The Dynamics of Threat and Challenge Appraisals prior to Stressful Achievement Events," *Journal of Personality & Social Psychology*, vol. 83(3), pp. 678–692 (2002)

Tenenbaum, Gershon, William A. Edmonds, & David W. Eccles, "Emotions, Coping Strategies, and Performance: A Conceptual Framework for Defining Affect-Related Performance Zones," *Military Psychology*, vol. 20(supp. 1), pp. S11–S37 (2008)

Yoshie, Michiko, Eriko Kanazawa, Kazutoshi Kudo, Tatsuyuki Ohtsuki, & Kimitaka Nakazawa, "Music Performance Anxiety and Occupational Stress among Classical Musicians," In: Janice Langan-Fo & Cary L. Cooper (Eds.), *Handbook of Stress in the Occupations*, ch. 20, pp. 409–429, Northampton, MA: Edward Elgar Publishing, Inc. (2011)

Yoshie, Michiko, Kazutoshi Kudo, Takayuki Murakoshi, & Tatsuyuki Ohtsuki, "Music Performance Anxiety in Skilled Pianists: Effects of Social-Evaluative Performance Situation on Subjective, Autonomic, and Electromyographic Reactions," *Experimental Brain Research*, vol. 199(2), pp. 117–126 (2009)

Yoshie, Michiko, Kazutoshi Kudo, & Tatsuyuki Ohtsuki, "Effects of Psychological Stress on State Anxiety, Electromyographic Activity, and Arpeggio Performance in Pianists," *Medical Problems of Performing Artists*, vol. 23(3), pp. 120–132 (2008)

Yoshie, Michiko, Kazutoshi Kudo, & Tatsuyuki Ohtsuki, "Motor/Autonomic Stress Responses in a Competitive Piano Performance," *Annals of the New York Academy of Sciences*, vol. 1169, pp. 368–371 (2009)

Yoshie, Michiko, & Kazuo Shigemasu, "Effects of State Anxiety on Performance in Pianists: Relationship between the Revised Competitive State Anxiety Inventory-2 Subscales and Piano Performance," Paper Presentation for 9th International Conference on Music Perception & Cognition, Bologna (2006)

Yoshie, Michiko, Kazuo Shigemasu, Kazutoshi Kudo, & Tatsuyuki Ohtsuki, "Effects of State Anxiety on Music Performance: Relationship between the Revised Competitive State Anxiety Inventory-2 Subscales and Piano Performance, *Musicae Scientiae*, vol. 3(1), pp. 55–84 (2009)

3.

The Difference between Positive Thinking, Fantasy, and Goal Achievement:

Beattie, Stuart, David Lief, Mark Adamoulas, & Emily Oliver, "Investigating the Possible Negative Effects of Self-Efficacy upon Golf Putting Performance," *Psychology of Sport & Exercise*, vol. 12(4), pp. 434–441 (2011)

Cohen, Patricia, "Author's Personal Forecast: Not Always Sunny, but Pleasantly Skeptical," *New York Times,* http://nyti.ms/vRXAe (10/10/2009)

Dennis, Paul, Interviews with Authors (2011)

Ehrenreich, Barbara, *Bright-Sided: How Positive Thinking Is Undermining America*, New York: Picador (2010)

Gawrilow, Caterina, Katrin Morgenroth, Regina Schultz, Gabriele Oettingen, & Peter M. Gollwizter, "Mental Contrasting with Implementation Intentions Enhances Self-Regulation of Goal Pursuit in Schoolchildren at Risk for ADHD," *Motivation & Emotion*, online early release, doi:10.1007/s11031-012-9288-3 (2012)

Gollwitzer, Anton, Gabriele Oettingen, Teri A. Kirby, Angela L. Duckworth, & Doris Mayer, "Mental Contrasting Facilitates Academic Performance," *Motivation & Emotion*, vol. 35(4), pp. 403–412 (2011)

Gollwitzer, Peter M., & Veronika Brandstätter, "Implementation Intentions and Effective Goal Pursuit," *Journal of Personality and Social Psychology*, vol. 73(1), pp. 186–199 (1997)

Hardy, James, "Speaking Clearly: A Critical Review of the Self-Talk Literature," *Psychology of Sport & Exercise*, vol. 7(1), pp. 81–87 (2006)

Highlen, Pamela S., & Bonnie B. Bennett, "Elite Divers and Wrestlers: A Comparison between Open- and Closed-Skill Athletes," *Journal of Sport Psychology*, vol. 5(4), pp. 390–409 (1983)

Kappes, Heather Barry, Gabriele Oettingen, & Doris Mayer, "Positive Fantasies Predict Low Academic Achievement in Disadvantaged Students," *European Journal of Social Psychology*, vol. 42(1), pp. 53–64 (2012)

Mahoney, Michael J., & Marshall Avener, "Psychology of the Elite Athlete: An Exploratory Study," *Cognitive Therapy & Research*, vol. 1(2), pp. 135–141 (1977)

Norem, Julie K., & Edward C. Chang, "The Positive Psychology of Negative Thinking," *Journal of Clinical Psychology*, vol. 58(9), pp. 993–1001 (2002)

Oettigen, Gabriele, "Expectancy Effects on Behavior Depend on Self-Regulatory Thought," *Social Cognition*, vol. 18(2), pp. 101–129 (2000)

Oettigen, Gabriele, "Free Fantasies about the Future and the Emergence of Developmental Goals," In: J. Brandstädter & R. M. Lerner (Eds.), *Action & Self-Development*, pp. 315–342, London: Sage (1999)

Oettingen, Gabriele, Interview with Author (2012)

Oettingen, Gabriele, "Positive Fantasy and Motivation," In: P. M. Gollwitzer & J. A. Bargh (Eds.), *Psychology of Action: Linking Cognition and Motivation to Behavior*, New York: Guilford (1996)

Oettigen, Gabriele, & Peter M. Gollwitzer, "Goal Setting and Goal Striving," In: Abraham Tesser & Norbert Schwarz (Eds.), *Blackwell Handbook of Social Psychology*: Intraindividual Processes, ch. 15, Malden, MA: Blackwell (2001)

Oettigen, Gabriele, & Peter M. Gollwitzer, "Turning Hope Thoughts into Goal-Directed Behavior," *Psychological Inquiry*, vol. 13(4), pp. 304–307 (2002)

Oettigen, Gabriele, Gaby Hönig, & Peter M. Gollwitzer, "Effective Self-Regulation of Goal Attainment," *International Journal of Educational Research*, vol. 33(7–8), pp. 705–732 (2000)

Oettigen, Gabriele, & Doris Mayer, "The Motivating Function of Thinking about the Future: Expectations versus Fantasies," *Journal of Personality & Social Psychology*, vol. 83(5), pp. 1198–1212 (2002)

Oettigen, Gabriele, Doris Mayer, Jennifer S. Thorpe, Hanna Janetzke, & Solvig Lorenz, "Turning Fantasies about Positive and Negative Futures into Self-Improvement Goals," *Motivation & Emotion*, vol. 29(4), pp. 236–266 (2005)

Oettigen, Gabriele, Hyeon-ju Pak, & Karoline Schnetter, "Self-Regulation of Goal Setting: Turning Free Fantasies about the Future into Binding Goals," *Journal of Personality & Social Psychology*, vol. 80(5), pp. 736–753 (2001)

Oettigen, Gabriele, & Thomas A. Wadden, "Expectation, Fantasy, and Weight Loss: Is the Impact of Positive Thinking Always Positive?," *Cognitive Therapy & Research*, vol. 15(2), pp. 167–175 (1991)

Peale, Norman Vincent, *The Power of Positive Thinking*, New York: Ballantine Books (1996)

Risen, Jane L., & Thomas Gilovich, "Why People Are Reluctant to Tempt Fate," *Journal of Personality and Social Psychology*, vol. 95(2), pp. 293–307 (2008)

Woodman, Tim, Sally Akehurst, Lew Hardy, & Stuart Beattie, "Self-Confidence and Performance: A Little Self-Doubt Helps," *Psychology of Sport & Exercise*, vol. 11(6), pp. 467–470 (2010)

Woodstock, Louise, "Think about It: The Misbegotten Promise of Positive Thinking Discourse," *Journal of Communication Inquiry*, vol. 31(2), pp. 166–189 (2007)

Counterfactuals:

Another perspective on the emotional significance of subtractive counterfactuals—Medvec et al. found that Olympic bronze medal winners are happier than silver medalists. The reason being that bronze medalists are thinking, "Wow, I made it! If anything else had been different, I wouldn't have gotten a medal at all!" But the silver medalists are consumed with, "If I just hadn't made that one mistake, I've have gotten the gold."

Barbey, Aron K., Frank Krueger, & Jordan Grafman, "Structured Event Complexes in the Medial Prefrontal Cortex Support Counterfactual Representations for Future Planning," *Proceedings of the Royal Society of Biological Sciences, B*, vol. 364, pp. 1291–1300 (2009)

Boorman, Erie D., Timothy E. Behrens, & Matthew F. Rushworth, "Counterfactual Choice and Learning in a Neural Network Centered on Human Lateral Frontopolar Cortex," *PLoS Biology*, vol. 9(6), e1001093, doi:10.1371/journal.pbio.1001093 (2011)

Epstude, Kai, & Neal J. Roese, "The Functional Theory of Counterfactual Thinking," *Personality & Social Psychology Review*, vol. 12(2), pp. 168–192 (2008)

Galinsky, Adam D., & Laura J. Kray, "From Thinking about What Might Have Been to Sharing What We Know: The Effects of Counterfactual Mind-Sets on Information Sharing in Groups," *Journal of Experimental Psychology*, vol. 40(5), pp. 606–618 (2004)

Galinsky, Adam D., Vanessa L. Seiden, Peter H. Kim, & Victoria Husted Medvec, "The Dissatisfaction of Having Your First Offer Accepted: The Role of Counterfactual Thinking in Negotiations," *Personality & Social Psycholology Bulletin*, vol. 28(2), pp. 271–283 (2002)

Kray, Laura, Interview with Author (2012)

Kray, Laura J., Adam D. Galinsky, & Keith D. Markman, "Adding versus Subtracting What Might Have Been: The Impact of Counterfactual Activation on Integrative Negotiations," IACM Meetings Paper, http://dx.doi.org/10.2139/ssrn.1080634 (2007)

Kray, Laura J., Adam D. Galinsky, & Keith D. Markman, "Counterfactual Structure and Learning from Experience in Negotiations," *Journal of Experimental Social Psychology*, vol. 45(4), pp. 979–982 (2009)

Kray, Laura J., Adam Galinsky, & Elaine M. Wong, "Thinking within the Box: The Relational Counterfactual Mind-Sets," *Journal of Personality & Social Psychology*, vol. 91(1), pp. 33–48 (2006)

Kray, Laura J., E. Layne Paddock, & Adam D. Galinsky, "The Effect of Past Performance on Expected Control and Risk Attitudes in Integrative Negotiations," *Negotiation and Conflict Management Research*, vol. 1(2), pp. 161–178 (2008)

Joung, Wendy, Beryl Hesketh, & Andrew Neal, "Using 'War Stories' to Train for Adaptive Performance: Is It Better to Learn from Error or Success?" *Applied Psychology*, vol. 55(2), pp. 282–302 (2006)

Markman, Keith D., Matthew J. Lindberg, Laura J. Kray, & Adam D. Galinsky, "Implications of Counterfactual Structure for Creative Generation and Analytical Problem Solving," *Personality & Social Psychology Bulletin*, vol. 33(3), pp. 312–324 (2007)

Medvec, Victoria Husted, Scott F. Madey, & Thomas Gilovich, "When Less Is More: Counterfactual Thinking and Satisfaction among Olympic Medalists," *Journal of Personality and Social Psychology*, vol. 69(4), pp. 603–610 (1995)

Morris, Michael W., & Paul C. Moore, "The Lessons We (Don't) Learn: Counterfactual Thinking and Organizational Accountability after a Close Call," *Administrative Science Quarterly*, vol. 45(4), pp. 737–765 (2000)

Naquin, Charles E., "The Agony of Opportunity in Negotiation: Number of Negotiable Issues, Counterfactual Thinking, and Feelings of Satisfaction," *Organizational Behavior and Human Decision Processes*, vol. 91(1), pp. 97–107 (2003)

Platt, Michael L., & Ben Hayden, "Learning: Not Just the Facts, Ma'am, but the Counterfactuals as Well," *PLoS Biology*, vol. 9(6), e1001092, doi:10.1371/journal.pbio.1001092 (2011)

Sim, Damien L. H., & Michael W. Morris, "Representativeness and Counterfactual Thinking: The Principle that Antecedent and Outcome Correspond in Magnitude," *Personality & Social Psychology Bulletin*, vol. 24(6), pp. 69–84 (1998)

Uphill, Mark A., & Katie Dray, "Giving Yourself a Good Beating: Appraisal, Attribution, Rumination, and Counterfactual Thinking," *Journal of Sports Science & Medicine*, vol. 8(CSSI 3), pp. 5–12 (2009)

Ursu, Stefan, & Cameron S. Carter, "Outcome Representations, Counterfactual Comparisons and the Human Orbitofrontal Cortex: Implications for Neuroimaging Studies of Decision-Making," *Cognitive Brain Research*, vol. 23(1), pp. 51–60 (2005)

Wong, Elaine M., Michael P. Haselhuhn, & Laura J. Kray, "Improving the Future by Considering the Past: The Impact of Upward Counterfactual Reflection and Implicit Beliefs on Negotiation Performance," *Journal of Experimental Social Psychology*, vol. 48(1), pp. 403–406 (2012)

4.

The Physiology of Challenges and Threats:

See also the Chapter 7 sources for challenge and threat (particularly Jones et al. 2009), and Denson's work on the neuroscience and physiology of anger.

Blascovisch, Jim, Wendy Berry Mendes, Brenda Major, & Mark Seery, "Social 'Facilitation' as Challenge and Threat," *European Journal of Social Psychology*, vol. 31(1), pp. 477–497 (2001)

Blascovisch, Jim, Wendy Berry Mendes, Joe Tomaka, & Kristen Salomon, "The Robust Nature of the Biopsychosocial Model Challenge and Threat: A Reply to Wright and Kirby," *Personality and Social Psychology Review*, vol. 7(3), pp. 234–243 (2003)

Devine, Dan, "Under Pressure: What Big Games Do to Players and How They Cope," Yahoo! Sports, http://yhoo.it/9LPyfz (7/3/2010)

Ehrhart-Bornstein, Monika, & Stefan R. Bornstein, "Cross-Talk between Adrenal Medulla and Adrenal Cortex in Stress," *Annals of the New York Academy of Sciences*, vol. 1148, pp. 112–117 (2008)

Goldstein, David S., "Adrenaline and Noradrenaline," *Encyclopedia of Life Sciences*, John Wiley & Sons (2010)

Harrison, Lesley K., Samantha Denning, Helen L. Easton, Jennifer C. Hall, Victoria E. Burns, Christopher Ring, & Douglas Carroll, "The Effects of Competition and Competitiveness on Cardiovascular Activity," *Psychophysiology*, vol. 38(4), pp. 601–606 (2001)

"Italy's Weapon Is All in Their Heads," *The Gazette* (7/8/2006)

Martin, Jennifer L., Jake Begun, Michael J. McLeish, Joanne M. Caine, & Gary L. Grunewald, "Getting the Adrenaline Going: Crystal Structure of the Adrenaline-Synthesizing Enzyme PNMT," *Structure*, vol. 9(10), pp. 977–985 (2001)

Mendes, Wendy Berry, Interview with Authors (2012)

Pohorecky, Larissa A., Michael Zigmond, Harvey Karten, & Richard J. Wurtman, "Enzymatic Conversion of Norepinephrine to Epinephrine by the Brain," *Journal of Pharmacology & Experimental Therapeutics*, vol. 165(2), pp. 190–195 (1969)

Seery, Mark D., "Challenge or Threat? Cardiovascular Indexes of Resilience and Vulnerability to Potential Stress in Humans," *Neuroscience and Biobehavioral Reviews*, vol. 35(7), pp. 1603–1610 (2011)

Seery, Mark D., Max Weisbuch, & Jim Blascovich, "Something to Gain, Something to Lose: The Cardiovascular Consequences of Outcome Framing," *International Journal of Psychophysiology*, vol. 73(3), pp. 308-312 (2009)

Skinner, Natalie, & Neil Brewer, "The Dynamics of Threat and Challenge Appraisals Prior to Stressful Achievement Events," *Journal of Personality & Social Psychology*, vol. 83(3), pp. 678–692 (2002)

Turner, Martin J., Marc V. Jones, David Sheffield, & Sophie L. Cross, "Cardiovascular Indices of Challenge and Threat States Predict Competitive Performance," *International Journal of Psychophysiology* (in press) (2012)

Waugh, Christian E., Sommer Panage, Wendy Berry Mendes, & Ian H. Gotlib, "Cardiovascular and Affective Recovery from Anticipatory Threat," *Biological Psychiatry*, vol. 84(2), pp. 169–175 (2010)

Wurtman, Richard J., "Control of Epinephrine Synthesis in the Adrenal Medulla by the Adrenal Cortex: Hormonal Specificity and Dose-Response Characteristics," *Endocrinology*, vol. 79(3), pp. 608–614 (1966)

Yamaguchi-Shima, Naoko, Shoshiro Okada, Takahiro Shimizu, Daisuke Usui, Kumiko Nakamura, Lianyi Lu, & Kunihiko Yokotani, "Adrenal Adrenaline- and Noradrenaline-Containing Cells and Celiac Sympathetic Ganglia Are Differentially Controlled by Centrally Administered Corticotropin-Releasing Factor and Arginine–Vasopressin in Rats," *European Journal of Pharmacology*, vol. 564(1–3), pp. 94–102 (2007)

Zaichkowsky, Leonard, "Stephen R. Heyman Memorial Keynote Lecture," Speech at Annual Convention of the American Psychological Assn., Washington, DC (2011)

Understanding Anger:

As we said above, researchers often examine multiple types of affect at the same time, so when considering the sources for anger, also look to our earlier-listed sources on anxiety.

Aarts, Henk, Kirsten I. Ruys, Harm Veling, Robert A. Renes, Jasper H. B. de Groot, Anna M. van Nunen, & Sarit Geertjes, "The Art of Anger: Reward Context Turns Avoidance Responses to Anger-Related Objects into Approach," *Psychological Science*, vol. 21(10), pp. 1406–1410 (2010)

Ahmadia, Sanaz Saeed, Mohammad Ali Besharata, Korosh Azizia, & Roja Larijanib, "The Relationship between Dimensions of Anger and Aggression in Contact and Noncontact Sports," *Procedia—Social & Behavioral Sciences*, vol. 30, pp. 247–251 (2011)

Ballard, Chris, "Where Does Greatness Come From?," *Sports Illustrated*, http://bit.ly/IYrwrs (5/14/2012)

Berkowitz, Leonard, & Eddie Harmon-Jones, "Toward an Understanding of the Determinants of Anger," *Emotion*, vol. 4(2), pp. 107–130 (2004)

Boekaerts, Monique, "Anger in Relation to School Learning," *Learning & Instruction*, vol. 3(4), pp. 269–280 (1993)

Chiodo, Keri, "Anger Makes People Want Things More," Press Release, Assn. for *Psychological Science* (11/1/2010)

Clarkson, Michael, *Competitive Fire*, Champaign, IL: Human Kinetics Publishers (1999)

Cutler, Andy, Interview with Author (2011)

D., Chuck, Interview with Author (2011)

Davis, Paul A., Tim Woodman, & Nichola Callow, "Better Out than In: The Influence of

Anger Regulation on Physical Performance," *Personality & Individual Differences*, vol. 49(5), pp. 457–460 (2010)

Denson, Thomas, Interview with Authors (2012)

Denson, Thomas F., Jessica R. Grisham, & Michelle L. Moulds, "Cognitive Reappraisal Increases Heart Rate Variability in Response to an Anger Provocation," *Motivation & Emotion*, vol. 35(1), pp. 114–122 (2011)

Denson, Thomas F., William C. Pedersen, Malte Friese, Aryun Hahm, & Lynette Roberts, "Understanding Impulsive Aggression: Angry Rumination and Reduced Self-Control Capacity Are Mechanisms Underlying the Provocation–Aggression Relationship," *Personality & Social Psychology Bulletin*, vol. 37(6), pp. 850–862 (2011)

Denson, Thomas F., William C. Pedersen, Jacklyn Ronquillo, & Anirvan S. Nandy, "The Angry Brain: Neural Correlates of Anger, Angry Rumination, and Aggressive Personality," *Journal of Cognitive Neuroscience*, vol. 21(4), pp. 734–744 (2009)

Ford, Brent Q., & Maya Tamir, "When Getting Angry Is Smart: Emotional Preferences and Emotional Intelligence," *Emotion*, vol. 12(4), pp. 685-689 (2012)

Gable, Philip A., & Eddie Harmon-Jones, "Attentional Consequences of Pregoal and Postgoal Positive Affects," *Emotion*, vol. 11(6), pp. 1358–1367 (2011)

Gadea, Marien, Raul Espert, Alicia Salvador, & Luis Martí-Bonmatí, "The Sad, the Angry, and the Asymmetrical Brain: Dichotic Listening Studies of Negative Affect and Depression," *Brain & Cognition*, vol. 76(2), pp. 294–299 (2011)

Halperin, Eran, Alexandra G. Russell, Carol S. Dweck, & James J. Gross, "Anger, Hatred, and the Quest for Peace: Anger Can Be Constructive in the Absence of Hatred," *Journal of Conflict Resolution*, vol. 55(2), pp. 274–291 (2011)

Herrero, Neus, Marien Gadea, Gabriel Rodríguez-Alarcón, Raúl Espert, & Alicia Salvador, "What Happens When We Get Angry? Hormonal, Cardiovascular and Asymmetrical Brain Responses," *Hormones & Behavior*, vol. 57(3), pp. 276–283 (2010)

Lane, Andrew, "Relationships between Perceptions of Performance Expectations and Mood among Distance Runners: The Moderating Effect of Depressed Mood," *Journal of Science & Medicine in Sport*, vol. 4(1), pp. 116–128 (2001)

Lane, Andrew M., & Peter C. Terry, "The Nature of Mood: Development of a Conceptual Model with a Focus on Depression," *Journal of Applied Sport Psychology*, vol. 12(1), pp. 16–22 (2000)

Lane, Andrew M., Peter C. Terry, Christopher J. Beedie, David A. Curry, & Niall Clark, "Mood and Performance: Test of a Conceptual Model with a Focus on Depressed Mood," *Psychology of Sport & Exercise*, vol. 2(3), pp. 157–172 (2001)

Lane, Andrew M., Gregory P. Whyte, Peter C. Terry, & Alan M. Nevill, "Mood, Self-Set Goals and Examination Performance: The Moderating Effect of Depressed Mood," *Personality & Individual Differences*, vol. 39(1), pp. 143–153 (2005)

Lelieveld, Gert-Jen, Eric Van Dijk, Ilja Van Beest, Wolfgang Steinel, & Gerben A. Van Kleef, "Disappointed in You, Angry about Your Offer: Distinct Negative Emotions Induce Concessions via Different Mechanisms," *Journal of Experimental Social Psychology*, vol. 47(3), pp. 635–641 (2011)

Lerner, Jennifer S., & Dacher Keltner, "Fear, Anger, and Risk," *Journal of Personality & Social Psychology*, vol. 81(1), pp. 146–159 (2001)

Love, Andrew, Interview with Author (2012)

Martinent, Guilluame, Mickaël Campo, & Claude Ferrand, "A Descriptive Study of Emotional Process during Competition: Nature, Frequency, Direction, Duration and Co-Occurrence of Discrete Emotions," *Psychology of Sport & Exercise*, vol. 13(2), pp. 142–151 (2012)

Mayan, Iddo, & Nachson Meiran, "Anger and the Speed of Full-Body Approach and Avoidance Reactions," *Frontiers in Emotion Science*, vol. 2, art. 22 (2011)

Overbeck, Jennifer R., Margaret A. Neale, & Cassandra L. Govan, "I Feel, Therefore You Act: Intrapersonal and Interpersonal Effects of Emotion on Negotiation as a Function of Social Power," *Organizational Behavior & Human Decision Processes*, vol. 112(2), pp. 126–139 (2010)

Peper, Erik, Interview with Author (2011)

Reifen-Tagar, Michal, Christoper M. Federico, & Eran Halperin, "The Positive Effect of Negative Emotions in Protracted Conflict: The Case of Anger," *Journal of Experimental Social Psychology*, vol. 47(1), pp. 157–164 (2011)

Robazza, Claudio, & Laura Bortoli, "Perceived Impact of Anger and Anxiety on Sporting Performance in Rugby Players," *Psychology of Sport & Exercise*, vol. 8(6), pp. 875–896 (2007)

Robazza, Claudio, Laura Bortoli, & Yuri Hanin, "Perceived Effects of Emotion Intensity on Athletic Performance: A Contingency-Based Individualized Approach," *Research Quarterly for Exercise & Sport*, vol. 77(3), pp. 372–385 (2006)

Ruiz, Montse C., & Yuri L. Hanin, "Idiosyncratic Description of Anger States in Skilled Spanish Karate Athletes: An Application of the IZOF Model," *Revista de Psicología del Deporte*, vol. 13(1), pp. 75–93 (2004)

Ruiz, Montse C., & Yuri L. Hanin, "Perceived Impact of Anger on Performance of Skilled Karate Athletes," *Psychology of Sport & Exercise*, vol. 12(3), pp. 242–249 (2011)

Sinaceur, Marwan, Gerben A. Van Kleef, Margaret A. Neale, Adam Hajo, & Christophe Haag, "Hot or Cold: Is Communicating Anger or Threats More Effective in Negotiation?" *Journal of Applied Psychology*, vol. 96(5), pp, 1018–1032 (2011)

Sinaceur, Marwan, & Larissa Z. Tiedens, "Get Mad and Get More Than Even: When and Why Anger Expression Is Effective in Negotiations," *Journal of Experimental Social Psychology*, vol. 42(3), pp. 314–322 (2006)

Steinel, Wolfgang, Gerben A. Van Kleef, & Fieke Harinck, "Are You Talking to *Me*?! Separating the People from the Problem when Expressing Emotions in Negotiation," *Journal of Experimental Social Psychology*, vol. 44(2), pp. 362–369 (2008)

Tamir, Maya, & Brett Q. Ford, "Should People Pursue Feelings that Feel Good or Feelings that Do Good? Emotional Preferences and Well-Being," *Emotion*, vol. 12(5), pp. 1061–1070 (2012)

Van Kleef, Gerben A., Christina Anastasopoulou, & Bernard A. Nijstad, "Can Expressions of Anger Enhance Creativity? A Test of the Emotions as Social Information (EASI) Model," *Journal of Experimental Social Psychology*, vol. 46(6), pp. 1042–1048 (2010)

Van Kleef, Gerben A., & Stéphane Côté, "Expressing Anger in Conflict: When It Helps and When It Hurts," *Journal of Applied Psychology*, vol. 92(6), pp. 1557–1569 (2007)

Van Kleef, Gerben A., Eric Van Dijk, Fieke Harinck, Wolfgang Steinel, & Ilja Van Beest, "Anger in Social Conflict: Cross-Situational Comparisons and Suggestions for the Future," *Group Decision & Negotiation*, vol. 17(1), pp. 13–30 (2008)

Chapter 9—The 'Roid Rage of Chess

1.

The 'Roid Rage and Other Hormones of Tournaments:

While the chess study by Booth and colleagues is perhaps the most famous study to find testosterone (or "T") levels could predict cognitive success prior to an event, it isn't the only study to have done so. For example, in 2011, Flegr had college students submit saliva samples before they took their final exam in a demanding science course. Those with the highest T levels before the exam received the highest grades.

Booth, Alan, Correspondence with Authors (2012)

Booth, Alan, Interview with Author (2012)

Edinger, Kassandra L., & Cheryl A. Frye, "Testosterone's Analgesic, Anxiolytic, and Cognitive-Enhancing Effects May Be Due in Part to Actions of Its 5 α-Reduced Metabolites in the Hippocampus," *Behavioral Neuroscience*, vol. 118(6), pp. 1352–1364 (2004)

Flegr, Jaroslav, Correspondence with Author (2011)

Flegr, Jaroslav, Interview with Author (2011)

Flegr, Jaroslav, & Lenka Príplatová, "Testosterone and Cortisol Levels in University Students Reflect Actual Rather Than Estimated Number of Wrong Answers on Written Exam," *Neuroendocrinology Letters*, vol. 31(4), pp. 577–581 (2010)

Frye, C. A., M. E. Rhodes, R. Rosellini, & B. Svare, "The Nucleus Accumbens as a Site of Action for Rewarding Properties of Testosterone and its 5 α-Reduced Metabolites," *Pharmacology Biochemistry & Behavior*, vol. 75(1), pp. 119–127 (2002)

Hermans, Erno J., Peter A. Bos, Lindsey Ossewaarde, Nick F. Ramsey, Guillén Fernández, & Jack van Honk, "Effects of Exogenous Testosterone on the Ventral Striatal BOLD Response during Reward Anticipation in Healthy Women," *NeuroImage*, vol. 52(1), pp. 277–283 (2010)

Keenan D. M., & J. D. Veldhuis, "Mathematical Modeling of Receptor-Mediated Interlinked Systems," In: Helen L. Henry & Anthony W. Norman (Eds.), *Encyclopedia of Hormones*, pp. 286–294, San Diego: Academic Press (2003)

Mazur, Allan, Alan Booth, & James M. Dabbs, Jr., "Testosterone and Chess Competition," *Social Psychology Quarterly*, vol. 55(1), pp. 70–77 (1992)

Ostojic, Sergej M., Julio Calleja-Gonzalez, & Marko Stojanovic, "Steroid Prohormones: Effects on Body Composition in Athletes," In: Gianluca Aimaretti, Paolo Marzullo & Flavia Prodam (Eds.), *Update on Mechanisms of Hormone Action—Focus on Metabolism, Growth, and Reproduction*, ch. 2, pp. 11–24, Rijeka, Croatia: InTech (2011)

2.

Testosterone as Motivation, Its Impact on Cognition, Aggression:

Adolph, Dirk, Sabine Schlösser, Maren Hawighorst, & Bettina M. Pause, "Chemosensory Signals of Competition Increase the Skin Conductance Response in Humans," *Physiology & Behavior*, pp. 666–671 (2010)

Aleman, André, Erik Bronk, Roy P. C. Kessels, Hans P. F. Koppeschaar, & Jack van Honk, "A Single Administration of Testosterone Improves Visuospatial Ability in Young Women," *Psychoneuroendocrinology*, vol. 29(5), pp. 612–617 (2004)

Archer, John, "Testosterone and Human Aggression: An Evaluation of the Challenge Hypothesis," *Neuroscience & Biobehavioral Reviews*, vol. 30(3), pp. 319–345 (2006)

Bhasin, Shalender, "Androgen Effects in Mammals," In: Helen Henry & Anthony W. Norman (Eds.), *Encyclopedia of Hormones*, San Diego: Academic Press, pp. 70 et seq. (2003)

Blue, Jeffrey G., & John A. Lombardo, "Steroids and Steroid-Like Compounds," *Clinics in Sports Medicine*, vol. 18(3), pp. 667–689 (1999)

Booth, Alan, Correspondence with Authors (2012)

Booth, Alan, Interview with Author (2012)

Booth, Alan, Douglas A. Granger, Allan Mazur, & Katie T. Kivlighan, "Testosterone and Social Behavior," *Social Forces*, vol. 85(1), pp. 179–204 (2006)

Bos, Peter A., Erno J. Hermans, Nick F. Ramsey, & Jack van Honk, "The Neural Mechanisms by Which Testosterone Acts on Interpersonal Trust," *NeuroImage*, vol. 61(3), pp. 730–737 (2012)

Bos, Peter A., Jaak Panksepp, Rose-Marie Bluthé, & Jack van Honk, "Acute Effects of Steroid Hormones and Neuropeptides on Human Social–Emotional Behavior: A Review of Single Administration Studies," *Frontiers in Neuroendocrinology*, vol. 33(1), pp. 17–35 (2012)

Brennan, P. A., M. K. Herd, R. Puxeddu, R. Anand, L. Cascarini, J. S. Brown, C. M. Avery, R. T. M. Woodwards, & D. A. Mitchell, "Serum Testosterone Levels in Surgeons during Major Head and Neck Cancer Surgery: A Suppositional Study," *British Journal of Oral & Maxillofacial Surgery*, vol. 49(3), pp. 190–193 (2011)

Carney, Dana R., Amy J. C. Cudy, & Andy J. Yap, "Power Posing: Brief Nonverbal Displays Affect Neuroendocrine Levels and Risk Tolerance," *Psychological Science*, vol. 21(10), pp. 1363–1368 (2010)

Carré, Justin M., Jenna D. Gilchrist, Mark D. Morrissey, & Cheryl M. McCormick, "Motivational and Situational Factors and the Relationship between Testosterone Dynamics and Human Aggression during Competition," *Biological Psychology*, vol. 84(2), pp. 346–353 (2010)

Carré, Justin M., & Pranjal J. Mehta, "Importance of Considering Testosterone–Cortisol Interactions in Predicting Human Aggression and Dominance," *Aggressive Behavior*, vol. 37(6), pp. 489–491 (2011)

Carré, Justin M., Susan K. Putnam, & Cheryl M. McCormick, "Testosterone Responses to Competition Predict Future Aggressive Behaviour at a Cost to Reward in Men," *Psychoneuroendocrinology*, vol. 34(4), pp. 561–570 (2009)

Denson, Thomas F., Richard Ronay, William von Hippel, & Mark M. Schira, "Endogenous Testosterone and Cortisol Modulate Neural Responses during Induced Anger Control," *Social Neuroscience*, in press (2012)

DiPaolo, Marc, *War, Politics and Superheroes: Ethics and Propaganda in Comics and Film*, Jefferson, NC: McFarland & Co. (2011)

Eubank, Martin, Dave Collins, Geoff Lovell, Debra Dorling, & Steve Talbot, "Individual Temporal Differences in Precompetition Anxiety and Hormonal Concentration," *Personality and Individual Differences*, vol. 23(6), pp. 1031–1039 (1997)

Geniole, Shawn N., Justin M. Carré, & Cheryl M. McCormick, "State, Not Trait, Neuroendocrine Function Predicts Costly Reactive Aggression in Men after Social Exclusion and Inclusion," *Biological Psychology*, vol. 87(1), pp. 137–145 (2011)

Hasegawa, Masako, Masahiro Toda, & Kanehisa Morimoto, "Changes in Salivary Physiological Stress Markers Associated with Winning and Losing," *Biomedical Research*, vol. 29(1), pp. 43–46 (2008)

Hasegawa-Ohira, Masako, Masahiro Toda, & Kanehisa Morimoto, "Stress Hormone Levels in Saliva after Shogi Competition Are Modified by Stress Coping Strategies," *Environmental Health & Preventive Medicine*, vol. 16(6), pp. 369–374 (2011)

Hermans, Erno J., Nick F. Ramsey, & Jack van Honk, "Exogenous Testosterone Enhances Responsiveness to Social Threat in the Neural Circuitry of Social Aggression in Humans," *Biological Psychiatry*, vol. 63(1), pp. 263–270 (2008)

Janowsky, Jeri S., "Thinking with Your Gonads: Testosterone and Cognition," *Trends in Cognitive Science*, vol. 10(2), pp. 77–82 (2006)

Kaplan, Arie, *From Krakow to Krypton: Jews and Comic Books*, Philadelphia: Jewish Publication Society (2008)

Mehta, Pranjal H., & Jennifer Beer, "Neural Mechanisms of the Testosterone-Aggression Relation: The Role of the Orbitofrontal Cortex," *Journal of Cognitive Neuroscience*, vol. 22(10), pp. 2357–2368 (2010)

Peper, Jiska S., Martijn P. van den Heuvel, René C. W. Mandl, Hilleke E. Hulshoff Pol, & Jack van Honk, "Sex Steroids and Connectivity in the Human Brain: A Review of Neuroimaging Studies," *Psychoneuroendocrinology*, vol. 36(8), pp. 1101–1113 (2011)

Peterson, Carly K., & Eddie Harmon-Jones, "Anger and Testosterone: Evidence that Situationally-Induced Anger Relates to Situationally-Induced Testosterone," *Emotion*, vol. 12(5), pp. 899–902 (2012)

Ronay, Richard, Interview with Authors (2012)

Ronay, Richard, & Adam D. Galinsky, "Lex Talionis: Testosterone and the Law of Retaliation," *Journal of Experimental Social Psychology*, vol. 47(3), pp. 702–705 (2011)

Salvador, Alicia, "Steroid Hormones and Some Evolutionary-Relevant Social Interactions," *Motivation & Emotion*, vol. 36(1), pp. 74–83 (2012)

Schutter, Dennis J. L. G., & Jack van Honk, "Decoupling of Midfrontal Delta-Beta Oscillation after Testosterone Administration," *International Journal of Psychophysiology*, vol. 53(1), pp. 71–73 (2004)

Stanton, Steven J., O'Dhaniel A. Mullette-Gillman, R. Edward McLaurin, Cynthia M. Kuhn, Kevin S. LaBar, Michael L. Platt, & Scott A. Huettel, "Low- and High-Testosterone Individuals Exhibit Decreased Aversion to Economic Risk," *Psychological Science*, vol. 22(4), pp. 447–453 (2011)

Terburg, David, Barak Morgan, & Jack van Honk, "The Testosterone–Cortisol Ratio: A Hormonal Marker for Proneness to Social Aggression," *International Journal of Law & Psychiatry*, vol. 32(4), pp. 216–223 (2009)

Van der Meija, Leander, Abraham P. Buunk, Mercedes Almela, & Alicia Salvador, "Testosterone Responses to Competition: The Opponent's Psychological State Makes it Challenging," *Biological Psychology*, vol. 84(2), pp. 330–335 (2010)

Van Honk, Jack, "Testosterone Decreases Trust and Empathy in Humans," Paper Presentation at Annual Convention for the Assn. for Psychological Science, San Francisco (2009)

Van Honk, Jack, Dennis J. L. G. Schutter, Erno J. Hermans, & Peter Putnam, "Testosterone, Cortisol, Dominance, & Submission: Biologically Prepared Motivation, No Psychological Mechanisms Involved," *Behavioral Brain Sciences*, vol. 27(1), p. 160 (2004)

Van Honk, Jack, Dennis J. L. G. Schutter, Erno J. Hermans, Peter Putnam, Adriaan Tuiten, & Hans Koppeschaar, "Testosterone Shifts the Balance between Sensitivity for Punishment and Reward in Healthy Young Women," *Psychoneuroendocrinology*, vol. 29(7), pp. 937–943 (2004)

Van Rijn, S., A. Aleman, L. de Sonneville, M. Sprong, T. Ziermans, P. Schothorst, H. van Engeland, & H. Swaab, "Neuroendocrine Markers of High Risk for Psychosis: Salivary Testosterone in Adolescent Boys with Prodromal Symptoms," *Psychological Medicine*, vol. 41(9), pp. 1815–1822 (2011)

Wu, F. C. W., "Endocrine Aspects of Anabolic Steroids," *Clinical Chemistry*, vol. 43(7), pp. 1289–1292 (1997)

Yildirim, Baris O., & Jan J. L. Derksen, "A Review on the Relationship between Testosterone and the Interpersonal/Affective Facet of Psychopathy," *Psychiatry Research*, vol. 197(3), pp. 181-198 (2012)

3.

Dog Agility Contests / Gender Differences in Handling the Stress of Competition:

While everyone agrees that female levels of testosterone are just a fraction of male levels, there is some variation in what that fraction exactly is—ranging from about 1/10th to as much as 1/5th. The discrepancy may be due to the fact that, as Stanton et al. has found, there are large seasonal variations in T for both men and women. (On average, testosterone is highest in the fall and lowest in the summer.) What is important to remember is that the overall pattern of T's effects is generally the same in women.

"A Beginner's Guide to Companion Events," American Kennel Club (2010)

"Colorful History of America's Dog Show," Westminster Kennel Club, http://bit.ly/w6FTj1 (u.d.)

Costa, Raquel, & Alicia Salvador, "Associations between Success and Failure in a Face-to-Face Competition and Psychobiological Parameters in Young Women," *Psychoneuroendocrinology*, vol. 37(11), pp. 1780-1790 (2012)

Denson, Thomas F., Pranjal H. Mehta, & D. Ho Tan, "Cortisol and Testosterone Jointly Influence Reactive Aggression in Women," Paper Presentation, Social Neuroendocrinology Pre-Conference, San Diego (2012)

Dugan, Michael, & Cathy Dugan, "Seven Secrets of Show Dog Success, Pt. 4," *Dogs in Review* (May 2011)

"Economic Benefits of AKC Dog Shows," American Kennel Club flyer (u.d.)

Goetz, Stefan J., S. K. Putnam, & Justin M. Carré, "Effect of Competition Ambiguity on Testosterone Release and Willingness to Compete in Women," Paper Presentation, Social Neuroendocrinology Pre-Conference, San Diego (2012)

Jiménez, Manuel, Raúl Aguilar, & José R. Alvero-Cruz, "Effects of Victory and Defeat on Testosterone and Cortisol Response to Competition: Evidence for Same Response Patterns in Men and Women," *Psychoneuroendocrinology*, vol. 37(9), pp. 1577–1581 (2012)

Jones, Amanda C., & Robert A. Josephs, "Interspecies Hormonal Interactions between Man and the Domestic Dog (Canis Familaris)," *Hormones & Behavior*, vol. 50(3), pp. 393–400 (2006)

Kennedy Melia, Marilyn, "Professional Dog Handler," *Chicago Tribune*, http://bit.ly/PvRtxL (4/2/2000)

Mazur, Allan, Elizabeth Susman, & Sandy Edelbrock, "Sex Difference in Testosterone Response to a Video Game Contest," *Evolution & Human Behavior*, vol. 18(5), pp. 317–326 (1997)

McClarty, Barbara, "In the Ring: The Life of a Dog Handler," *Modern Dog*, http://bit.ly/S3TOpv (1992)

Mehta, Pranjal, Correspondence with Authors (2012)

Mehta, Pranjal, Interviews with Authors (2012)

Mehta, Pranjal H., Stefan M. Goetz, & Justin Carré, "The Social Neuroscience of Human Aggression: Genetic, Hormonal, and Neural Underpinning," In: D. Frank & J. Turner, *Handbook of Neurosociology*, ch. 5, pp. 47-65, New York: Springer (2013)

Mehta, Pranjal H., Amanda C. Jones, & Robert A. Josephs, "The Social Endocrinology of Dominance: Basal Testosterone Predicts Cortisol Changes and Behavior Following Victory and Defeat," *Journal of Personality & Social Psychology*, vol. 94(6), pp. 1078–1093 (2008)

Mehta, Pranjal H., & Robert A. Josephs, "Testosterone and Cortisol Jointly Regulate Dominance: Evidence for a Dual-Hormone Hypothesis," *Hormones & Behavior*, vol. 58(5), pp. 898–906 (2010)

Mehta, Pranjal H., & Robert A. Josephs, "Testosterone Change after Losing Predicts the Decision to Compete Again," *Hormones & Behavior*, vol. 50(5), pp. 684–692 (2006)

Mehta, Pranjal H., Elizabeth V. Wuehrmann, & Robert A. Josephs, "When Are Low Testosterone Levels Advantageous? The Moderating Role of Individual versus Intergroup Competition," *Hormones & Behavior*, vol. 56(1), pp. 158–162 (2009)

Oliveira, T., M. J. Gouveia, & R. F. Oliveira, "Testosterone Responsiveness to Winning and Losing Experiences in Female Soccer Players," *Psychoneuroendocrinology*, vol. 34(7), pp. 1056–1064 (2005)

Stanton, Steven J., O'Dhaniel A. Mullette-Gillman, & Scott A. Huettel, "Seasonal Variation of Salivary Testosterone in Men, Normally Cycling Women, and Women Using Hormonal Contraceptives," *Physiology & Behavior*, vol. 104(5), pp. 804–808 (2011)

Taylor, Shelley E., Laura Cousino Klein, Brian P. Lewis, Tara L. Gruenewald, Regan A. R. Gurung, & John A. Updegraff, "Biobehavioral Responses to Stress in Females: Tend-and-Befriend, Not Fight-or-Flight," *Psychological Review*, vol. 107(3), pp. 411–429 (2000)

Testosterone Responds When You Care about the Outcome / Testosterone in Home Field Advantage:

Bateman, Chris, & Lennart E. Nacke, "The Neurobiology of Play," Paper Presentation at Futureplay '10 Proceedings of the International Academic Conference on the Future of Game Design and Technology, New York (2010)

Carré, Justin, Correspondence with Authors (2012)

Carré, Justin, Interviews with Authors (2012)

Carré, Justin M., "No Place Like Home: Testosterone Responses to Victory Depend on Game Location," *American Journal of Human Biology*, vol. 21(3), pp. 392–394 (2009)

Carré, Justin, Cameron Muir, Joey Belanger, & Susan K. Putnam, "Pre-Competition Hormonal and Psychological Levels of Elite Hockey Players: Relationship to the 'Home Advantage,'" *Physiology & Behavior*, vol. 89(3), pp. 392–398 (2006)

Fuxjager, Matthew J., Robin M. Forbes-Lorman, Dylan J. Coss, Catherine J. Auger, Anthony P. Auger, & Catherine A. Marlera, "Winning Territorial Disputes Selectively Enhances Androgen Sensitivity in Neural Pathways Related to Motivation and Social Aggression," *Proceedings of the National Academy of Sciences*, vol. 107(27), pp. 12393–12398 (2010)

Fuxjager, Matthew J., Gabriel Mast, Elizabeth A. Becker, & Catherine A. Marler, "The 'Home Advantage' Is Necessary for a Full Winner Effect and Changes in Post-Encounter Testosterone," *Hormones & Behavior*, vol. 56(2), pp. 214–219 (2009)

Oxford, Jonathan, Davidé Ponzi, & David C. Geary, "Hormonal Responses Differ When Playing Violent Video Games against an Ingroup and Outgroup," *Evolution & Human Behavior*, vol. 31(3), pp. 201–209 (2010)

Putnam, Susan K., & Justin Carré, "Game Location Moderates the Relationship between Anticipatory Testosterone Changes and Athletic Performance," *International Journal of Sports Physiology*, vol. 7(3), pp. 301-303 (2012)

Van Anders, Sari M., & Neil V. Watson, "Effects of Ability- and Chance-Determined Competition Outcome on Testosterone," *Physiology & Behavior*, vol. 90(4), pp. 634–642 (2007)

Wagner, John D., Mark V. Flinn, & Barry G. England, "Hormonal Response to Competition among Male Coalitions," *Evolution & Human Behavior*, vol. 23(6), pp. 437–442 (2002)

4.

A New Understanding of Cortisol...:

For additional research on stress responses, please see the sources listed in Chapter 4, as well as Rohleder et al. and Deinzer et al., discussed in Chapter 1. The cited research on the biochemical aspects of anxiety and challenge/threat states is also relevant.

Akinola, Modupe, & Mendes, Wendy Berry, "Stress-Induced Cortisol Facilitates Threat-Related Decision Making among Police Officers," *Behavioral Neuroscience*, vol. 126(1), pp. 167–174 (2012)

Bourdeau, Isabelle, & Constantine A. Stratakis, "Pharmacology of Glucocorticoids," In: Helen L. Henry & Anthony W. Norman (Eds.), *Encyclopedia of Hormones*, pp. 104 et seq., San Diego: Academic Press (2003)

Ehrhart-Bornstein, Monika, & Stefan R. Bornstein, "Cross-Talk between Adrenal Medulla and Adrenal Cortex in Stress," *Annals of the New York Academy of Sciences*, vol. 1148, pp. 112–117 (2008)

Ell, Shawn W., Brandon Cosley, & Shannon K. McCoy, "When Bad Stress Goes Good: Increased Threat Reactivity Predicts Improved Category Learning Performance," *Psychonomic Bulletin & Review*, vol. 18(1), pp. 96–102 (2011)

Filaire, Edith, Deborah Alix, Claude Ferrand, & Michel Verger, "Psychophysiological Stress in Tennis Players during the First Single Match of a Tournament," *Psychoneuroendocrinology*, vol. 34(1), pp. 150–157 (2009)

Gonzalez-Bono, E., A. Salvador, M. A. Serrano, & J. Ricarte, "Testosterone, Cortisol, and Mood in a Sports Team Competition," *Hormones & Behavior*, vol. 35(1), pp. 55–62 (1999)

Het, Serkan, Daniela Schoofs, Nicolas Rohleder, & Oliver Wolf, "Stress-Induced Cortisol Level Elevations Are Associated with Reduced Negative Affect after Stress: Indications for a Mood-Buffering Cortisol Effect," *Psychosomatic Medicine*, vol. 74(1), pp. 23–32 (2012)

Joëls, Marian, Gullen Fernandez, & Benno Roozendaal, "Stress and Emotional Memory: A Matter of Timing," *Trends in Cognitive Sciences*, vol. 15(6), pp. 280–288 (2011)

Kivlighan, Katie T., Douglas A. Granger, & Alan Booth, "Gender Differences in Testosterone and Cortisol Response to Competition," *Psychoneuroendocrinology*, vol. 30(1), pp. 58–71 (2005)

Koolhaas, J. M., A. Bartolomucci, B. Buwalda, S. F. de Boer, G. Flügge, S. M. Korte, P. Meerlo, R. Murison, B. Olivier, Pl. Palanza, G. Richter-Levin, A. Sgoifo, T. Steimer, O. Stiedl, G. van Dijk, M. Wöhr, & E. Fuchs, "Stress Revisited: A Critical Evaluation of the Stress Concept," *Neuroscience & Biobehavioral Reviews*, vol. 35(5), pp. 1291–1301 (2011)

Kudielka, Brigitte M., D. H. Hellhammer, & Stefan Wüst, "Why Do We Respond So Differently? Reviewing Determinants of Human Salivary Cortisol Responses to Challenge," *Psychoneuroendocrinology*, vol. 34(1), pp. 2–18 (2009)

Kyrou, Ioannis, & Constantine Tsigos, "Stress Hormones: Physiological Stress and Regulation of Metabolism," *Current Opinion in Pharmacology*, vol. 9(6), pp. 787–793 (2009)

Montoya, Estrella R., David Terburg, Peter A. Bos, & Jack van Honk, "Testosterone, Cortisol, and Serotonin," *Motivation & Emotion*, vol. 36(1), pp. 65–73 (2012)

Putman, Peter, Niki Antypa, Panagiota Crysovergi, & Willem A. J. van der Does, "Exogenous Cortisol Acutely Influences Motivated Decision Making in Healthy Young Men," *Psychopharmacology*, vol. 208(2), pp. 257–263 (2010)

Putman, Peter, Erno J. Hermans, Hans Koppeschaar, Alexandra van Schijndel, & Jack van Honk, "A Single Administration of Cortisol Acutely Reduces Preconscious Attention for Fear in Anxious Young Men," *Psychoneuroendocrinology*, vol. 32(7), pp. 793–802 (2007)

Putman, Peter, & Karin Roelofs, "Effects of Single Cortisol Administrations on Human Affect Reviewed: Coping with Stress through Adaptive Regulation of Automatic Cognitive Processing," *Psychoneuroendocrinology*, vol. 32(7), pp. 793–802 (2007)

Rimmele, Ulrike, Roland Seiler, Bernard Marti, Petra H. Wirtz, Ulrike Ehlert, & Markus Heinrichs, "The Level of Physical Activity Affects Adrenal and Cardiovascular Reactivity to Psychosocial Stress," *Psychoneuroendocrinology*, vol. 34(2), pp. 190–198 (2009)

Soravia, Leila M., Markus Heinrichs, Amanda Aerni, Caroline Maroni, Gustav Schelling, Ulrike Ehlert, Benno Roozendaal, & Dominique J-F de Quervain, "Glucocorticoids Reduce Phobic Fear in Humans," *Proceedings of the National Academy of Sciences*, vol. 103(14), pp. 5585–5590 (2006)

Van Peer, Jacobien M., Karin Roelofs, & Philip Spinhoven, "Cortisol Administration Enhances the Coupling of Midfrontal Delta and Beta Oscillations," *International Journal of Psychophysiology*, vol. 67(2), pp. 144–150 (2008)

Wurtman, Richard J., "Stress and the Adrenocortical Control of Epinephrine Synthesis," *Metabolism—Clinical & Experimental*, vol. 51(6), Pt. B, pp. 11–14 (2002)

Zilioli, Samuele, & Neil V. Watson, "The Hidden Dimensions of the Competition Effect: Basal Cortisol and Basal Testosterone Jointly Predict Changes in Salivary Testosterone after Social Victory in Men," *Psychoneuroendocrinology*, vol. 37(11), pp. 1855-1865 (2012)

…And Oxytocin…:

Baron-Cohen, Simon, *The Essential Difference: Men, Women, and the Truth about Autism*, New York: Basic Books (2004)

Baron-Cohen, Simon, Sally Wheelwright, Jacqueline Hill, Yogini Raste, & Ian Plumb, "The 'Reading the Mind in the Eyes' Test Revised Version: A Study with Normal Adults, and Adults with Asperger Syndrome or High-Functioning Autism," *Journal of Child Psychology & Psychiatry*, vol. 42(2), pp. 241–251 (2001)

Bartz, Jennifer, "Interactionist Perspective on the Prosocial Effects of Oxytocin in Humans," Paper Presentation, Social Neuroendocrinology Pre-Conference, San Diego (2012)

Bartz, Jennifer, Daphne Simeon, Holly Hamilton, Suah Kim, Sarah Crystal, Ashley Braun, Victor Vicens, & Eric Hollander, "Oxytocin Can Hinder Trust and Cooperation in Borderline Personality Disorder," *Social Cognitive & Affective Neuroscience*, vol. 6(5), pp. 556–563 (2011)

Bos, Peter A., Jaak Panksepp, Rose-Marie Bluthé, & Jack van Honk, "Acute Effects of Steroid Hormones and Neuropeptides on Human Social–Emotional Behavior: A Review of Single Administration Studies," *Frontiers in Neuroendocrinology*, vol. 33(1), pp. 17–35 (2012)

Bullock, Sandra, Quinton Aaron (perfs.), Hancock, John Lee (dir./scr.), *The Blind Side*, Warner Bros., Film (2009)

Churchland, Patricia S., & Piotr Winkielman, "Modulating Social Behavior with Oxytocin: How Does It Work? What Does It Mean?," *Hormones & Behavior*, vol. 61(3), pp. 392–399 (2012)

De Dreu, Cartsen, Interviews with Authors (2012)

De Dreu, Carsten K. W., "The Neuroendocrinology of 'Tend-and-Defend' Responding in Intergroup Conflict," Paper Presentation, Social Neuroendocrinology Pre-Conference, San Diego (2012)

De Dreu, Carsten K. W., "Oxytocin Modulates Cooperation within and Competition between Groups: An Integrative Review and Research Agenda," *Hormones & Behavior*, vol. 61(3), pp. 419–428 (2012)

De Dreu, Carsten K. W., "Oxytocin Modulates the Link between Adult Attachment and Cooperation through Reduced Betrayal Aversion," *Psychoneuroendocrinology*, vol. 37(7), pp. 871–880 (2012)

De Dreu, Carsten K. W., Lindred L. Greer, Michel J. J. Handgraff, Shaul Shalvi, & Gerben A. Van Kleef, "Oxytocin Modulates Selection of Allies in Intergroup Conflict," *Proceedings of the Royal Society of Biological Sciences, B*, vol. 279(1731), pp. 1150–1154 (2012)

De Dreu, Carsten K. W., Lindred L. Greer, Gerben A. Van Kleef, Shaul Shalvi, & Michel J. J. Handgraff, "Oxytocin Promotes Human Ethnocentrism," *Proceedings of the National Academy of Sciences*, vol. 108(4), pp. 1262–1266 (2011)

Domes, Gregor, Markus Heinrichs, Jan Gläscher, Christain Büchel, Dieter F. Braus, & Sabine C. Herpertz, "Oxytocin Attenuates Amygdala Responses to Emotional Faces Regardless of Valence," *Biological Psychiatry*, vol. 62(10), pp. 1187–1190 (2007)

Domes, Gregor, Markus Heinrichs, Andre Michel, Christop Berger, & Sabine C. Herpertz, "Oxytocin Improves 'Mind-Reading' in Humans," *Biological Psychiatry*, vol. 61(6), pp. 731–733 (2007)

Fischer-Shofty, Meytal, Yechiel Levkovitz, & Simone G. Shamay-Tsoory, "Oxytocin Facilitates Accurate Perception of Competition in Men and Kinship in Women," *Social Cognitive & Affective Neuroscience*, online early release, doi:10.1093/scan/nsr100524 (2012)

Gamer, Matthias, Bartosz Zurowski, & Christian Büchel, "Different Amygdala Subregions Mediate Valence-Related and Attentional Effects of Oxytocin in Humans," *Proceedings of the National Academy of Sciences*, vol. 107(20), pp. 9400–9405 (2010)

Gamer, Matthias, Bartosz Zurowski, & Christian Büchel, "Oxytocin Specifically Enhances Valence-Dependent Parasympathetic Responses," *Psychoneuroendocrinology*, vol. 37(1), pp. 87–93 (2012)

Gordon, Ilanit, Carina Martin, Ruth Feldman, & James F. Leckman, "Oxytocin and Social Motivation," *Developmental Cognitive Neuroscience*, vol. 1(4), pp. 471–493 (2011)

Guastella, Adam J., Philip B. Mitchell, & Mark R. Dadds, "Oxytocin Increases Gaze to the Eye Region of Human Faces," *Biological Psychiatry*, vol. 63(1), pp. 3–5 (2008)

Hahn-Holbrook J., M. Haselton, J. Holt-Lunstad, C. Holbrook, L. Glynn, & C. Dunkel Schetter, "The Role of Breastfeeding and Oxytocin in Shaping the Maternal Mind," Paper Presentation, Social Neuroendocrinology Pre-Conference, San Diego (2012)

Hahn-Holbrook, Jennifer, Julianne Holt-Lunstad, Colin Holbrook, Sarah M. Coyne, & E. Thomas Lawson, "Maternal Defense: Breast Feeding Increases Aggression by Reducing Stress," *Psychological Science*, vol. 22(10), pp. 1288–1295 (2011)

Heinrichs, Markus, & Gregor Domes, "Neuropeptides and Social Behaviour: Effects of Oxytocin and Vasopressin in Humans," *Progress in Brain Research*, vol. 170, pp. 337–350 (2008)

Kubzansky, Laura D., Wendy Berry Mendes, Allison A. Appleton, Jason Block, & Gail K. Adler, "A Heart Felt Response: Oxytocin Effects on Response to Social Stress in Men and Women," *Biological Psychology*, vol. 90(1), pp. 1–9 (2012)

Mendes, Wendy Berry, "Psychological States Potentiate the Effect of Hormones on Affective Experiences," Paper Presentation, Social Neuroendocrinology Pre-Conference, San Diego (2012)

Rimmele, Ulrike, Karin Hediger, Markus Heinrichs, & Peter Klaver, "Oxytocin Makes a Face in Memory Familiar," *Journal of Neuroscience*, vol. 29(1), pp. 38–42 (2009)

Simeon D., J. Bartz, H. Hamilton, S. Crystal, A. Braun, S. Ketay, & E. Hollander, "Oxytocin Administration Attenuates Stress Reactivity in Borderline Personality Disorder: A Pilot Study," Paper Presentation, Social Neuroendocrinology Pre-Conference, San Diego (2012)

Van Anders, Sari M., Katherine L. Goldey, & Patty X. Kuo, "The Steroid/Peptide Theory of Social Bonds: Integrating Testosterone and Peptide Responses for Classifying Social Behavioral Contexts," *Psychoneuroendocrinology*, vol. 36(9), pp. 1265–1275 (2011)

Young, Larry, & Hans H. Zingg, "Oxytocin," In: Anne M. Etgen & Donald W. Pfaff (Eds.), *Molecular Mechanisms of Hormones Actions on Behavior*, ch. 25, pp. 783–802, San Diego: Academic Press (2009)

Zak, Paul J., *The Moral Molecule: The Source of Love and Prosperity*, New York: Dutton / Penguin Group (2012)

5.

Testosterone Responds to What Society Values:

Aarts, Henk, & Jack van Honk, "Testosterone and Unconscious Positive Priming Increase Human Motivation Separately," *NeuroReport*, vol. 20(14), pp. 1300–1303 (2009)

Carré, Justin, "The Social Neuroendocrinology of Human Aggression," Paper Presentation, Social Neuroendocrinology Pre-Conference, San Diego (2012)

Edwards, David A., "Competition and Testosterone," *Hormones & Behavior*, vol. 50, pp. 681–683 (2006)

Edwards, David A., Correspondence with Author (2012)

Edwards, David A., & Lauren S. Kurlander, "Women's Intercollegiate Volleyball and Tennis: Effects of Warm-Up, Competition, and Practice on Saliva Levels of Cortisol and Testosterone," *Hormones & Behavior*, vol. 58(4), pp. 606–613 (2010)

Edwards, David A., Jennifer Waters, Alexis Weiss, & Amalia Jarvis, "Intercollegiate Athletics: Competition Increases Saliva Testosterone in Women Soccer, Volleyball, and Softball Players," In: L. I. Ardis (Ed.), in *Testosterone Research Trends*, ch. 1, pp. 159–209, New York: Nova Science Publishers, Inc. (2007)

Edwards, David A., Karen Wetzel, & Dana R. Wyner, "Intercollegiate Soccer: Saliva Cortisol and Testosterone Are Elevated during Competition, and Testosterone Is Related to Status and Social Connectedness with Teammates," *Physiology & Behavior*, vol. 87(1), pp. 135–143 (2006)

Eisenegger, C., M. Naef, R. Snozzi, M. Heinrichs, & E. Fehr, "Prejudice and Truth about the Effect of Testosterone on Human Bargaining Behavior," *Nature*, vol. 463, pp. 356–359 (2010)

Fannin, Noel, & James M. Dabbs, Jr., "Testosterone and the Work of Firefighters: Fighting Fires and Delivering Medical Care," *Journal of Research in Personality*, vol. 37(2), pp. 107–115 (2003)

Gesquiere, Laurence R., Niki H. Learn, M. Carolina M. Simao, Patrick O. Onyango, & Susan C. Alberts, "Life at the Top: Rank and Stress in Wild Male Baboons," *Science*, vol. 333(6040), pp. 357–360 (2011)

Gleason, Erin D., Matthew J. Fuxjager, Temitayo O. Oyegbile, & Catherine A. Marler, "Testosterone Release and Social Context: When It Occurs and Why," *Frontiers in Neuroendocrinology*, vol. 30(4), pp. 460–469 (2009)

Gordon, Ilanit, Carina Martin, Ruth Feldman, & James F. Leckman, "Oxytocin and Social Motivation," *Developmental Cognitive Neuroscience*, vol. 1(4), pp. 471–493 (2011)

Josephs, Robert A., Pranjal H. Mehta, & Justin M. Carré, "Gender and Social Environment Modulate the Effects of Testosterone on Social Behavior: Comment on Eisenegger et al.," *Trends in Cognitive Sciences*, vol. 15(11), p. 509 (2011)

Josephs, Robert A., Jennifer Guinn Sellers, Matthew L. Newman, & Pranjal H. Mehta, "The Mismatch Effect: When Testosterone and Status Are at Odds," *Journal of Personality and Social Psychology*, vol. 90(6), pp. 999–1013 (2006)

Liening, S. H., P. H. Mehta, & R. A. Josephs, "Competition," In: Vilanayur S. Ramachandran (Ed.), *Encyclopedia of Human Behavior*, New York: Academic Press (2012)

Miller, Saul L., Jon K. Maner, & James K. McNulty, "Adaptive Attunement to the Sex of Individuals at a Competition: The Ratio of Opposite- to Same-Sex Individuals Correlates with Changes in Competitors' Testosterone Levels," *Evolution & Human Behavior*, vol. 33(1), pp. 57–63 (2012)

Ronay, Richard, Interview with Authors (2012)

Sapolsky, Robert M., "Sympathy for the CEO," *Science*, vol. 333(6040), pp. 293–294 (2011)

Sellers, Jennifer, Interview with Authors (2012)

Sellers, Jennifer Guinn, Matthais R. Mehl, & Robert A. Josephs, "Hormones and Personality: Testosterone as a Marker of Individual Differences," *Journal of Research in Personality*, vol. 14(1), pp. 126–138 (2007)

Stanton, Stephen, Interview with Authors (2012)

Van Anders, Sari M., Katherine L. Goldey, & Patty X. Kuo, "The Steroid/Peptide Theory of Social Bonds: Integrating Testosterone and Peptide Responses for Classifying Social Behavioral Contexts," *Psychoneuroendocrinology*, vol. 36(9), pp. 1265–1275 (2011)

Van Honk, Jack, "Testosterone Decreases Trust and Empathy in Humans," Paper Presentation at Annual Convention for Assn. for Psychological Science, San Francisco, CA (2009)

Van Honk, Jack, Dennis J. L. G. Schutter, Erno J. Hermans, & Peter Putnam, "Testosterone, Cortisol, Dominance, & Submission: Biologically Prepared Motivation, No Psychological Mechanisms Involved," *Behavioral Brain Sciences*, vol. 27(1), p. 160 (2004)

Zitzmann, M., & E. Nieschlag, "Testosterone Levels in Healthy Men and the Relation to Behavioural and Physical Characteristics: Facts and Constructs," *European Journal of Endocrinology*, vol. 144(3), pp. 183–197 (2001)

PART IV

The Patti Smith quote is from Scott Cohen's article, "Patti Smith: Can You Hear Me Ethiopia?" *Circus Magazine* (Dec. 14, 1976).

Chapter 10—The Hierarchy of Teams

1.

Jason Lezak, the Emotions and Neuroscience of Being on a Team:

Please see the citations for Chapter 1 for information relating to Lezak's performance. Additionally, research relating to the Chapter 7 discussion of the neuroscience of mistakes—particularly studies done in cooperation and competition (e.g., de Bruijn et al.'s studies, and Decenty et al.)—is also an important addition.

Cikara, Mina, Matthew M. Botvinick, & Susan T. Fiske, "Us versus Them: Social Identity Shapes Neural Responses to Intergroup Competition and Harm," *Psychological Science*, vol. 22(3), pp. 306–313 (2011)

Lezak, Jason, Interview with Author (2012)

Molenberghs, Pascal, Veronika Halász, Jason B. Mattingley, Eric J. Vanman, & Ross Cunnington, "Seeing is Believing: Neural Mechanisms of Action–Perception Are Biased by Team Membership," online early release, doi:10.1002/hbm.22044 (2012)

Schloss, Karen B., Rosa M. Poggesi, & Stephen E. Palmer, "Effects of University Affiliation and 'School Spirit' on Color Preferences: Berkeley versus Stanford," *Psychonomic Bulletin & Review*, vol. 18(3), pp. 498–504 (2011)

Walton, Gregory M., Geoffrey L. Cohen, David Cwir, & Steven J. Spencer, "Mere Belonging: The Power of Social Connections," *Journal of Personality & Social Psychology*, vol. 102(3), pp. 513–532 (2012)

2.

Rise, Popularity and Rewards for Use of Teamwork:

Allen, Natalie J., & Tracy D. Hecht, "The 'Romance of Teams': Toward an Understanding of Its Psychological Underpinnings and Implications," *Journal of Occupational and Organizational Psychology*, vol. 77(4), pp. 439–461 (2010)

Bikfalvi, Andrea, "Teamwork in Production: Implementation, Its Determinants, and Estimates for German Manufacturing," *Human Factors and Ergonomics in Manufacturing & Service Industries*, vol. 21(3), pp. 244–259 (2011)

Cain, Susan, *Quiet: The Power of Introverts in a World that Can't Stop Talking*, New York: Crown Publishers (2012) (regarding use of teams in American classrooms)

Erev, Ido, Gary Bornstein, & Rachely Galili, "Constructive Intergroup Competition as a Solution to the Rider Problem: A Field Experiment," *Journal of Experimental Social Psychology*, vol. 29, pp. 463–478 (1993)

Garvey, Charlotte, "Focus on Compensation-Steer Teams with the Right Pay," *HR Magazine*, vol. 47(5), http://bit.ly/O7TIHl (2002) (reporting on USC analysis of the rise of companies using team-based compensation)

Gibson, Cristina B., Christine L. Porath, George S. Benson, & Edward E. Lawler III, "What Results When Firms Implement Practices: The Differential Relationship between Specific Practices, Firm Financial Performance, Customer Service, and Quality," *Journal of Applied Psychology*, vol. 92(6), pp. 1467–1480 (2007)

Maymin, Allan, Philip Maymin, & Eugene Shen, "NBA Chemistry: Positive and Negative Synergies in Basketball," http://ssrn.com/abstract=1935972 (10/7/2011)

Maynard, M. Travis, John E. Mathieu, Tammy L. Rapp, & Lucy L. Gilson, "Something(s) Old and Something(s) New: Modeling Drivers of Global Virtual Team Effectiveness," *Journal of Organizational Behavior*, vol. 33(3), pp. 342–365 (2012)

Naquin, Charles E., & Renee O. Tynan, "The Team Halo Effect: Why Teams Are Not Blamed for Their Failures," *Journal of Applied Psychology*, vol. 88(2), pp. 332–340 (2003)

Rapp, Adam, Michael Ahearne, John Mathieu, & Tammy Rapp, "Managing Sales Teams in a Virtual Environment," *International Journal of Research in Marketing*, vol. 27(3), pp. 213–224 (2010)

Staw, Barry M., "Attribution of the 'Causes' of Performance: A General Alternative Interpretation of Cross-Sectional Research on Organizations," *Organizational Behavior & Human Performance*, vol. 13(3), pp. 414–432 (1975)

Staw, Barry M., & Lisa D. Epstein, "What Bandwagons Bring: Effects of Popular Management Techniques on Corporate Performance, Reputation, and CEO Pay," *Administrative Science Quarterly*, vol. 45(3), pp. 523–556 (2000)

Tannenbaum, Scott I., John Mathieu, Eduardo Salas, & Debra Cohen, "Teams Are Changing: Are Research and Practice Evolving Fast Enough?" *Industrial and Organizational Psychology*, vol. 5(1), pp. 2–24 (2012)

Wageman, Ruth, Heidi Gardner, & Mark Mortensen, "The Changing Ecology of Teams: New Directions for Teams Research," *Journal of Organizational Behavior*, vol. 33(3), pp. 301–315 (2012)

West, Michael A., & Joanne Lyubovnikova, "Real Teams or Pseudo Teams? The Changing Landscape Needs a Better Map," *Industrial and Organizational Psychology*, vol. 5(1), pp. 25–28 (2012)

Team Size, Connections and Communication:

Aubé, Caroline, Vincent Rousseau, & Sébastien Tremblay, "Team Size and Quality of Group Experience: The More the Merrier?," *Group Dynamics: Theory, Research, and Practice*, vol. 15(4), pp. 357–375 (2011)

Barkan, Rachel, Ido Erev, Einat Zinger, & Mayan Tzach, "Tip Policy, Visibility and Quality of Service in Cafés," *Tourism Economics*, vol. 10(4), pp. 449–462 (2004)

Barnes, Christopher M., John R. Hollenbeck, David T. Wagner, D. Scott DeRue, Jennifer D. Nahrgang, & Kelly M. Schwind, "Harmful Help: The Costs of Backing-Up Behavior in Teams," *Journal of Applied Psychology*, vol. 93(3), pp. 529–539 (2008)

"A Call for Raising Industry Benchmarks in IT Service Delivery," Tata Consultancy Services (TCS), http://bit.ly/OwMc9N (2012)

Carron, Albert V., Shauna M. Burke, & Kim M. Shapcott, "Enhancing Team Effectiveness," In: Britton W. Brewer, *Sport Psychology*, ch. 7, Oxford: Wiley-Blackwell (2009)

Dalenberg, Sander, Ad L. W. Vogelaar, & Bianca Beersma, "The Effect of a Team Strategy Discussion on Military Team Performance," *Military Psychology*, vol. 21(supp. 2), pp. S31–S46 (2009)

Driskell, James E., & Eduardo Salas, "Groupware, Group Dynamics, and Team Performance," In: Clint Bowers, Eduardo Salas, & Florian Jentsch (Eds.), *Creating High-Tech Teams: Practical Guidance on Work Performance and Technology*, Washington, DC: American Psychological Assn. (2006)

Ellis, Aleksander P. J., "System Breakdown: The Role of Mental Models and Transactive Memory in the Relationship between Acute Stress and Team Performance," *Academy of Management Journal*, vol. 49(3), pp. 576–589 (2006)

Fincannon, Thomas, Joseph R. Keebler, Florian Jentsch, Elizabeth Phillips, & A. William Evans III, "Team Size, Team Role, Communication Modality, and Team Coordination in the Distributed Operation of Multiple Heterogeneous Unmanned Vehicles," *Journal of Cognitive Engineering & Decision Making*, vol. 5(1), pp. 106–131 (2011)

Gardner, Heidi K., "Performance Pressure as a Double-Edged Sword Enhancing Team Motivation but Undermining the Use of Team Knowledge," *Administrative Science Quarterly*, vol. 57(1), pp. 1–46 (2012)

Johnson, Michael D., John R. Hollenbeck, Stephen E. Humphrey, Daniel R. Ilgen, Dustin Jundt, & Christopher J. Meyer, "Cutthroat Competition: Asymmetrical Adaptation to Changes in Team Reward Structures," *Academy of Management Journal*, vol. 49(2), pp. 103–119 (2006)

Mueller, Jennifer S., "Why Individuals in Larger Teams Perform Worse," *Organizational Behavior & Human Decision Processes*, vol. 117(1), pp. 111–124 (2012)

Noe, Raymond A., Ali McConnell Dachner, Brian Sexton, & Kathryn E. Keeton, "Team Training for Long-Duration Missions in Isolated and Confined Environments: A Literature Review, an Operational Assessment, and Recommendations for Practice and Research," NASA/TM-2011-216162, Houston: NASA (2011)

Nokes-Malach, Timothy J., Michelle L. Meade, & Daniel G. Morrow, "The Effect of Expertise on Collaborative Problem Solving," *Thinking & Reasoning*, vol. 18(1), pp. 32–58 (2012)

Salas, Eduardo, Diana R. Nichols, & James E. Driskell, "Testing Three Team Training Strategies in Intact Teams: A Meta-Analysis," *Small Group Research*, vol. 38(4), pp. 471–488 (2007)

Staats, Bradley R., Correspondence with Author (2012)

Staats, Bradley R., Katherine L. Milkman, & Craig R. Fox, "The Team Scaling Fallacy: Underestimating the Declining Efficacy of Teams," *Organizational Behavior & Human Decision Processes*, vol. 118(2), pp. 132–142 (2012)

3.

60-30-10 Rule: Importance of Defining Team Roles, Structuring to Improve Team Performance:

Carron, Albert V., Shauna M. Burke, & Kim M. Shapcott, "Enhancing Team Effectiveness," In: Britton W. Brewer, *Sport Psychology*, ch. 7, Oxford: Wiley-Blackwell (2009)

Edmondson, Amy C., "Teamwork on the Fly," *Harvard Business Review*, vol. 90(4), (Apr. 2012)

Hackman, J. Richard, *Collaborative Intelligence: Using Teams to Solve Hard Problems*, San Francisco: Berrett-Koehler Publishers, Inc. (2011)

Hackman, J. Richard, "From Causes to Conditions in Group Research," *Journal of Organizational Behavior*, vol. 33(3), pp. 428–444 (2012)

Hackman, J. Richard, "Why Teams Don't Work," *Leader to Leader*, vol. 1998(7), pp. 24–31 (1998)

Hackman, J. Richard, & Ruth Wageman, "When and How Team Leaders Matter," *Research in Organizational Behavior*, vol. 26, pp. 37–74 (2005)

Klein, Cameron, Deborah DiazGranados, Eduardo Salas, Huy Le, & C. Shawn Burke, "Does Team Building Work?," *Small Group Research*, vol. 40(1), pp. 181–222 (2009)

Salas, Eduardo, Nancy J. Cooke, & Michael A. Rosen, "On Teams, Teamwork, and Team Performance: Discoveries and Developments," *Human Factors: The Journal of the Human Factors and Ergonomics Society*, vol. 50(3), pp. 540–547 (2008)

Shuffler, Marissa L., Deborah DiazGranados, & Eduardo Salas, "There's a Science for That," *Current Directions in Psychological Science*, vol. 20(6), pp. 365–372 (2011)

Valentine, Melissa, Interview with Author (2012)

Valentine, Melissa A., & Amy C. Edmondson, "Team Scaffolds: How Minimal In-Group Structures Support Fast-Paced Teaming," Harvard Business School Working Paper, No. 12-062 (1/18/2012)

Weaver, Sallie J., Michael A. Rosen, Eduardo Salas, Karyn D. Baum, & Heidi B. King, "Integrating the Science of Team Training: Guidelines for Continuing Education," *Journal of Continuing Education in the Health Professions*, vol. 30(4), pp. 208–220 (2010)

Woolley, Anita, Interview with Author (2012)

Woolley, Anita Williams, "Responses to Adversarial Situations and Collective Intelligence," *Journal of Organizational Behavior*, vol. 32(7), pp. 978–983 (2011)

4.

The Disharmony in Teams:

Bradley, Bret H., Bennett E. Postlethwaite, Anthony C. Klotz, Maria R. Hamdani, & Kenneth G. Brown, "Reaping the Benefits of Task Conflict in Teams: The Critical Role of Team Psychological Safety Climate," *Journal of Applied Psychology*, vol. 97(1), pp. 151–158 (2012)

Driskell, James E., Gerald F. Goodwin, Eduardo Salas, & Patrick Gavan O'Shea, "What Makes a Good Team Player? Personality and Team Effectiveness," *Group Dynamics: Theory, Research, and Practice*, vol. 10(4), pp. 249–271 (2006)

Feynman, Richard P., *Surely, You're Joking Mr. Feynman*, New York: W. W. Norton (1997)

Fischer, Bill, & Andy Boynton, "Virtuoso Teams," *Harvard Business Review*, vol. 83(7), pp. 116–123 (2005)

Gelfand, Michele Joy, Jeanne M. Brett, Lynn Imai, Hwa-Hwa Tsai, & Daphne Huang, "Team Negotiation across Cultures: When and Where Are Two Heads Better Than One?" Paper Presentation at IACM 18th Annual Conference, Amsterdam, http://bit.ly/O7TNuJ (2005)

Gibson, Cristina B., & Dana M. McDaniel, "Moving beyond Conventional Wisdom: Advancements in Cross-Cultural Theories of Leadership, Conflict, and Teams," *Perspectives on Psychological Science*, vol. 5(4), pp. 450–462 (2010)

Gleick, James, *Genius: The Life of Science of Richard Feynman*, New York: Vintage Books (1993)

Hong, Sung-Mook, & Salvatora Faedda, "Refinement of the Hong Psychological Reactance Scale," *Educational and Psychological Measurement*, vol. 56(1), pp. 173–182 (1996)

Kearns Goodwin, Doris, *Team of Rivals*, New York: Simon & Schuster (2005)

Kozlowski, Steve W. J., & Daniel R. Illgen, "Enhancing the Effectiveness of Work Groups and Teams," *Psychological Science in the Public Interest*, vol. 7(3), pp. 77–124 (2006)

Leander, N. Pontus, Interview with Author (2012)

Leander, N. Pontus, Tanya L. Chartrand, & Wendy Wood, "Mind Your Mannerisms: Behavioral Mimicry Elicits Stereotype Conformity," *Journal of Experimental Social Psychology*, vol. 47(1), pp. 195–201 (2011)

Moll, Tjerk, Geir Jordet, & Gert-Jan Pepping, "Emotional Contagion in Soccer Penalty Shootouts: Celebration of Individual Success is Associated with Ultimate Team Success," *Journal of Sports Sciences*, vol. 28(9), pp. 983–992 (2010)

Pierro, Antonio, Fabio Presaghi, E. Tory Higgins, Kristen M. Klein, & Arie W. Kruglanski, "Frogs and Ponds: A Multilevel Analysis of the Regulatory Mode Complementarity Hypothesis," *Personality and Social Psychology Bulletin*, vol. 38(2), pp. 269–279 (2012)

Reiter-Palmon, Roni, Remarks at Session on Team Creativity in Science, Technology, Engineering, & Mathematics (STEM), Annual Convention of the American Psychological Assn., Orlando (2012)

Reiter-Palmon, Roni, "Team Creativity and Innovation: Current Findings and Future Research Needs," Remarks at Annual Convention of the American Psychological Assn., Washington, DC (2011)

Wolfe, Tom, *The Right Stuff*, New York: Bantam / Farrar, Straus & Giroux (1979/1980)

Woolley, Anita Williams, Christopher F. Chabris, Alex Pentland, Nada Hashmi, & Thomas W. Malone, "Evidence for a Collective Intelligence Factor in the Performance of Human Groups," *Science*, vol. 330(6004), pp. 686–688 (2010)

Team Hierarchy, Team Stars:

Allmendinger, Jutta, & J. Richard Hackman, "The More, the Better? A Four-Nation Study of the Inclusion of Women in Symphony Orchestras," *Social Forces*, vol. 74(2), pp. 423–460 (1995)

Allmendinger, Jutta, & J. Richard Hackman, "Organizations in Changing Environments: The Case of East German Symphony Orchestras," *Administrative Science Quarterly*, vol. 41(3), pp. 337–369 (1996)

Allmendinger, Jutta, J. Richard Hackman, & Erin V. Lehman, "Life and Work in Symphony Orchestras," *Musical Quarterly*, vol. 80(2), pp. 194–219 (1996)

Berri, David J., Michael A. Leeds, Eva Marikova Leeds, & Michael Mondello, "The Role of Managers," *International Journal of Sport Finance*, vol. 4, pp. 75–93 (2009)

Bucciol, Alessandro, & Marco Piovesan, "Pay Dispersion and Work Performance," Harvard Business School Research Paper Series, No. 12-075, http://ssrn.com/abstract=2012514 (2012)

Chan, Tat Y., Jia Li, & Lamar Pierce, "Compensation and Peer Effects in Competing Sales Teams," http://ssrn.com/abstract=1367441 (2012)

Hackman, J. Richard, "Learning More by Crossing Levels: Evidence from Airplanes, Hospitals, and Orchestras," *Journal of Organizational Behavior*, vol. 24(8), pp. 905–922 (2003)

Hackman, J. Richard, & Nancy Katz, "Group Behavior and Performance," In: S. T. Fiske, D. T. Gilbert, & G. Lindzey (Eds.), *Handbook of Social Psychology*, 5th Ed., New York: Wiley (2010)

Halevy, Nir, Eileen Y. Chou, & Adam D. Galinsky, "A Functional Model of Hierarchy," *Social Psychological & Personality Science*, vol. 3(4), pp. 398–406 (2012)

Halevy, Nir, Eileen Y. Chou, Adam D. Galinsky, & J. Keith Murnighan, "When Hierarchy Wins Evidence from the National Basketball Association," *Social Psychological & Personality Science*, vol. 3(4), pp. 398–406 (2012)

Holliday, Emma, Clifton David Fuller, Lynn D. Wilson, & Charles R. Thomas, Jr., "Success Breeds Success: Authorship Distribution in the Red Journal, 1975–2011," *International Journal of Radiation Oncology * Biology * Physics*, in press (2012)

Kuhn, Peter, & Marie Claire Villeval, "Do Women Prefer a Co-operative Work Environment?" IZA Discussion Paper No. 5999 (2011)

Oettl, Alexander, "Productivity, Helpfulness and the Performance of Peers: Exploring the Implications of a New Taxonomy for Star Scientists," University of Toronto, http://bit.ly/PTVH2y (2009)

Simmons, Rob, & David J. Berri, "Mixing the Princes and the Paupers: Pay and Performance in the National Basketball Association," *Labour Economics*, vol. 18(3), pp. 381–388 (2011)

Sitkin, Sim B., & J. Richard Hackman, "Developing Team Leadership: An Interview with Mike Kryzyzewski," *Academy of Management Learning & Education*, vol. 10(3), pp. 494–501 (2011)

Stribeck, Agnes, "The Downside of Looking for Team Players—An Empirical Analysis of the Effects of Requiring Teamwork Skills in Job Advertisements on the Applicant Pool," http://bit.ly/O0eaOC (2010)

Stribeck, Agnes, & Kerstin Pull, "Do Lame Ducks Sort into Teams," Working Paper (u.d.)

Stribeck, Agnes, & Kerstin Pull, "Self-Selection into Teamwork, A Theoretical and Experimental Analysis," Beiträge zur Jahrestagung des Vereins für Socialpolitik 2010: Ökonomie der Familie—Session: Organisational Design, No. B15-V2 (2010)

Chapter 11—Michelangelo Had an Agent

1.

Linux and TopCoder:

"2012 Grand Prize Winners," Technology Academy of Finland, http://bit.ly/HVLu5t (2012)

Andersen-Gott, Morten, Gheorghita Ghinea, & Bendik Bygstad, "Why Do Commercial Companies Contribute to Open Source Software?," *International Journal of Information Management*, vol. 32(2), pp. 106–117 (2012)

Boudreau, Kevin J., Nicola Lacetera, & Karim R. Lakhani, "Incentives and Problem Uncertainty in Innovation Contests: An Empirical Analysis," *Management Science*, vol. 57(5), pp. 843–863 (2011)

Corbet, Jonathan, Greg Kroah-Hartman, & Amanda McPherson, "Linux Kernel Development: How Fast It Is Going, Who Is Doing It, What They Are Doing, and Who Is Sponsoring It," The Linux Foundation (2012)

Crainer, Stuart, & Julian Birkinshaw, "Who Needs Employees?" *Business Strategy Review*, vol. 19(3), pp. 18–21 (2008)

David, Paul A., & Joseph S. Shapiro, "Community-Based Production of Open-Source Software: What Do We Know about the Developers Who Participate?" *Information Economics & Policy*, vol. 20(4), pp. 364–398 (2008)

Goldberg, Corey, "Linus Torvalds on Competition by Technical Merit," Goldb.org, http://bit.ly/T0y2Rf (4/19/2007)

Gulley, Ned, & Karim R. Lakhani, "The Determinants of Individual Performance and Collective Value in Private-Collective Software Innovation," Harvard Business School Working Paper, No. 10-065 (2010)

Hertel, Guido, Sven Niedner, & Stefanie Hermann, "Motivation of Software Developers in Open Source Projects: An Internet-Based Survey of Contributors to the Linux Kernel," *Research Policy*, vol. 32(7), pp. 1159–1177 (2003)

Jdamato12, "TopCoder Celebrates 400,000 Members as Payments Top $36 Million," Top-Coder.com, http://bit.ly/O0ehd4 (4/12/2012)

Lakhani, Karim, Correspondence with Authors (2011, 2012)

Lakhani, Karim, Interview with Author (2012)

Lakhani, Karim R., "TopCoder (A): Developing Software through Crowdsourcing," Harvard Business School Teaching Note, No. 5-611-071 (2011)

Lakhani, Karim R., & David A. Garvin, "TopCoder (A): Developing Software through Crowdsourcing," Harvard Business School Case Study, No. 9-610-032 (2010)

Lakhani, Karim R., & Jill A. Panetta, "The Principles of Distributed Innovation," *Innovations*, vol. 2(3), pp. 97–113 (2007)

McKeown, Jim, "TopCoder One of *Inc.* Magazine's 500 Fastest-Growing Companies in America for Second Consecutive Year," Press Release (8/27/2008)

Moon, Jae Yun, & Lee Sproull, "Essence of Distributed Work: The Case of the Linux Kernel," *First Monday*, vol. 5(11) (2000)

Noyes, Kathleen, "Top Honor for Linus Torvalds Highlights Linux's Importance," Operating Systems Blog, *PC World*, http://bit.ly/HTceE4 (4/19/2012)

Peyrache, Eloic, Jacques Cremer, & Jean Tirole, "Some Reflections on Open Source Software," *Communications & Strategies*, vol. 40, pp. 139–159 (2000)

Raymond, Eric, "The Cathedral and the Bazaar: Musings on Linux and Open Source by an Accidental Revolutionary, Revised Edition," Sebastopol, CA: O'Reilly & Assoc., Inc. (2001)

Terwiesch, Christian, & Yi Xu, "Innovation Contests, Open Innovation, and Multiagent Problem Solving," *Management Science*, vol. 54(9), pp. 1529–1543 (2008)

Torvalds, Linus, "Re: [Announce] [patch] Modular Scheduler Core and Completely Fair Scheduler [CFS]," E-mail exchange, http://bit.ly/wxQVcQ (4/15/2007)

Torvalds, Linus, & David Diamond, *Just for Fun: The Story of an Accidental Revolutionary*, New York: Harper Business (2002)

Watson, Andrew, "Reputation in Open Source Software," Working Paper (2005)

"Who Uses TopCoder?" http://bit.ly/GAJERz (u.d.)

The Rise of Open Source Development:

"Collaboration Is the New Revolution," *The Guardian*, http://bit.ly/RswGdC (8/17/2008)

Lakhani, Karim R., "InnoCentive.com (A)," Harvard Business School Case Study, No. 9-608-170 (2009)

Lakhani, Karim R., "Threadless: The Business of Community," Harvard Business School Teaching Note, No. 5-608-169 (2008)

McGann, Matt, "Match Game," MIT Admissions Blog, http://bit.ly/R0hhAP (1/27/2005)

"Politicians Need to Learn Virtue of Collaboration," *USA Today*, http://usat.ly/rKwl2w (1/1/2012)

von Hippel, Eric, & Georg von Krogh, "Open Source Software and the 'Private-Collective' Innovation Model: Issues for Organization Science," *Organization Science*, vol. 14(2), pp. 209–223 (2003)

The Role of Competition, Personality, etc., in Scientific Innovation:

Many of the innovations we take for granted in modern life were created in response to a formal competition. Chemical fire extinguishers are based on Ambrose Godfrey's 1761 prize-winning entry for a contest to come up with ideas for putting out fires. Hyppolyte Mège-Mouriés's margarine was the winning entry for Napoleon III's competition for a butter-substitute that could be sent to the troops in the field. (Napoleon I's contest to feed the troops was the catalyst for Nicholas Appert's 1809 innovation in bottling food.) Charles

Lindbergh's 1927 transcontinental flight was for a contest sponsored by Raymond Orteig, a French hotel owner who hoped to spur the French tourism and hotel industries. In 2006, an Apple user started publicly asking for donations to sponsor a competition for software that would translate PC software for Macs. He received so many donations that Apple itself decided to develop the software.

Beersman, Bianca, John R. Hollenbeck, Henry Moon, Stephen E. Humphrey, Donald E. Coglin, & Daniel R. Ilgen, "Cooperation, Competition, and Team Performance: Toward a Contingency Approach," *Academy of Management Journal*, vol. 46(5), pp. 572–590 (2003)

Feist, Gregory, Interview with Author (2012)

Feist, Gregory J., "How Development and Personality Influence Scientific Thought, Interest, and Achievement," *Review of General Psychology*, vol. 10(2), pp. 163–182 (2006)

Feist, Gregory J., "The Influence of Personality on Artistic and Scientific Creativity," In: Robert J. Sternberg (Ed.), *Handbook of Creativity*, ch. 14, pp. 273–296, Cambridge, UK: Cambridge University Press (1999)

Feist, Gregory J., "A Meta-Analysis of Personality in Scientific and Artistic Creativity," *Personality and Social Psychology Review*, vol. 2(4), pp. 290–309 (1998)

Hsieh, An-Tien, & Chin-Show Tarng, "Clarifying the Relationship between Competition and Employee Creativity," Paper Presentation at International Conference on Market Development and Investment Strategies, ShenZhen, China (2008)

Masters, William A., & Benoit Delbecq, "Accelerating Innovation with Prize Rewards," International Service for National Agricultural Research, IFPRI Discussion Paper, No. 00835 (Dec. 2008)

Simonton, Dean, Interviews with Author (2011, 2012)

Wigert, B., & R. Reiter-Palmon, "The Influence of Perfectionism and Regulatory Focus on Creativity," Paper Presentation for Annual Meeting of the Society for Industrial / Organizational Psychology, San Diego (2012)

2.

Competitions in Renaissance Art and Baroque Music:

Brecht, Martin, *Martin Luther: Shaping and Defining the Reformation, 1521–1532*, Minneapolis: Fortress Press (1990)

Butt, John, *Bach: Mass in B Minor*, Cambridge: Cambridge University Press (1991/1999)

Caldwell, John, "Music," In: Adrian Hastings, Alistair Mason, & Hugh Pyper (Eds.), *The Oxford Companion to Christian Thought*, Oxford: Oxford University Press (2000)

David, Hans T., Arthur Mendel, & Christoph Wolf, *The New Bach Reader: A Life of Johann Sebastian Bach in Letters and Documents*, New York: W. W. Norton & Co. (1998)

Durant, Will, *The Story of Civilization*, vol. 4, *The Age of Faith*, ch. 33, New York: Simon & Schuster (1950)

Durant, Will, *The Story of Civilization*, vol. 5, *The Renaissance*, ch. 17, New York: Simon & Schuster (1953)

Durant, Will, *The Story of Civilization*, vol. 6, *The Reformation*, ch. 34, New York: Simon & Schuster (1957)

Eire, Carlos M. M., "The Reformation," In: James J. Buckley, Frederick Christian Bauerschmidt, & Trent Pomplun (Eds.), *The Blackwell Companion to Catholicism*, ch. 5, pp. 64–80, Essex, UK: Wiley (2007)

Geck, Martin, *Bach* (Anthea Bell, Trans.), London: Haus Publishing Ltd. (2003)

Geck, Martin, *Johann Sebastian Bach: Life and Work* (John Hargraves, Trans.), Orlando: Harcourt (2000)

Goffen, Rona, *Renaissance Rivals: Michelangelo, Leonardo, Raphael, Titian*, New Haven, CT: Yale University Press (2002)

"History of the JMM," Jesuit Communications Foundation, Inc., http://bit.ly/RswOKl (u.d.)

Jones, Jonathan, "And the Winner Is," *The Guardian*, http://bit.ly/Q6awkx (10/22/2002)

"Michelangelo vs. Leonardo," Reuters via *China Daily*, http://bit.ly/OARcbQ (4/1/2010)

Ratzinger, Joseph, Cardinal, "Theological Problems of Church Music" (1983)

Rich, Norman, "The Historical Setting: Politics and Patronage," In: Raymond Erickson (Ed.), *The Worlds of Johann Sebastian Bach*, ch. 1, pp. 67–104, Milwaukee: Amadeus Press (2009)

Sherry, Patrick, "Art and Literature," In: James J. Buckley, Frederick Christian Bauerschmidt, & Trent Pomplun (Eds.), *The Blackwell Companion to Catholicism*, ch. 31, pp. 465–476 (2007)

Schluter, Joseph, *A General History of Music* (Mrs. Robert Tubbs, Trans.), London: Richard Bentley (1865)

Vaubel, Roland, Correspondence with Author (2011)

Vaubel, Roland, "The Role of Competition in the Rise of Baroque and Renaissance Music," *Journal of Cultural Economics*, vol. 29(5), pp. 277–297 (2005)

Williams, Peter, *The Life of Bach*, Cambridge: Cambridge University Press (2004)

Wolf, Christoph, *Johann Sebastian Bach: The Learned Musician*, New York: W. W. Norton & Co. (2000)

3.

Challenges in Post-Unification Germany:

Albinsson, Pia A., Marco Wolf, & Dennis A. Kopf, "Anti-Consumption in East Germany: Consumer Resistance to Hyperconsumption," *Journal of Consumer Research*, vol. 9(6), pp. 412–425 (2010)

Anscombe, Nadya, "A Passion for Politics and a Head for Business," *Opto & Laser Europe*, http://bit.ly/PRnq6E (Jan. 2002)

"Architects of Unification—Lothar Späth," *Deutsche Welle*, http://bit.ly/SY2uge (5/9/2010)

Carlin, Wendy, "Good Institutions Are Not Enough: Ongoing Challenges of East German Development," CESifo Working Paper Series No. 3204, http://ssrn.com/abstract=1691496 (2010)

Carlin, Wendy, & Peter Richthofen, "Finance, Economic Development and the Transition: The East German Case," *Economics of Transition*, vol. 3(2), pp. 169–195 (1995)

"CNN Interview of Kurt Kasch, SVP Deutsche Bank" (video), http://bit.ly/R0hDaD (3/17/1993)

Cooper, Belinda, "Questions of National Identity Still Swirl in Post-Unification Germany, with the Pursuit of Cultural Unity Still Ongoing," *ISN Insight* (11/3/2009)

Czarnitzki, Dirk, & Georg Licht, "Additionality of Public R&D Grants in a Transition Economy: the Case of Eastern Germany," *Economics of Transition*, vol. 14(1), pp. 101–131 (2006)

Eickelpasch, Alexander, & Michael Fritsch, "Contests for Cooperation—A New Approach in German Innovation Policy," *Research Policy*, vol. 34(8), pp. 1269–1282 (2005)

Ewing, Jack, & William Boston, "Germany: A Brighter Sun in the East," *Bloomberg Businessweek*, http://buswk.co/NFIUyM (10/4/2004)

Fay, Doris, & Michael Frese, "Working in East German Socialism in 1980 and in Capitalism 15 Years Later: A Trend Analysis of a Transitional Economy's Working Conditions," *Applied Psychology: An International Review*, vol. 49(4), pp. 636–657 (2000)

Frese, Michael, Correspondence with Author (2012)

Frese, Michael, Wolfgang Kring, Andrea Soose, & Jeannette Zemple, "Personal Initiative at Work: Differences between East and West Germany," *Academy of Management Journal*, vol. 39(1), pp. 37–63 (1996)

Furhmans, Vanessa, "Eastern, Western German Firms See Sides of Labor Reverse Roles," *Wall Street Journal* (1/4/2001)

"German City of Jena Recovering from Reunification Blues," Expatica.com, http://bit.ly/T0yXRv (5/26/2008)

Greenhouse, Steven, "It's Sink or Swim in East Germany, *New York Times*, http://nyti.ms/RvDjQA (6/24/1990)

Herbst, Moira, "A Bright Light in Eastern Germany," *Der Spiegel*, http://bit.ly/TCnZzk (10/21/2009)

Hitchens, D. M. W. N., "A Matched Plant Comparison of Productivity in East and West Germany: Transition to the Market Economy," *Omega*, vol. 24(3), pp. 321–335 (1996)

Hummel, Wolfgang, "Twenty Years of Stimulus for East Germany," *Wall Street Journal*, http://on.wsj.com/318c38 (11/8/2009)

"Jenoptik under Fire," *Der Spiegel* (2002)

Kogut, Bruce, & Udo Zander, "Did Socialism Fail to Innovate? A Natural Experiment of the Two Zeiss Companies" (Feb. 1999)

Köhler, Fabian, "Jena—What's the Price of Paradise?" German Academic Exchange Service / Deutscher Akademischer Austausch Dienst, http://bit.ly/LKMndV (u.d.)

Maier, Charles S., "The Travails of Unification East Germany's Economic Transition Since 1989," United Nations University Working Paper No. 2010/60 (2010)

Mitchener, Brandon, "Optical Company Rises from Remains of State Firm: Jena Sees Its Future Come into Focus," *New York Times*, http://nyti.ms/O7USTc (3/24/1994)

Omland, Nils, & Holger Ernst, "Vitalisation of Industry through the Regional Promotion of Knowledge Intensive New Firms—The Case of German Biotechnology," Paper for Japan Institute for Labour Policy and Training (2004)

Orosz, Gábor, "Good Citizens? The Dark Side of the Hungarian Competitive Business Life," In: A. Ross (Ed.), *Citizenship Education in Society*, pp. 663–674, London: CiCe (2007)

Protzman, Ferdinand, "East Germany's Economy Far Sicker than Expected," *New York Times*, http://nyti.ms/ODO16F (9/20/1990)

Protzman, Ferdinand, "A Worry in West Germany: Indolence," *New York Times*, http://nyti.ms/NApMIn (4/4/1990) (secretaries, other examples of East Germans' sloth)

Ragnitz, Joachim, "Explaining the East German Productivity Gap—The Role of Human Capital," Working Paper No. 1310, Kiel (2007)

Schmid, John, "Main Parties Rediscover the East, Where Kingmakers Live in Anger," *New York Times*, http://nyti.ms/TCok59 (9/26/1998)

"Späth Era Ends at Jenoptik," *Heise Online* (6/15/2003)

Stephan, Johannes, "Firm-Specific Determinants of Productivity Gaps between East and West German Industrial Branches," *Journal of Economics & Business*, vol. 7(2), pp. 11–38 (2004)

"Universitätsklinikum Jena," North American Service Center, M+D Europe, http://bit.ly/ON0m76 (u.d.)

Wallace, Charles P., "A Tale of Two Cities," *Time*, http://ti.me/N2F1bs (10/9/2000)

Woodruff, David, "Eastern Germany's Jenoptik Rises from the Rubble," *Business Week* (international ed.) http://buswk.co/Q6bdKQ (1998)

World Fact Book, Washington, DC: Central Intelligence Agency (1990)

Wulf, Torsten, & Harald Hungenberg, "Jenoptik (A): The Famous Zeiss in Ruins," University of Erlangen-Nuremberg Case Study, Reference No. 300-166-1 (2000)

Psychological Predictors of Success or Struggle in Post-Unification Germany:

Little, Todd D., Mara Brendgen, Brigitte Wanner, & Lothar Krappmann, "Children's Reciprocal Perceptions of Friendship Quality in the Sociocultural Contexts of East and West Berlin," *International Journal of Behavioral Development*, vol. 23(1), pp. 63–89 (1999)

Little, Todd D., Anna Stetsenko, & Heiner Maier, "Action-Control Beliefs and School Performance: A Longitudinal Study of Moscow Children and Adolescents," *International Journal of Behavioral Development*, vol. 23(3), pp. 799–823 (1999)

Merkl, Christian, & Dennis Snower, "Escaping the Unemployment Trap: The Case of East Germany," *Journal of Comparative Economics*, vol. 36(4), pp. 542–556 (2008)

Oettingen, Gabriele, "Cross-Cultural Perspectives on Self-Efficacy," In: A. Bandura (Ed.) *Self-Efficacy in Changing Societies*, pp. 149–176, New York: Cambridge University Press (1995)

Oettingen, Gabriele, Interview with Author (2012)

Oettingen, Gabriele, Todd D. Little, Ulman Lindenberger, & Paul B. Baltes, "Causality, Agency, and Control Beliefs in East versus West Berlin Children: A Natural Experiment on the Role of Context," *Journal of Personality & Social Psychology*, vol. 66(3), pp. 579–595 (1994)

Pinquart, Martin, Rainer K. Silbereisen, & Linda P. Juang, "Moderating Effects of Adolescents' Self-Efficacy Beliefs on Psychological Responses to Social Change," *Journal of Adolescent Research*, vol. 19(3), pp. 340–359 (2004)

Speier, Christa, & Michael Frese, "Generalized Self-Efficacy as a Mediator and Moderator Between Control and Complexity at Work and Personal Initiative: A Longitudinal Field Study in East Germany," *Human Performance*, vol. 10(2), pp. 171–192 (1997)

Stetsenko, Anna, Todd D. Little, Matthais Grasshof, & Gabriele Oettingen, "Gender Effects in Children's Beliefs about School Performance: A Cross-Cultural Study," *Child Development*, vol. 71(2), pp. 517–527 (2000)

Stetsenko, Anna, Todd D. Little, Gabriele Oettingen, & Paul B. Baltes, "Agency, Control, and Means–Ends Beliefs about School Performance in Moscow Children: How Similar Are They to Beliefs of Western Children?" *Developmental Psychology*, vol. 31(2), pp. 285–299 (1995)

4.

Competition in the Development of Creativity, Role of Agency, etc.:

Abra, Jock C., "Competition: Creativity's Vilified Motive," *Genetic, Social, & General Psychology Monographs*, vol. 119(3), pp. 289–342 (1993)

Amabile, Teresa M., & Colin M. Fisher, "Stimulate Creativity by Fueling Passion," In: Edwin A. Locke (Ed.), *Handbook of Principles of Organizational Behavior*, 2nd Ed., ch. 26, pp. 481–498, West Sussex, UK: Wiley (2009)

Attle, Simon, & Bob Baker, "Cooperative Learning in a Competitive Environment: Classroom Applications," *International Journal of Teaching and Learning in Higher Education*, vol. 19(1), pp. 77–83 (2007)

Boser, Ulrich, "Diamonds on Demand," *Smithsonian Magazine* (June 2008)

Conti, Regina, Correspondence with Author (2011, 2012)

Conti, Regina, Interview with Author (2011)

Conti, Regina, Mary Ann Collins, & Martha L. Picariello, "The Impact of Competition on Intrinsic Motivation and Creativity: Considering Gender, Gender Segregation and Gender Role Orientation," *Personality & Individual Differences*, vol. 31(8), pp. 1273–1289 (2001)

Csikszentmihalyi, Mihaly, *Creativity*, New York: Harper Perennial (1997)

Eisenberg, Jacob, & William Forde Thompson, "The Effects of Competition on Improvisers' Motivation, Stress, and Creative Performance," *Creativity Research Journal*, vol. 23(2), pp. 129–136 (2011)

Kim, Kyung-Hee, "Can We Trust Creativity Tests? A Review of the Torrance Tests of Creative Thinking," *Creativity Research Journal*, vol. 18(1), pp. 3–14 (2006)

Kim, Kyung-Hee, Correspondence with Authors (2010)

Kim, Kyung-Hee, "Critique on the Torrance Tests of Creative Thinking: Assessment of Gifted Children and Youth" (2002)

Kim, Kyung-Hee, Interviews with Authors (2010)

Kim, Kyung-Hee, "Meta-Analyses of the Relationship of Creative Achievement to Both IQ and Divergent Thinking Scores," *Journal of Creative Behavior*, vol. 42(2), pp. 106 (2008)

Knudson, M. D., M. P. Desjarlais, & D. H. Dolan, "Shock-Wave Exploration of the High-Pressure Phases of Carbon," *Science*, vol. 322(5909), pp. 1824–1825 (2008)

Oxford English Dictionary, 2nd Ed., Oxford: Oxford University Press (1991/2000)

Plucker, Jonathan, Correspondence with Authors (2010)

Plucker, Jonathan, Interviews with Authors (2010)

Plucker, Jonathan A., "Is the Proof in the Pudding? Reanalyses of Torrance's (1958 to Present) Longitudinal Data," *Creativity Research Journal*, vol. 12(2), pp. 103–114 (1999)

Raina, M. K., "A Study into the Effect of Competition," *Gifted Child Quarterly*, vol. 12, pp. 217–220 (1968)

Shalley, Christina E., & Greg R. Oldham, "Competition and Creative Performance: Effects of Competitor Presence and Visibility," *Creativity Research Journal*, vol. 10(4), pp. 337–345 (1997)

Ybarra, Oscar, Matthew C. Keller, Emily Chan, Stephen M. Garcia, Jeffrey Sanchez-Burks, Kimberly Rios Morrison, & Andrew S. Baron, "Being Unpredictable; Friend or Foe Matters," *Social Psychological and Personality Science*, vol. 1(3), pp. 259–267 (2010)

Chapter 12—How the Black Sox Cleaned Up Wall Street

1.

How Sports Catalyze Democracy and Politics:

For additional sources on the Ancient Olympics, please refer to the Chapter 1 references.

Carr, David, "On the Moral Value of Physical Activity: Body and Soul in Plato's Account of Virtue," *Sport, Ethics & Philosophy*, vol. 4(1), pp. 3–15 (2010)

Daqing, Wang, "On the Ancient Greek αγων," *Procedia Social & Behavioral Sciences*, vol. 2(5), pp. 6805–6812 (2010)

Fisher, Nick, "The Culture of Competition," In: Kurt A. Raaflaub & Hans van Wees (Eds.), *A Companion to Archaic Greece*, ch. 27, pp. 524–541, West Sussex, UK: Blackwell Publishing Ltd. (2009)

Fleck, Robert K., & F. Andrew Hanssen, "The Origins of Democracy: A Model with Application to Ancient Greece," *Journal of Law & Economics*, vol. 49(1), pp. 115–146 (2006)

Golden, Mark, "Equestrian Competition in Ancient Greece: Difference, Dissent, Democracy," *Phoenix*, vol. 51(3-4), pp. 327–344 (1997)

Gómez-Lobo, Alfonso, "The Olympics in the Ancient World," *Estudios Públicos* (John Bell, Trans.), vol. 65, pp. 1–21 (1997)

Hemingway, Colette, & Seán Hemingway, "Athletics in Ancient Greece," Heilbrunn Timeline of Art History, New York: Metropolitan Museum of Art, http://bit.ly/RvDz1U (u.d.)

Hubbard, Thomas, "Contemporary Sport Sociology and Ancient Greek Athletics," *Leisure Studies*, vol. 27(4), pp. 379–393 (2008)

Liddel, Peter, "Democracy Ancient and Modern," In: Ryan K. Balot (Ed.), *A Companion to Greek and Roman Political Thought*, ch. 9, pp. 133–148, West Sussex, UK: Blackwell Publishing Ltd. (2009)

Paphitis, Nicholas, "Greece Approves Replanting at Ancient Olympia," MSNBC.com, http://nbcnews.to/TCoDgb (2008)

Pritchard, David M., "Sport, War and Democracy in Classical Athens," *International Journal of the History of Sport*, vol. 26(2), pp. 212–245 (2009)

Reid, Heather L., "Athletic Competition as Socratic Philosophy," *Acta Universitatis Palackianae Olomucensis Gymnica*, vol. 36(2), pp. 73–77 (2006)

Reid, Heather L., "Contemporary Athletics and Ancient Greek Ideals," *Sport, Ethics & Philosophy*, vol. 4(3), pp. 359–361 (2010)

Reid, Heather L., "The Political Heritage of the Olympic Games: Relevance, Risks, and Possible Rewards," *Sport, Ethics & Philosophy*, vol. 6(2), pp. 108–122 (2012)

Spivey, Nigel, *The Ancient Olympics*, New York: Oxford University Press (2005)

Swaddling, Judith, "Ancient Greek Olympics Gallery," http://bbc.in/PvTny9 (u.d.)

"Text of John Roberts' Opening Statement," *USA Today*, http://usat.ly/8qWwP3 (9/12/2005)

Wallach, John R., "Demokratia and Arete in Ancient Greek Political Thought," *Polis*, vol. 28(2), pp. 181–215 (2011)

Washington, Robert, "Bringing Sport Back In: Sport as a Model of Meritocracy: Theoretical Implications and a Research Agenda," Paper Presentation at Annual Meeting of the American Sociological Assn., Las Vegas (2011)

Washington, Robert, Interview with Author (2012)

History of the Black Sox, the Progressive Era, etc.:

Anderson, William B., "Saving the National Pastime's Image: Crisis Management during the 1919 Black Sox Scandal," *Journalism History*, vol. 27(3), pp. 105–111 (2001)

Asinof, Eliot, *Eight Men Out: The Black Sox and the 1919 World Series*, New York: Holt, Rinehart, & Winston (1987)

Bachin, Robin F., "At the Nexus of Labor and Leisure: Baseball, Nativism, and the 1919 Black Sox Scandal," *Journal of Social History*, vol. 36(4), pp. 941–962 (2003)

Derickson, Alan, "Making Human Junk: Child Labor as a Health Issue in the Progressive Era," *American Journal of Public Health*, vol. 82(9), pp. 1280–1290 (1992)

Fitzgerald, F. Scott, *The Great Gatsby* (Cambridge Ed.), Matthew J. Bruccoli (Ed.), Cambridge: Cambridge University Press (1991)

Law, Marc T., & Gary D. Libecap, "The Determinants of Progressive Era Reform: The Pure Food and Drugs Act of 1906," In: Edward L. Glaeser & Claudia Goldin (Eds.), *Corruption & Reform: Lessons from America's Economic History*, Chicago: University of Chicago Press (2006)

Nathan, Daniel A., "The Big Fix," *Legal Affairs*, http://bit.ly/ON0yDA (2004)

Panacy, Peter, "Major League Baseball Finds Its Roots in Progressive America," *Bleacher Report*, http://bit.ly/fUpsZ0 (4/11/2011)

Pietruska, David, *Rothstein: The Life, Times and Murder of the Criminal Genius Who Fixed the 1919 World Series*, New York: Basic Books (2011)

Riess, Steven A., "Professional Baseball and American Culture in the Progressive Era," *NASHH Proceedings*, pp. 40–41 (1975)

Rosenberg, Norman L., "Here Comes the Judge! The Origins of Baseball's Commissioner System and American Legal Culture," *Journal of Popular Culture*, vol. 20(4), pp. 129–146 (1987)

"SEC Historical Summary of Chairmen and Commissioners," Securities & Exchange Commission, http://1.usa.gov/awO9hl (u.d.)

Tosches, Nick, *King of the Jews: The Greatest Mob Story Never Told*, New York: Harper Perennial (2006) (regarding Henry Ford's editorial on Rothstein)

Cricket and Corruption in India:

The quote "You can steal land…" is from Khan (2010); similar views were expressed in Magnier 2010. The statement that the corruption wasn't cricket nor Indian culture was said by former federal finance minister Yashwant Sinha. The quote was reported by a number of media outlets, but we first learned of it in *Sun Daily*'s 2012 piece.

Abdulraheem, A., "Corruption in India: An Overview," *Social Action*, vol. 59, pp. 351–363 (2009)

Burke, Jason, "Corruption in India: 'All Your Life You Pay for Things that Should Be Free,'" *The Guardian*, http://bit.ly/oEVemW (8/19/2011)

"Cricket Scandals? What Scandals? IPL Hailed as Success," AFP, *Sun Daily*, http://bit.ly/Km2Etl (5/29/2012)

Khan, Adnan R., "Cricket Scandal Consumes India," *AOL News*, http://aol.it/OASvaN (4/29/2010)

Lakshmi, Rama, "Indian Premier League Cricket Stung by Scandals," Washingtonpost.com, http://wapo.st/JcjVFB (5/18/2012)

Lall, Rashmee Roshan, "An 'Emerged' India Is Still Submerged in Corruption," *The National*, http://bit.ly/R0jfBk (11/26/2010)

Magnier, Mark, "India Rocked by Cricket Scandal," *Los Angeles Times*, http://lat.ms/UfoLV9 (4/19/2010)

"Ministers May Oppose, Ex-Cricketers Welcome," *India Today*, http://lat.ms/UfoLV9 (8/30/2011)

Nayyar, Dhiraj, Padmaparna Ghosh, & Shafi Rahman, "The Best of India Today: Cancer of Corruption," *India Today*, http://bit.ly/PRofwh (4/25/2011)

Nelson, Dean, "Shashi Tharoor: The Poster-Boy of 'New India' Falls from Grace," *Daily Telegraph*, http://bit.ly/db6CTE (4/21/2010)

Sarangi, Y. B., "It's Not Cricket, Says Kirti Azad," *The Hindu*, http://bit.ly/KESIIi (5/20/2012)

Tharoor, Shashi, "India's Anti-Corruption Contest," Project Syndicate, http://bit.ly/PDsUxI (1/3/2012)

Tummala, Krishna K., "Combating Corruption: Lessons out of India," *International Public Management Review*, vol. 10(1), pp. 34–58 (2009)

Westhead, Rick, "Fighting the Culture of Corruption in India," *The Star*, http://bit.ly/hLePNB (11/22/2010) (noting criminal defendants running for office)

Yardley, Jim, "As Cricket Grew in India, Corruption Followed," *New York Times*, http://nyti.ms/S3WymT (5/10/2010)

2.

Responses to Competition and Competitive Outcomes:

While there are other published forms of the Pausanias quote, our version comes from Spivey (2005).

Behrens, Timothy E. J., Mark W. Woolrich, Mark E. Walton, & Matthew F. S. Rushworth, "Learning the Value of Information in an Uncertain World," *Nature Neuroscience*, vol. 10(9), pp. 1214–1221 (2007)

Fisher, Nick, "The Culture of Competition," In: Kurt A. Raaflaub & Hans van Wees (Eds.), *A Companion to Archaic Greece*, West Sussex, UK: Blackwell Publishing Ltd., ch. 27, pp. 524–541 (2009)

Fülöp, Márta, "Competition in Educational Settings," Paper Presentation, University of Ljubljana, Slovenia (2002)

Fülöp, Márta, "Happy and Unhappy Competitors: What Makes the Difference?" *Psychological Topics*, vol. 18(2), pp. 345–367 (2009)

Fülöp, Márta, "Research on Social Capital in the Visegrad Context: The Case of Business and Competition," In: A. Ross (Ed.), *Human Rights & Citizenship Education*, pp. 17–25, London: CiCe (2009)

Fülöp, Márta, & Mihály Berkics, "A Gyözelemmel és a Vesztéssel Való Megküzdés Mintázatai Serdülőkorban / Patterns of Coping with Winning and Losing in Adolescence," Pszichológia: Az MTA *Pszichológiai Intézéenek folyóirata*, vol. 27(3), pp. 199–220 (English abstract) (2007)

Fülöp, Márta, Tamas Nagy, Mihaly Berkics, & Xuejun Bai, "Competitiveness, Coping with Winning and Losing and School Motivation among Chinese and Hungarian Adolescents," Poster Presentation at ISSBD 2012 Conference, Alberta, Canada (2012)

Fülöp, Márta, & Mónika Sándor, "Cross-Cultural Understandings from Social Psychology on Cooperation and Competition," In: A. Ross (Ed.), *Citizenship Education: Europe & the World*, pp. 75–88, London: CiCe (2006)

Nathanson, Craig, Delroy L. Paulhus, & Kevin M. Williams, "Predictors of a Behavioral Measure of Scholastic Cheating: Personality and Competence but Not Demographics," *Contemporary Educational Psychology*, vol. 31(1), pp. 97–122 (2006)

Spivey, Nigel, *The Ancient Olympics*, New York: Oxford University Press (2005)

"Zanes," Hellenic Ministry of Culture and Tourism, http://bit.ly/T0BrQ0 (u.d.)

3.

The Thrill of Testing Ourselves:

Rozin, Paul, Correspondence with Author (2012)

Rozin, Paul, "Food and Eating," In: Shinobu Kitayama & Dov Cohen (Eds.), *Handbook of Cultural Psychology*, ch. 16, pp. 391–416, New York: Guilford Press (2007)

Rozin, Paul, "One-Trial Acquired Likes and Dislikes in Humans: Disgust as a US, Food Predominance, and Negative Learning Predominance," *Learning & Motivation*, vol. 17(2), pp. 180–189 (1986)

Rozin, Paul, "Preadaptation and the Puzzles and Properties of Pleasure," In: D. Kahneman, E. Diener & N. Schwarz (Eds.), *Well Being: The Foundations of Hedonic Psychology*, pp. 109–133, New York: Russell Sage (1999)

Rozin, Paul, "Psychobiological Perspectives on Food Preferences and Avoidances," In: Marvin Harris & Eric B. Ross (Eds.), *Food & Evolution: Toward a Theory of Human Food Habits*, ch. 7, pp. 181–205, Philadelphia: Temple University Press (1987)

Rozin, Paul, "Spicing Up Psychological Science," Presentation at Annual Convention for Assn. for Psychological Science, Boston (2010)

Rozin, Paul, Lori Ebert, & Jonathan Schull, "Some Like It Hot: A Temporal Analysis of Hedonic Responses to Chili Pepper," *Appetite: Journal or Intake Research*, vol. 3(1), pp. 13–22 (1982)

Rozin, Paul, Michael Mark, & Deborah Schiller, "The Role of Desensitization to Capsaicin in Chili Pepper Ingestion and Preference," *Chemical Senses*, vol. 6(1), pp. 23–31 (1981)

Rozin, Paul, & Deborah Schiller, "The Nature and Acquisition of a Preference for Chili Pepper by Humans," *Motivation & Emotion*, vol. 4(7), pp. 77–101 (1980)

ACKNOWLEDGMENTS

We wish to thank our publisher, Twelve, special thanks going to Cary Goldstein, Jamie Raab, and Brian McClendon, each of whom, from the very first, was as excited about the science of competition as we were. Peter Ginsberg at Curtis Brown Ltd. has long been our stalwart, as have Shirley Stewart and Dave Barbor.

Of course, we couldn't do our work without the dozens of scholars and others who were instrumental in helping us with our research. We've been pestering some of them for years now, and we're so appreciative that they're still willing to return our calls, and they smile when we show up for another conference presentation with yet more questions. Dozens of researchers were kind enough to agree to be interviewed and shared working drafts of their papers and presentations. They patiently answered our questions as we trailed after them through the halls of conventions, interrupted their sabbaticals with repeated rounds of telephone calls and e-mails, and so on.

We are especially thankful to Chun-Yen Chang of National Taiwan Normal University for generously allowing us to use the oh-so-difficult sample test questions included in Chapter 4, and to Simon Baron-Cohen of Cambridge University who equally graciously allowed us to use the image from his *Reading the Mind in the Eyes* test.

Then, we're also very appreciative of the time, drafts, e-mails, et cetera, from: American University's Jennifer L. Lawless; Brandeis University's Nicolas Rohleder; Robert E. Washington of Bryn Mawr

College; Neil Lutsky, Carleton College; Anita Williams Woolley at Carnegie Mellon University; Jaroslav Flegr at Prague's Charles University; Regina Conti, Colgate University; Richard Ronay, Columbia University; Kyle Siler, Cornell University; Duke University's Stephen Stanton; David A. Edwards, Emory University; Robert Dur, Erasmus University; Gordon Goodman, Fielding Graduate University; John V. C. Nye, George Mason University; Green Mountain College's Jennifer Sellers; at Harvard University, Joyce Benenson, Zoë Chance, J. Richard Hackman, Karim R. Lakhani, and Melissa Valentine; Renate Deinzer of the Justus Liebig University of Giessen; Michael Frese, of NUS Business School in Singapore; Naval Postgraduate School's Quinn Kennedy; Joshua M. Aronson and Gabriele Oettingen of New York University; Northwestern University's Adam Galinsky and C. Kirabo Jackson; Alan Booth at Pennsylvania State University; Gilda Morales of Rutgers University's Center for American Women and Politics; Gregory Feist, San Jose State University; Stanford University's Muriel Niederle; Anna Dreber Almenberg, Stockholm School of Economics and Patrik Gränsmark at Stockholm University; Sarah A. Fulton of Texas A&M University; Carsten De Dreu, University of Amsterdam; University of British Columbia's Adele Diamond; at the University of California, Berkeley, Laura Kray and Frank Sulloway; Scott Carrell and Dean Keith Simonton at the University of California, Davis; Wendy Berry Mendes, University of California, San Francisco; N. Pontus Leander, University of Groningen; University of Mannheim's Roland Vaubel; Stephen M. Garcia at the University of Michigan; Aldo Rustichini, University of Minnesota; David A. Bergin and Donald O. Granberg at the University of Missouri; Thomas Denson, University of New South Wales; Bradley R. Staats, University of North Carolina–Chapel Hill; University of Oregon's Pranjal H. Mehta and Michael I. Posner; Paul Rozin, University of Pennsylvania; Alok Kumar, University of Texas at Austin; Paul Dennis of the University of Toronto and York University; Jeanne

M. Liedtka, University of Virginia; and Wayne State University's Justin M. Carré.

Additionally, Amy Adler at Walter Reed Army Institute of Research; Cornell University's Michael H. Goldstein; University at Buffalo's Jamie Ostrov; University of Wisconsin–Madison's B. Bradford Brown; and James C. Kaufman at California State University, San Bernadino, were helpful in pointing us in new directions to research. The Sherif family (Joan, Sue, and Ann) gave us some insight into their parents' Robbers Cave experiment.

Still others took time out of their schedules to give us their invaluable input—notably UNC's Anson Dorrance, Jason Lezak, NASA's Edward Rogers, Chuck D., and Andrew Love.

From the political world, our friend Kirk Hanlin answered many calls, e-mails, and texts. For political background on candidacy, life in state legislatures, and other information, we are grateful to have spoken to our friends Paul Begala and Jeffrey Eller. Samantha Kenner of the Eisenhower Presidential Library and Museum came to our aid, as did Mark Twain guru Barbara Schmidt.

For help getting other details right, we're thankful to: Richard Eisinger; Karen Bosko; Evan Carmichael; Jason Goldberg and Christian Schoenherr; Andy Cutler; Erik Peper; Daniel Fowler of the American Sociological Association; and Jolyn Matsumoto. Thank-yous also go to Jim Gilden at SAGE Publications, Sacha Boucherie of Elsevier B.V., and Jennifer Beal at Wiley-Blackwell, for granting us access to their publishers' journals.

INDEX

ABOUT THE AUTHORS

Po BRONSON and ASHLEY MERRYMAN are the authors of the *New York Times* best seller *NurtureShock: New Thinking about Children*. Additionally, they've written for *Newsweek*, *New York*, the *Guardian*, and numerous other publications. For their reporting, Bronson and Merryman have won nine national awards, including the PEN Center USA Literary Award for Journalism; the American Association for the Advancement of Science (AAAS) Award for Science Journalism; an "Audie" from the Audio Publishers Association; and two Clarion Awards.

Prior to collaborating with Merryman, Bronson authored five books, including the #1 *New York Times* best seller, *What Should I Do with My Life?* Merryman has also written for *Time*, the *Washington Post*, and the *Daily Beast*.

Bronson lives in San Francisco with his wife and their two children; he is a founder of the San Francisco Writers' Grotto and serves as volunteer president of the San Francisco Vikings Youth Soccer League.

Merryman lives in Los Angeles; an attorney, she previously served in the Clinton administration and currently volunteers as the head of a small inner-city tutoring program.

ABOUT TWELVE

TWELVE

TWELVE was established in August 2005 with the objective of publishing no more than twelve books each year. We strive to publish the singular book, by authors who have a unique perspective and compelling authority. Works that explain our culture; that illuminate, inspire, provoke, and entertain. We seek to establish communities of conversation surrounding our books. Talented authors deserve attention not only from publishers, but from readers as well. To sell the book is only the beginning of our mission. To build avid audiences of readers who are enriched by these works—that is our ultimate purpose.

For more information about forthcoming TWELVE books, please go to www.twelvebooks.com.